Innovating Counseling for Self- and Career Construction

Jacobus Gideon (Kobus) Maree

Innovating Counseling for Self- and Career Construction

Connecting Conscious Knowledge with Subconscious Insight

Springer

Jacobus Gideon (Kobus) Maree
Department of Educational Psychology
University of Pretoria
Pretoria, Gauteng, South Africa

ISBN 978-3-030-48647-1 ISBN 978-3-030-48648-8 (eBook)
https://doi.org/10.1007/978-3-030-48648-8

This Springer imprint is published by the registered company Springer Nature Switzerland AG
The registered company address is: Gewerbestrasse 11, 6330 Cham, Switzerland

Dedicated to Mark Savickas, my personal role model, career counseling's most eminent scholar, and the person that I look up to and try to emulate always.

Foreword

Around the globe, people are facing complex challenges arising from the spectacular social, technological, economic, and demographic developments of the past two centuries. Solutions to the climate crisis and ways of reducing our ecological footprint and promoting sustainable development will, for example, have to be found. These developments have led also to the increasing global movement of goods, resources, people, and knowledge. The power of the voices of smaller groups of people at this time has increased while that of nations has decreased. Among the social consequences are the precarization, tertiarization, and dualization of the labor market. While the changes and consequences may vary, people around the world all experience them, whether living in, for example, Brazil, Indonesia, Canada, South Africa, or Switzerland. Accompanying these changes are seemingly higher levels of social, economic, and ecological insecurity and watered-down social norms. The complexity of this changing world can be seen in more complex education systems and labor markets and more ambiguous social norms, making the work of career counselors accordingly also more complex. For a start, they have to process more information following the diversification of populations and career trajectories (paths).

Vocational and career guidance have always been seen as ways to promote social justice and advocacy (Butler, 2012; Ratts, 2009). Moreover, Cardoso, Savickas, and Gonçalves (2020) state that "Fostering change is the main aim of any psychological practice including career construction counseling" (p. 1). However, if we as career counselors really want to achieve this goal, our interventions must be accessible to everyone. In order to promote sustainable careers, we have to do all we can to increase access to "decent' work and ensure successful career transitions. We need, therefore, not only to develop life-long learning (to help people develop their employability) but also life-long counseling and training (to help them reposition themselves in the changing labor market). This has, among things, implications for how people situate and define themselves in the social space. If vocational psychology and, more specifically, the life-design paradigm are to promote sustainability, contextualized interventions will have to be developed to accommodate a diversity of needs and situations. These interventions should be holistic, inclusive, and context- and culture-sensitive in order to meet the needs of all career, social, and life spheres. This holistic approach implies considering an individual's entire life course, with its temporal and unique dimensions, different features of the Self (dispositions, values, life stories, life themes, and identities), as well as cultural contexts. Many new intervention strategies have been developed for specific marginalized groups, for example, migrants or those not in employment or training. These interventions involve more than vocational guidance. They often require specialists (e.g., social workers, nurses, and career counselors) to work together in a network of competencies. They can include coaching or supportive counseling extending beyond the typical three to five career counseling sessions. Here, group interventions are particularly relevant.

This book contributes meaningfully to the career counseling field because of its many ideas on how interventions can be adapted and expanded to promote career counseling for all. In terms of the useful life-design paradigm, it can help counselees link their past, present, and future during deconstruction, reconstruction, and co-construction processes. It explains also how new assessment instruments can be used with a diversity of counselees in various settings. The career interventions discussed in the book will help counselees become the main actors in the counseling process and also help them develop their career management abilities. The explanation of the articulation between narrativity and enaction, which promotes intentionality, is another important contribution of the book. All interventions should stimulate counselees' reflexivity (need for meaning) and intentionality (need for continuity in a changing world).

Finally, policy-makers need to be convinced of the importance of developing not only life-long learning but also life-long counseling for all. For career counseling to help provide security in an insecure world, career counselors need to develop new assessment instruments and interventions, adapt existing theories, and widen the accessibility of these interventions, especially to unserved and underserved populations, as proposed in this significant book.

Jérôme Rossier
Research Center in Vocational Psychology
and Career Counseling (CePCO)
Institute of Psychology
University of Lausanne
Lausanne, Switzerland

References

Butler, S. K. (2012). Issues of social justice and career development. *Career Planning & Adult Development Journal, 28*(1), 140–151.

Cardoso, P., Savickas, M. L. & Gonçalves, M. M. (2020). Facilitating narrative change in career construction counselling. *Journal of Career Development, 29*(1), 1–14. DOI: 10.1177/0894845319898872

Ratts, M. J. (2009). Social justice counseling: toward the development of a fifth force among counseling paradigms. *Journal of Humanistic Counseling, Education and Development, 48*, 160–172.

Acknowledgements

Thanks to the entire Springer publishing team for assisting me in converting my ideas about innovation in career counseling into a scholarly narrative. Special thanks to Shinjini Chatterjee, our senior editor (psychology and health), for her exceptional guidance, commitment, patience, and passion, and whose smile always lifted my spirits in challenging times; Chris Wilby, our ever-kind and approachable assistant editor; as well as Gowtham Chakravarthy, Prashanth Ravichandran and Ameena Jaffar, our accomplished, committed, and patient project manager, project coordinator, and Editorial Assistant, respectively. In addition, I also thank Tim Steward, who has been editing my work as only he can over so many years.

A very special thanks to Mark Savickas, the world's pre-eminent scholar in the field of career counseling, without whose inspiration and guidance this book would not have been possible. Thank you for sharing your invaluable insights with me and for changing the course of career counseling forever. Thank you, too, for shaping my career-life and the career-lives of many others. I admire particularly the way in which you steadfastly not only teach but also actually live out the value and essence of true scholarliness.

A special thanks to Paul Hartung for his unfailing kindness and willingness to advise me on all matters related to career counseling, innovation in career counseling, and scholarliness in general. You are a true example of a scholar who practises what he preaches in all facets of life.

To Chris Briddick and Hande Sensoy-Briddick, thank you for your incisive and constructive comments and for contributing far more than I had hoped for. I value our friendship and collegiality.

To Paul Hartung, Marcelo Ribeiro, Paulo Cardoso, Melinde Coetzee, Chris Beukes, my critical readers, thank you for your constructive and uplifting comments. It was a privilege to have worked with and learned from you.

To Jérôme Rossier and Peter McIlveen for graciously accepting my invitation to write the Foreword and Epilogue, thank you for your illuminating contributions.

I thank everyone else with whom I had the pleasure of working with and learning from. This includes the many thousands of research participants—often from backgrounds of extreme poverty—who always embraced me and lifted my spirits when our research task threatened to become too daunting and overwhelming.

To Dolly Parton, whose remarkable career-life story and music never cease to amaze and inspire me, thank you for your music, humanitarian endeavors, social contributions, and especially, the remarkable manner in which you demonstrate in such a natural way what we as career counseling theorists can only theorize about. I doubt whether anyone in the history of our field and in the field of music has managed to illustrate more convincingly the principle of converting hurt into hope and lasting social upliftment.

Lastly, I thank my loving mother, who unfailingly and unreservedly encouraged me, made me feel special, and cared about all people in "pain". Mother, your story will inspire, encourage, and motivate me until my life's journey ends. Likewise, I thank my father for always motivating and displaying confidence in me. I conclude by thanking my son who never complains when "I burn the midnight oil" or seek his invaluable input.

Contents

About the Author

Prof. Jacobus Gideon (Kobus) Maree (D.Ed (Career Counseling); Ph.D. (Learning Facilitation in Mathematics); D.Phil (Psychology)) is a full Professor in the Department of Educational Psychology at the University of Pretoria. His main research interests are facilitating sustainable decent work for all, counseling for self- and career construction, life design counseling, emotional–social intelligence, social responsibility, and learning facilitation in mathematics. Past Editor of a number of scholarly journals, for instance, the *South African Journal of Psychology*, he is the current Editor of the *African Journal of Career Development* and the regional Editor for Southern Africa: *Early Child Development and Care*. Kobus is the sole African representative on the following core scientific (UNESCO) committees: a. UNESCO Chair on Lifelong Guidance and Counseling, and b. the UNESCO University Network and Twinning (UNITWIN) Chair. In addition, he was elected as a Member of the Board of Directors of the International Association of Applied Psychology (IAAP) (Division 16) in 2018. Moreover, he serves as Registrar of the South African Career Development Association, and he accepted appointments as a Research Fellow at the University of the Free State and as Professor Extraordinaire at the University of Stellenbosch and the University of Southern Queensland.

Kobus has received multiple awards for his research. In 2010, he was, for instance. awarded the Stals Prize for exceptional research and contributions to psychology. In 2014, he was awarded the Stals Prize for exceptional research and contributions to Education and he received the Psychological Society of South Africa's Award for Excellence in Science in 2014. He also received Honorary Membership of the Golden Key International Honour Society for exceptional academic achievements, leadership skills, and community involvement in 2014. He was awarded the Chancellor's Medal for Teaching and Learning from the University of Pretoria in 2010 and has been nominated successfully as an Exceptional Academic Achiever on four consecutive occasions. He has a B1 rating from the National Research Foundation.

Kobus has authored or co-authored 90^{+} peer-reviewed articles and 75 books/ book chapters on career counseling, research, and related topics since 2010. In the same period, he supervised 38 doctoral theses and Master's dissertations and read keynote papers at 25^{+} international conferences (e.g., Australia, Belgium, Canada, Croatia, Czechia, Egypt, England, France, Hungary, India, Italy, Mauritius, Namibia, Poland, Slovakia, South Africa, The Republic of Korea, Turkey, and the United States of America), and at 22^{+} national conferences. He has also presented invited workshops at conferences in 40^{+} countries across the world on (a) integrating qualitative and quantitative approaches in career counseling, and (b) the art and science of writing scholarly articles in his career-lifetime. Over the past seven years, he has spent a lot of time abroad as a visiting Professor at various universities where he presented workshops on, for instance, contemporary developments in career counseling, the art and science of scholarly article writing, and research methodology. He was awarded a fellowship of the IAAP in 2014 and received the Psychological Society of South Africa's Fellow Award (Lifetime Award in recognition of a person who has made exceptional contributions to Psychology in her/his life) in 2017.

List of Figures

List of Tables

List of Photographs

Part I
Orientation

Chapter 1
Connecting What We Know Consciously with What We Are Aware of Subconsciously: Orientation of and Rationale for the Book

Never doubt that a small group of thoughtful, committed citizens can change the world; indeed, it's the only thing that ever has (Margaret Mead)

To improve is to change often, so to be perfect is to have changed very often (Winston Churchill)

Abstract In this chapter, I first dwell briefly on important events in the field of career counseling over the past few decades and explain why innovation in the field is needed. I draw on one of my earliest recollections to set the scene for what is to follow in later chapters and elaborate on my own personal Damascene moment—a moment that convinced me forever of the need for as well as the power and value of an integrative QUALITATIVE-quantitative approach to career counseling, particularly at a time when many speculate that work itself is at risk. I conclude by outlining the contents of the book and explaining its aims—to help people connect what they know about themselves consciously with what they are aware of subconsciously (elicited by activities such as asking clients for their most hurtful experiences or for their earliest recollections).

1.1 Orientation

For the purposes of this book, I accept the following definition of the word "innovate": The Collins Dictionary (n.d.) explains that the word "innovation" stems from the word *innovationem* (Latin for renew or change).[1,2] It refers to something new or a novel way of doing something that already exists or even introducing novel or new ideas, strategies, methods, or features. The word thus comprises a process that innovates or

---

[1]It is typical to refer to a person's early recollections. During career construction counseling, however, career counselors often ask their clients to share their three earliest recollections with them.

[2]I am aware of the view of some people that it is not always necessary or even advisable to elicit people's most painful stories (Eramian & Denov, 2019). I respect this view; however, it does not fall within the scope of this book to debate the issue. Clearly, more research is needed on the subject.

J. G. (Kobus) Maree, *Innovating Counseling for Self- and Career Construction*,
https://doi.org/10.1007/978-3-030-48648-8_1

renews something that already exists. It does not introduce something that either has not been there before or something entirely new. The word "renewal" probably best describes the essence of what innovation means. Fraser (2014, n.p.) adds: "For this renewal to take place it is necessary for people (counselors as well as their clients) to change the way they make decisions … they must choose to do things differently, make choices outside of their norm."

This book should be read against the background of the following premise: The future is here already and the unpredictable world of work is changing continually, rapidly, and fundamentally. Moreover, the pace of change is accelerating all the time; something that career counseling needs to respond to in a proactive, timeous, appropriate, and innovative manner. The situation differs from country to country—Work 4.0 is impacting workers in different ways. The situation in Global North countries in particular differs widely from that in the Global South. The industrial sector, especially in the Global South, has been shrinking, and people have increasingly been turning to the service sector and informal settings for employment opportunities. This will continue to be the case (M. Ribeiro, personal communication, September 29, 2019).

Whereas the situation of many workers in the Global South or developing countries has not changed markedly, with these workers still functioning in what can be classified as "fixed" hierarchical structures, in typical Global North contexts such structures are fast disappearing and work contexts are becoming more unstable and insecure (Rossier, Ginevra, Bollmann, & Nota, 2017)—to a large extent because of the Fourth Industrial Revolution (Work 4.0) and more particularly the upsurge in networking and connectivity (Gurri, 2013). To an increasing extent, people are working in non-traditional environments. London (2018), for example, maintains that the erstwhile "pyramidal" or ladder-type of occupational hierarchy or occupational order (where relationships are clearly structured) is changing. According to London (2018, n.p.):

> In the more dynamic Fourth Industrial Revolution (4IR), people will increasingly find that they have to work with a larger variety of people at different times, some above and some below them in terms of rank, expertise, or experience; this constant rotation means that an ability to manage up – which can mean anticipating needs and coming up with solutions without being asked – is that much more important.[3]

Likewise, McPherson (2018, n.p.) maintains that "[w]hat we are really looking at is the emergence of an entirely new economy … What differentiates the 4IR from former revolutions is the quantum of change and the convergence of global factors (such as climate change, rising populations, and terrorism) of a magnitude quite unprecedented in human history". There is every chance that Work 4.0 and Work 5.0 will increase the already significant divide between people without adequate access to resources and those with sufficient access, thereby also increasing the "Matthew effect" (Merton, 1968). Workers in less "fixed" work environments are often engulfed by the discourse that those who manage to find work should consider themselves fortunate to be in any job at all, that robots are rapidly taking over the work

[3]Many Global South occupational contexts still resemble pyramidal hierarchies.

of humans (in lower order work positions in particular), and that, in many instances, work opportunities advertised in future may carry the disclaimer: "Humans should not apply" (Grey, 2014). Many people are losing their jobs, work opportunities are dwindling, and the key question has now become: What sense does work make? In such circumstances, it is not strange that workers and work-seekers in particular find it difficult to make meaning of their work-lives, find a sense of purpose, and rekindle a sense of hope for the future. This at a time when the general belief is that all people have a right to "decent work [that] helps all workers attain a sense of self-respect and dignity, experience freedom and security in the workplace, and … [allows them] opportunity to choose and execute productive, meaningful, and fulfilling work that will enable them to construct themselves adequately and without restrictions and make social contributions" (Di Fabio & Maree, 2016, p. 9).

What has been discussed above would be incomplete without a brief reference to the 'arrival' of the coronavirus (Covid-19) globally. Even though the full impact of the virus will only become clearer over time, it is safe to predict that its ripple effect will influence the world of work globally extremely negatively. Kelly (2020, p. 1), for instance, says that "[t]he coronavirus has changed the job market almost overnight. The global outbreak has seriously impacted the economy and job security. It will have long-lasting, game-changing ramifications". Hooley, Sultana, and Thomsen (2020) maintain that the coronavirus' primary threat is to people's health but that its threat to the economy "is likely to have an even greater impact. We can expect unemployment to rise, occupational shifting to increase, and job content to change" (p. 3). Speculation is rife, but there seems to be general agreement that many millions of jobs will be lost and that those jobs that remain will become increasingly sought after. More specifically, there will be an increase in the demand for jobs that can be executed online. It is therefore clear that a prompt and decisive local and global response by all stakeholders is required to address the fundamental changes in people's work-lives following the coronavirus pandemic. The need for telehealth (including telepsychology and especially, from the perspective of this book, tele-career counseling), too, will increase substantially.

In my opinion, too much negative emphasis is placed on matters such as predicted job losses. I support those who have a more balanced outlook such as Pring et al. (2018) who say: "In the future, work will change but won't go away … a world without work is a fantasy that is no closer to reality in 2017 than it was more than 500 years ago upon the publication of Thomas More's Utopia" (p. 4). Gaskell (2018), too, believes that the discourse on the future of work focuses too much on envisaged job losses resulting from Work 4.0-related developments. He argues that "[i]t's a narrative that doesn't really provide an accurate reflection of the true state of things … there is a growing consensus that AI-driven technology will change the kind of work we do, which will require adaptation both of the roles themselves and the skills required to perform them. It will automate some entirely (although not as many as predicted), and the productivity gains will result in new jobs emerging" (p. 1). Of relevance here is Pring et al.'s (2018) observation that "human imagination and ingenuity will be the source of human work ad infinitum" (p. 4).

Irrespective, however, of whether one agrees or disagrees with the gloomy predictions, career counseling theory, research, practice, and policy need to be revamped and updated regularly. Kuhn (1996) and Kuhn and Hacking (2012) believe that paradigms in general lose their power and validity after a period of about 20 years. Savickas (2007) maintains that career counseling paradigms last only 50 years or so, after which they lose their effectiveness as lenses for observing the career-related behavior of people. They also lose their capacity to help career counseling theorists and practitioners plan appropriate and timeous career counseling interventions. Career theorists, researchers, and practitioners need to ensure that their counseling prepares people for the numerous transitions and challenges they will face in the occupational world. This includes increased levels of work-related anxiety and trauma caused by changes in unpredictability-filled workplaces (Maree, 2013a). Career counselors will have to help clients deal with work-related anxieties and help them set viable short-, medium-, and long-term goals for making meaning of and attaining a sense of purpose in their career-lives[4] (Hartung, 2011; Strauser, Lustig, & Ciftci, 2008). In summary: A practical local and global response is needed that will enable us as career counselors to respond practically to events in local and global economies that impact modern-day occupational contexts as well as the career-lives of workers.

1.2 Why This Book? Rationale for the Book

As stated earlier (Maree, 2013a), the plight of impoverished people has always been a profound concern of mine. Given the extent of recent changes in the workplace and the concomitant escalation in job losses and poverty, now, more than ever, career counseling needs to ensure that different categories of people benefit from career counseling interventions: (a) a gifted school student in a private school in Wroclaw who wants to become an architect; (b) a bright student in a public school in Nigeria who wants to become a medical doctor; (c) an inmate of a Pakistani correctional services facility wanting to study law; (d) a young woman from a small school in a little town in Japan who is interested in becoming a plumber; and (e) a learner with an intellectual disability in Pyongyang who has no idea what she[5] wants to study. Career counseling should also be offered in group contexts, for example (a) to a group of homeless migrants living in an informal settlement outside Paris; (b) to destitute people living on the outskirts of Sao Paolo; (c) to a group of displaced people in a part of Homs that was almost completely destroyed during the Syrian civil war; (d)

[4]According to Hartung (P. J. Hartung, personal communication, October 21, 2019), human life consists of three domains, namely love (intimacy), work (including career), and friends (community, avocational interests, and relationships). Hartung contends that "life story" refers to the narrative about all three of these domains in general, and he uses the term "life-career story" to refer to the narrative about the work domain specifically. I agree but prefer the term "career-life story" to "life-career story".

[5]Feminine and masculine pronouns (she, he, her, him, hers, or his) should be regarded as interchangeable.

to groups of Indian graduates in Mumbai who cannot find employment; and (e) to a group of unemployed women who have not received formal after-school training and live in poverty outside Bloemfontein (see Winslade, 2011).

Of course, not all people will agree with the above exposition. Bassot (2015), for instance, in reviewing an earlier book of mine (*Counseling for career construction,* Maree, 2013a, 2013b) said that "it is difficult to imagine that any single approach could achieve [the aim of finding a contemporary, contextualized approach that will be of value to every person irrespective of color, creed, financial situation, or geographic location] … in this respect perhaps the author simply gave himself an impossible task" (p. 370). I respectfully disagree with this comment. What I was in fact trying to say was that career counselors should be able to contextualize their interventions in a way that makes them helpful, useful, and valuable to all people and not to just a select, privileged few. Moreover, I argue in favor of an approach that will address the work-related needs of all people and help them find sustainable, decent work.[6]

My goal in life is therefore to reach out to people in general and to the "voiceless",[7] the homeless, the forgotten, and the disadvantaged in particular. A quote by Mother Teresa of Calcutta, now Saint Teresa of Calcutta, has always inspired me and neatly sums up how I feel about life, work, and research. She said: "The other day I dreamed that I was at the gates of heaven. And St. Peter said, 'Go back to Earth. There are no slums up here'".

My life goal is consistent also with the UNESCO goals of ensuring that career counseling is always contextualized, that all people receive career counseling, and that sustainable decent work is made accessible to everyone. Moreover, with reference to Lincoln's famous Gettysburg address (Herndon & Welk, 1892), I believe in career counseling of people (construction of their life stories), career counseling with people (themselves co-, de-, and reconstructing these stories), career counseling for people (by career counselors), and career counseling by people (themselves) or self-advising. Ultimately, regarding career counseling, I agree that "[h]eaven is something that each and every one of us can hold in her or his hand" (Lofts, 1958, p. 15). Or, in the words of Dolly Parton, whose inspiring "career-life story" encapsulates the essence of postmodern career counseling (see Chap. 12): "One is only poor if [one] wants to be poor." By this is meant that we cannot and should not be defined by our contexts. With the necessary support structures and mechanisms to respond to challenges, people have the power and innovativeness to act proactively, convert challenges into opportunities, inaction into actionality and action, "problems" into growth areas and strengths, questions into answers (and answers into further questions), and subconscious life themes into conscious motivations to make a success of our lives—as humankind has done consistently throughout the ages, no matter how daunting the challenges facing them. Allen (2015), for instance, reminds us

[6] I acknowledge the different conceptualizations of "decent work" as a result of the reality of different socioeconomic and cultural contexts.

[7] I agree with Canham and Langa's (2017) view that "We do not [subscribe to] the tradition of 'giving voice to the voiceless'. It is not possible or desirable to speak on behalf of the other" (p. 6).

that, in the 1800s, the Luddites in Yorkshire and Nottinghamshire smashed weaving machines in the belief that they would take over their jobs. Today, retail staff members are concerned about automatic checkouts, and taxi drivers worry about self-driving cars. A research study by Deloitte found that, rather than jobs being "destroyed" by technology, the latter has consistently shown itself to be "a great job-creating machine" (Allen, p. 3). There are thus different perspectives on the future of work, and one should carefully consider the various viewpoints if one wishes to arrive at an informed opinion on the matter.

1.3 Main Innovation to the Field of Career Counseling I Am Proposing

1.3.1 General Introduction

Changing times call for regular adaptation of older and conceptualization and development of contemporary assessment instruments, both quantitative and qualitative (Duarte, 2017a, 2017b; Hartung, 2011; Savickas et al., 2009; Soresi & Nota, 2010). Moreover, general consensus exists today on the merits of storied (qualitative) approaches to career counseling in conjunction with narrative-based theories and the design, development, and use of appropriate assessment instruments and interventions alongside objective or quantitative approaches (Hartung, 2011; Maree, 2013b, 2018c; Savickas, 2005, 2011; Subich, 2011). Many qualitative, storied questionnaires have been developed during the past few decades thanks largely to the work and leadership of Mark Savickas, supported by a number of other scholars. Bimrose and Hearne (2012) maintain that while general consensus exists about the effectiveness of quantitative methods, techniques, strategies, and interventions in career intervention (Savickas, 2001), the effectiveness of approaches or modalities that do not blend quantitative and qualitative modalities should be questioned (Blustein, 2006). This chapter covers this topic and describes an attempt to address the lacunae highlighted by, for instance, Bimrose and Hearne (2012), Hartung (2018), Maree (2018a, 2018b), and Savickas (2015a, 2015b).

Niles, in (1997), urged those of us working in career counseling to think innovatively in the interests of clients and to conceptualize, implement, and examine the value of new paradigms and associated interventions on an ongoing basis. This will help ensure the lasting value of career counseling theory and practice across time, space, and location.

1.3.2 Main Innovation I Am Proposing

The main innovation to the field of career counseling that I am proposing is my integrative model. The theoretical background to the advances in the pre-existing theories and practices proposed by this model is elucidated in the first part of the book, after which the practical application in various contexts is explicated. The following should be stated up front: It is my conviction that (self- and) career construction and life design counseling do not exclude the use of tests. Quite the opposite. For purposes of triangulation, and to improve the rigor of intervention, personally, I prefer to draw on all three of the fundamental theoretical paradigms on which (self- and) career construction theory is based.

1.4 Looking Back Over the Past to Help Us Map and Shape the Way Forward

Practicing as a career counselor (and psychologist) for more than four decades has been something that I would not have missed for anything in the world. The journey has been rewarding and memorable.

Looking back over the years reminds me of being on a flight late in the evening, sitting in my window seat and casting my eyes down from about 1000 meters on the scene below: a few lonely lights somewhere in the vast, encompassing darkness. A lonely farmhouse or two. A few more lights; seemingly, a small town. Many lights; clearly a city. The lights neatly dotted. These sights always excite me. What can be more hauntingly beautiful than looking out of the window, early in the morning, outside Istanbul, for instance? Ships (small and large) in the harbor. Many lights mystically dotting the contours of that timeless city; the aerial perspective enabling one literally and figuratively to see the "bigger picture".

Now, in your mind's eye, picture yourself on the airplane during your return flight in broad daylight. See Mother Nature's topographical features and natural boundaries such as winding river courses, mountains, hills, and forests. By contrast, see human-made structures such as houses, towns, informal settlements, cities, dams, canals, farms, corn, and lucerne fields.

From a height of some 1000 meters it is relatively easy to obtain a bird's eye view of the scene below and to decide where and how to intervene—to "reshape" Mother Nature's features in the interests of progress. This could include building new dams and new roads and highways. All in the cause of improving living conditions and promoting the best interests of humanity.

Similarly, with the advantage of distance and perspective, career counseling theorists, researchers, practitioners, and policy makers can gain useful insight into what has worked in the profession, what no longer works, and what needs to be changed, adapted, or even discarded in order to respond appropriately to global changes, changing contexts, and new challenges in the occupational world. The entire book should be read and interpreted through this lens.

1.5 Setting the Scene for This Book: An Earliest Recollection

I realized early in my life that most learners across the world do not receive adequate career counseling. It was clear to me also that using the traditional approach to career counseling in relative isolation does not enable career counselors to address people's career counseling needs properly. I have therefore dedicated most of my professional life to the design of an integrative[8] QUALITATIVE-quantitative career counseling strategy to meet these needs—if only in my home country to begin with.

My mother was an English-speaking (Catholic) woman of Lebanese origin, while my father was of Afrikaans (Protestant) stock. Living in an almost exclusively Afrikaans environment at the height of apartheid, a member of one of many minority groups, I was almost "lost" in an intersectionality trap—it just never felt as if I really belonged to any group. Always an outsider, I felt "at home" among marginalized people and people with poverty in general. At the age of six, I and my family lived in a rented house in a little town called Holpan in the Northern Cape Province of South Africa where my father was the head of a very small primary school (the school did not have more than 30 learners in total). Some of the farmers grew grapes and employed black women to harvest the grapes. During that time, in the late afternoon, many of the women would walk down the road in front of our house with sizeable baskets on their heads. I was curious to find out whether the baskets were not hurting them and what they had inside those baskets. One afternoon, I waited next to the road until the women came past. I started walking next to one of them and put my questions to her. She smiled, stopped, put the basket down, and assured me that she was accustomed to carrying heavy "stuff" on her head. Then, to my surprise, she put her hand in the basket and took out two delicious bunches of grapes, which she presented to me. It did not seem right to accept the gift, and I tried to decline her offer, but she smilingly insisted and proceeded to hand me the two bunches of grapes. I thanked her and watched her turn around and walk away.

When I got home, I told my mother what had happened and offered her one bunch. In her gentle manner, she explained that while she understood why I had taken the grapes from a poor woman, it was far better to give than to receive. I still clearly remember her words: "This woman, like so many others, is really struggling to make ends meet. Giving you some of the little food she had is saddening but

---

[8]Given the nature of the *CIP* and the *MCM*, my design almost inevitably comprises a mixed-methods (QUALITATIVE + quantitative) (uppercase denoting the greater weight given to the qualitative part of the design) assessment and intervention design. The "+" is used to indicate that qualitative and quantitative data are gathered simultaneously. For the sake of convenience, though, from here on, I use the term "QUALITATIVE-quantitative" to denote my design.

also inspiring. Tomorrow, we will prepare a parcel containing food and household goods you can give to her." Even though my mother was running the household on a shoestring budget, she managed to put together a decent food parcel, which I handed to the same woman the next day. Her humble "thank you", accompanied by her sense of gratitude, will always linger in my mind. To this day, I derive great satisfaction from giving whatever I can to people who have very little. Wherever I travelled during later stages of my life, I would notice and be drawn to impoverished people, for example beggars, male or female, black, white, brown, young or old, but also to people with any other form or disadvantage. Later, I learned about the reticular activating system (RAS) (Van Schneider, 2017). Stated briefly, the RAS takes what we focus on and creates a filter for it; for instance, if on any given day we decide to spot red cars while driving to work, we will succeed in seeing some. Likewise, if we focus on positive news about the future of work, we are likely to find reasons to be upbeat (and vice versa). That to some extent explained why I was and remain drawn to people experiencing major challenges in life; consciously and subconsciously noticing them and trying to find a way to improve their situation. Over time, I began to realize that every poverty-related challenge carried with it the opportunity to make a small contribution to a person in need. And each time any of us makes a difference in the life of a distressed person, we benefit as much from the "good deed" as the recipient of that deed.

1.6 My Personal Damascene Moment

At university, we were all trained to give career counseling in a positivist, quantitative, test-and-tell manner. During the early part of my career, I therefore practiced the way I was taught: "Testing" people and "telling" them what to do. However, even during that time, I was asked by the head of our department to develop an "*individual workbook for career guidance investigation*" (see Chap. 8), which contained multiple qualitative questions. The information obtained from the use of this "workbook" was subsequently used to gain insight into aspects of people's personalities other than just the outcomes of career inventories in isolation. Later, when teaching honors and master's degree students about the theory underlying the *Jung Personality Questionnaire (JPQ)* (1983) (Hall, Halstead, & Taylor, 1986a, 1986b) and showing them how actually to administer the questionnaire, it struck me that testees' responses to the fourth basic preference pair of type theory (Martin, 1995) did not make sense. (Testees' preferences are indicated on four dichotomous scales, namely (a) extraversion (E) versus introversion (I); (b) sensing (S) versus intuition (I); (c) thinking (T) versus feeling (F); and (d) judging (J) versus perceiving (P).) I accordingly suggested that the students should carefully (re-)consider all their clients' responses to the fourth basic preference pair responses. All their clinical observations and other information should be considered when they interpreted the *JPQ* profiles. Then, in 1993, I attended a course on the administration of the *Myers-Briggs Type Inventory* (Martin, 1995), which was a turning point in my career. I noticed a serious error on the *JPQ* answer sheet, which had been used in South Africa for more than 40 years. The fourth basic preference pair recorded on the answer sheet (J versus P) should be anchored by the J (or judging) on the left and P (or perceiving) on the right. Instead it read: P (left) and J (right). An inattentive typist had made a serious typing mistake many years previously.

Misleading information had thus been given to people for more than 40 years. I brought the error to the attention of the test distributors, who eventually made the correction. However, sadly, many psychologists are still using the incorrect version of the answer sheet. To appreciate the seriousness of the oversight, readers should note that this questionnaire was used to select prospective medical and engineering students at some tertiary institutions in South Africa.

That was the turning point in my life as a career counseling lecturer, researcher, and practitioner. Never again would I allow myself to be coerced into accepting an approach that did not make proper sense to me. Noticing the mistake, soon afterwards, I was privileged to read the 1993 article "Career counseling in the post-modern era" of Mark Savickas, my personal and all-time role model. After its publication, career counseling would never be the same again. In it, Savickas (1993) stated that present-day career counseling is characterized by numerous innovations. Above all, Savickas argued that people are the sole experts (authorities) on themselves. They are thus the main sources of trustworthy, valid, and reliable (authoritative) information on themselves and their life stories (the profiling of which can uncover a great deal about their psychological DNA/psychological fingerprinting).

Instead of plotting clients on the normal curve of "average" traits, it is our job as career counselors to empower them by encouraging them to compare themselves with themselves only. We need also to show a genuine interest in them and elicit **their** unique life stories irrespective of how their traits "compare with" other people's traits. This assertion is consistent with McAdams's (1997) observation that "[i]f you want to know me, then you must know my story, for my story defines who I am. And if *I* want to know *myself*, to gain insight into the meaning of my own life, then I, too, must come to know my own story" (p. 11). Eliciting people's stories comprises a universal methodology and intervention to enhance understanding and promote reflection, reflexivity,[9] and forward movement. Reflection involves contemplating one's past experiences (including one's earliest memories), emotions, and cognitions to connect the past with the present, while reflexivity involves thinking processes that presume dynamic self-conscious assessment of one's conscious knowledge to uncover psychologically healthier ways of self-construction (Guichard, 2009) and career construction (Savickas, 2015a, 2015b) in the future. All of this is brought about by connecting the past, the present, and the future prospectively. Once people's stories have been elicited, and narrativizing of the stories has concluded, the personal stories of trauma remain and call for our intervention. We then help[10] people rewrite

[9]Reflexivity develops narratability and biographicity and promotes clarification and co-construction of people's life stories (Maree, 2013a; M. L. Savickas, personal communication, July 26, 2018).

[10]I am aware that using the word "help" in a career counseling context may be seen as maintaining the "power" discourse (positioning counselors in a powerful position in relation to clients)

their idiosyncratic stories and turn them into living stories (Boje, 2008). Boje (2008) explains that living stories enhance the restorying of people's past narratives. He adds that a "living story has many authors and as a collective force has a life of its own. We live in living stories" (p. 338). We as career counselors act as co-authors and co-facilitators of clients' career-life stories and help them articulate their careers through stories. Themes and patterns as well as tensions in their stories and storylines are pointed out, and they (the clients) are helped to script the next chapters in their stories. All the way through, we highlight the trio of roles that clients assume, namely the roles of clients as social actors, as motivated agents, and as autobiographical authors (McAdams, 1993, 2013; Savickas, 2016a, 2016b). Seen from this perspective, career choices reflect profoundly personal predispositions that stem from people's uniqueness and matchlessness. Where an integrative QUALITATIVE-quantitative approach is followed, the process of career counseling prioritizes people's stories instead of their "scores" in "objective" tests. People's central life themes add meaning to their career interest patterns and are integrated with their "measured" interests and abilities.

My sole concern since those early days has been the best interests of my clients, and I believe that an integrative QUALITATIVE-quantitative[11] approach to career counseling-related challenges best serves those interests. The usefulness of narrative approaches to career counseling has been widely reported in publications across the world over the past three decades (McIlveen, 2012; McIlveen & Patton, 2007). People consistently report their experience of the strategy as respectful and helpful. For these and other reasons, I decided that I would in the future only in the rarest of instances consider the use of any quantitative approach on its own during research. Instead, wherever possible, I would use an integrative (qualitative-quantitative) approach. In certain cases, though, I might use a qualitative or narrative approach on its own (see Chap. 10).

1.7 What the Book Sets Out to Achieve

This book sets out to show readers how to connect career counseling history and best practices with contemporary models and methods in a way that gives them insight into the theory underlying an innovative, integrative qualitative-quantitative approach to career counseling. I also elaborate on the development of two career counseling instruments, both specifically designed to promote the integrative approach and facilitate career counseling in individual and group contexts. While the *Career Interest Profile* (*CIP*) (Maree, 2017a, 2017b) emphasizes storytelling, the *Maree Career*

instead of promoting the idea of a collaborative counseling partnership. However, in my opinion, it is what actually happens during the intervention that defines this relationship; hence my consistent emphasizing of the importance of establishing an atmosphere of mutual trust, respect, and collaboration.

[11] For instance, QUALITATIVE-quantitative, QUALITATIVE + quantitative, as well as QUALITATIVE → quantitative approaches (Ivankova, Creswell, & Plano Clark, 2019).

Matrix (*MCM*) (2016) draws on established approaches. I explain the need to provide context for career construction counseling as it enhances career counselors' ability to help clients uncover, understand, and interpret their key life themes. In addition, it promotes clients' understanding of their areas for development (growth areas) and helps them identify (qualitatively) their career values and career interest patterns. It facilitates (quantitatively) an integrated assessment of clients' self-estimates of their career interests and confidence in their aptitude to follow certain careers. This intervention strategy should enable career counselors to help clients identify, interpret, and draw on their central life themes, their areas for development, and their career values and link them to their self-estimates of their career interests and confidence in their aptitude to execute certain careers. The strategy also facilitates the triangulation and crystallization of clients' scores and their life stories and explains their trio of roles as social actors, motivated agents, and autobiographical authors (McAdams, 2010; Savickas, 2019).

Three key ideas recur throughout the book. First, the idea of not **dispensing "advice"** to clients—instead, enabling them to advise themselves. After all, we should not act as self-appointed experts or authorities on any other person. People should not be "actors" following a script written by others for them. Second, the idea of **listening for instead of to people's stories** (Hartung, 2018; Savickas, 2019; Welty, 1998) to help them choose and construct careers and themselves, become adaptable and employable, shape their career identities, design purposeful lives, and make meaningful social contributions. Third, the idea of helping people connect what they know about themselves **consciously** with what they are aware of **subconsciously**. The book endeavors to promote career counselors' ability to help clients "thrive" rather than merely "survive" in turbulent times. It confronts some of the main challenges posed by Work 4.0 but also foreshadows the imminent advent and impact of Work 5.0 on the workplace. It shows how narrative questionnaires that yield qualitative interest-related information and quantitative instruments can be used (individually and together) to integrate technological advances with career counseling practice to ensure "best practice" while promoting self-exploration and self-advising.

To summarize: In this book, I attempt to point out the usefulness and effectiveness of the postmodernist career construction approach and the strategies, techniques, and methods used to enhance career counseling in the 21st century. Grounded in self- and career construction principles and practices, the integrative strategy and concept I propose can facilitate critical reflection, reflection on reflection, reflexivity (which helps join insight and activity), innovation, action, and forward momentum in career counseling.

1.8 Outline of What Can Be Expected in the Book

This book is a response to global change and its impact on people's career-lives. The frameworks and interventions discussed in the book deal with (but are not limited to) self- and career construction and life design counseling. The book also promotes the

UNESCO goal of ensuring that career counseling is contextualized, that all people receive career counseling, and that sustainable decent work is accessible to everyone.

In Part 1, Chap. 1, I explain the rationale for the book and elaborate on its objectives. An overview is given of the essence of the book, namely how to integrate stories and scores in career counseling and how to help people connect what they (and we) know consciously with what they (and we) are aware of subconsciously to help them make meaning of their career-lives, find a sense of purpose, and (re-)discover a sense of hope for the future.

In Part 2, the focus shifts to a discussion of the book's theoretical and conceptual framework. Chapter 2 discusses the pressing need for an innovative approach to career counseling as well as several personality theories that have influenced the development of career counseling theory and practice. Chapter 3 discusses career construction counseling, self-construction counseling, and life design counseling. The focus then shifts again to an integrative career counseling framework as the foundation for the implementation of integrative career (construction) counseling. Chapter 4 elaborates on the link between the four waves in career counseling, psychology, the global economy, and the Fourth Industrial Revolution, while fifth wave-related developments are also touched on. The four economic waves relate to the four helping models in career counseling; the attributes or traits of each wave are highlighted, and associated career interventions are explained. Here, too, I reflect briefly on fifth wave developments. The chapter builds on and links economic, industrial, psychology, and career counseling waves and highlights the various traits in each of the waves. The challenges and opportunities associated with the Fourth Industrial Revolution (or Work 4.0) are discussed, and a call is made for a balanced view of and approach to Work 4.0 developments. Also discussed is the need to re-invent career counseling in the 21st century to anticipate challenges and opportunities that may result from the Fifth Industrial Revolution (or Work 5.0).

Chapter 5 considers how innovation can be enhanced in career counseling by appropriately indigenizing and contextualizing (decontextualizing, recontextualizing, and co-contextualizing) career counseling theory and practice in contexts that differ from those where career counseling was originally conceptualized to promote its relevance and applicability and ensure the necessary rigor. Above all, the expert opinions of "local" people must be sought and considered. Chapter 6 reviews changes in the vocabulary of the career counseling discourse and how these changes are reflected in the changing of shop names by businesses (the economy) across the world. Whereas many Global North[12] countries have accepted and embraced the need for a changed approach to career counseling and the changes in the world of work that have taken place globally over the past few decades, the same cannot be said of most Global South countries where the need for career counseling and the promotion of sustainable decent work is at its greatest. Chapter 7 accordingly considers the importance of promoting social justice (advocacy) (Butler, 2012; Ratts,

[12]The terms "Global North" and "Global South" are used interchangeably with the terms "developed countries" and "developing and underdeveloped countries" respectively in this book.

2009) and sustainable decent work for all. It considers also the need to provide career counseling for seriously disadvantaged people.

Part 3 moves from theorizing about matters relating to innovative assessment in career counseling to explicating the practical aspects of such counseling. Here, the emphasis is largely on two new career counseling instruments that can be used to elicit people's "stories" and "scores"; help them craft their identity, value, or power statements; integrate their stories and scores to arrive at specific career choices; and, ultimately, help them draft their mission and vision statements. These instruments are the *Career Interest Profile* (*CIP*, version 6), a narrative questionnaire that yields qualitative interest-related information, and the *Maree Career Matrix* (*MCM*), which measures people's (a) career interests and (b) self-estimates of confidence about their aptitude to follow certain careers. First, in Chap. 8, I explain how the *CIP* can be used to draw on and promote people's universal propensity for storytelling. It has been designed to elicit, qualitatively, a sufficiently rich bouquet (formerly referred to as a representative sample) of people's numerous micro- or "small" life stories to enable career counselors not only to enhance their understanding of their clients but, especially, to help their clients retain the momentum needed to bring about change and progress in their career-lives. Chapter 9 focuses on the elicitation of "scores" quantitatively with the help of the *MCM*. Following on this, in Chap. 10, I explain how people's "scores" (obtained through the *MCM*) can be integrated with their "stories" (obtained through the *CIP*). I explain also that, while scores are useful in career choice, stories promote the notions of "meaning", "mattering", and "finding purpose". The chapter shows how career counseling theorists, researchers, and practitioners can integrate paradigms in career counseling with actual career intervention practice.

In Part 4, Chap. 11, I use a broad array of individual and collective intervention case studies to demonstrate how integrative QUALITATIVE-quantitative career counseling intervention can promote innovation in career counseling in individual as well as group-based contexts across people's life span and help people connect what they know about themselves consciously with what they are aware of subconsciously.

I have long maintained that career counseling was inspired and practiced by artists and entertainers long before we started building our theory from such practice. Part 5, Chap. 12, confirms Mark Savickas' (2019) assertion that career counseling practice precedes theory, and not the other way around. Much of what we theorize about in career counseling has thus already been practiced by artists and entertainers. The chapter reflects the innovative nature of the book by focusing on the career-life of a rare living legend, Dolly Parton. This chapter shows how counseling for self- and career construction theory is built on practice, exemplified by the inspiring career-life story of Dolly Parton—a story that encapsulates the essence of what postmodern career counseling should be about.

Part 6 concludes the book. In the final chapter (Chap. 13), I review key aspects of the "storyline" of the book before discussing the "lens" or "prism" through which it should be read. I consider the key issue of whether it is advisable to continue using tests (in conjunction with qualitative assessment instruments) in career counseling. Conditions for the professional implementation of the integrative approach are discussed, and key aspects of the career counselor's role in career counseling are examined and clarified before the chapter is concluded.

1.9 Summary

At the first level, the book is informed by the words (often attributed to Albert Einstein): "The definition of insanity is doing the same thing over and over again but expecting different results." Faced with mounting challenges in the occupational world, we, as career counselors, have to devise proactively innovative ways to remain useful and valuable to our clients by helping them do things that no longer work in a postmodern occupational environment in a new, changed way. To this end, the book draws on and develops Mark Savickas' career construction counseling[13] approach (2005) and, to a lesser extent, Jean Guichard's (2009) self-construction approach, the life design group's (Savickas et al., 2009) life design approach, and also related theoretical and conceptual approaches. At the second level, the book aims to help career counselors and their clients connect what clients know about themselves consciously with what they (clients) are aware of about themselves subconsciously. At the third level, it endeavors to direct these approaches towards further utility in individual and group contexts in Global North as well as Global South countries. At the fourth level, it shows how career counseling (counseling for self- and career construction) can be adapted and applied in a way that renews career counseling generally. At the fifth level, it shows how innovative counseling for self- and career construction can be used to bring about best practice in the profession. At the sixth level, it examines the career-life of Dolly Parton and demonstrates how her inspiring "story" encapsulates the essence of what postmodern career counseling is about. At the seventh level, the book sets out to show that career counseling can be exciting, creative, inspirational, and life-changing and can be used to help people across their life span experience meaning and purpose in their career-lives. Ultimately, though, the book fully supports Trull and Phares' (2001) contention that career counselors' primary allegiance in career counseling should be to find the best ways to help and be of value and use to their clients instead of adhering to any particular theoretical approach or technique—we have to stay abreast of global developments that impact our clients and consequently also our profession. The book also supports and illustrates the truth of Savickas' (2009a, 2009b, 2009c, 2009d) assertion that theory follows practice, and not the other way around.

[13]I use the terms "counseling for self- and career construction" and "career construction counseling" interchangeably in this book. The approach that I advocate when using the *CIP* and the *MCM* emphasizes the importance of both self- and career construction; hence the title of the book.

References

Allen, K. (2015, August 15). Technology has created more jobs than it has destroyed, says 140 years of data. *The Guardian*. Retrieved from https://www.theguardian.com/business/2015/aug/17/technologycreatedmorejobsthandestroyed140yearsdatacensus.

Bassot, B. (2015). Book review: Counseling for career construction—connecting life themes to construct life portraits: Turning pain into hope. *British Journal of Guidance and Counselling, 43*, 369–370. https://doi.org/10.1080/03069885.2015.1019313.

Bimrose, J., & Hearne, L. (2012). Resilience and career adaptability: Qualitative studies of adult career counseling. *Journal of Vocational Behavior, 8*(3), 338–344. https://doi.org/10.1016/j.jvb.2012.08.002.

Blustein, D. L. (2006). *The psychology of working: A new perspective for career development, counseling, and public policy*. New York, NY: Routledge.

Boje, D. M. (2008). *Storytelling organizations*. London, England: SAGE.

Butler, S. K. (2012). Issues of social justice and career development. *Career Planning & Adult Development Journal, 28*(1), 140–151.

Canham, H., & Langa, M. (2017). Narratives of everyday resistance from the margins. *PINS, 55*, 3–13. Retrieved from https://doi.org/10.17159/2309-8708/2017/n55a2.

Collins Dictionary. (n.d.). *Definition of 'innovation'*. Retrieved from https://www.collinsdictionary.com/dictionary/english/innovation.

Di Fabio, A., & Maree, J. G. (2016). Using a transdisciplinary interpretive lens to broaden reflections on alleviating poverty and promoting decent work. *Frontiers in Psychology, 6*. https://doi.org/10.3389/fpsyg.2016.00503.

Duarte, M. E. (2017a, June). *Sustainable decent work*. Invited public lecture at University of Pretoria, Pretoria, South Africa.

Duarte, M. E. (2017b, June). *Sustainable decent work and life design*. Invited public lecture at JvR Psychometrics, Randburg, South Africa.

Eramian, L. & & Denov, M. (2019). *Silence can be healing for Rwandan youth born of genocide rape*. Retrieved from http://theconversation.com/silence-can-be-healing-for-rwandan-youth-born-of-genocide-rape-96493.

Fraser, J. (2014). *Etymology of innovation*. Retrieved from https://www.innovationexcellence.com/blog/2014/04/29/etymology-of-innovation/.

Gaskell, A. (2018). *New report suggests 21 jobs of the future*. Retrieved from https://www.forbes.com/sites/adigaskell/2018/11/15/new-report-suggests-21-jobs-for-the-future/#4ff22c7549d8.

Grey, C. D. P. (2014). *Humans need not apply*. Retrieved from https://www.youtube.com/watch?v=7Pq-S557XQU.

Guichard, J. (2009). Self-constructing. *Journal of Vocational Behavior, 75*, 251–258.

Gurri, M. (2013). *The revolt of the public and the crisis of authority in the new millennium*. [Kindle DX version]. Retrieved from Amazon.com.

Hall, B. A., Halstead, M. E., & Taylor, T. R. (1986a). *Rothwell-Miller Interest Blank*. Pretoria: Human Sciences Research Council.

Hall, B. A., Halstead, M. E., & Taylor, T. R. (1986b). *Test administrator's manual for the Rothwell-Miller Interest Blank*. Pretoria, South Africa: HSRC.

Hartung, P. J. (2011). Career construction: Principles and practice. In K. Maree (Ed.), *Shaping the story: A guide to facilitating narrative counselling* (pp. 103–120). Rotterdam, The Netherlands: Sense.

Hartung, P. J. (2018, July). Life design: *A unifying paradigm for international Counseling Psychology. Paper prepared for Division 16*. Presidential Address at the 29th International Congress of Applied Psychology. Montréal, Quebec, Canada.

Hartung, P. J. (2019). Life design: A paradigm for innovating career counselling in global context. In J. G. Maree (Ed.), *Handbook of innovative career counseling* (pp. 3–18). New York, NY: Springer.

Herndon, W. H., & Welk, J. W. (1892). *Abraham Lincoln: The true story of a great life* (Vol II., p. 65). New York, NY: D. Appleton and Company.

Hooley, T., Sultana, R., & Thomsen, R. (2020). *Why a social justice informed approach to career guidance matters in the time of coronavirus*. https://careerguidancesocialjustice.wordpress.com/2020/03/23/why-a-social-justice-informed-approach-to-career-guidance-matters-in-the-time-of-coronavirus/.

Ivankova, N. V., Creswell, J. W., & Plano Clark, V. L. (2019). Foundations and approaches to mixed methods research. In J. G. Maree (Ed.), *First steps in research* (3rd ed., pp. 326–356). Pretoria, South Africa: van Schaik Publishers.

Kelly, J. (2020). *The coronavirus effect: Here are the jobs that will be added and lost*. Retrieved from https://www.forbes.com/sites/jackkelly/2020/03/19/the-coronavirus-effect-here-are-the-jobs-that-will-be-added-and-lost/?utm_source=newsletter&utm_medium=email&utm_campaign=career&cid=5cbf279f1802c8c524aef51c#3878564f2a1cKelly.

Kuhn, T. S. (1996). *The structure of scientific revolutions* (3rd ed.). Chicago, IL: University of Chicago Press.

Kuhn, T. S., & Hacking, I. (2012). *The structure of scientific revolutions* (4th ed.). Chicago, Il: The University of Chicago Press.

Lofts, N. (1958). *Heaven in your hand*. Greenwich, CT: Fawcett Publications.

London, T. (2018). *How to future proof a career in finance*. Retrieved from https://www.howwemadeitinafrica.com/how-to-future-proof-a-career-in-finance/62266/.

Maree, J. G. (2013a). *Counseling for career construction: Connecting life themes to construct life portraits: Turning pain into hope*. Rotterdam, The Netherlands: Sense.

Maree, J. G. (2013b). Latest developments in career counselling in South Africa: Towards a positive approach. *South African Journal of Psychology, 43*(4), 409–421.

Maree, J. G. (2016). *Maree Career Matrix (MCM)*. Randburg, South Africa: JvR Psychometrics.

Maree, J. G. (2017a). *The Career Interest Profile (Version 6)*. Randburg, SA: JvR Psychometrics.

Maree, J. G. (2017b). *The Career Interest Profile (CIP) (version 6): Obtaining, qualitatively, a profile of personal career-life themes and interests*. Randburg: JvR Psychometrics.

Maree, J. G. (2018a). Perspective: Promoting career development in the early years of people's lives through self- and career construction counselling to promote their career resilience and career adaptability. *Early Child Development and Care, 188*(4), 421–424. https://doi.org/10.1080/03004430.2018.1438748.

Maree, J. G. (2018b). Promoting career development and life design in the early years of a person's life. *Early Child Development and Care, 188*(4), 425–436. https://doi.org/10.1080/03004430.2017.1345892.

Maree, J. G. (2018c). Using life design counseling for career construction to facilitate sustainable employability and decent work in a developing country context. In V. Cohen-Scali, J. Pouyaud, M. Podgórny, V. Drabik-Podgórny, G. Aisenson, J-L. Bernaud, I. Moumoula., J. Guichard (Eds.). *Interventions in career design and education* (pp. 195–214). New York, NY: Springer.

Martin, C. R. (1995). *Looking at type and careers*. Gainesville, FL: Center for Applications of Psychological Type.

McAdams, D. P. (1993). *The stories we live by: Personal Myths and the making of the self*. New York, NY: William Morrow.

McAdams, D. P. (1997). *The stories we live by: Personal myths and the making of the self*. New York, NY: Guilford.

McAdams, D. P. (2010). The problem of meaning in personality psychology from the standpoints of dispositional traits, characteristic adaptations, and life stories. *Japanese Journal of Personality, 18*, 173–186.

McAdams, D. P. (2013). The psychological self as actor, agent, and author. *Perspectives on Psychological Science, 8*(3), 272–295.

McIlveen, P. (2012). Extending the metaphor of narrative to dialogical narrator. In P. McIlveen & D. E. Schultheiss (Eds.), *Social constructionism in vocational psychology and career development* (pp. 59-75). Rotterdam, The Netherlands: Sense Publishers.

McIlveen, P., & Patton, W. (2007). Narrative career counseling: Theory and exemplars of practice. *Australian Psychologist, 42,* 226–235.

McPherson, S. (2018). *Three things Africa must get right if it wants to leapfrog into the 4th industrial revolution.* Retrieved from https://www.gsb.uct.ac.za/po-3-things-africa-must-get-right-to-leapfrog-4th-industrial-revolution.

Merton, R. K. (1968). The Matthew effect in science. *Science, 159,* 56–63.

Niles, S. G. (1997). Annual review: Practice and research in career counseling and development—1996. *The Career Development Quarterly, 46,* 115–136.

Pring, B., Brown, R. H., Davis, E., Bahl, M., Cook, M., Styr, C., et al. (2018). *More jobs of the future: A guide to getting and staying employed through 2029.* Teaneck, NJ: Center for the future of work.

Ratts, M. J. (2009). Social justice counseling: Toward the development of a Fifth Force among counseling paradigms. *Journal of Humanistic Counseling, Education and Development, 48,* 160–172.

Ribeiro, M. A., & Gama de Almeida, M. C. C. (2019). A socio-constructionist career counseling grounded on intersectionality of gender, class and race/ethnicity. In J. G. Maree (Ed.), *Handbook of innovative career counseling)* (pp. 597–614). New York, NY: Springer.

Rossier, J., Ginevra, M. C., Bollmann, G., & Nota, L. (2017). The importance of career adaptability, career resilience, and employability in designing a successful life. In J. G. Maree (Ed.), *The psychology of career adaptability, career resilience, and employability* (pp. 65–82). New York, NY: Springer.

Savickas, M. L. (1993). Career counseling in the postmodern era. *Journal of Cognitive Psychotherapy: An International Quarterly, 7,* 205–215.

Savickas, M. L. (2001). Toward a comprehensive theory of career development: Disposition concerns and narratives. In F. T. L. Leong & A. Barak (Eds.), *Contemporary models in vocational psychology: A volume in honor of Samuel H. Osipow* (pp. 295–320). Mahwah, NJ: Lawrence Erlbaum.

Savickas, M. L. (2005). The theory and practice of career construction. In S. Brown & R. W. Lent (Eds.), *Career development and counseling: Putting theory and research to work* (pp. 42–70). New York, NY: John Wiley.

Savickas, M. L. (2007). Internationalization of counseling psychology: Constructing cross-national consensus and collaboration. *Applied Psychology: An International Review, 56*(1), 182-188.

Savickas, M. L. (2009a, April). *The essentials of life design counseling.* Invited public lecture, the University of Pretoria, Pretoria, South Africa.

Savickas, M. L. (2009b, April). *Utilizing early anecdotes in counseling in the 21st century.* Keynote presentation, SA Society for Clinical Hypnosis. Pretoria, South Africa.

Savickas, M. L. (2009c, June). *The role of values in careers: Meaning and mattering in life design.* Keynote at the Biennial Society for Vocational Psychology Conference, University of St Louis, Missouri.

Savickas, M. L. (2009d). Career-style counseling. In T. J. Sweeney (Ed.), *Adlerian counseling and psychotherapy: A practitioner's approach* (5th ed., pp. 183–207). New York, NY: Routledge.

Savickas, M. L. (2011). Reshaping the story of career counseling. In K. Maree (Ed.), Shaping the story—A guide to facilitate narrative counseling (pp. 1–3). Boston/Rotterdam, The Netherlands: Sense.

Savickas, M. L. (2015a). Career counseling paradigms: Guiding, developing, and designing. In P. Hartung, M. Savickas, & W. Walsh (Eds.), *The APA handbook of career intervention* (Vol. 1, pp. 129–143). Washington, DC: APA Books.

Savickas, M. L. (2015b). *Life-design counseling manual.* Rootstown, OH: Author.

Savickas, M. L. (2016a, July). *Meaning at work: Work at meaning.* Closing keynote presentation, National Career Development Association Conference, Chicago, United States of America.

Savickas, M. L. (2016b). Reflection and reflexivity during life-design interventions: Comments on Career Construction Counseling. *Journal of Vocational Behavior, 97,* 84–89.

Savickas, M. L. (2019). *Theories of psychotherapy series. Career counseling* (2nd ed.). Washington, DC: American Psychological Association.

Savickas, M. L., Nota, L., Rossier, J., Dauwalder, J. P., Duarte, M. E., Guichard, J., ...Van Vianen, A. E. M. (2009). Life designing: A paradigm for career construction in the 21st century. *Journal of Vocational Behavior, 75*, 239–250.

Soresi, S., & Nota, L. (2010). Alcune procedure qualitative per il career counseling [Some qualitative procedures for career counseling]. In L. Nota & S. Soresi (Eds.), *Sfide e nuovi orizzonti per l'orientamento. Metodologie e nuove pratiche* (pp. 100–135). Firenze, Italy: Giunti O.S.

Strauser, D. R., Lustig, D. C., & Çiftçi, A. (2008). Psychological well-being: Its relation to work personality, vocational identity, and career thoughts. *The Journal of Psychology, 142*(1), 21–35.

Subich, L. M. (2011, August). Tracing the evolution of career counseling theory. In P. J. Hartung, Chair. *Career counseling. Definitions and new directions.* Paper read at the 119th annual meeting of the American Psychological Association, Washington, D.C.

Trull, T. J., & Phares, E. J. (2001). *Clinical psychology* (6th ed.). Belmont, CA: Wadsworth.

Van Schneider, T. (2017). If you want it, you might get it. *The reticular activating system.* Retrieved from https://medium.com/desk-of-van-schneider/if-you-want-it-you-might-get-it-the-reticular-activating-system-explained-761b6ac14e53.

Welty, E. (1998). *One writer's beginnings.* Cambridge, MA: Harvard University Press.

Winslade, J. (2011). Constructing a career narrative through the care of the self. In K. Maree (Ed.), *Shaping the story: A guide to facilitating narrative counseling* (pp. 52–62). Rotterdam, The Netherlands: Sense.

Part II
Theoretical and Conceptual Framework

Chapter 2
Innovating Counseling for Self- and Career Construction: Theoretical Premises, Antecedents, and Associations

Innovation is taking two things that already exist and putting them together in a new way (Tom Freston)

Abstract In this chapter, I first discuss the need for an innovative approach to career counseling. A few examples of key life transitions are given. Several personality theories that have influenced the development of career counseling theory and practice are considered. Next, humanistic and related perspectives on human performance, development, choice-making, and execution that relate to counseling for self- and career construction and life design are covered. I also discuss different perspectives on the notion of "Active mastering of passive suffering".

2.1 Need for an Innovative and Proactive Approach to Career Counseling

The world of work is changing rapidly largely because of major work-defining technological advances brought about by the Fourth Industrial Revolution (Work 4.0) (Urbanaviciute, Udayar, & Rossier, 2019).[1] Work contexts are transforming mainly due to information and communication (ICT) innovations, and in the process many workers are feeling alienated and losing their sense of safety and security in the work environment. Many jobs are likely to disappear and many human beings may well be replaced by robots in the workplace. Thousands of people are either losing their jobs or are unable to access work. Underemployment and unemployment rates across the world are rising steadily, and inequality is spiraling. Big business is gathering large data sets and hiring data analysts to identify and predict work-related trends, and career counselors should do the same. In the midst of the changes taking place in

[1]For the purposes of this book, career counseling is defined as "helping people to develop and accept an integrated and adequate picture of themselves and of their role in the work world, to test this concept against reality, and to convert it into reality with satisfaction to themselves and benefit to society" (Savickas, 2019a, p. 161; also see Super, 1951).

J. G. (Kobus) Maree, *Innovating Counseling for Self- and Career Construction*,
https://doi.org/10.1007/978-3-030-48648-8_2

Table 2.1 Examples of key life transitions

	Transition from	To
1	Womb	World
2	Home	Crèche
3	Crèche	Primary school
4	Primary school	Secondary school
5	Secondary school	Tertiary training
6	Tertiary training	World of work
7	One work environment	Next … (and so on)
8	Etc.	

the workplace, a high premium is placed on workers' ability to deal effectively with repeated work-related transitions, work insecurity, and work-related trauma.

People need to be reminded that they have already successfully navigated many crossroads in their lives, that facing a crossroads is a natural phenomenon in the life of everyone, and that people should draw inspiration from these crossroads experiences. Table 2.1 shows a few examples of life transitions.

Questions I am frequently asked by research participants, students, congress and workshop attendees, colleagues, and clients include the following: Will all jobs disappear in the future or change to such an extent that I will no longer be able to do my work competently? Will robots take the place of most human workers? Will I still fit into my current work environment? How will I deal with the additional free time at my disposal since robots will increasingly take over "routine" tasks? Is it true that people will change jobs up to 20 times and more? Will I be allowed to work after the age of, for instance, 40? Will non-regulated jobs increase? These questions often reveal insecurity, low self-esteem, feelings of worthlessness, depression, and even thoughts of suicide (Pillay, 2019). Individually and collectively these questions reflect people's concern about an occupational environment over which they have seemingly lost control. They indicate that we as career psychology theorists, researchers, and practitioners must respond timeously and appropriately to ensure that we continue to provide a career counseling service that meets the changing career counseling needs of our clients. Of course, this also means that we as human beings and workers ourselves need to attend to and make sense of these changes and draw on our experiences to guide and enable us to meet adequately and professionally the needs of clients.

2.2 Changing and Innovating Our Approach to Career Counseling Routinely

Several economic downturns, globalization, technological advances, downsizing, retrenchments, and organizational mergers are changing the occupational world and impacting career theory and practice irreversibly (Maree & Di Fabio, 2019; Reid & West, 2011, 2016; Savickas, 2019a).[2] The unprecedented hardships caused by the economic, financial, and psychological impact of the coronavirus pandemic illustrate what I mean. Reid and West (2016) maintain that "[i]n the context of mass migration and unstable labor markets … traditional career guidance is no longer sufficient … the need for a paradigm shift is becoming more urgent" (p. 573). Arulmani (2019) contends that "More than two thirds of the world follow occupations where work is mainly in the informal sector" and asks: "Does "career" really exist in these contexts?" (n.p.) The search is on for a model that supplements, updates, and innovates current interventions to address numerous key changes in the occupational world impelled by information communication technology developments fast-tracked by networking and increased connectivity (Gurri, 2013). The chances of finding "stable" work and working for one organization throughout one's life are fast disappearing; causing insecurity and uncertainty among present-day workers. Research is therefore needed on how the occupational world is changing, how these changes are impacting workers, and what the reasons for the changes are. We then need to project into the future and devise innovative career counseling interventions to ensure that the service we offer remains relevant, helpful, and valuable, bearing in mind technological advances and the advent of Work 4.0 and Work 5.0 as well as the envisaged effect of artificial intelligence developments.

To a smaller or larger extent, the counseling for self- and career construction approach advocated in this book correlates positively with several personality and identity theories. Some of these theories are discussed below.

2.3 Influence of Personality and Identity Theories on the Development of Career Counseling Theory and Practice

It is generally agreed that the development of career counseling theory and practice has been strongly influenced by personality theories (Cherry, 2018; Maree, 2002, 2009, 2013; Overview of…, n.d.; Phares, 1992; Trull & Phares, 2001). To a smaller or larger extent, the counseling for self- and career construction approach advocated in

[2]The discipline of career counseling has witnessed innovation in Global North countries (Western European and North American countries in particular) during the past three to four decades especially. However, this has not quite been the case in Global South (i.e. developing) countries. However, the inspiring efforts of colleagues and researchers such as Arulmani (2019) and Ribeiro (2016) in this regard are acknowledged and appreciated.

this book correlates positively with the psychodynamic and humanistic perspectives on human performance, the narrative perspective, the socio-constructionist perspective, the systems theory perspective but also with psycho-social development as well as self-concept development (a key aspect of life span, life-space career development theories). All these perspectives are reflected in the integrative strategy advocated in the book and discussed below.

2.3.1 Psychodynamic Approach as an Important Premise of Career Construction Counseling

People are influenced by the dynamic forces that begin to shape their lives at a very young age (Bordin, 1994). How they interact with significant others (close family members in particular) are key aspects of their future storylines. Negative experiences (e.g. trauma, sadness, and rejection) as well as positive experiences (e.g. emotional support, encouragement, and approval) and unresolved issues (e.g. parents' divorce) in the early years remain with people throughout their lives. People's lives are also shaped by a wide array of experiences later in life. These influences provide the foundation for decision-making as and when new crossroads are experienced, such as going to school for the first time, transitioning from one grade to another, losing a friend, leaving the parental home to study, taking up a new job, and dealing with perceived "failure"[3] or success. Here, it is important to stress the word "perceived" as an achievement (e.g. achieving 75% in a test) may signify failure for one person (who tried to achieve 80% in the test) and success for another person. A lot depends on how achievement (or lack thereof) is perceived (or perceived to be perceived) by significant others. Put differently: People's life stories (autobiographies) (Savickas, 2019a) or life narratives (Edwards, 2018) are constantly shaped, co-shaped, and reshaped; scripted, co-scripted, and rescripted in the course of interaction that includes both verbal and non-verbal communication and conversation as well as reflection (reflecting on one's life story) and reflexivity (drawing on one's reflections to bring about change and forward movement in one's life). In the process, a wealth of information (on how people can deal with transitions) is built up that people can draw on whenever they experience repeated transitions that must be negotiated.

Essentially, the psychodynamic approach holds that powerful **conscious as well as subconscious motivations and determinations will** influence people throughout their lives. The **storied approach with its narrative framework** (Brott, 2001) draws on the underpinnings outlined above by acknowledging the power and influence of past experiences on people's lives and is premised on the assumption that **every person's life story starts with hurt, pain, or suffering** (Savickas, 2011a). However,

[3]The word 'fail' has no place in current education parlance. Instead the phrase 'insufficient achievement' is more appropriate. I am using the word here merely because it has become ingrained in our education vocabulary.

it should be emphasized that this approach essentially focuses on the creation or construction of new possibilities and transforming past experiences of hurt into positive stories that promote the transcending of a hurtful past and inadequate access to resources of various kinds. Elicitation of these stories sets in motion the dynamic process of construction, deconstruction, reconstruction, and co-construction of the stories to help people make meaning of their lives (choose and construct meaningful careers and lives), find a sense of purpose, and (re-)kindle a sense of hope for the future.

Here it may be worth noting Enright's (2018) assertion that experiencing (emotional) pain of whatever kind ("challenges") early in one's life almost always serves a useful purpose. The author contends that the growth of young people who have had almost all their needs met and who have experienced little suffering may be stifled (Enright, 2018). In my opinion, the search for a sense of meaning and purpose is humankind's most profound search, irrespective of the context in which one finds oneself. I frequently present workshops on the art and science of writing scholarly articles and participants' single most important question generally is: "Why do we have to write these articles that, in most cases, mean nothing to society and are read by a very small number of people at best?"

2.3.2 The Humanistic Approach as a Keystone of the Narrative Approach

Rogers (1951, 1961, 1977) has a non-deterministic view of human functioning and development that emphasizes the effect of human motivation and preferences on how people think and act. Rogers foregrounded the power of people's inner world but also their perceptions of the world on how they behaved. In similar vein, Seeman (2008), Teixeira and Gomes (2000), and Young and Valach (2004) maintain that people's personal choice and agency are crucial shaping forces in their key life decisions. Cochran (1997), too, underscores the importance of agency in actively making things happen instead of letting things happen to one. Also, from a social cognitive career theory perspective, many authors (e.g. Bandura, 2011; Lent, Brown, & Hackett, 1994, 1996) stress the importance of people's self-efficacy or the belief that they can achieve desired outcomes or aims.

The person-centered perspective (humanistic perspective) holds that people are free to choose and are not "condemned" by or subject to "chance" or circumstances beyond their control (Rogers, 1951). Hartung (2011, 2015), McAdams (2010), and Savickas (2019a) argue that adapting oneself to the life-long (perpetual or continuous) progression of fitting oneself to work-related roles (as social actors), accomplishing career-life goals (as motivated agents), and constructing oneself and one's career to make personal and social meaning (as autobiographical authors) already commences in the early childhood years. Maree (2018a, 2018b) maintains that experiences during early childhood constitute happenings that comprise "a series of happenstances", developmental crises, and areas for growth" (p. 421) that collectively form psychic footprints or life themes that acquire particular prominence later in life. This implies that self- and career construction (and, ultimately, life design intervention) should be introduced early in life to enable people to attain stable work-life identities that may help them deal with challenges and transitions during their work-lives (Maree, 2018a, 2018b).

Factors emphasized by humanistic perspectives include the importance of self-authorship, accepting responsibility for one's actions, the elicitation of people's career and personal stories, the importance of meaning-making (achieving a meaningful existence), and people's continual search for a purposeful life and meeting their destiny. It is believed also that people can transcend perceived or real barriers and challenges imposed on them by their environments by taking ownership of and accepting responsibility for their actions. (Maslow's (1987) view that having an occupation contributes meaningfully to people's need satisfaction is relevant here too.)

The notions of active mastering of passive suffering. The humanistic view implicitly advances the idea that reflection and, subsequently, reflexivity are key elements in career counseling. Once people arrive at a good understanding of their private world, they are more likely to rise above life's vicissitudes, view their idiosyncratic restrictions ("limitations") as opportunities for growth (development), and actively master what they have suffered (Freud, 1963; Savickas, 2019a).

Table 2.2 Different perspectives on the notion of "Active mastering of passive suffering"

	Distinctive explication of the notion "Active mastering of passive suffering"	Author
1	Active mastering of passive suffering	Savickas (2005, 2019a, 2019b)
2	The wound is the place where the light enters you	Sehgal (2016)
3	Our torments also may, in length of time, become our elements	Milton (2002)
4	Every opportunity has a difficulty, and every difficulty has an opportunity	Ryan (2016)
5	"Where id was, there ego shall be" (p. 112)	Freud (1991)
6	From a felt negative [sense of failure] to a perceived plus	Adler (1958); Slavik and Carlson (2007)
7	From tragedy to triumph	Frankl (2006)
8	From identity crisis (role confusion) to adequate identity formation	Cherry (2020); Erikson (1994)
Etc.		

Challenging developments in children's storylines signify unresolved issues they have passively experienced (key developmental tasks they have failed to master successfully) (Erikson, 1994). His strong emphasis on the importance of young children mastering key developmental tasks is a fundamental contribution to current thinking on the essence of career counselling (Erikson, 1968)

The principle of converting pain or hurt into hope and a social contribution (Savickas, 2016, 2019a, 2019b) has been elaborated on by many leading scholars in the twin fields of psychology and career counseling (see Table 2.2). Typically, career counselors seek to identify the unresolved challenges/pain clients suffered during their early lives and enable them to turn their hurt into hope. 'Problematic' (challenging) "twists" in clients' storylines (unresolved issues they have passively experienced) are thus resolved. In reality, and even though this may seem unlikely at first, these "opposites" are in fact very close and to a certain extent relate to the notion of "graduating" from feeling disempowered to feeling empowered. Needless to say, from a self- and career construction perspective, this also implies that **people's "pain" (feeling disempowered) can and should be linked to their future careers (that should 'empower' them to heal others but also themselves**. The following examples illustrate the point. Suzanne cited the fact that she "could not pronounce words correctly and was mocked because of that" as her most painful experience when she was young. After three unsuccessful attempts, she succeeded in enrolling for a degree in speech and language. Jane said: "I was fat and 'ugly' and was the butt of many sick jokes by my friends". She is now studying to become a dietician.

The "every thesis has an antithesis" principle. Here, the authors draw on the "every thesis has an antithesis" assumption (all beliefs or emotions have contrasting opposites). Every preoccupation (compulsion or obsession) has a diametric opposite, for instance, feeling 'invisible' (unacknowledged) is the diametric opposite of feeling 'visible' (acknowledged) (see Table 2.3). Ultimately, the aim of career counseling is to bring about change in clients by facilitating progress in meaning-making within them. For instance, an individual who feels "hurt" should be assisted to find a way to **convert her or his hurt into hope and social contributions (potentially even into a business model)**. The success of such intervention requires career counselors to guide clients practically on how to achieve progress in identifying the kind of meaning they attach to key life experiences.

There are, of course, numerous examples of this kind of change that demonstrates progress in the meaning people attach to life experiences. The point is that staying at an abstract, theoretical level when dealing with preoccupations is not helpful. Career counselors and their clients should rather work together to devise action plans to bring about positive change in the negative meaning people often attach to life experiences. It is also important to understand that there is never a single 'accurate, 'valid', or 'objective' analysis of people's stories (Savickas, 2016) or "right" or "wrong" ways of dealing with preoccupations. Certain "action plans" may, however, be less appropriate than others and, consequently, following up on clients' progress and renegotiating action strategies as and when needed are crucial.

This perspective resonates positively with me. Early in my career as a psychologist, I was interested in the influence of "subconscious personality challenges" on my clients' career-related decisions. At the time, under the guidance of a respected mentor, I used the *Zulliger ink blots* and the *Thematic Apperception Test* (Murray, 1943; Zulliger, 1969) to illuminate clients' "subconscious personality challenges". Having identified such challenges, I tried to find a way to link them to future occupations. I wondered about the wisdom and, especially, the theoretical and scientific

Table 2.3 Demonstrating the thesis vs antithesis assumption: Examples of changes demonstrating progress in making meaning of life experiences

Thesis	Antithesis	Action steps to bring about progress in such meaning-making
"Stuckness", impediment, or constriction (preoccupation; key life experience and theme)	Change demonstrating progress in making meaning of life experiences (purposeful resolution)	Practical examples
Hurt	Hope	A mother loses her daughter to cancer and starts a support group for parents of children with terminal illnesses
Invisibility	Visibility	A woman who feels unacknowledged ("invisible") by her peers offers her "help" to an orphanage where she helps abandoned children with their homework
Victim	Survivor	A hijacking survivor writes a book on what to do during hijacking situations and how to deal with emotional scarring that may occur after a hijacking. He gives talks at schools to promote learners' alertness to possible hijacking situations
Hardship	Opportunity	A young black man from a seriously disadvantaged region completes school, becomes an engineer, and starts to give extra classes in mathematics and physical sciences to disadvantaged high school learners on Saturday afternoons to help them achieve better marks so that they can qualify for sought-after fields of study
Symptom	Strength	A young girl suffers from severe acne and is mocked by her peers. She later becomes a medical specialist specializing in skin-related problems such as acne

(continued)

Table 2.3 (continued)

Thesis	Antithesis	Action steps to bring about progress in such meaning-making
Demoralized	Inspirational	A woman loses the "love of her life" in a motorcar accident. She writes a song about her traumatic experience and starts a support group for others who have had similar experiences. She is amazed at the healing they find by writing songs or poems about their experiences
Denied	Acknowledged	A young man who was denied access to a private school establishes an NGO that secures funding for talented learners from resource-constrained environments
Unloved	Loved	A young man is "sold" by his parents at the age of five. He completes his university studies, becomes a hugely successful construction manager, and devotes his life to finding money to establish facilities for homeless children
Silenced	Articulation	A young man who stuttered early in his life (and still struggles with certain sounds) studies speech-language pathology to help children with speech-language impediments
Suffering	Surviving	A young woman from a destitute background writes an inspiring teenage novel on how she managed to deal with what she described as an almost "hopeless" situation

(continued)

Table 2.3 (continued)

Thesis	Antithesis	Action steps to bring about progress in such meaning-making
Vulnerable	Resilient	A young woman gives birth to a baby girl while in Grade 11 and is compelled to give her baby up for adoption (a day that she describes as "the saddest day of my life"). She completes school and becomes a social worker who works with pregnant adolescents. Travelling and lecturing across the world helps her not only heal others as well as herself but also make a decent living–a good example of innovatively converting pain into hope and a viable business model[a]
Receiving	Giving	A young student from an affluent family who has "everything" in life starts taking drugs and is expelled from university on account of his addiction. He befriends a counselor while in an institution for victims of substance abuse, enrols for a degree in teaching, and becomes a youth counselor in a township school, specializing in working with learners with substance abuse problems

[a]Sugars (2013) asserts that "Having an idea for a business is great, but knowing the difference between a good idea and a good commercial idea is literally money in the bank" (p. 2)

justification and appropriateness of encouraging a person who presented with, for instance, a history of having been bullied or even abused as a child to venture into fields such as teaching or law. After all, there is a strong likelihood that such a person will repeatedly be confronted with challenges like the very she or he had experienced in early (or earlier) life. I still recall the popular but somewhat denigrating observation that psychologists venture into the field of psychology precisely because they have themselves experienced the "problems" they would have to deal with as psychologists. It was only after I had met Mark Savickas that the realization began to dawn on me that we can all heal ourselves through our daily work by helping to heal others with similar experiences.

Enright (2018) maintains that when people are treated unreasonably, they suffer and subsequently develop feelings of anger, disappointment, anxiety, and sadness (sentiments that can impede healthy development). They can choose to internalize the negativity that results from suffering (which can stifle their growth and development forever) or they can choose **not** to internalize their suffering and concomitant anger by making a conscious effort to make meaning of their suffering, absolve those who have hurt them, and work through their suffering in a way that prevents others from being hurt in the process. Frankl is globally renowned for having stressed the value of finding meaning in one's suffering. Seen from this perspective, external trauma and suffering can be converted into motivations for growth and development. According to Enright (2018), "[h]ow we respond to the suffering, internally and not just behaviorally, may make all the difference in our lives" (p. 2). Ziller (2000) concisely summarizes the humanistic perspective by stating that we all have the capacity to become our "own agents of change" (p. 265).

2.4 Narrative Counseling as the Bedrock of Career Construction Counseling

Cochran (1997, 2011), Hatch and Cunliffe (2006), Jones (1996), Lieblich, Tuval-Mashiach, and Zilber (1998), Logan (2004), Maree (2013), Savickas (2019a), Sonn, Stevens, and Duncan (2013), and Stevens, Duncan, and Hook (2013) contend that narrative counseling is founded on several premises and assumptions, including the following:

- People's individual life stories give significance and meaning to and help them construct their career-lives.
- People's life stories revolve around several central life themes.
- People author and perform their general life stories and their life stories.
- Various people, events, environments, and other influences jointly shape people's life stories.
- People's life stories filter their interpretations and perceptions either constructively or destructively.
- People are the key protagonists (social actors, motivated agents, and autobiographical authors) in their life stories.
- Storytelling comes to people naturally. Moreover, people's life stories enhance a sense of consistency or coherence and continuity to their lived experiences and interactions.
- Narrative counseling comprises more than a mere technique or strategy—its key characteristic vests in its capacity to enhance meaning-making.
- Narratives should not be regarded as "a" or "the" story because they have multiple meanings for different people (interviewers and interviewees).
- How the concepts of social actorship, motivated agency, and autobiographical authorship are intertwined either promotes or inhibits the extension and promotion of people's career-life stories (McAdams, 2013; Savickas, 2011a, 2016).

- People's micro-stories are personal, self-scripted, and self-constructed and can be gathered and connected or woven into a macro-story (emplotment).
- Integrated, these small or micro-stories constitute people's "grand life story" in microcosm. The meaning we make in our stories potentially predisposes us to either destructive or constructive thinking, feeling, understanding, and behavior patterns.
- Many people are not offered appropriate opportunities to narrate or articulate their life stories and elicit inner advice regarding appropriate ways to deal with challenges and navigate numerous life transitions.
- The conversion of "problem-saturated" narratives or stories (White & Epston, 1990) into positive, healing, and inspiring ones is key to meaning-making and living a purposeful life. People can choose whether to accept passively unconstructive "storylines" imposed on them by life or actively convert them into stories of hope and inspiration. Counseling for self- and career construction counseling intervention can contribute to the transformation of destructive stories into positive ones.
- Autobiographical reasoning enables people to conceptualize ways to manage numerous career-life transitions.

The quality of the counseling relationship will co-determine the success or failure of narrative (storied) career counseling. So too will the extent to which career counselors succeed in facilitating safe holding environments or safe spaces for clients (Winnicott, 1964). The latter substantially enhance the construction, deconstruction, reconstruction, and co-construction (sharing, unpacking, re-authoring, and co-authoring) of people's life stories.

2.5 Social Constructionism

The emphasis in social constructionism is on how people themselves, their knowledge construction, and their life stories are shaped and influenced by their idiosyncratic sociocultural and historical contexts (Hutchison, 2003; Robbins, Chatterjee, & Canda, 2005). Stated differently: Social constructionism relates to self- and career identity construction (which includes both objective and subjective facets). Career counselors adopt a "not-knowing" position (Anderson & Goolishian, 1992). The social constructionist emphasis is on eliciting and understanding people's idiosyncratic cultural scripts and narratives (life stories). A collaborative relationship is established between counselors and clients with the aim of promoting authentic self- and career construction by clients.

2.6 Systems Theory

This theory espouses the idea of a closely interconnected series of micro-, meso-, or macro-level, individual systems "within which is depicted a range of intrapersonal influences on career development, such as personality, ability, gender, and sexual orientation" (Patton & McMahon, 2006a, p. 154). People's individual systems are embedded in numerous interconnected, open systems that relate to many other influences that encompass their unique environmental and social systems. Systems theory correlates positively with the storied approach (the idea that people's life stories comprise a series of closely intertwined consecutive chapters). New chapters emerge from and are intrinsically linked to earlier chapters and vice versa. People's many stories are embedded in the stories of their communities—many cultural scripts (broader sub- and sub-subsystems) are available that shape people's individual life stories. Hatch and Cunliffe (2006) argue that our stories are "intertwined with organizational, social, and historical narratives" (p. 198). All systems form part of an overall all-inclusive system (Patton & McMahon, 1999, 2006a, 2006b). Any happening at any level has a ripple effect on the other levels in a given hierarchy. Whatever happens in a person's life influences that person in toto.

2.7 Psychosocial Development Theory: The Importance of Focusing on Key Developmental Tasks

Erikson's (1963, 1968) psychoanalytic theory distinguishes between eight stages in human development, beginning in infancy and culminating in late adulthood, namely 1. Basic trust versus Mistrust (infancy, 1–2 years); 2. Autonomy versus Shame and doubt (early childhood, 2–4 years); 3. Initiative versus Guilt (preschool age, 4–5 years); 4. Industry versus Inferiority (school age, 5–12 years); 5. Identity versus Role confusion (adolescence, 13–19 years); 6. Intimacy versus Isolation (early adulthood, 20–40 years); 7. Generativity versus Stagnation (adulthood, 40–65 years); and 8. Ego integrity versus Despair (maturity, 65-) (Erikson, 1994; Sprouts, 2017). These stages unfold naturally after birth and are influenced by people's environmental and culture-related nurturing, rearing, and education. People encounter and must deal with different challenges in each consecutive stage, and, ideally, they succeed in mastering these challenges. If certain challenges are not dealt with successfully, they often recur as "problems" in later stages. People nevertheless move from one stage to another irrespective of whether challenges encountered during previous stages have been dealt with successfully or not.

Erikson (1968) singles out identity formation as a key developmental task during adolescence in particular but also during the next stage when people transition from adolescence to early adulthood (i.e. the two stages when people normally choose fields of study, careers, and/or jobs). Stringer, Kerpelman, and Skorikov (2011, p. 158) define career identity as "the sense of self derived from one's development of an occupational career ... [it] is an important component of one's overall identity". Erikson (1963) argues that being unable to choose an appropriate career and find satisfying work or having an insufficient sense of self (or a negative career identity) renders career-related transitions particularly challenging. He emphasizes the social aspects of identity formation while acknowledging that broader contexts shape and co-determine people's various career-life roles. McAdams, Josselson, and Lieblich (2001) and Savickas (2011a) view identity formation as a self-construction process that develops over time.

2.8 Self-Concept Development/Identity Formation as a Key Facet of Life Span, Life Space Theory

Identity formation is also an integral element of Super's (1951, 1957) developmental perspectives on vocational choice. The notion of identity formation is especially relevant in his discussion of the exploratory stage of life, which he sees as the period between the ages of 14 and 24 years. Developmental theories are central to the approach discussed in this book because they promote our understanding of childhood and adolescence and the challenges faced while negotiating career-related transitions during this stage of life—a time when adolescents strive not only to gather information about themselves but, at a deeper level, also to authenticate their sense of self (self-concept or self-view). The fundamental question they endeavor to answer is, "Who am I?" (See Chap. 9 for a more detailed discussion.)

2.9 Summary

This chapter brought together insights into and perspectives on the theory base in relation to postmodernizing (a key component of which is innovation) career counseling across the world. The emergence and advancement of qualitative perspectives on career counseling coincided with and were strongly influenced by personality theories such as different and divergent career development theories, humanistic theories, and systems theory. Humanistic and phenomenological perspectives, in tandem with narrative and socio-constructionist perspectives, have had a major bearing on the emergence, general acceptance, and implementation of qualitative career counseling theory, research, practice, and policy. The latter manifested particularly in life, career, and life design counseling in Global North countries especially. Looking back over the past three decades in particular, it seems clear that the successful postmodernizing of career counseling can be ascribed largely to the stellar contributions of Savickas (2019a) (career construction counseling), Guichard (2005) (self-construction), and the life design group (Savickas et al., 2009) (life design counseling). The next chapter (Chap. 3) discusses the postmodernizing and innovating influence on career counseling of the above trio of contributions.

References

Adler, A. (1958). *What life should mean to you*. New York, NY: Capricorn Books.

Anderson, H., & Goolishian, H. (1992). Human systems as linguistic systems: Evolving ideas about the implications for theory and practice. *Family Process, 27,* 371–393.

Arulmani, G. (2019, September). *Career guidance in transition economies: New lamps for old?* Keynote address at the 43rd International Association for Educational and Vocational Guidance Conference, Bratislava, Slovakia.

Bandura, A. (2011). Social cognitive theory. In P. A. M. van Lange, A. W. Kruglanski, & E. T. Higgins (Eds.), *Handbook of theories of social psychological* (pp. 349–373). Thousand Oaks, CA: Sage.

Bordin, E. S. (1994). Intrinsic motivation and the active self: Convergence from a psychodynamic perspective. In M. L. Savickas & R. W. Lent (Eds.), *Convergence in career development theories* (pp. 53–62). Palo Alto, CA: CPP Books.

Brott, E. (2001). The storied approach: A postmodern perspective for career counseling. *The Career Development Quarterly, 49,* 304–313.

Cherry, K. (2018). *Perspectives in modern psychology*. Retrieved from https://www.verywellmind.com/perspectives-in-modern-psychology-2795595.

Cherry, K. (2020-03-20). *Biography of Erik Erikson (1902–1994)*. Retrieved from https://www.verywellmind.com/erik-erikson-biography-1902-1994-2795538.

Cochran, L. R. (1997). *Career counseling: A narrative approach*. Pacific Grove, CA: Thousand Oaks.

Cochran, L. R. (2011). The promise of narrative career counseling. In K. Maree (Ed.), *Shaping the story—A guide to facilitating narrative counseling* (pp. 7–19). Rotterdam, The Netherlands: Sense.

Edwards, L. H. (2018). *Dolly Parton: Gender and country music*. Bloomington, IN: Indiana University Press.

Enright, R. (2018). *Why Maslow's self-actualization theory is not quite right: Having all needs met and living with little suffering may stifle grow*th. Retrieved from https://www.psychologytoday.com/us/blog/the-forgiving-life/201805/why-maslows-self-actualization-theory-is-not-quite-right.

Erikson, E. H. (1963). *Childhood and society* (2nd ed.). New York, NY: Norton.

Erikson, E. H. (1968). *Identity: Youth and crisis*. New York, NY: W. W. Norton.

Erikson, E. H. (1994). *Identity: Youth and crisis (No. 7)*. New York, NY: WW Norton.

Frankl, V. (2006). *Man's search for meaning*. Boston, MA: Beacon Press.

Freud, S. (1963). *The standard edition of the complete psychological works of Sigmund Freud*. London, England: Hogarth.

Freud, S. (1991). *The dissection of the psychical personality (Lecture 31). In new introductory lectures on psychoanalysis* (1932, James Strachey, Trans.). London & New York. Penguin.

Guichard, J. (2005). Life-long self-construction. *International Journal for Educational and Vocational Guidance, 5,* 111–124.

Gurri, M. (2013). *The revolt of the public and the crisis of authority in the new millennium*. [Kindle DX version]. Retrieved from Amazon.com.

Hartung, P. J. (2011). Career construction: Principles and practice. In K. Maree (Ed.), *Shaping the story: A guide to facilitating narrative counselling* (pp. 103–120). Rotterdam, The Netherlands: Sense.

Hartung, P. J. (2015). Life design in childhood: Antecedents and advancement. In L. Nota & J. Rossier (Eds.), *Handbook of life design: From practice to theory, and from theory to practice* (pp. 89–101). Göttingen, Germany: Hogrefe.

Hatch, M. J., & Cunliffe, A. L. (2006). *Organization theory modern, symbolic, and postmodern perspectives* (2nd ed.). New York: Oxford University Press.

Hutchison, E. D. (2003). *Dimensions of human behavior: Person and environment* (2nd ed.). Thousand Oaks, CA: Sage.

Jones, M. O. (1996). *Studying organisational symbolism: What, how, why*. Thousand Oaks, CA: Sage.

Lent, R. W., Brown, S. D., & Hackett, G. (1994). Toward a unifying social cognitive theory of career and academic interest, choice, and performance. *Journal of Vocational Behavior, 45,* 79–122.

Lent, R. W., Brown, S. D., & Hackett, G. (1996). Career development from a sociocognitive perspective. In D. Brown & L. Brooks (Eds.), *Career choice and development* (3rd ed., pp. 373–422). San Francisco: Jossey-Bass.

Lieblich, A., Tuval-Mashiach, R., & Zilber, T (1998). *Narrative research. Reading, analysis, and interpretation.* (Applied Social Research Methods Series, 47.) Thousand Oaks, CA: Sage.

Logan, B. (2004). *Narrative therapy.* Retrieved from http://www.bl.co.nz/Counseling/Narrative_therapy.htm.

Maree, J. G. (2002). Theoretical approaches: An overview. In J. G. Maree, & L. Ebersöhn (Eds.), *Lifeskills and career counselling* (pp. 3–32). Cape Town, South Africa: Heinemann.

Maree, J. G. (2009). Career counseling in the 21st century: South African institutions of higher education at the crossroads. *South African Journal of Higher Education, 23,* 429–435.

Maree, J. G. (2013). *Counseling for career construction: Connecting life themes to construct life portraits: Turning pain into hope.* Rotterdam, The Netherlands: Sense.

Maree, J. G. (2018a). Perspective: Promoting career development in the early years of people's lives through self- and career construction counselling to promote their career resilience and career adaptability. *Early Child Development and Care, 188*(4), 421–424. https://doi.org/10.1080/03004430.2018.1438748.

Maree, J. G. (2018b). Promoting career development and life design in the early years of a person's life. *Early Child Development and Care, 188*(4), 425–436. https://doi.org/10.1080/03004430.2017.1345892.

Maree, J. G., & Di Fabio, A. (2019). Integrating personal and career counseling to promote sustainable development and change. *Personality and Individual differences, 10*(11). https://doi.org/10.3390/su10114176.

Maslow, A. H. (1987). *Motivation and personality* (2nd ed.). New York, NY: Addison-Wesley.

McAdams, D. P. (2010). The problem of meaning in personality psychology from the standpoints of dispositional traits, characteristic adaptations, and life stories. *Japanese Journal of Personality, 18,* 173–186.

McAdams, D. P. (2013). The psychological self as actor, agent, and author. *Perspectives on Psychological Science, 8*(3), 272–295.

McAdams, D. P., Josselson, R., & Lieblich, A. (Eds.). (2001). *Turns in the road: Narrative studies of lives in transition.* Washington, DC: APA Books.

Milton, J. (2002). *Paradise lost (Book 2).* Retrieved from http://triggs.djvu.org/djvu-editions.com/MILTON/LOST/Download.pdf.

Murray, H. A. (1943). *Thematic apperception test: Manual.* Cambridge, MA: Harvard University Press.

Overview of theories of human behavior and the social environment. (n.d.). Retrieved from https://www.slideshare.net/JonathanUnderwood1/overview-of-theories-of-human-behavior-the-social-environment.

Patton, W., & McMahon, M. (1999). *Career development and systems theory: A new relationship.* Pacific Grove, CA: Brooks/Cole.

Patton, W., & McMahon, M. (2006a). The systems theory framework. In M. McMahon & W. Patton (Eds.), *Career counselling: Constructivist approaches* (pp. 94–109). London, England: Routledge.

Patton, W., & McMahon, M. (2006b). *Career development and systems theory: Connecting theory and practice.* Rotterdam: Sense.

Phares, E. J. (1992). *Clinical psychology: Concepts, methods and profession.* Pacific Grove, CA: Brooks/Cole Publishing Company.

Pillay, A. (2019, June). *The need for career practitioners.* Keynote Address at the Annual Career Development Practitioner Congress, Emperors Palace Conference Centre, Kempton Park, South Africa.

Reid, H., & West, L. (2011). "Telling tales": Using narrative in career guidance. *Journal of Vocational Guidance, 78,* 174–183.

Reid, H., & West, L. (2016). Negotiating professional and personal biographies in a liquid world: Creating space for reflexive innovation in career counselling. *British Journal of Guidance and Counselling, 44,* 562–575. https://doi.org/10.1080/03069885.2016.1145014.

Ribeiro, M. A. (2016). Career counseling for people in psychosocial situations of vulnerability and flexicurity: A social constructionist proposal. In T. V. Martin (Ed.), *Career development: Theories, practices and challenges* (pp. 79–110). New York, NY: Nova.

Robbins, S., Chatterjee, P., & Canda, E. (Eds.). (2005). *Contemporary human behavior theory: A critical perspective for social work* (2nd ed.). Boston: Allyn and Bacon.

Rogers, C. R. (1951). *Client-centered therapy.* Boston, MA: Houghton Mifflin.

Rogers, C. R. (1961). *On becoming a person.* Boston, MA: Houghton Mifflin.

Rogers, C. R. (1977). *Carl Rogers on personal power.* New York, NY: Delacorte.

Ryan, L. (2016). *Every opportunity has a difficulty, and every difficulty has an opportunity* (J. Sidlo Baxter). Retrieved from https://lisaryanspeaks.com/every-opportunity-has-a-difficulty-and-every-difficulty-has-an-opportunity/.

Savickas, M. L. (2005). The theory and practice of career construction. In S. Brown & R. W. Lent (Eds.), *Career development and counseling: Putting theory and research to work* (pp. 42–70). New York, NY: John Wiley.

Savickas, M. L. (2011). Reshaping the story of career counseling. In K. Maree (Ed.), *Shaping the story—A guide to facilitate narrative counseling* (pp. 1–3). Boston/Rotterdam, The Netherlands: Sense.

Savickas, M. L. (2016, July). *Meaning at work: Work at meaning.* Closing keynote presentation, National Career Development Association Conference, Chicago, United States of America.

Savickas, M. L. (2019a). *Theories of psychotherapy series. Career counseling* (2nd ed.). Washington, DC: American Psychological Association.

Savickas, M. L. (2019b, September). *Designing a self and constructing a career in post-traditional societies.* Keynote address at the 43rd international association for educational and vocational guidance Conference, Bratislava, Slovakia.

Savickas, M. L., Nota, L., Rossier, J., & Dauwalder, J. P., Duarte, M. E., Guichard, J., ... Van Vianen, A. E. M. (2009). Life designing: A paradigm for career construction in the 21st century. *Journal of Vocational Behavior, 75,* 239–250.

Seeman, J. (2008). *Psychotherapy and the fully functioning person.* Bloomingon, IN: AuthorHouse.

Sehgal, M. (2016). *The wound is the place where the light enters you (Rumi).* Retrieved from https://www.linkedin.com/pulse/wound-place-where-light-enters-you-mamta-sehgal/.

Slavik, S., & Carlson, J. (2007). *Readings in the theory of individual psychology.* New York, NY: Routledge.

Sonn, C. C, Stevens, G., & Duncan, N (2013). Decolonization, critical methodologies, and why stories matter. In G. Stevens, G, N. Duncan, & D. Hook (Eds.), *Race, memory and the apartheid archive: Towards a transformative psychosocial praxis* (pp 295–314). London/Johannesburg: Palgrave Macmillan/Wits University Press.

Sprouts. (2017, April 23). *8 Stages of development by Erik Erikson.* Retrieved from https://www.youtube.com/watch?v=aYCBdZLCDBQ&t=46s.

Stevens, G., Duncan, N., & Hook, D. (Eds.). (2013). *Race, memory and the apartheid archive: Towards a transformative psychosocial praxis.* New York, NY: Springer.

Stringer, K., Kerpelman, J., & Skorikov, V. (2011). Career preparation: A longitudinal, process-oriented examination. *Journal of Vocational Behavior, 79,* 158–169.

Sugars, B. (2013, August 16). *How to turn your business idea into a business model.* Retrieved from https://www.entrepreneur.com/article/227907.

Super, D. E. (1951). Vocational adjustment: Implementing a self-concept. *Occupations: The Vocational Guidance Journal, 30,* 88–92.

Super, D. E. (1957). *The psychology of careers.* New York, NY: Harper & Row.

Teixeira, M. A. P., & Gomes, W. B. (2000). Autonomous career change among professionals: An empirical phenomenological study. *Journal of Phenomenological Psychology, 3,* 78–96.
Trull, T. J., & Phares, E. J. (2001). *Clinical psychology* (6th ed.). Belmont, CA: Wadsworth.
Urbanaviciute, I., Udayar, S., & Rossier, J. (2019). Career adaptability and employee well-being over a two-year period: Investigating cross-lagged effects and their boundary conditions. *Journal of Vocational Behavior*. https://doi.org/10.1016/j.jvb.2018.10.013.
White, M., & Epston, D. (1990). *Narrative means to therapeutic ends*. New York, NY: Norton.
Winnicott, D. W. (1964). *The child, the family and the outside world*. Cambridge, MA: Perseus.
Young, R. A., & Valach, L. (2004). The construction of career through goal-directed action. *Journal of Vocational Behavior, 64,* 499–514.
Ziller, R. C. (2000). Self-counseling through re-authored photo-self-narratives. *Counseling Psychology Quarterly, 13,* 265–278.
Zulliger, H. (1969). *The Zulliger individual and group test*. New York, NY: International Universities Press.

Chapter 3
Counseling for Self- and Career Construction and Life Design as the Basis for Eliciting Inner Advice Regarding Career Choice Decision-Making

Every answer you are seeking is already inside of you. Look within. Do the inner work (Akiroq Brost)

Abstract The chapter commences with a brief discussion of career construction counseling, self-construction counseling, and various life design counseling constructs. This is followed by a discussion on a framework for implementing integrative counseling for self- and career construction and life design in different contexts. This framework is used to promote understanding of the psychology of career choice decision-making and, especially, the idea of eliciting advice from within for answers to people's career-related questions, requests, and decision-making. The chapter ends on this note.

3.1 Orientation

Maree (2018a, 2018b, 2018c), Savickas (2019a), and others state that fundamental changes in the world of work pose major challenges to workers. They emphasize the need to postmodernize the psychology of career choice decision-making and promote the idea of enabling people to elicit advice from within. New approaches to career counseling are needed to manage and pre-empt rising unemployment and underemployment (Graham, Hjorth, & Lehdonvirta, 2017; ILO, 2019). As mentioned earlier, drawing on the traditional positivist "test-and-tell" approach in relative isolation is no longer regarded as sufficient to address the needs of people seeking career counseling in rapidly changing times (Maree, 2018a, 2018b; Savickas, 2016). Chiaradonna (2017) adds that the single most important challenge confronting workers today is becoming and remaining employable. Doyle (2017) argues that repeated transitions from one job or career to another complicate efforts to conserve work-life balance, which is further complicated by erstwhile sought-after competencies and abilities becoming obsolete and redundant. Doyle's view supplants the outdated perspective

J. G. (Kobus) Maree, *Innovating Counseling for Self- and Career Construction*,
https://doi.org/10.1007/978-3-030-48648-8_3

that helping people find proper paid employment is the ultimate aim of career counseling. Instead, it underscores the importance of blending work and life roles and pursuing a career trajectory that will promote lifelong personal growth and improved self-awareness.

3.2 Career Construction Theory

Career construction theory moves developmental theories towards increased utility by updating the notion that identity construction evolves constantly as people advance "linearly" through "fixed" career-life stages. It builds on the naturalistic (interpretive) paradigm (Hartung, 2007, 2010a, 2010b; Savickas, 2002, 2005, 2006a, 2007a, 2017b). Career construction theory uses social constructionism as a metatheory on how knowledge is constructed. It holds that language is the conduit for enabling people to "make meaning" and find purpose (Hartung, 2015a, 2018; Savickas, 2005, 2011a). Career construction theory (Savickas, 2005) incorporates and updates Super's (1957, 1983, 1990) life span, life-space career development theories in a way that shows that people's work roles should not be seen in isolation (Hartung, 2011). At the same time, Savickas (2008) stresses the value of identifying the personality traits, needs, values, and interests that are part of people's self-view or self-concept (Maree, 2009). Starting with Super's (1990) model, Savickas (2005) progressed to career construction, and, later, the life design team advanced the life design paradigm for careers (Rossier et al., 2015; Rossier, Ginevra, Bollmann, & Nota, 2017; Savickas et al., 2009a, 2009b, 2009c, 2009d). Super's interpretation and developmental view on how people choose careers, become mature enough to make career decisions and adaptive, and adjust to change was updated by career construction theory in the sense that three fundamental career choice theoretical traditions were merged. The three traditions were

a. the tradition of focusing on the individual differences between people (also referred to as the differential approach or personality-environment fit) (Parsons, 1909).
b. the tradition of focusing on people's individual development over several distinguishable life phases (also referred to as the developmental approach) (Super, 1990); and
c. the tradition of emphasizing the power of people's psychodynamic motivation (including the storied or narrative or qualitative traditions, all of which aim to identify people's central life themes).

This blend of traditions gave rise to the Career construction theory as a "grand", inclusive theory of vocational and/or career choice and behavior. Seen from this perspective, counseling for self- and career construction includes

a. measuring people's traits through psychometric tests,
b. examining ways in which these traits can be developed to promote adaptive behavior, and

c. eliciting people's key life themes (indicating how people move forward in certain directions) (Hartung, 2007).

At the heart of counseling for career construction is the *Career Construction Interview* (*CCI*) (Savickas, 2019a) (see Table 3.1).

The *CCI* promotes narrative intervention and "inspires participation from shy, reluctant, or withdrawn people and deeper thinking from others" (Reid, 2018, n.p.) (also see Maree, 2015a, 2015b, 2016b, 2016c).

I am regularly invited to present papers, workshops, and keynotes at national and international conferences where I have come to expect the following types of questions almost routinely:

a. "How do you reconcile qualitative, narrative, or storied intervention with the use of tests?"

Table 3.1 Career Construction Interview

	Question	Rationale
	How can I be useful to you?	People are regarded as the sole experts on their lives. This question aims to elicit their session goals and sets the scene for career counseling
1	Whom did you admire/Who were your three role models (heroes or heroines) when you were young, and what did or do you admire about them?	Role models represent the ideal self people[a] wish to attain and shed light on their key life goals. They also present people with possible answers to or solutions for their key life challenges ("problems"). Savickas (M. L. Savickas, personal communication, October 3, 2019) avoids any discussion on parents unless clients refer to them as their role models. After asking for three role models other than parents, as a token of respect to clients, he asks them for three words to describe each parent (Savickas, in press)
2	What is your favorite (a) magazine, (b) TV program, (c) website, and why?	Together and/or individually, answers to these questions shed light on those settings that suit or "fit" people's way of life (lifestyles that people prefer in order to perform themselves)
3	What is your favorite story (either book or movie or book turned into a movie)?	The favorite story or book (cultural script) often reveals characters who deal with challenges similar to those people have had to deal with. Moreover, it shows how these characters resolve the challenges. The story or book thus provides people with a script to connect their "self" to a particular setting[b]
4	What are your three favorite mottos or quotations?	The mottos or quotations shed light on people's advice to themselves at the time of assessment

(continued)

Table 3.1 (continued)

	Question	Rationale
5	What are the first three things you can remember about your life (what are your earliest recollections[c])? Tell me three stories about things you remember happening to you when you were young.	Earliest recollections reveal key "challenges" (preoccupations) people face and shed light on people's central life themes. More particularly, they signify the central plot or main scenario of people's life stories.[d] Savickas (M. L. Savickas, personal communication, October 3, 2019) initially agreed with Adler (1958) that earliest recollections reveal people's pain. However, on discovering that many clients had earliest recollections without pain, he began to refer to earliest recollections as recollections about preoccupations. He emphasizes that earliest recollections are about the present, not the past, and that they reveal how clients are currently viewing their present "problems" (career concerns). I believe career counselors can better serve clients by following this approach

[a]The terms people, clients, assessees, testees, and participants are largely interchangeable (depending on context) but, generally speaking, people should be understood in a more general sense, clients in a more clinical sense, assessees and testees in a more assessment ("testing") sense, and participants in a more research sense

[b]Readers are cautioned about concentrating too much on a particular character because usually by this point, they have their role models to utilize. However, the role models and the main character someone might like often have things in common (C. Briddick, personal communication, September 27, 2019)

[c]It should be emphasized that an "[earliest recollection] is not an [earliest recollection] unless an event is described" (Signorelli, 2016, p. 2)

[d]According to Savickas (2019a, 2019b), skipping the earliest recollections might be necessary if trauma is involved as the trauma could be reflected in the earliest recollections and may not necessarily be useful to the situation at hand

b. "You pledge allegiance to self- and career construction and life design counseling. Yet, you say that it is in order to still use tests when you assess people. How do you explain and motivate that?"
c. "Can you explain the relationship between the tests you sometimes use (e.g. the *MCM*) and the theoretical model (counseling for self- and career construction counseling) you advocate?"

In such instances, I explain the rationale for administering tests while drawing on counseling for self- and career construction counseling as a theoretical framework and lens (prism) for the interpretation of outcomes. From a career construction point of view, career counselors are free to use scores (objective perspective) as well as stories (subjective perspective) to generate data to help their clients and themselves arrive at informed career choice and construction decisions. Since one of the three cornerstones of career construction theory is the differential approach—which directly alludes to quantitative assessment (the use of tests)—there is actually no contradiction in using tests when administering career construction (as well as life design) counseling. The above questions are therefore based on a misunderstanding and/or misinterpretation of the key tenets of career construction (and life design) counseling and intervention. Therefore, I confirm the following once again: Career construction does not exclude the use of tests. Quite the opposite. For purposes of triangulation, and to improve the rigor of intervention, I, personally, prefer to draw on all three of the fundamental theoretical traditions on which career construction theory is based.

3.2.1 Key Aspects of Career Construction Counseling (CCC) (Savickas, 2019a)

Cardoso, Savickas, and Gonçalves (2019) state that "the fundamental goal of CCC is to enable clients to enact career change in the real world by first constructing new plans that elaborate their career themes and reconstruct a narrative identity with greater coherence and continuity" (p. 189). To this end, career construction counseling (CCC) aims to help people narrate and use their own life stories (autobiographies) to sculpt their careers (Savickas, 2001, 2005). This kind of counseling manifests in dynamic, action-oriented interventions and assessments that also promote the revisiting of earliest memories but, especially, the reframing and reinterpretation of such memories in the context of people's current career-related challenges and questions. Painful memories from the past are converted into action steps that rekindle people's sense of meaning and purpose in their career-lives. In essence, CCC helps people re-experience and reframe their earliest stories, connect their present understandings and insights with their past (subconscious) insights, and construct elicited key life themes in their career-lives. An 'autobiographical bridge' is thus built linking their past experiences, their present aspirations and challenges, and their future career-lives and linking these three aspects is promoted. This equips them with the know-how to negotiate future transitions successfully (Savickas, 2011a, 2011b).

Career construction counseling comprises a creative mix of the following features: First, a **safe (sacred) space** or a **holding environment** (Winnicott, 1964) must be created to ensure that a trusting relationship develops between counselor and client (a key requirement for the success of any intervention) (Savickas, 2011b). Inasmuch as this is possible, counselors need to elicit an "uncut", truthful version of clients' life stories. If mutual trust is lacking, the successful elicitation and narration (referred to as narratability) of clients' life stories, which will eventually serve as the basis for eliciting inner advice regarding their reasons for seeking career counseling (**autobiographicity**) (Maree, 2018a, 2018b; Savickas, 2019a), is likely to be inhibited. Hartung (2013a, 2013b) states that CCC promotes **narrativity** and "emphasizes **narratability** to tell one's story coherently, adaptability to cope with changes in self and situation, and intentionality to design a successful life" (p. 11). Career counselors using CCC (which builds on a social constructionist perspective) endeavor to help clients **identify life themes or key patterns of personal meaning**. These themes can be identified by analyzing past (earliest) memories (a psychodynamic view) (see, for instance, Adler, 1958, 1998; Savickas, 2019a), examining present experiences, contemplating future hopes and desires, and focusing on clients' most profound feelings and emotions. Career counselors and clients work collaboratively to construct, deconstruct, reconstruct, and co-construct hope- and purpose-filled career-life stories. Eventually, a narrative is constructed that weaves together clients' numerous micro-narratives into a larger, grand macro-narrative. Savickas (2019a) conceptualized and used the term "life portrait"[1] as a "macro-narrative that organizes a client's perspective, self-concepts, preferred settings, script, and advice to self into a portrayal of the occupational plot, career theme, and character arc" (p. 162). Eliciting people's evolving-life stories is key to clarifying the subjective meaning they attach to their stories and promotes understanding of their sense of who they are (sense of self) (Savickas, 2005, 2015a, 2015b). Savickas (1995) contends that career counselors attempt to elicit two kinds of career counseling stories, namely "those that reveal the client's preoccupation or central life concern and those that reveal the plot or what they plan to do about the preoccupation. The counselor then connects these stories with the thread of continuity that is the life theme" (p. 4). In the career construction approach, counselors occupy a very special position as they are the first supportive audience of their clients (Briddick & Sensoy-Briddick, 2013).

Uncovering these stories incentivizes and calls for **action**, **forward movement, and maintaining momentum** in people's career-lives. These three activities contribute to clarification and authentication of people's career identities, which encompasses the "practice of articulating, performing and negotiating identity positions in narrating career decisions" (LaPointe, 2010, p. 2). Confirmation of who people are from a career choice perspective (e.g. a data analyst, a solar energy technician, a medical doctor, a plumber, a cyber-attack agent, a medical mentor, a smart home design manager, a flying car developer, or a robot engineer) paves the way for deciding on a kind of work that will enable them to construct themselves by "actualizing" or enacting their preoccupations or central life themes (Krieshok, Black, & McKay, 2009; Savickas, 2019b). Advancing people's self-awareness, promoting critical self-reflection, and bolstering their reflexivity helps them shape and fine-tune their sense of self and identity, which empowers them to approach the future with a clear, proven plan of action (Savickas, 2011a). LaPointe (2010), too, maintains that people's career identities are authorized when they narrate, share, and act upon their

[1]A life portrait is a brief, integrated account of the outcomes of assessing a person for career counseling. Whereas, previously, the term "career counseling report" was used to refer to the narrative that comprises these outcomes, currently, terms such as "life portrait" (Savickas, 2019a), "career story", "career-life story", and "living portrait" are preferred by many career counselors. The choice of an appropriate term depends on the personal orientation and choice of individual career counselors. Personally, I prefer the term "career-life story narrative (or portrait)" instead of "report". (After playing around with many terms to describe the integrated career-life story, I devised the term "living story" and was quite surprised and pleased to learn that it had in fact been used before by, for instance, Boje (2008)).

stories. Moreover, those who listen to these stories being recounted and "performed" are transformed into a corroborating and authenticating audience (Di Fabio & Maree, 2013a, 2013b).

Sharing their stories enhances people's career adaptability, adaptivity, and career resilience, which is described by Masten (2014) as "the capacity of a dynamic system to adapt successfully to disturbances that threaten system function, viability, or development" (p. 6). In other words, sharing their stories enhances people's capacity to function proficiently in "standard" but also in exigent and/or disabling work contexts and under demanding circumstances (Rochat, Masdonati, & Dauwalder, 2017).

Below, I briefly discuss the twin constructs career adaptability and employability.

Career adaptability. Career adaptability is associated with different attitudes, beliefs, and competencies (ABCs) (Hartung, 2011; Rossier, 2015a, 2015b). Career construction theory holds that what distinguishes one person from another is their readiness to master key developmental tasks at different life stages. Accordingly, it is argued that people should be helped to develop novel and key attitudes, beliefs, and competencies (ABCs) to advance their careers. Viewed from a career construction perspective, however, as well as in terms of the avant garde, contemporary "project perspective of individual design" (Savickas, 2019a, p. 12), people are seen as "autobiographical authors", and their autobiographies are regarded as fundamentally important.

Individual adaptability dimensions and their related actions can promote people's overall career adaptability by reinforcing and augmenting their actions (Savickas, 2003). Individually and collectively, these dimensions signify the adaptability resources people have at their disposal as well as their style of coping with important transitions and traumas during their career-related endeavors (Hartung, 2011). Perera and McIlveen (2017), Rottinghaus, Falk, and Eshelman (2017) and Savickas (2013) maintain that adaptivity includes career readiness and commitment to deal with the often poorly defined and complex challenges inherent in many career-related assignments and transitions. Hirschi, Herrmann, and Keller (2015) describe adaptivity as the ability to act proactively and flexibly and to evaluate and reflect on the self appropriately.

They add that, according to career construction theory, career adaptive responses ensue along four interrelated dimensions of adaptability (Hartung, 2011; Savickas, 2005, 2013, 2015a, 2015b; Savickas & Porfeli, 2012), each of which is associated with a central question that are connected with central career-related questions, attitudes, beliefs, and competencies (ABCs).

Hartung (2015a, b) and Savickas (2005, 2015a) relate each of the four C's of career adaptability to specific questions, attitudes, beliefs, and attitudes:

a. Career Concern relates to the question, "Do I have a future?" and talks to people's awareness of, their involvement in, and their active planning for their future (McLennan, McIlveen, & Perera, 2017).
b. Career Control relates to the question, "Who owns my future?" and manifests in how people obtain and exert control over their future.

c. Career Curiosity relates to the question, "What do I want to do with my future?" and correlates positively with people's level of mindfulness of and their curiosity about the world of work.
d. Career Confidence relates to the question, "Can I do it?" and refers to people's capacity to resolve career-related issues (solve career-related problems, including their proficiency in recognizing and utilizing work-related opportunities) (Ginevra, Pallini, Vecchio, Nota, & Soresi, 2016; Santili, Marcionetti, Rochat, Rossier, & Nota, 2017).

Van der Horst and Klehe (2019, p. 92) contend that "most empirical research on career adaptation has stayed close to its roots in vocational maturity (Super, 1955) by studying students and graduates in the context of their school-to-work transition". These authors further maintain that "a key challenge is, therefore, how best to support individuals in honing their career adaptive responding (Bimrose & Hearne, 2012, p. 95). Moreover, they concur with Hirschi, Hermann, and Keller's (2015) view that people draw on adaptive responses to attend successfully to developmental tasks that relate to career, the changing world of work, and constantly changing work environments. Relevant stakeholders often express their support for and concern about students who receive little or no career counseling, drop out of school or university (do not complete their training), do not find work, or end up in careers they dislike especially. However, these well-intended sentiments (expressions of concern) mean very little without the planning and implementation of action steps to help such people deal with their quandaries. This includes planning and conducting research aimed at promoting the effectiveness of integrative career counseling assessments in group contexts especially (Di Fabio & Maree, 2013a, 2013b; Hartung, 2013a, 2013b; Maree & Di Fabio, 2019; Ribeiro & Guilherme de Oliveira, 2018; Van der Horst & Klehe, 2019; Whiston, Li, Mitts, & Wright, 2017).

Career Adaptability and employability. According to Savickas (2011a):

> Vocational psychology ... and career counseling have been asking new questions during the first decade of the 21st century. The questions arise from the demise of jobs. The employment premise of matching individuals to jobs is fading as the digital revolution produces jobless work. In response to the recurring transitions that they will face as they move from project to project, individuals cannot maintain their employment, so they must maintain their employability (p. 6).

An interesting link seems to exist between employability and people's adaptability (Guilbert, Bernaud, Gouvernet, & Rossier, 2016). According to Fugate, Kinicki, & Ashforth, (2004), employability is a psychosocial concept that relates to and is dependent on adaptive cognition, behavior, and feelings. Seen through this lens, people's employability helps them advance their career situation proactively by consciously adapting to changing situations instead of waiting for others to assist them to do so. Fugate, Kinicki, & Ashforth, (2004) and Koen (2013) differentiate between three key aspects of employability, namely career identity, career adaptability, and (social and human) capital. While these three aspects involve different skills, knowledge, and behaviors, jointly they enhance people's capacity to find and retain work. Dispositional employability is regarded as "a constellation of individual differences that predispose employees to (pro-)actively adapt to their work and career environments" (p. 504). Adaptability is thus seen as the vehicle that guides people's employability potential. Employable people pro-actively pursue their occupational interests, experience increased job satisfaction, and perform better in their work (Crant, 2000; Fugate, Kinicki, & Ashforth, 2004).

3.3 Self-Construction Theory (SCT)

Guichard's (2005) self-construction theory is associated with career construction theory-related intervention dynamics. Self-construction theory, too, advances the narration of people's life stories, which are linked to practicable and imminent career-life projects. It aims to help people (re-)construct their fluctuating identities and help them attain a less fluid, stable, consistent, and authenticated identity to inspire meaning-making and purposeful lives. Stabilized identities manifest in overt and covert answers to questions such as "Who am I?", "Where am I?", "Where am I going?", "Why do I live and work?" What is the meaning of my life?", and "What is the purpose of my life?" (Guichard, 2005). Central to Guichard's (2005, 2010) theory of self-construction is the belief that people's identities unfold unremittingly. Self-construction theory holds also that people actively construct their selves through narratives used during social interaction, conversation, and communication. Initially, Guichard focused on self- and life construction (Collin & Guichard, 2011; Guichard, 2005; Guichard, 2009) but later tended to confine himself to self-construction. While Savickas' (2005) career construction theory holds that people "construct their careers by imposing meaning on their vocational behavior and occupational experiences" (p. 43) and that "occupation provides a mechanism for social integration" (p. 48) and for making social contributions, self-construction relates primarily to essential aspects of people's personal development.

Guichard (2008a, 2008b, 2009) distinguishes between the primary factors and later developments that influence the way in which people design their lives to enable them to deal with multiple and repeated transitions in their lives. I personally believe that construction of the self serves as an inner compass that enables people to negotiate transitions and that, in this way, the essential meaning given to personal experience and the search for fulfilment is captured (Maree, 2017a, 2017b).

To summarize: Self-construction theory is associated with and relates to a more general kind of human construction than career construction theory. In other words, it focuses predominantly on the construction of the self but not, in the first instance, in relation to the construction of a career and the designing of a life. In practice, self-construction theory-related intervention aims to answer the question regarding what makes people's lives meaningful and how career counselors and their clients can jointly "work" towards consolidating clients' present situation by advancing their future possibilities and, especially, their future selves (Guichard, 2005; Savickas, 2005, 2010).

3.4 Merging Career Construction Theory and Self-Construction Theory

Career construction theory and self-construction theory alike hold that people's reality, roles, proficiencies, and competencies in social contexts are shaped and constructed through accepted, shared, and mutually agreed-upon meanings regarding their career-lives. These two theoretical conventions hold also that people's identities develop as and while they actively participate in social spaces. Career construction theory and self-construction theory are both grounded in the belief that (a) people have the capacity to construct personal meaning from a large number of life experiences (happenstances or fortuitous meetings), (b) scrutinizing these happenstances can promote their self-insight, and (c) enhanced self-insight can promote career management and self-elaboration (Maree, 2016a, 2016b). In reality, the Adlerian approach (Adler, 1958, 1998), particularly the concept of mattering, is a cornerstone of the career construction approach. Self-reflection and reflexivity are central features of career construction. Reflection relates to people's reflection on (a) certain actual events in their career-lives (i.e. objective experiences) and (b) private and subjective meanings they associate with these events. Reflexivity occurs when people are inspired by reflection to effect key adjustments (and changes) in their lives that may positively shape their future career-lives. Reflexivity promotes narratability and (auto)biographicity and facilitates the clarification and construction of life stories. Career construction theory and self-construction theory hold that people can become more adaptive by drawing personal meaning from their actions while they construct their careers and themselves. Savickas (2015a) maintains that people's private or personal identities produce the "adhesive" that merges or blends their life stories.

3.5 Life Design Counseling

Three different yet corresponding life design traditions can be distinguished.

3.5.1 Zunker's Model of Life Design Counseling

This model is characterized by its use of several career counseling techniques that are still in use today. These include the lifeline technique, collages, identifying people's idiosyncratic roles, and guided fantasy to advance the design of meaningful career-lives. This model relates especially to the implementation of life design counseling in group contexts by means of interactive group discussions (Zunker, 1998).

3.5.2 *Campbell and Ungar's Model of Life Design Counseling*

This life design model, too, relates to the use of postmodern assessment and intervention techniques. It can also be described as holistic, developmental, context-responsive, pre-emptive, and preventive. Moreover, the model acknowledges that careers are inseparably intertwined with those distinctive issues that manifest in the career-lives of people at specific moments (Campbell & Ungar, 2004).

The "thread" that runs through both these life design models is the notion of helping people make (instead of find) meaning in their career-lives.

3.5.3 *Savickas et al.'s Model of Life Design Counseling*

The key constructs of the third life design counseling model are self- and career identity, narratability (narrating or telling the story of one's identity), and the actualization of intentionality (Savickas, 2015c) by taking meaningful action (Lent, 2012). The most fundamental change brought about by the third life design approach is the view that people's search for meaning and purpose lies at the heart of life design endeavors. This life design model started gaining traction in 2009 and rapidly achieved global recognition. Guichard (J. Guichard, personal communication, May 17, 2015) explains that life design at the turn of the previous century was the career psychology equivalent of the 16th century Copernican revolution. Previously, vocational guidance and career development centered on the idea of "paid work" as a key feature of the system of financial exchanges (much like the presumption of the Ptolemaic system that the universe revolved around the earth). From this perspective, life design can perhaps be conceptualized as an extension of Adlerian social interest (Adler, 1958) (H. Sensoy-Briddick, personal communication, October 10, 2019).

Savickas (2019a) explains that it is not the purpose of career construction theory, self-construction theory, and life design counseling to replace previous paradigms but rather to take its place beside them for the benefit of clients. Life design holds that the activity of working should be seen as a much more encompassing experience than just a so-called "paid job". Remuneration is only one (albeit important) facet of meaning-making promoted by life design. This fundamental shift concerning the essence of work had major consequences for career counseling intervention, which strove to help people in terms of the defined purposes of such intervention. Central to the appreciation of the importance of life design is an understanding and acceptance that traditional career counseling intervention (i.e. vocational guidance) in the main endeavored to help people adapt to their current occupational contexts by helping them develop a vocational self-concept and self-esteem needed to meet prevailing employability standards. By contrast, life design counseling focuses on helping people consider the kind of work they wish to choose and do and also to reflect on how their work-related endeavors may enhance their chance of experiencing a sense of meaning and purpose in their career-lives. The emergence of the life design approach has thus contributed substantially to the shift in career psychology towards promoting sustainable, decent work for all.

In general, life design counseling involves an intervention model that draws on stories and actions rather than on test scores and profile interpretations only. Savickas (M. Savickas, personal communication, September 16, 2015) explains that the life design paradigm comprises a broader paradigm (Duarte & Cardoso, 2015) that includes career construction counseling (Savickas, 2011a), dialogical self-construction theory (Guichard, 2005), chaos theory (Pryor & Bright, 2011), and systems theory (Patton & McMahon, 2006a, 2006b). Collin & Guichard (2011) argue that the aim of life design counseling is threefold: First, it helps people clarify their major life themes. Second, it helps them understand the role and meaning of work in their career-lives. Third, it helps them identify and, most importantly, put into practice the key perspectives that will help them make meaning, kindle or rekindle their sense of positivity and hope, and, ultimately, live purposeful lives. Duarte (2009) contends, similarly, that the primary aim of self- and career counseling intervention is to develop people's sense of self, of who they really are, of identity. Duarte adds that life design is wholly psychological in nature and involves people in critical self-reflection and reflexivity-related behavior. Furthermore, life design promotes the integration of education, training, counseling, and psychological conduits into a (career-)life that is worth living.

For a variety of reasons, people's 'original' life designing does not yield the desired outcomes. In such instances, life redesigning may be(-come) necessary.

3.6 Life Redesigning

Del Corso (2013), Hartung (2015a, b), and Savickas (2015a, 2015b) associate career adaptability with repeated choice-making, transitioning, and managing work-related traumas in volatile and unpredictable work environments. In essence, then, when people require redesigning of their career-lives, intervention is needed that will help them reflect critically on the many twists and turns in their career-lives, focusing on those issues that may have influenced their career adaptability in terms of their career control, career curiosity, career concern, and career confidence (see below) negatively (Briddick & Sensoy-Briddick, 2017). People of all ages often turn to career counselors for "help" when they no longer experience a sense of meaning-making in their careers and/or a sense of purpose in their career-lives after having been in a particular career for a number of years (when their career is not meaningful or purposeful to them anymore). To me, in such instances, they are seeking help in the redesigning of their lives. These are instances when the need for uncovering key life themes or motifs (shedding light on subconscious motivations and reasons for their lack of meaning-making and loss of purpose in life) becomes almost irresistible. Since their initial attempts to design successful, purposeful lives failed to yield satisfactory outcomes, a different, new strategy needs to be devised to help them rekindle their sense of meaning and purpose (Hartung, 2018; Savickas, 2019a, b). Even people who achieve fame and wealth during their career-lives and find themselves at the pinnacle of their careers often experience a deep sense of aimlessness and lack of purpose. The song *Plamondon* (Celine Dion—visit YouTube to listen to this beautiful song) (Music Story, 2018) shows that financial success and fame are no guarantee for experiencing a sense of purpose in one's life.

As mentioned earlier, a variety of contextual factors can influence people adversely, even to the extent of necessitating serious rethinking of their career-related situation. In such instances, it is necessary to encourage people's thoughtful reflection on what is causing them to feel "stuck" and unable to experience a sense of meaning-making and purpose in their career-lives. Once clarified, these issues should be converted into responses to the career counselor's initial question regarding their reasons for seeking career counseling. The aim of career counseling in such cases is to foster change and forward movement in these people's career-lives. What is therefore needed is redesigning of their career-lives by enhancing their self-construction (restoring their sense of self (Law, Bunning, Byng, Farrelly, & Heyman, 2005)) and rekindling their career construction to revitalize their experience of a sense of meaning-making and of living a purposeful life. Moreover, it is essential to elicit and co-constructively link key life themes with people's stated reasons for presenting for career counseling when it is evident that their previous attempts to design purposeful lives failed to yield the results or outcomes they had hoped for.

Below, I elaborate on an integrative career counseling framework that indicates how career counseling intervention is currently provided in different contexts (Duarte, 2017a, 2017b; Hartung & Cadaret, 2017; Savickas, 2015a). This framework (see Table 3.2) reflects Savickas' belief that all the different paradigms, foci, applications, and perspectives on people, as well as intervention aims, are valid and useful. How career counseling is provided, as well as its value, depends largely on the nature of a country's economy at any given moment (Savickas, 2006a, 2006b). The state of the economy influences career counseling's conceptual foundation as well as the associated research methodology and career counselors' preferred application strategy. All three approaches listed in Table 3.2 are "valuable and effective for [their] intended purpose" (Savickas, 2019a, p. 12). People's unique career counseling needs will co-determine the mode of service that will be most appropriate for each person when they seek career counseling. Regardless of people's life circumstances (whether they are poor or wealthy, for instance), they have the right to learn more about themselves in a career context. In other words, even when a trait-factor model is used to help people choose a career (or a job/work) that is in line with their abilities, interests, and personality, they are still entitled to uncover and learn about their life themes as such knowledge can have a healing effect on them (H. Sensoy-Briddick, personal communication, October 19, 2019).

Table 3.2 Integrative career counseling framework

Paradigm	Vocational guidance	Career development	Life design
Perspective	Positivism	Humanism	Social constructionism
Focus is on	Resemblance	Careers and how people develop careers over time	Reflection, reflexivity, addressing the life-designing needs of insecure workers with unstable jobs
Application	Guide, advise	Educate, guide, advise, and coach	Design a life, heal
Client regarded as	Social actor	Motivated agent	Autobiographical author
Aim of intervention	Enhance self-knowledge; increase information about opportunities and conditions for success; and match individual to other people	Assess development status; orient person to developmental tasks (challenges); identify resources needed; and develop the attitudes, beliefs, and competencies needed to master developmental tasks appropriate to life stages	Construct self and career by selecting and organizing incidents and episodes from the micro-narratives to craft an identity narrative and life story narrative, and then help them make meaning of these stories; reconstruct micro- and meso-stories into an identity narrative; and co-construct the next chapter in the person's life

3.7 Integrative Career Counseling Framework

3.7.1 Difference Between Vocational Guidance, Career Education, and Career Counseling

Career counseling and career decision-making should be recognized as a complex, multidimensional process that draws on numerous data sources (both qualitative and quantitative). Savickas (2011a) explains that career (construction) counseling does not "replace anything. Instead, it takes its place alongside vocational guidance and career education" (p. 41). Career counselors who practice from a vocational guidance perspective regard people as "social actors". Assessing people comprises obtaining their scores on tests regarding several personality traits (the so-called objectivist, individual differences, or differential approach). Based on their test scores, people are helped to match their traits with what is required by certain occupations to find an "optimal" fit. The aim is to achieve a match or fit that will bring them into contact with people who resemble themselves (the notion of ensuring "resemblance" in occupational contexts based on the view that "birds of a feather flock together") (Krumboltz, 2003). In contrast, career education is premised on the subjective view of the importance of foregrounding people's individual development. People are regarded as "motivated agents". Counseling for self- and career construction counseling, on the other hand, regards people as autobiographical authors and endeavors to help them choose and enact careers that will enable them to design meaningful and purposeful work-lives.

To a lesser or greater extent, each of the following three different yet intertwined kinds of intervention should feature in every career (construction) counseling intervention (See Table 3.2—compiled from Duarte (2017a, 2017b), Hartung (2018), and Savickas (2010, 2015a). The table assembles and integrates several seemingly divergent career counseling ideas. The table indicates also that all assessments and interventions should be conceptualized and executed in a way that renders them appropriate and suitable for their intended purpose (Savickas, 2011b). Moreover, it shows how ideas and conceptualizations in career counseling can be put into practice.

The link between and progression from vocational guidance to career guidance/education to life design is shown in Table 3.3 (compiled from Duarte, 2017a, 2017b; Savickas, 2015a, 2015b), and the relationship between career counseling waves (helping models), theoretical underpinnings, and associated interventions is summarized.

The associated interventions listed in Table 3.3 are discussed below.

Table 3.3 Relationship between career counseling waves (helping models), theoretical underpinnings, and interventions

Career counseling wave (helping model)	Theoretical underpinning	Associated intervention (Duarte, 2017a, 2017b; Guichard, 2005, 2009; Savickas, 2011a, 2015a)	Example: Demonstrative question
Vocational Guidance	Differential	Provide information; matching	Which career will "fit" my personality?
Career guidance/education	Developmental	Provide a. psychoeducational, and b. psychosocial information	a. How should I conduct job analysis? b. How do I go about improving my interpersonal relationships?
Life design and career counseling	Storied (psychodynamic)	Help people identify key life themes, reflect, and draw on their reflexivity	a. What are my key life themes? b. Which career will enable me to make meaning and experience a sense of purpose in my career-life?

a. General information. This includes "basic" information such as where to study and what the requirements for acceptance into a certain field of study are.
b. i. Psychoeducational information. This concerns, for instance, appropriate study methods, the kind of attitude towards study habits, motivating learners to apply themselves, to work hard, and to persist when struggling to solve challenging contents.
   ii. Psychosocial information. This concerns matters such as where people should look for help when needed; the importance of establishing, maintaining, and promoting sound interpersonal relationships; the strategic value of emotional-social intelligence, of emotional stability, and of persisting with attempts to solve problems despite feeling unhappy or demotivated.
c. Self- and career construction interventions and, ultimately, life design. This relates to "deeper-seated" aspects of career counseling and concerns existential questions such as "Why am I studying?" and "What is my ultimate purpose or reason for studying, working, and living?" This intervention also promotes people's understanding that career comprises a mechanism to integrate into society as well as a mechanism to contribute to the wellbeing of other people in addition to simply finding work. Career counseling intervention at this level is associated with "psychological" or "personal" intervention. The need for life design intervention is confirmed by Chen (2004) who argues that "[c]areer counselors are frequently challenged to work with a career dilemma that encompasses a range of diverse issues and factors in their clients' personal lives" (p. 524).

It should thus be clear that the integrative career counseling framework outlined above does not make provision for giving advice per se. Below, I elaborate on how people should be enabled to advise themselves.

3.7.2 Narrating and Drawing on One's Own Stories to Elicit Advice from Within Oneself

Career counselors who advocate eliciting advice from within draw on a **humanistic (including an existential and phenomenological perspective as well as elements of transpersonal theory) and social constructionism** framework or lens through which to examine and enrich their understanding of how people can be helped to uncover advice from within themselves to deal with career counseling decision-making challenges. They support Crites' (1981) view that the advice provided by "experts" can never be regarded as the ultimate or even correct answer to people's career counseling questions. Instead, enabling people to make their own decisions (facilitated by career counselors) should be encouraged where people are considered capable of making age- and life phase-appropriate career decisions.

Cardoso, Savickas, and Gonçalves (2019) maintain that the goal of career construction counseling is normally achieved in three phases. In phase 1, "clients formulate their career problem and explore micronarratives or narrow stories about the constructs (e.g., role models, interests, values, and scripts) with which they have formed their careers so far" (p. 189). In phase 2, they "identify life themes and reconstruct the micronarratives into a macronarrative that revises the career story" (p. 189). In phase 3, they draw on "the new story to coconstruct career plans and perform change. Ideally, counselors devote one full 50-minute session to each of the three phases" (p. 189). While the first two phases normally happen one week apart, the third phase happens a month after phase two. However, these time frames depend on the "depending on the flow of the relationship between client and counselor" (p. 190) and are highly flexible.

Put differently, counselors **elicit** people's life stories by asking questions that prompt their critical self-reflection (listening to and hearing themselves) and meta-reflection (reflecting on their own reflections) during the first phase[2] of the intervention. In the second phase, they are asked to **authorize** (validate) these stories, which are read to them by career counselors. In the third phase, action plans and strategies to bring about action and forward movement are devised and implemented. People are encouraged and enabled to participate actively in their self- and career construction. They are thus helped to connect or integrate what they know consciously with what they only "know" subconsciously. This enables them to connect unconnected dots in their life stories while they transcend faulty cognitions, become active, and elicit advice from within regarding how to negotiate career decision-making crossroads.

Helping people connect what they consciously know or are aware of with their subconscious advice can be facilitated by examining their responses to the question about their three earliest recollections (in the case of individual counseling). Earliest recollections often help reveal their mission and vision in life (see Sect. 3.2). In group contexts, people's responses to the question about their three most hurtful experiences or to the question about their biggest challenges ("problems") when they were young (see Sect. 8.6.2) shed light on their key life themes and help them make this connection.[3] It is essential to find a link between people's elicited integrated life themes (subconscious motivations and strivings) and their responses to Part 2 of the *CIP* (their conscious insights) (see Chap. 8) regarding their reason for seeking career counseling.

I am aware of the fine line between dispensing advice and facilitating self-decision-making by people. We all have our own preferences and style of counseling. However, I maintain that it is not helpful to "advise" people regarding what career counseling

---

[2]The unique situation and needs of assessees will be the key considerations that determine the number of sessions in each of the counseling for self- and career construction phases. Moreover, career counselors' unique styles and preferences will co-determine how the *CIP* and the *MCM* are used. Sufficient information and guidance should be provided unassumingly to promote assessees' reflection and meta-reflection in an effort to nudge them subtly towards connecting dots that may sometimes appear to be random, unconnected, and/or unrelated.

[3]The earliest recollections question (used in individual career counseling intervention) as well as the question about three hurtful things ("The following three things have hurt me so much when I was young/younger that I do not want other people to suffer the same hurt/pain" OR "What were your three biggest challenges ("problems") when you were young?" (which can also be used in group settings) may elicit major traumatic experiences of assessees. The questions should therefore be asked only by registered psychologists.

decisions they should make. In my view, it is better to provide them with enough information to make decisions by themselves. As the following example illustrates, it is important to refrain from making "alarmistic" pre-hypnotic suggestions, albeit unintentionally. When John started to gain weight, he was referred to a medical practitioner concerning his tendency to eat too much when he was stressed. He was warned (negative pre-hypnotic suggestion or nocebo) that he will suffer a heart attack after turning 20 unless he changed his diet (which he did not do). Two years later, in his mid-year examinations in his second year at university, he began to display classical symptoms of a heart attack. Hypnotherapeutic intervention, however, revealed that the symptoms had nothing to do with an actual physical condition but rather with the pre-hypnotic suggestion of the medical doctor two years before.

In the same vein, if a psychologist is approached by an abused wife, the recommended strategy is to counsel her in way that enhances her feelings of self-worth and assertiveness. The aim is to enable her to become strong enough emotionally to take appropriate steps to counter the abuse.

3.8 Summary

The interrelated trio of constructs, namely self-construction counseling, career construction counseling, and life design counseling, provides an ideal theoretical and conceptual framework for the development and implementation of innovative integrative counseling for career construction (see Chaps. 9, 10, 11, and 12). This framework gives career counseling theorists, researchers, and practitioners a practical strategy for administering and postmodernizing career counseling. It also promotes understanding of the psychology of career decision-making challenges and, especially, the idea of eliciting advice from within for answers to people's career-related questions, requests, and decision-making.

References

Adler, A. (1958). *What life should mean to you.* New York, NY: Capricorn Books.

Adler, A. (1998). Understanding children with emotional problems. *The Journal of Humanistic Psychology, 38*(1), 121–127.

Bimrose, J., & Hearne, L. (2012). Resilience and career adaptability: Qualitative studies of adult career counseling. *Journal of Vocational Behavior, 8*(3), 338–344. https://doi.org/10.1016/j.jvb.2012.08.002.

Boje, D. M. (2008). *Storytelling organizations.* London, England: SAGE.

Briddick, W. C., & Sensoy-Briddick, H. (2013). The role of audience in life design. In A. Di Fabio & J. G. Maree (Eds.), *Psychology of career counseling: New challenges for a new era* (pp. 69–83). New York, NY: Nova Science.

Briddick, W., & Sensoy-Briddick, H. (2017). Psychology of career adaptability, employability and resilience. *Paradigm and promise: Life design, psychology of working, and decent work* (pp. 317–327). Cham, Switzerland: Springer.

Campbell, C., & Ungar, M. (2004). Constructing a life that works. Part 1: Blending postmodern family therapy and career counseling. *The Career Development Quarterly, 53*(1), 16–27.

Cardoso, P., Savickas, M. L., & Gonçalves, M. M. (2019). Career construction counseling: Proposal for an integrative model. *Career Development Quarterly, 67,* 188–204.

Chen, C. P. (2004). Positive compromise: A new perspective for career psychology. *Australian Journal of Career Development, 13*(2), 17–28.

Chiaradonna, A. (2017). *Staying relevant: Managing yourself and your career.* Retrieved from https://register.gotowebinar.com/register/359872737676269315?utm_source=Sailthruandutm_.

Collin, A., & Guichard, J. (2011). Constructing self in career theory and counseling interventions. In P. J. Hartung & L. M. Subich (Eds.), *Constructing self in work and career. Concepts, cases and contexts* (pp. 89–106). Washington, DC: American Psychological Association.

Crant, J. M. (2000). Proactive behavior in organizations. *Journal of Management, 26,* 435–462.

Del Corso, J. J. (2013). The theory of career adaptability. In A. Di Fabio & J. G. Maree (Eds.), *Psychology of career counseling: New challenges for a new era* (pp. 117–130). Hauppauge, NY: NOVA.

Di Fabio, A., & Maree, J. G. (2013a). Career counseling: The usefulness of the *Career Interest Profile* (*CIP*). *Journal for Psychology in Africa, 23*(1), 41–51.

Di Fabio, A., & Maree, J. G. (2013b). The effectiveness of the *Career Interest Profile* (*CIP*). *Journal of Employment Counseling, 50,* 110–123.

Doyle, A. (2017). *How often do people change jobs?* Retrieved from https://www.thebalance.com/how-often-do-people-change-jobs-2060467.

Duarte, M. E. (2009). The psychology of life construction. *Journal of Vocational Behavior, 75,* 259–266.

Duarte, M. E. (2017a, June). *Sustainable decent work.* Invited public lecture at University of Pretoria, Pretoria, South Africa.

Duarte, M. E. (2017b, June). *Sustainable decent work and life design.* Invited public lecture at JvR Psychometrics, Randburg, South Africa.

Duarte, M. E., & Cardoso, P. (2015). The life design paradigm: From practice to theory. In L. Nota & J. Rossier (Eds.), *Life design handbook: From practice to theory and from theory to practice* (pp. 41–57). Göttingen, Germany: Hogrefe.

Fugate, M., Kinicki, A. J., & Ashforth, B. E. (2004). Employability: A psycho-social construct, its dimensions, and applications. *Journal of Vocational Behavior, 65,* 14–38.

Ginevra, M. C., Pallini, S., Vecchio, G. M., Nota, L., & Soresi, S. (2016). Future orientation and attitudes mediate career adaptability and decidedness. *Journal of Vocational Behavior, 95,* 102–110.

Graham, M., Hjorth, I., & Lehdonvirta, V. (2017). Digital labour and development: Impacts of global digital labour platforms and the gig economy on worker livelihoods. *Transfer, 23*(2), 135–162. https://doi.org/10.1177/1024258916687250.

Guichard, J. (2005). Life-long self-construction. *International Journal for Educational and Vocational Guidance, 5,* 111–124.

Guichard, J. (Ed.). (2008a). *La nouvelle découverte des activités professionnelles et projets personnels [The discovery of occupational activities and personal plans: An updated workshop method].* Paris, France: Editions qui plus est.

Guichard, J. (2008b). Proposition d'un schema d'entretien constructiviste de conseil en orientation pour des adolescents ou de jeunes adultes [Outline of a life designing counseling interview for adolescents and young adults]. *L'orientation Scolaire et Professionnelle, 37,* 413–440.

Guichard, J. (2009). Self-constructing. *Journal of Vocational Behavior, 75,* 251–258.

Guichard, J. (2010, March). *Les théories de la construction des parcours professionnels et de la construction de soi: Deux approches de la construction de la vie individuelle.* Paper presented at Colloque International INETOP, Paris, France.

Guilbert, R., Bernaud, J., Gouvernet, B., & Rossier, J. (2016). Employability: Review and research prospects. *International Journal for Educational and Vocational Guidance, 16*(1), 69–89.

Hartung, P. J. (2007). Career construction: Principles and practice. In K. Maree (Ed.), *Shaping the story: A guide to facilitating narrative counseling* (pp. 103–120). Pretoria, South Africa: Van Schaik.
Hartung, P. J. (2010a). Career assessment: Using scores and stories in life designing. In J. G. Maree (Ed.), *Career counselling: Methods that work* (pp. 1–10). Cape Town, South Africa: Juta & Company, Ltd.
Hartung, P. J. (2010b). Identifying life-career themes with the career story interview. In J. G. Maree (Ed.) *Career counselling: Techniques that work* (pp. 161–166). Cape Town, South Africa: Juta & Company, Ltd.
Hartung, P. J. (2011). Career construction: Principles and practice. In K. Maree (Ed.), *Shaping the story: A guide to facilitating narrative counselling* (pp. 103–120). Rotterdam, The Netherlands: Sense.
Hartung, P. J. (2013a). The life-span, life-space theory of careers. In S. D. Brown & R. W. Lent (Eds.), *Career development and counseling: Putting theory and research to work* (2nd ed., pp. 83–113). Hoboken, NJ: John Wiley & Sons.
Hartung, P. J. (2013b). Career construction counselling. A. Di Fabio & J. G. Maree (Eds.), *Psychology of career counseling: New challenges for a new era* (pp. 15–28). Hauppauge, New York: Nova Science.
Hartung, P. J. (2015a). Life design in childhood: Antecedents and advancement. In L. Nota & J. Rossier (Eds.), *Handbook of life design: From practice to theory, and from theory to practice* (pp. 89–102). Göttingen, Germany: Hogrefe Publishing.
Hartung, P. J. (2015b). The career construction interview. In M. McMahon, & M. Watson (Eds.), *Career assessment: Qualitative approaches* (pp. 115–121). Rotterdam, The Netherlands: Sense Publishers.
Hartung, P. J. (2018, July). Life design: *A unifying paradigm for international Counseling Psychology. Paper prepared for Division 16*. Presidential Address at the 29th International Congress of Applied Psychology. Montréal, Quebec, Canada.
Hartung, P. J., & Cadaret, M. J. (2017). Career adaptability: Changing self and situation for satisfaction and success. In J. G. Maree (Ed.), *Psychology of career adaptability, employability, and resilience* (pp. 15–28). New York, NY: Springer.
Hirschi, A., Hermann, & Keller, A. C. (2015). Career adaptivity, adaptability, and adapting: A conceptual and empirical investigation. *Journal of Vocational Behavior, 87,* 1–10. https://doi.org/10.1016/j.jvb.2014.11.008.
International Labor Organization. (2019). *World employment and social outlook: Trends 2019.* Retrieved from https://www.ilo.org/global/research/global-reports/weso/2019/lang--en/index.htm.
Koen, J. (2013). *Prepare and pursue: Routes to suitable (re-)employment* (PhD thesis). Amsterdam, The Netherlands: University of Amsterdam. Retrieved from http://hdl.handle.net/11245/2.120347.
Krieshok, T. S., Black, M. D., & McKay, R. A. (2009). Career decision making: The limits of rationality and the abundance of non-conscious processes. *Journal of Vocational Behavior, 75,* 75–290.
Krumboltz, J. D. (2003). Creating and capitalizing on happenstance in educational and vocational guidance. In R. Kunz, J. P. Dauwalder, & J. Renz (Eds.), *Quality development in vocational counselling and training* (pp. 30–32). Zürich, Switzerland: SVB.
LaPointe, K. (2010). Narrating career, positioning identity: Career identity as a narrative practice. *Journal of Vocational Behavior, 77,* 1–9.
Law, J., Bunning, K., Byng, S., Farrelly, S., & Heyman, B. (2005). Making sense in primary care: Levelling the playing field for people with communication difficulties. *Disability & Society, 20,* 169–184.
Lent, R. W. (2012). Social cognitive career theory. In S. D. Brown & R. W. Lent (Eds.), *Career development and counseling: Putting theory and research to work* (2nd ed., pp. 115–146). Hoboken, NJ: John Wiley & Sons.
Maree, J. G. (2009). Career counseling in the 21st century: South African institutions of higher education at the crossroads. *South African Journal of Higher Education, 23,* 429–435.

Maree, J. G. (2015a, September 6). *DVD trailer: A guide to reflective career counselling*. Retrieved from https://www.youtube.com/watch?v=3Rb8oIJTd6Y.
Maree, J. G. (2015b). Research on life design in (South) Africa: A qualitative analysis. *South African Journal of Psychology, 45*, 332-348.
Maree, J. G. (2016a). *Maree Career Matrix (MCM)*. Randburg, South Africa: JvR Psychometrics.
Maree, J. G. (2016b). Career construction counseling with a mid-career black male. *Career Development Quarterly, 64*, 20–35.
Maree, J. G. (2016c). Using interpersonal process during career construction counseling to promote reflexivity and expedite change. *Journal of Vocational Behaviour, 96*, 22–30.
Maree, J. G. (2017a). Life design counselling. In G. Stead & M. Watson (Eds.), *Career psychology* (3rd ed., pp. 105–118). Pretoria, South Africa: Van Schaik.
Maree, J. G. (2017b). Utilizing career adaptability and career resilience to promote employability and decent work and alleviate poverty. In J. G. Maree (Ed.), *Handbook of career adaptability, employability, and resilience* (pp. 349-373). New York, NY: Springer.
Maree, J. G. (2018a). Perspective: Promoting career development in the early years of people's lives through self- and career construction counselling to promote their career resilience and career adaptability. *Early Child Development and Care, 188*(4), 421–424. https://doi.org/10.1080/03004430.2018.1438748.
Maree, J. G. (2018b). Promoting career development and life design in the early years of a person's life. *Early Child Development and Care, 188*(4), 425–436. https://doi.org/10.1080/03004430.2017.1345892.
Maree, J. G. (2018c). Advancing career counselling research and practice using a new quantitative + qualitative approach to elicit clients' advice from within. *South African Journal of Higher Education, 32*(4), 149–170.
Maree, J. G., & Di Fabio, A. (2019). Integrating personal and career counseling to promote sustainable development and change. *Personality and Individual Differences, 10*(11). https://doi.org/10.3390/su10114176.
Masten, A. (2014). Global perspectives on resilience in children and youth. *Child Development, 85*(1), 6–20.
McLennan, B., McIlveen, P., & Perera, H. N. (2017). Pre-service teachers' self-efficacy mediates the relationship between career adaptability and career optimism. *Teacher and Teacher Education, 63*, 176–185.
Music Story. (2018, April 26). *Le blues du businessman—Celine Dion*. Retrieved from https://www.youtube.com/watch?v=oWWny-tu9No.
Parsons, F. (1909). *Choosing a vocation*. Boston, MA: Houghton Mifflin.
Patton, W., & McMahon, M. (2006a). The Systems Theory Framework. In M. McMahon & W. Patton (Eds.), *Career counselling: Constructivist approaches* (pp. 94–109). London, England: Routledge.
Patton, W., & McMahon, M. (2006b). *Career development and systems theory: Connecting theory and practice*. Rotterdam: Sense.
Perera, H. N., & McIlveen, P. (2017). Profiles of career adaptivity and their relations with adaptability, adapting, and adaptation. *Journal of Vocational Behavior, 98*, 70–84.
Pryor, R., & Bright, J. (2011). *The chaos theory of careers*. New York, NY: Routledge.
Reid, H. (2018, July). Prompting reflection and learning in career construction counseling: Three research studies evaluating process and practice in the UK. In P. J. Hartung (Chair), *Reflexivity and change in life designing: Perspectives from process research*. 29th International Congress of Applied Psychology (ICAP 2018) conducted at the Palais des Congrès, Montréal, Québec, Canada.
Ribeiro, M. A., & Guilherme de Oliveira, S. F. (2018). Impacts of a group-based career counseling model for unskilled adults in crisis: A case study. In A. Di Fabio & J.-L. Bernaud (Eds.), *Narrative interventions in post-modern guidance and career counseling* (pp. 87–118). Retrieved from https://doi.org/10.1007/978-3-319-98300-4_6.

Rochat, S., Masdonati, J., & Dauwalder, J. (2017). Determining career resilience. In J. G. Maree (Ed.), *The psychology of career adaptability, career resilience, and employability* (pp. 125–141). New York, NY: Springer.

Rossier, J. (2015a). Career adaptability and life designing. In L. Nota & J. Rossier (Eds.), *Handbook of the life design paradigm: From practice to theory and from theory to practice* (pp. 154–164). Boston, MA: Hogrefe.

Rossier, J. (2015b). Personality assessment and career interventions. In P. J. Hartung, M. L. Savickas, & W. B. Walsh (Eds.), *APA handbook of career intervention: Foundations* (Vol. 1, pp. 327–350). Washington, DC: American Psychological Association. https://doi.org/10.1037/1438-018.

Rossier, J., Nota, L., Dauwalder, J.-P., Duarte, M. E., Guichard, J., Savickas, M., et al. (2015). Conclusion. In L. Nota & J. Rossier (Eds.), *Handbook of the life design paradigm: From practice to theory, from theory to practice* (pp. 285–290). Göttingen, Germany: Hogrefe.

Rossier, J., Ginevra, M. C., Bollmann, G., & Nota, L. (2017). The importance of career adaptability, career resilience, and employability in designing a successful life. In J. G. Maree (Ed.), *The psychology of career adaptability, career resilience, and employability* (pp. 65–82). New York, NY: Springer.

Rottinghaus, P. J., Falk, N. A., & Eshelman, A. (2017). Assessing career adaptability. In J. G. Maree (Ed.), *The psychology of career adaptability, career resilience, and employability* (pp. 85–105). New York, NY: Springer.

Santili, S., Marcionetti, J., Rochat, S., Rossier, J., & Nota, L. (2017). Career adaptability, hope, optimism, and life satisfaction in Italian and Swiss adolescents. *Journal of Career Development, 44*(1), 62–76. https://doi.org/10.1177/0894845316633793.

Savickas, M. L. (1995). Examining the personal meaning of inventoried interests during career counseling. *Journal of Career Assessment, 3*(2), 188–201.

Savickas, M. L. (2001). Toward a comprehensive theory of career development: Disposition concerns and narratives. In F. T. L. Leong & A. Barak (Eds.), *Contemporary models in vocational psychology: A volume in honor of Samuel H. Osipow* (pp. 295–320). Mahwah, NJ: Lawrence Erlbaum.

Savickas, M. L. (2002). Career construction: A developmental theory of vocational behavior. In D. Brown (Ed.), *Career choice and development* (pp. 149–205). San Francisco, CA: Jossey-Bass.

Savickas, M. L. (2003). Advancing the career counseling profession: Objectives and strategies for the next decade. *The Career Development Quarterly, 52,* 87–95.

Savickas, M. L. (2005). The theory and practice of career construction. In S. Brown & R. W. Lent (Eds.), *Career development and counseling: Putting theory and research to work* (pp. 42–70). New York, NY: John Wiley.

Savickas, M. L. (2006a, April). *Counseling for career construction (facilitating the storied approach in (career) counseling: Practical implementation*). Paper presented at the 15th Australian Career Counseling Conference, Sydney, Australia.

Savickas, M. L. (2006b, July). *A vocational psychology for the global economy.* Keynote presentation, American Psychological Association Annual Conference. New Orleans.

Savickas, M. L. (2007a). Internationalization of counseling psychology: Constructing cross-national consensus and collaboration. *Applied Psychology: An International Review, 56*(1), 182–188.

Savickas, M. L. (2007b). Internationalization of counseling psychology: Constructing cross-national consensus and collaboration. *Applied Psychology, 56,* 182–188.

Savickas, M. L. (2008, July). Interactive workshop on life design counseling at the XXXIXth International Congress of Psychology, Berlin, Germany.

Savickas, M. L. (2009a, April). *The essentials of life design counseling.* Invited public lecture, the University of Pretoria, Pretoria, South Africa.

Savickas, M. L. (2009b, April). *Utilizing early anecdotes in counseling in the 21st century.* Keynote presentation, SA Society for Clinical Hypnosis. Pretoria, South Africa.

Savickas, M. L. (2009c, June). *The role of values in careers: Meaning and mattering in life design.* Keynote at the Biennial Society for Vocational Psychology Conference, University of St Louis, Missouri.

Savickas, M. L. (2009d). Career-style counseling. In T. J. Sweeney (Ed.), *Adlerian counseling and psychotherapy: A practitioner's approach* (5th ed., pp. 183–207). New York, NY: Routledge.
Savickas, M. L. (2010, July). *Life Designing: Framework and introduction.* Paper presented at the 27th International Congress of Applied Psychology, Melbourne, Australia.
Savickas, M. L. (2011a). Reshaping the story of career counseling. In K. Maree (Ed.), *Shaping the story—A guide to facilitate narrative counseling* (pp. 1–3). Boston/Rotterdam, The Netherlands: Sense.
Savickas, M. L. (2011b). *Career counseling.* Washington, DC: American Psychological Association.
Savickas, M. L. (2013). Career construction theory and practice. In R. W. Lent & S. D. Brown (Eds.), *Career development and counseling: Putting theory and research into work* (pp. 147–183, 2nd ed.). Hoboken, NJ: Wiley.
Savickas, M. L. (2015a). Career counseling paradigms: Guiding, developing, and designing. In P. Hartung, M. Savickas, & W. Walsh (Eds.), *The APA handbook of career intervention* (Vol. 1, pp. 129–143). Washington, DC: APA Books.
Savickas, M. L. (2015b). *Life-design counseling manual.* Rootstown, OH: Author.
Savickas, M. L. (2015c). Designing projects for career construction. In ed. R. A. Young, J. F. Domene, & L. Valach (Eds.), *Counseling and action: Toward life-enhancing work, relationships, and identity*, (pp. 13–31). New York, NY: Springer.
Savickas, M. L. (2016, July). *Meaning at work: Work at meaning.* Closing keynote presentation, National Career Development Association Conference, Chicago, United States of America.
Savickas, M. L. (2019a). *Theories of psychotherapy series. Career counseling* (2nd ed.). Washington, DC: American Psychological Association.
Savickas, M. L. (2019b, September). *Designing a self and constructing a career in post-traditional societies.* Keynote address at the 43rd international association for educational and vocational guidance Conference, Bratislava, Slovakia.
Savickas, M. L. (in press). Career construction theory and counseling model. In R. W. Lent & S. D. Brown (Eds.), *Career development and counseling: Putting theory and research into work* (3rd ed., pp. …). Hoboken, NJ: Wiley.
Savickas, M. L., & Porfeli, E. J. (2012). *Career Adapt-Abilities Scale*: Construction, reliability, and measurement equivalence across 13 countries. *Journal of Vocational Behavior, 80,* 661–673. https://doi.org/10.1016/j.jvb.2012.01.011.
Signorelli, J. (2016, February, 14). *How to elicit stories from others.* Retrieved from https://www.business2community.com/branding/elicit-stories-others-01450948.
Super, D. E. (1955). The dimensions and measurement of vocational maturity. *Teachers College Record, 57,* 151–163.
Super, D. E. (1957). *The psychology of careers.* New York, NY: Harper & Row.
Super, D. E. (1983). Assessment in career guidance: Toward truly developmental counseling. *Personnel and Guidance Journal, 61,* 555–562.
Super, D. E. (1990). Career and life development. In D. Brown & L. Brooks (Eds.), *Career choice and development* (2nd ed., pp. 192–234). San Francisco, CA: Jossey-Bass.
Van der Horst, A. C., & Klehe, U.-C. (2019). Enhancing career adaptive responses among experienced employees: A mid-career intervention. Advance online publication. *Journal of Vocational Behavior, 111,* 91–106.
Whiston, S. C., Li, Y., Goodrich Mitts, N., & Wright, L. (2017). Effectiveness of career choice interventions: A meta-analytic replication and extension. *Journal of Vocational Behavior, 100,* 175–184.
Winnicott, D. W. (1964). *The child, the family and the outside world.* Cambridge, MA: Perseus.
Zunker, V. G. (1998). *Career counseling: Applied concepts of life planning* (5th ed.). Pacific Grove, CA: Brooks/Cole Publishing Company.

Chapter 4
How Global Change Necessitates Innovation in Career Counseling: Linking Economic, Industrial, Psychology, and Career Counseling Waves

If you look at history, innovation doesn't come just from giving people incentives; it comes from creating environments where their ideas can connect (Steven Johnson)

Abstract This chapter elaborates on the link between successive waves in career counseling, psychology, the global economy, and successive industrial revolutions. The waves in career counseling are then linked to prominent helping models in each wave, the attributes or traits emphasized during each wave are highlighted, and associated career interventions are explained. The influence of concurrent "business models" on career counseling helping models are examined, and associated personality traits are clarified before the chapter is concluded.

4.1 Orientation

Any innovation in the theory and practice of career counseling should be considered against the background of Collin and Young's (1986, p. 827) comment: "[Career counseling] provides the basis for action in the real world." The authors contend that such action should impact people positively in an ever-changing world "in which occupational certainties are [constantly and progressively] being eroded" (p. 827). They argue that a career counseling theory needs to be consistent, coherent, appropriate, and sufficiently pertinent to change and its effect to qualify for informing policy and practice. Likewise, Pryor (2008) states that career counselors should adopt an accommodating approach to changes in the occupational world and to their impact. He contends also that considering global occupational trends and technological advances through an integrative lens is key to career counselors renewing themselves to meet the growing need for contemporary skills and attitudes. We as career counselors need to identify and inculcate such skills, attitudes, and traits in order to help our clients not only survive but become adaptive and thrive. Today, referring to "people skills" as "soft skills" is no longer acceptable (Agarwal, 2018), and there is growing global consensus that people skills are actually the key skills

J. G. (Kobus) Maree, *Innovating Counseling for Self- and Career Construction*,
https://doi.org/10.1007/978-3-030-48648-8_4

in any corporation and should rather be referred to as "hard skills". Villiers (2020) contends that "Career development professionals do clients a major disservice by using the flawed 'hard'/'soft' skills distinction. It perpetuates the false idea that there is little rigor in learning and applying emotional intelligence, persuasion, negotiation, and team leadership" (p. 1). These sentiments merely serve to confirm Savickas' (2006a) view: "I keep repeating that the vocational guidance model is a superb model for countries that are still organized the way we were from 1900 to 1950. I am not saying any of these models are no good; depends though on which type of economy you are working in" (p. 5).

What is happening in South Africa and in most developing country contexts supports this observation and is the main reason for the model I am proposing. Extensive research (as discussed in this book) has confirmed that the approach works well in both Global North and Global South contexts.

4.1.1 Overview of the Different Waves in the Economy, Industry (Industrial Revolutions), Psychology in General, and Career Counseling

I agree with the authors cited above that an innovative approach to career counseling should be designed and assessed against the following four criteria, namely, it should be (a) consistent, (b) appropriate, (c) relevant, and (d) sufficiently attuned and sensitive to change and its impact if it is to inform policy and practice meaningfully. Any new strategy should therefore be based on a thorough examination of the identifiable, consecutive, and largely overlapping waves or cycles in the economy, industry (culminating in the Fourth Industrial Revolution or Work 4.0 and the impending Fifth Industrial Revolution or Work 5.0), psychology in general, and career counseling in particular over the past 100 years or more (Maree, 2010a, 2010b, 2013).

Understanding and appreciating the factors that have guided the career counseling profession since the beginning of the 20th century requires some knowledge of the connection between the different waves in the economy, industry (industrial revolutions), psychology in general, and career counseling during successive periods in the past millennium or so. This will help explain why counseling for self- and career construction has emerged so strongly during the past three decades as a key theoretical component of the contemporary theory base for career counseling research and practice. Table 4.1 shows the link or overlap between these different waves over the past 120^{+} years or so.[1] An overview is given below of the link between the different waves in the economy, industry (industrial revolutions), psychology in general, and career counseling.

[1] All time frames in this section date back to the beginning of the 20th century. Tables 4.1 and 4.2 have been designed to help readers see the overall pattern; the "big" picture and should not be seen as "final" or 100% precise. It is impossible to be entirely accurate when it comes to discussions of this kind and to surmising about the future.

Table 4.1 Horizontal (across fields) and vertical (over the past 120 years) overview of waves in the economy, industry (industrial revolutions), psychology in general, and career counseling

Wave	Economy (Goldschmidt & Hilbert, 2009; Molitor, 1999, 2000; Moody & Nogrady, 2010)	Six Industrial revolutions (Lindsay & Hudson, 2019; Salimi, 2015; Seymour, 2016)	Technological waves (Kondratiev waves; Waves of innovation) (Silva & Di Serio, 2016; Yegorov, 2011)	Psychology: Epistemological basis (Henriques, 2011, 2012; Leontiev, 2005; Maree, 2018; O'Hanlon, 1994)	Helping model in career counseling (Lindsay & Hudson, 2019; Maree, 2019a, 2019b, 2019c, 2019d; Ratts, 2009; Savickas, 2006a, 2006b)
First	Agricultural wave (late 18th and early 19th centuries)	First: Work 1.0: Mechanization	Industrial Revolution (1770–1830)	Psychodynamic theory	Friendly volunteers
Second	Industrial wave (late 19th and early 20th centuries)	Second: Work 2.0: Mass production	Steam and railways (1830–1880)	Cognitive-behavioral theory and problem-focused therapies	Vocational guidance
Third	Service wave (later part of 20th century)	Third: Work 3.0: Automation	Steel, electricity, and engineering (1880–1910)	Existential-phenomenological/humanistic assumptions; narrative, postmodern, constructivist (storied) approach	Career education/guidance
Fourth	Information communication technology wave (last part of 20th century and first few decades of 21st century (evolving)	Fourth: Work 4.0: Robotization	Automobile, oil, and mass production (1910–1970–80)	Transpersonal psychology and diversity or multicultural counseling theory. Added contextual perspective. Reaction to European and North American models	Career counseling and life design

(continued)

Table 4.1 (continued)

Wave	Economy (Goldschmidt & Hilbert, 2009; Molitor, 1999, 2000; Moody & Nogrady, 2010)	Six Industrial revolutions (Lindsay & Hudson, 2019; Salimi, 2015; Seymour, 2016)	Technological waves (Kondratiev waves; Waves of innovation) (Silva & Di Serio, 2016; Yegorov, 2011)	Psychology: Epistemological basis (Henriques, 2011, 2012; Leontiev, 2005; Maree, 2018; O'Hanlon, 1994)	Helping model in career counseling (Lindsay & Hudson, 2019; Maree, 2019a, 2019b, 2019c, 2019d; Ratts, 2009; Savickas, 2006a, 2006b)
Fifth-Sixth	Artificial intelligence wave (midway during the third decade of 21st century)	Fifth: Work 5.0: Artificial Intelligence and a focus on human healthcare and wellbeing as well as meaning, hope, and purpose. Understanding the association between "the changing human-nature relationship, and its impact" (Seymour, 2016, p. 1) on human health and wellbeing	Information and telecommunications (1970/80-)	Innovating and creatively reconsidering psychology; emphasis on sustainable psychosocial health; reconnecting personal and professional selves	Life purpose counseling: focus on inspiration, social justice (advocacy), purpose, ethical behavior, and the common good–marrying the needs of humans with the skills of robots. Ensuring "optimal health at the human-environmental interface" (Seymour, 2016, p. 9)

Below, I elaborate on the meaning and implications of this table. The reader is reminded that my comments about the fifth wave are purely hypothetical and based on my idiosyncratic reading of future events.

4.1.2 Association Between Successive Waves in Career Counseling, Psychology,[2] the Global Economy, and Successive Industrial Revolutions

Influence of the economy on career counseling. The state of the economy of any given country impacts the career counseling profession. Many impoverished people (including learners from socioeconomically disadvantaged contexts and other disabling conditions in rural areas and townships in particular) struggle to access education and training and also to adapt to university studies (Ribeiro, 2016). In South Africa, for instance, which is categorized as a developing, Global South country (with small sections of the economy having a Global North character), only a small percentage of the population ever receive career counseling.

According to the Quarterly Labour Force Survey (QLFS) (2019), during the third quarter of 2019, the official unemployment rate in South Africa increased to 29.1%. Moreover, one in every six South African workers in the informal economy (referred to as the 'forgotten economy'). The situation of unemployed people who are neither in education nor in training is particularly dire. Of the 3.4 million 15 to 24-year-olds, roughly 33.2% were "Not in Education, Employment, or Training" (NEETs), and of the 20.3 million 15 to 34-year-olds, 40.7% were NEETs. Currently (Staff writer, 2019), four months after the release of the QLFS report, the unemployment figure has increased to 29.0%. In addition, the so-called "expanded unemployment rate" has risen to 38.5%.

There are many reasons for the high unemployment in South Africa:

a. The national unemployment rate is hovering in the region of 29%, which means that many people have to accept any form of employment as long as the job can help them secure an income and eke out a living. The overwhelming majority of these people need an income so badly that merely finding a job overrides the notion of searching for work that will promote their sense of meaning, help them find meaning in the workplace, and kindle their sense of hope for the future.
b. There are too few trained career counselors to meet the career counseling needs of the entire population.

---

[2]This is merely a tentative attempt at generalizing (one that applies to Global North contexts especially). While one time frame may, for instance, apply to Global North contexts, other frames may apply to Global South contexts. Time frames also often intersect. Other authors may very well have different views on the matter.

c. Only a small percentage of career counselors have been trained in contemporary career counseling approaches and associated interventions.[3]
d. Career counseling is expensive, which means very few people can afford this service.
e. "Testing and telling" is the standard mode of assessing people and administering career counseling in group contexts especially. For various reasons, this is not ideal.

The next section covers the use of traditional career counseling approaches in different contexts.

Pervasive influence of traditional (trait-and-factor) career counseling. Interest in qualitative (storied) approaches together with quantitative (objective) approaches has increased significantly in their use in individual contexts (Hartung & Santili, 2018). However, despite the fact that postmodern approaches have begun to gain traction during the past three decades in developed (Global North) countries, the traditional style of career counseling, based on the interpretation of test results and the recommendation of a few fields of study by an 'expert' career counselor, still prevails in large parts of Global South, underdeveloped countries especially. Besides, traditional career counseling still serves a useful purpose in developing, less affluent, third world countries, especially because very few of these countries have as yet made the "narrative turn". This "turn" can be described as the transition from using tests in career counseling to helping people identify and describe who they really are by articulating their career-lives in words (Hartung, 2013a, 2013b; White & Epston, 1990). However, the traditional approach to career counseling still predominates even in many affluent, primarily first world (Global North) countries. Furthermore, insufficient research has been done on the viability of group-based career counseling intervention, self- and career construction, and life design intervention (in developing countries in particular). This is the case even though drawing on group-based career counseling models is key to meeting the career counseling needs of large numbers of people who currently have little or no access to any career counseling. It should be emphasized, though, that while working in groups has the advantage of reaching more people, it has other advantages as well (see, for instance, Lehman, Ribeiro, Uvaldo, and Silva (2015).

Influence of economic and industrial waves on the occupational world. Irrespective of the socioeconomic situation in any given country, and the career counseling approach followed, the impact of consecutive economic and industrial waves on the occupational world is felt in all work contexts in post-industrial societies. Guichard (2004, 2013a, 2013b), Hartung (2016), Maree (2016), Savickas (2011a, 2011b, 2011c) and others explain how the changed and ever-changing occupational environments are increasingly failing either to maintain or create "safe spaces" for their workers. Recent occupational trends such as the gig economy and digital nomads (Krapivin, 2018) (also see Chap. 6) confirm that these and related developments will merely intensify people's sense of insecurity and uncertainty. Here, I agree with

[3]A major project by the South African Career Development Association (SACDA) is under way to make career counseling available to the entire South African population (see Chap. 5).

Doyle's (2017, p. 1) assertion that "upgrading one's employment status has become an ongoing process" and that workers should develop skills that cannot easily be automated or performed by robots. Using a similar lens, I also believe that we should approach the future from a 'positive uncertainty' perspective (Gelatt, 1989). In other words, we accept and feel positive about the uncertainty.

Workers are increasingly being offered short-term work assignments today (the new "normal") rather than longer term or even lifelong work contracts. They are being left to their own devices to become employable (as opposed to merely attempting to find work), to become career resilient, and to become adaptable (formerly referred to as "maturing"). The fourth economic wave, driven by the Fourth Industrial Revolution, has accelerated the need for skilled workers and decreased the demand for un-, low-, or inappropriately skilled workers—a cause for considerable concern.

Need to balance work-life roles and making social contributions. Some of the pressing challenges workers and work-seekers will increasingly experience include blending their work and life roles, becoming and remaining employable (Savickas & Porfeli, 2012), becoming and remaining career resilient (Maree, 2017a, 2017b), and becoming and remaining career agile to retain and enhance their employability. Finding a way somehow to stay relevant in the rapidly shifting and changing occupational world will therefore require revisiting and renegotiating the contracts between employees and employers and ensuring that the criterion of "facilitating sustainable decent work for every worker" supersedes all other considerations. This lofty aim is achievable, but it depends on if and how much we want to achieve it. Each of us is capable of contributing in this regard in seemingly unrelated contexts. I, personally, value obtaining information from workers in lowly work situations (and even jobless people) such as waiters, cleaners, newspaper vendors, postmen, security people, farm workers, shop assistants, cashiers, and domestic workers. My questions normally revolve around those aspects of their work they enjoy most and those they enjoy least. I also try to find out what it is about their jobs that makes them believe they are (or are not) doing meaningful work—why or why not they believe their work enhances their overall sense of living a purposeful life and makes them feel wanted, appreciated, acknowledged, or worth something in the workplace. Then, I ask them what they really want to do in life: What will make them happy and feel that their work-life is meaningful and purposeful. Their responses unfailingly humble and inspire me. Many of them, for instance, want to become teachers, nurses, social workers, lawyers, medical doctors, electricians, architects, and engineers. Their reasons for not having pursued their dreams differ, but a few common themes run through their collective responses. First, they feel that circumstances beyond their control prevented them from pursuing their desired career-lives, such as poverty, lacking the money to enroll in and pursue a field of study, and having had to take care of an ailing family member, usually a parent. Second, most of them want to do work they consider more professional—work that will make them feel proud of themselves and earn the respect of others. Third, they experience feelings of sadness, unfulfilment, frustration, and being "trapped" in an unsatisfactory work situation. Fourth, they experience little or no work satisfaction. Fifth, the money they earn is often regarded as less important than a sense of "belonging" where they work and being made to feel "wanted" in their workplace.

In most cases, though, a brief counseling for self- and career construction discussion with these workers is enough to bring about a change in their lives, to ignite processes that promote the rewriting of their life stories, redesigning their lives, and setting them on a career trajectory that can enhance their sense of personal and social meaning in their lives. The following example illustrates this point. About a year ago, I was on a visit to the little town of Hazyview, Mpumalanga; a seriously disadvantaged, impoverished part of South Africa where I am collaborating with colleagues from the Good Work Foundation (GWF) to assess the effectiveness of a postmodern life design intervention on the career adaptability and decision-making capacity of impoverished and unemployed people. Staying at a nearby guesthouse, I was one morning served breakfast by a humble and friendly young woman. In response to my question about how she felt about her work, she said that she was working at the guesthouse because she desperately needed money as she could not afford to apply for admission to and study at a tertiary training institution. Asked what she wanted to do, her eyes lit up when she said, "I want to become a nurse". A brief interview with her after hours confirmed that she was interested in and might become a nurse to enact her key life themes. Asked further whether she had heard about the Sector Education and Training Authorities (SETA) system, she shook her head. I scribbled the contact details of the Health SETA on a piece of paper. Before too long she was accepted into a nursing learnership and, judging by her feedback, participating in the program has changed her life irrevocably. She felt that she was doing what she had always wanted to do.

Linking economic waves, helping models in career counseling, attributes or traits emphasized, and associated career interventions (Maree, 2019a, 2019b, 2019c, 2019d; Savickas, 2006a, 2006b). Table 4.2 shows the linking of economic waves, helping models in career counseling, attributes or traits emphasized, and associated career interventions.

Friendly volunteers. The practice of friendly volunteers providing informal career counseling to people who wished to leave the farms of their parents and thus needed career counseling (the precursor of vocational guidance) (Savickas, 2006a) emerged as the first helping model in career counseling during the first economic wave, which is associated with the First Industrial Revolution (Work 1) (Salimi, 2015; Schwab, 2017; The four industrial revolutions, 2017). In this era, land was cultivated to make a living, and work was mostly an extension of the work of one's parents—children (workers) by and large stayed on the farms of their parents.

Vocational guidance. During the industrial era (the second economic wave, ca. 1900-1950), vocational guidance (Parsons, 2005) emerged as the second career counseling helping model in career counseling. This period corresponded with Work 2.0 (the Second Industrial Revolution) (Salimi, 2015) when the mass manufacturing was the prevalent mode of production (Molitor, 2000), numerous "jobs" were generated, and people gathered together in cities.

Career education or career guidance. The third helping model (associated with career education or career guidance) appeared during the third economic wave (ca. 1940–1990) (also known as the service wave), which was associated with Work 3.0 or the Third Industrial Revolution (Salimi, 2015). Automation was the order of

Table 4.2 Overview of consecutive waves in the economics field, helping models in career counseling, associated traits, and career interventions

Wave	Helping model in career counseling (Savickas, 2006a, 2006b)	Attributes or traits emphasized (Savickas, 2006a, 2006b)	Associated career intervention (Savickas, 2011b).
First (late 18th and early 19th century)	Friendly volunteers	Character was articulated through self-expression and individual effort. People were expected to "be the same"; have the same values	Informal help from "friendly visitors"
Second (early to middle 19th century)	Vocational guidance	People are seen as social actors ("objectivist", individual differences, how they resemble others approach). Insufficient evidence of exploration, development, and self-reflection	Provision of general information
Third (middle to late 19th century	Career guidance. education	People seen as motivated agents differentiated by their readiness to deal with developmental tasks consistent with their particular life stages	Provision of psychoeducational and psychosocial information and guidance/educatio.
Fourth (late 19th to the present; still evolving)	Self- and career construction counseling and life design	People seen as autobiographical authors of career identity. Adaptability, resilience, and creativity are paramount	Career counseling (or "counseling for (self- and) career construction", self-construction, and life design)
Fifth (early 21st century -)	Innovative, creative career counseling **for all**	People are seen as designers of their "self" and "constructors" of their careers with the aid of established digital infrastructure and technology	Tele-career counseling, tele-counseling, and tele-therapy

the day. In this period, the pendulum swung towards using the skills of third-party providers to access specialized know-how. The "test-and-tell" approach prevailed with career counselors telling or advising people about suitable fields of study that "matched" their personalities. The expectation was that people would choose a career and "actualize" (develop) themselves and their careers, get promoted, and gradually work their way up the corporate ladder (Savickas, 2002). Holland's (1997) trait and factor theory and Super's (1955, 1957) life span, life-space theory are theories associated with the third wave.

Self- and career construction counseling and life design. The emergence of information communication technology (ICT) signaled the fourth economic wave, which is associated with Work 4.0 or the Fourth Industrial Revolution (1990-). The outstanding feature of this period is rapid technological and artificial intelligence advances, including robotization (Salimi, 2015). In line with these advances, the language of the career counseling discourse has also changed (see Chap. 6). Many communication and computer technology developments were and still are characterized by the loss of conventional jobs and the emergence of short-term work assignments, dejobbing, protean and boundaryless careers, increased connectivity and networking, and artificial intelligence. The attendant uncertainty, insecurity, and loss of work identity led to work trauma in many employees. During this period, life design intervention (the fourth helping model) emerged in Global North countries in particular. Savickas (2000) summarized the outcome of these developments by stating that "[c]areer must become more personal and self-directed to flourish in the postmodern information age" (p. 59).

Life purpose counseling. I believe that life purpose counseling will lie at the heart of fifth wave counseling, and its focus will be on inspiring clients and helping them experience a sense of purpose in a world of work that will differ vastly from the workplace of today. The notion of "work" will most likely be renegotiated, and the emphasis in counseling will be on promoting social justice, ethical behavior, and the common good—thus marrying the needs of human beings with the abilities of robots. Currently, for instance, robots and drones are used to monitor, fight, and/or prevent the spread of the coronavirus by delivering medicine and food and disinfecting locations (Ackerman, Guizzo, & She, 2020; Marr, 2020).

Fifth Industrial Revolution. Even at this stage, the internet is already abuzz with conjectures, hypotheses, and predictions about the Fifth Industrial Revolution and especially its possible effect on the future of work and, consequently, the wellbeing and future of humankind (see, for instance, Lindsay, 2019; Lindsay & Hudson, 2019; Naidoo, 2019; Rundle, 2019). Some of the predictions are the following:

a. Artificial intelligence will enable human beings to answer instead of simply keeping on asking bigger and more complex questions than before (Sterry, in Lindsay, 2019).
b. Endeavors to ensure that all people receive a basic income will gain momentum (Lewis, in Lindsay, 2019; Reich, in Lindsay & Hudson, 2019).
c. Whereas the Fourth Industrial Revolution appears intent on removing human beings from the work environment, the Fifth Industrial Revolution will bring

them back (Lindsay & Hudson, 2019), thus posing the question: "How can you make the world 'better' rather than just 'more efficient' or 'more productive'?" (p. 1).

d. To an increasing extent, people will be able to work from where they live.
e. The way in which employees are treated in small and large businesses will increasingly impact on their psychological, social, and emotional wellbeing.
f. Given the disparity in access to the internet between Global South and Global North countries, learners and workers in poor countries will be negatively affected by the introduction of artificial intelligence and robots into the workplace (and inadequate preparation of learners by education fraternities and of the workforce by employers) as opposed the situation in Global North countries.
g. Naidoo's (2019) observation is worth considering here: "In robot utopia, the importance of innovation and advancement is not only embraced but celebrated without fear of a total machine takeover or the extinction of man ... whatever side of the fence you're on in predicting humanity's fate, there's no stopping the technology bullet train or the robots it is carrying" (n.p.).

Naidoo (2019) mentions the following two future scenarios.

First, the dystopian possibility (referred to as singularity) that human beings may eventually be reduced to extinction by their own creations (robots) if robots become "cleverer" (artificial super-intelligence) and refuse to accept instructions from human beings and, instead, begin to issue instructions themselves.

Second, what the author terms robot utopia may eventuate. In this scenario, AI and robotics will reduce human beings' workload by eradicating boring, repetitive work and help them take "wise" decisions. Human beings will have more time to do what adds meaning and purpose to their career-lives. Most of the world's population will benefit from "the democratization of technology; where ordinary people will have access to some of the most powerful technologies on earth and exist in harmony with it all ... the importance of innovation and advancement is not only embraced but celebrated without fear of a total machine takeover or the extinction of [hu]man[s]" (Naidoo, 2019, n.p.) (Photograph 4.1).

4.1.3 *Influence of Contemporaneous "Business Models" on Career Counseling Helping Models and the Foregrounding of Certain Personality Traits (Savickas, 2006a, 2006b; Maree & Morgan, 2012)*

As discussed earlier, the state of a country's economy at any particular stage, the nature and impact of the corresponding industrial revolution, and the associated "manufacturing paradigm [will] transform the way in which we work and do business" (Salimi, 2015, p. 1). Our approach to career counseling intervention is informed by the feature (e.g. identity) that is focused on at any given time. This focus shapes our intervention and co-determines how we administer career counseling in

Photograph 4.1 Celebrating innovation and advancement

a given context and at a given time. Providing context for our chosen career counseling approach and style (e.g. a "test-and-tell" approach or a life design approach) (Guichard, 2009; Savickas, 2011a; Savickas et al., 2009a, 2009b, 2009c, 2009d) is key to ensuring that the service we render is in the best interests of clients (Taber, Hartung, Briddick, Sensoy-Briddick, & Rehfuss, 2011). Today, probably more than ever before, a sense of hope and purpose needs to be rekindled in clients in a world in which many people have lost hope in the future. People need to rediscover a sense of purpose and meaning in the face of the message that robots are replacing workers and at a time when "work" as we know it is losing meaning in occupational contexts that no longer "hold" workers in the way they used to.

Traits such as integrity, autonomy, humility, and frugality were valued during the first economic wave, and, accordingly, work success was achieved through people's individual endeavors (Savickas, 1993). During the second wave, following the example set by natural scientists, people working in the field of career counseling began to develop "objective" assessment instruments. The aim was to find a way to "test" people objectively to establish their personality traits (e.g. interests, aptitudes, and intelligence). It was believed that testing or measuring was sufficient to obtain objective information that could predict people's success in given work environments for the duration of their career-lives. Intervention was aimed at establishing a satisfactory fit or match between people and their careers as it was thought this would ensure success in a career (Maree, 2013; Watson, McMahon, Mkhize, Schweitzer, & Mpofu, 2011). During the third economic wave[4] the idea of "making meaning"

[4]Here again I emphasise the difficulty of generalizing in these matters. As mentioned, different time frames applied to what happened in the Global South and the Global North in particular.

in one's occupation or work began to emerge. The emphasis shifted from relying almost exclusively on measuring people's "objective" traits (Hergenhahn, 2005) to emphasizing their individuality, enhancing their career adaptability, improving their attitudes, developing their (self-)belief, and enhancing their competencies (ABCs). Today, career counseling emphasizes people as individuals and promotes understanding of their idiosyncratic situations rather than how they resemble or differ from one another (Byars-Winston, 2013). Logical positivism (with its emphasis on how people resemble one another) as the predominant guiding theory was gradually replaced by subjective, existential-humanistic approaches (with their emphasis on people themselves and their distinctiveness) (Hergenhahn, 2005; Lent, 1996). The pendulum thus swung from measuring people's "objective", "fixed" traits towards revealing their unique style of seeing things (constructing reality). Helping people not only move forward but actually take the action needed to bring about therapeutically relevant change in their lives and advance their sense of who they are began to take center stage in career counseling (Rogers, 1942; Seligman, 1994).

The trend that emerged during the third economic wave, namely an increased emphasis on people's identity (Who am I? Where do I "fit in"?) instead of on their "personality profiles" became even more pronounced during the fourth wave. There is today less emphasis on "climbing the corporate ladder". Modern career counseling intervention is thus to a large extent aimed at promoting the stability of career identities (Savickas, 2010). Helping people narrate their life stories is key, with the emphasis on helping them attain lucid, coherent, and stable life-story narratives or self-portraits.

To manage change in the workplace, people should increasingly be encouraged to examine, understand, appreciate, and embrace, rather than fear, the new and changing dynamics of the world of work. This includes accepting the idea of lifelong learning and becoming more employable, more adaptable, and more career resilient (Hartung & Cadaret, 2017; Maree, 2017a, 2017b). Wolfe (2017) maintains that acquiring competencies such as curiosity, creativity, conscientiousness, critical thinking, collaboration, and intellectual agility is essential in this regard. Palti (2017) rates the quality of creativity as particularly important today and argues that this trait sets human beings apart from machines (robots). Speaking of the words "creative" and innovative": Here is a simple way of informally 'assessing' people's sense of creativity and innovation before any formal assessment. Provide them with a blank piece of paper and ask them what they see on the piece of paper. In most cases, they will struggle to give creative, innovative responses—until they discover that what they see depends to a large extent on what they choose to see.

4.2 Summary

During the past 130 years or so, the guiding theoretical and conceptual underpinnings of career counseling theory, research, intervention, and policy making have been informed and influenced by, and have also coincided with, general global advances in fields such economics and different industrial revolutions. During this time, premodernism was gradually replaced by modernism, modernism by high modernism, and, eventually, high modernism by postmodernism (Watson & Kuit, 2007). It may seem logical to use the term "post-postmodernism" here, but it is too unwieldly and awkward to the liking of many. Terms such as altermodernism, cosmodernism, digimodernism, metamodernism, performatism, postdigitalism, and posthumanism have therefore been put forward (Basulto, 2011; Gibbons, 2017), but the jury is still out as to which term is the most appropriate.

What is clear, though, is that career counseling theorists, researchers, practitioners, and policy makers need to constantly revisit, reconsider, update, and adapt their theory base, research endeavors, career counseling intervention, and policy making in line with changing economic, industrial, and social circumstances to ensure that the profession retains its currency and value for people. This includes examining critically the influence of different business models on career counseling (Kinkar, Põld, Ümarik, & Õun, 2019). It also includes making a connection between different economic waves, helping models in career counseling, and, especially, those attributes or traits that were emphasized during each successive wave in these subject fields. This will help us understand the influence of contemporaneous "business models" on career counseling helping models and foreground certain personality traits to help people manage change in the workplace by examining, understanding, appreciating, and embracing, instead of fearing, the new and changing dynamics of the world of work. Put differently, people should be encouraged to develop those traits (survival or thriving skills) that will enable them to transition successfully and repeatedly from one work context to another. These skills include being able to code and knowing more than one programming language.

In the next chapter, the spotlight falls on the key issue of providing context for career counseling in contexts that differ from those in and for which it was initially conceptualized and implemented.

References

Ackerman, E., Guizzo, E., & Shi, F. (2020, January 21). *How robots are helping to fight the coronavirus outbreak*. Retrieved from https://spectrum.ieee.org/automaton/robotics/robotics-hardware/robots-helping-to-fight-coronavirus-outbreak.

Agarwal, A. (2018). *Data reveals why the 'soft' in 'soft skills' is a major misnomer*. Retrieved from https://www.forbes.com/sites/anantagarwal/2018/10/02/data-reveals-why-the-soft-in-soft-skills-is-a-major-misnomer/#74c799f76f7b.

Basulto, D. (2011, February 22). On the Internet, what comes after post-Modernism? Retrieved from https://bigthink.com/endless-innovation/on-the-internet-what-comes-after-post-modernism.

Byars-Winston, A. (2013). Career stages. In M. L. Savickas (Ed.), *Ten ideas that changed career development* (p. 13). Broken Arrow, OK: NCDA.

Collin, A., & Young, R. A. (1986). New directions for theories of career. *Human Relations, 39*(8), 837–853.

Doyle, A. (2017). *How often do people change jobs?* Retrieved from https://www.thebalance.com/how-often-do-people-change-jobs-2060467.

Gelatt, H. B. (1989). Positive uncertainty: A new decision-making framework for counseling. *Journal of Counseling Psychology, 36*, 252–256.

Gibbons, A. (2017, June 12). Postmodernism is dead. What comes next? Retrieved from https://www.the-tls.co.uk/articles/public/postmodernism-dead-comes-next/.

Goldschmidt, A J. W., & Hilbert, J. (2009). *Health economy in Germany – economical field of the future (Gesundheitswirtschaft in Deutschland - Die Zukunftsbranche).* Germany: Wikom Publishing House.

Guichard, J. (2004). Se faire soi [To make oneself self]. *L'Orientation Scolaire et Professionnelle, 33,* 499–534.

Guichard, J. (2009). Self-constructing. *Journal of Vocational Behavior, 75,* 251–258.

Guichard, J. (2013a, November). *Career guidance, education, and dialogues for a fair and sustainable human development*. Inaugural conference of the UNESCO chair of Lifelong guidance and counselling, University of Wroclaw, Poland.

Guichard, J. (2013b). What competencies need people living in liquid societies to design their lives and direct their careers? In A. Di Fabio & J. G. Maree (Eds.), *Psychology of career counseling: New challenges for a new era* (pp. 41–60). New York, NY: Nova.

Hartung, P. J. (2013a). The life-span, life-space theory of careers. In S. D. Brown & R. W. Lent (Eds.), *Career development and counseling: Putting theory and research to work* (2nd ed., pp. 83–113). Hoboken, NJ: John Wiley & Sons.

Hartung, P. J. (2013b). Career construction counselling. A. Di Fabio & J. G. Maree (Eds.), *Psychology of career counseling: New challenges for a new era* (pp. 15–28). Hauppauge, New York: Nova Science.

Hartung, P. J. (Ed.) (2016). Advancing career intervention for life design [Special issue]. *Career Development Quarterly, 64*(1), 2–3.

Hartung, P. J., & Cadaret, M. J. (2017). Career adaptability: Changing self and situation for satisfaction and success. In J. G. Maree (Ed.), *Psychology of career adaptability, employability, and resilience* (pp. 15–28). New York, NY: Springer.

Hartung, P. J., & Santili, S. (2018). *My Career Story*: Description and initial validity evidence. *Journal of Career Assessment, 26*(2), 308–321.

Henriques, G. (2011). *A new unified theory of psychology* (11th ed.). New York, NY: Springer.

Henriques, G. (2012). Psychotherapy's fifth wave. Retrieved from https://www.psychologytoday.com/intl/blog/theory-knowledge/201205/psychotherapy-s-fifth-wave.

Hergenhahn, B. R. (2005). *An introduction to the history of psychology* (5th ed.). Belmont, CA: Thomson Wadsworth.

Holland, J. L. (1997). *Making vocational choices: A theory of vocational personalities and work environments* (3rd ed.). Lutz, FL: Psychological Assessment Resources.

Kinkar, V., Põld, M., Ümarik, M., & Õun, T. (2019). *Guidelines for career counsellors on addressing gender equality and gender stereotypical career choices in career counselling.* Tallinn, Estonia: Tallinn University.

Krapivin, P. (2018). *The study, work, retire model is broken as we live until 100.* Retrieved from https://www.forbes.com/sites/pavelkrapivin/2018/08/13/the-study-work-retire-model-is-broken-as-we-live-until-one-hundred/#62f6fa8f7bd4.

Lehman, Y. P., Ribeiro, M. A., Uvaldo, M. C. C., & Silva, F. F. (2015). A psychodynamic approach on group career counseling: A Brazilian experience of 40 years. *International Journal for Educational and Vocational Guidance, 15*(1), 23–36. https://doi.org/10.1007/s10775-014-9276-0.

Lent, E. B. (1996). The person focus in career theory and practice. In M. L. Savickas & B. Walsh (Eds.), *Handbook of career counseling theory and practice* (pp. 109–120). Palo Alto, CA: Davies-Black Publishing.

Leontiev, D. (2005). Existential psychology as a response to the challenges of the 21st century. *International Journal of Existential Psychology & Psychotherapy, 1,* 103–105.

Lindsay, J. (2019). *What if the future of work was no work at all?* Retrieved from https://metro.co.uk/2019/05/09/future-work-no-work-9385679/.

Lindsay, J., & Hudson, A. (2019). *What is the Fifth Industrial Revolution and how will it change the world?* Retrieved from https://metro.co.uk/2019/06/10/fifth-industrial-revolution-will-change-world-9738825/.
Maree, J. G. (2010a). Brief overview of the advancement of postmodern approaches to career counseling. *Journal of Psychology in Africa, 20,* 361–369.
Maree, J. G. (2010b). Using early memories in career-story interviewing. In J. G. Maree (Ed.), *Career counseling: Methods that work* (pp. 167–199). Cape Town, South Africa: Juta Academic.
Maree, J. G. (2013). *Counseling for career construction: Connecting life themes to construct life portraits: Turning pain into hope.* Rotterdam, The Netherlands: Sense.
Maree, J. G. (2016). Using interpersonal process during career construction counseling to promote reflexivity and expedite change. *Journal of Vocational Behaviour, 96,* 22–30.
Maree, J. G. (2017a). Life design counselling. In Stead, G. & Watson, M. (Eds.), *Career psychology* (3rd ed.) (pp. 105–118). Pretoria, South Africa: Van Schaik.
Maree, J. G. (2017b). Utilizing career adaptability and career resilience to promote employability and decent work and alleviate poverty. In J. G. Maree (Ed.), *Handbook of career adaptability, employability, and resilience* (pp. 349–373). New York, NY: Springer.
Maree, J. G. (2018). Using life design counseling for career construction to facilitate sustainable employability and decent work in a developing country context. In V. Cohen-Scali, J. Pouyaud, M. Podgórny, V. Drabik-Podgórny, G. Aisenson, J-L. Bernaud, I. Moumoula., J. Guichard (Eds.), *Interventions in career design and education* (pp. 195–214). New York, NY: Springer.
Maree, J. G. (2019a, June). *Career Development in Africa: Decent work for all: Brief photomontage.* Keynote Address at the Annual Career Development Practitioner Congress, Emperors Palace Conference Centre, Kempton Park, South Africa.
Maree, J. G. (2019b). Postmodernising career counseling in a deep rural context. In J. G. Maree (Ed.), *Handbook of innovative career counseling* (pp. 577–596). New York, NY: Springer.
Maree, J. G. (2019c). Group career construction counseling: A mixed-methods, intervention study with high school students. *Career Development Quarterly, 67*, 47–61.
Maree, J. G. (2019d). Innovative career construction counselling for a creative adolescent. *British Journal of Guidance and Counselling.* https://doi.org/10.1080/03069885.2018.1504202.
Maree, J. G., & Morgan, B. (2012). Toward a combined qualitative-quantitative approach: Advancing postmodern career counselling theory and practice. *Cyprian Journal of Educational Sciences, 7,* 311–325.
Marr, B. (2020, March 18). *Robots and drones are now used to fight Covid-19.* Retrieved from https://www.forbes.com/sites/bernardmarr/2020/03/18/how-robots-and-drones-are-helping-to-fight-coronavirus/#7b106d302a12.
Molitor, G. T. T. (1999). The next 1,000 years: The "Big Five" engines of economic growth. *The Futurist, 33,* 13–18.
Molitor, G. T. T. (2000). Emerging economic sectors in the third millennium: Introduction and overview of the 'big five'. *Foresight, 2,* 323–329.
Moody, J. B., & Nogrady, B. (2010). *The sixth wave: How to succeed in a resource-limited world.* Sydney, Australia: Random House.
Naidoo, V. (2019). *The Fifth Industrial Revolution looms.* Retrieved from https://www.itweb.co.za/content/WnxpE74D2jg7V8XL.
O'Hanlon, B. (1994). The Third Wave. *Family Therapy Networker, 18*(6), 19–29.
Palti, I. (2017). *Creativity will be the source of our next industrial revolution, not machines.* Retrieved from https://qz.com/954338/creativity-will-bethe-source-of-our-next-industrial-revolution-not-machines.
Parsons, F. (2005). *Choosing a vocation.* Broken Arrow, OK: National Career Development Association.
Pryor, R. (2008). Does career counseling matter? A personal reflection. *Australian Journal of Career Development, 17*(2), 55–59.
Quarterly Labour Force Survey (QLFS). (2019). *Statistical release P0211.* Pretoria, South Africa: Statistics, SA.

Ratts, M. J. (2009). Social justice counseling: Toward the development of a Fifth Force among counseling paradigms. *Journal of Humanistic Counseling, Education and Development, 48,* 160–172.

Ribeiro, M. A. (2016). Career counseling for people in psychosocial situations of vulnerability and flexicurity: A social constructionist proposal. In T. V. Martin (Ed.), *Career development: Theories, practices and challenges* (pp. 79–110). New York, NY: Nova.

Rogers, C. R. (1942). *Counseling and psychotherapy. Newer concepts in practice.* Boston, MA: Houghton Mifflin.

Rundle, E. (2019). *The 5th Industrial Revolution: When it will happen and how*? Retrieved from https://devops.com/5th-industrial-revolution-will-happen/.

Salimi, M. (2015). Work 4.0: An enormous potential for economic growth in Germany. *ADAPT Bulletin,* 16 December. Retrieved from http://englishbulletin.adapt.it/wp-content/uploads/2015/12/work4.0_sam.pdf.

Savickas, M. L. (1993). Career counseling in the postmodern era. *Journal of Cognitive Psychotherapy: An International Quarterly, 7,* 205–215.

Savickas, M. (2000). Renovating the psychology of careers for the twenty-first century. In R. A. Young & A. Collin (Eds.), *The future of career* (pp. 53–68). Cambridge, England: Cambridge University Press.

Savickas, M. L. (2002). Career construction: A developmental theory of vocational behavior. In D. Brown (Ed.), *Career choice and development* (pp. 149–205). San Francisco, CA: Jossey-Bass.

Savickas, M. L. (2006a, April). *Counseling for career construction (facilitating the storied approach in (career) counseling: Practical implementation).* Paper presented at the 15th Australian Career Counseling Conference, Sydney, Australia.

Savickas, M. L. (2006b, July). *A vocational psychology for the global economy.* Keynote presentation, American Psychological Association Annual Conference. New Orleans.

Savickas, M. L. (2009a, April). *The essentials of life design counseling.* Invited public lecture, the University of Pretoria, Pretoria, South Africa.

Savickas, M. L. (2009b, April). *Utilizing early anecdotes in counseling in the 21st century.* Keynote presentation, SA Society for Clinical Hypnosis. Pretoria, South Africa.

Savickas, M. L. (2009c, June). *The role of values in careers: Meaning and mattering in life design.* Keynote at the Biennial Society for Vocational Psychology Conference, University of St Louis, Missouri.

Savickas, M. L. (2009d). Career-style counseling. In T. J. Sweeney (Ed.), *Adlerian counseling and psychotherapy: A practitioner's approach* (5th ed., pp. 183–207). New York, NY: Routledge.

Savickas, M. L. (2010, July). *Life Designing: Framework and introduction.* Paper presented at the 27th International Congress of Applied Psychology, Melbourne, Australia.

Savickas, M. L. (2011a). Reshaping the story of career counseling. In K. Maree (Ed.), *Shaping the story—A guide to facilitate narrative counseling* (pp. 1–3). Boston/Rotterdam, The Netherlands: Sense.

Savickas, M. L. (2011b). *Career counseling.* Washington, DC: American Psychological Association.

Savickas, M. L. (2011c). *Career counseling [DVD].* Washington, DC: American Psychological Association.

Savickas, M. L., & Porfeli, E. J. (2012). *Career Adapt-Abilities Scale*: Construction, reliability, and measurement equivalence across 13 countries. *Journal of Vocational Behavior, 80,* 661–673. https://doi.org/10.1016/j.jvb.2012.01.011.

Schwab, K. (2017). *The Fourth Industrial Revolution.* New York, NY: Crown Business.

Seligman, L. (1994). *Developmental career counseling and assessment* (2nd ed.). Thousand Oaks, CA: Sage.

Seymour, V. (2016). The human-nature relationship and its impact on health: A critical review. *Frontiers in Public Health, 4,* 260. https://doi.org/10.3389/fpubh.2016.00260.

Silva, G., & Di Serio, L. C. (2016). The sixth wave of innovation: Are we ready?. *Revista de Administração e Inovação, 13,* 128–134.

Staff Writer. (2019, July 31). *Skills vs employment in South Africa and the truth about getting a job.* Retrieved from https://businesstech.co.za/news/business/332367/skills-vs-employment-in-south-africa-and-the-truth-about-getting-a-job.

Super, D. E. (1955). The dimensions and measurement of vocational maturity. *Teachers College Record, 57,* 151–163.

Super, D. E. (1957). *The psychology of careers.* New York, NY: Harper & Row.

Taber, B. J., Hartung, P. J., Briddick, H., Briddick, W. C., & Rehfuss, M. C. (2011). Career style interview: A contextualized approach to career counseling. *The Career Development Quarterly, 59*(3), 274–287.

The four industrial revolutions. (2017). Retrieved from https://people.hofstra.edu/geotrans/eng/ch2en/conc2en/four_industrial_revolutions.html.

Villiers, A. (2020). *Why we should stop using 'soft' skills.* Retrieved from https://www.ncda.org/aws/NCDA/pt/sd/news_article/278124/_PARENT/CC_layout_details/false.

Watson, M., & Kuit, W. (2007). Postmodern career counselling and beyond. In K. Maree (Ed.), *Shaping the story: A guide to facilitating narrative counselling* (pp. 73–86). Pretoria, South Africa: Van Schaik.

Watson, M., McMahon, M., Mkhize, N., Schweitzer, R. D., & Mpofu, E. (2011). Career counseling people of African ancestry. In E. Mpofu (Ed.), *Counselling people of African ancestry* (pp. 281–293). New York, NY: Cambridge University Press.

White, M., & Epston, D. (1990). *Narrative means to therapeutic ends.* New York, NY: Norton.

Wolfe, I. (2017). *Entrepreneurs' network interview: What will the future of work and jobs look like?* Retrieved from www.perfectlaborstorm.com/2016/12/future-jobs-future-work.

Yegorov, Y. (2011, May). *Long economic waves as innovation cycles.* Paper read at Simon Kuznets International Symposium, SKKISD. Kiev, Ukraine.

Chapter 5
Innovating Career Counseling Through Contextualization

When the winds of change blow, some people build walls and others build windmills (Unknown)

Abstract This chapter discusses the main background argument for the integrative model that I am proposing and elaborates on the value of dealing innovatively with contextual challenges in career counseling. It begins with an explanation of the need for the contextualization of career counseling in different contexts and why I believe global change, contextualization, and innovation are an inextricably interwoven trio of concepts that should be considered jointly during discussions about career counseling in a changing world. Next, I elaborate on the differences between, but also the golden thread running through, concepts related to contextualization. Also discussed is the importance of contextualization during the adaptation or modification of theory, assessment, or intervention to ensure that their implementation will be advantageous and fit for their intended purpose. Practical examples are given. The focus then shifts to the need for multilevel contextualization to address diversity needs when different career counseling paradigms are implemented in typical Global South contexts. Next, contextualizing the implementation of counseling for self- and career construction in such contexts is discussed based on how it is being done in Africa, after which the chapter is concluded.

J. G. (Kobus) Maree, *Innovating Counseling for Self- and Career Construction*,
https://doi.org/10.1007/978-3-030-48648-8_5

5.1 Dealing Innovatively with Contextual Challenges in Career Counseling

I (Maree, 2019b) believe that a closely interwoven synergy exists between the following trio of concepts: global change, contextualization, and innovation. Using a particular career counseling theory, assessment strategy, or intervention in socioeconomic contexts[1] that differ from the context in which that particular career counseling theory, technique, or intervention strategy was initially developed can be considered useful only if it can be applied in a valid, reliable, and trustworthy manner in the new socioeconomic context. In addition, accepting and understanding that "context is all" (Reid, 2018, n.p.) is particularly important in collectivist, Global South (third world) countries where large numbers of people have been subjugated and colonized for centuries and where the culture often differs widely from that in the countries where the theories and practice were originally developed. Maree (2017c) as well as Ntinda, Maree, Mpofu, and Seeco (2014) state that those who design, develop, and adapt assessment instruments should carefully consider the socioeconomic contexts in which they will be implemented and used because constructs such as "career adaptability", "individual resilience", and even the word "career" itself may be foreign to some Global South contexts especially and regarded as overly progressive or liberal. Contextualization of career counseling should be managed and executed in a way that customizes such counseling in terms of factors such as ethnicity, age, intellectual and health status, social and economic situation, and geographic setting. Only in this way can career counseling be contextualized to ensure its value for all people and promote the ideal of an inclusive career counseling service.

Fundamental, rapid, and escalating global changes inevitably change people's socioeconomic and occupational situations. This implies that people's career counseling needs, too, change all the time, demanding an appropriate response from the career counseling profession. The theory of, research on, and interventions in career counseling can therefore never remain static. Existing theories, techniques, and interventions need to be recontextualized, updated, and innovated constantly to ensure that they continue to meet clients' ever-changing needs.

The next few sections cover the constructs contextualization, decontextualization, recontextualization, and co-contextualization. The link between these constructs is also discussed.

5.1.1 Contextualization

To gain a proper understanding of any phenomenon or activity, examining and considering all aspects of that phenomenon or activity are essential (Macmillan Dictionary,

[1]The term "socioeconomic contexts" is used here to denote cultural, social, economic, socioeconomic, and sociocultural contexts.

n.d.). Given the dearth of home-grown or indigenous career counseling theory development, we mostly have to use career counseling intervention styles, techniques, and other content developed in and imported from other countries to stay abreast of developments and promote career counseling in developing country contexts (Watson, Nota, & McMahon, 2015). However, this means that all imported theory, practice, and/or research must be considered carefully upfront to ensure its applicability in the "new" context. This includes considering the nature of imported assessment instruments (qualitative and/or quantitative) and establishing the usefulness and effectiveness of interventions associated with the imported material.

In Africa, for instance, the beliefs and behavior of people are influenced by notions such as *Ubuntu*. This construct refers to the strong emphasis Africans place on collective needs such as connecting with other human beings and showing kindness, compassion, and respect for others' sense of dignity. Likewise, the notion of *iSinti*, which holds that the needs and identity of individual people can best be understood by considering the collective identity (Nussbaum, Palsule, & Mkhize, 2010). *Ujamaa* (i.e. collectivism, emphasizing the importance of the extended family as a collective holding environment) (Winnicott, 1965, 1969, 1987) and the belief that we are only human because of others), too, meaningfully shapes African worldviews and associated behavior (Cranford, 1999; Ibdawoh & Dibua, 2003). For these and other reasons, it makes little sense to try to advance either career counseling theory or practice without considering the role of individualism versus collectivism, the narrative tradition, and the interrelatedness and interdependence of people in their contexts.

Savickas' (2015) career construction theory itself is an example of the contextualization of a theory, model, and associated approach. By including the traditional differential approach in career construction theory, he has shown career counseling theorists, researchers, and practitioners how an approach (in this case the person-environment fit approach) can be contextualized in way that ensures its continued worth and currency in changing and changed times (the 21st century) and in different contexts (such as postmodern, fourth wave career counseling contexts). By advancing the idea of drawing on scores and stories, Savickas (2015) shows the profession how to use the best of both worlds (qualitative and quantitative assessment and intervention) to promote the best interests of people in rapidly changing contexts where using the "differential" (test-and-tell) approach in relative isolation simply no longer yields satisfactory outcomes.

Contextualization actually comprises the following trio of actions: decontextualization, recontextualization, and co-contextualization.

5.1.2 Decontextualization

Removing something (e.g. a theory, assessment technique, intervention strategy, or approach developed in a specific country) from its original context and implementing it in a new context is an example of decontextualization. This includes using a person-environment fit (positivist) model (developed in North America many years ago) in a Global South, developing country context without first considering the effectiveness of the model in the "new" or different context (Collins Dictionary, n.d.; Psychology Dictionary, n.d.). Decontextualization implies the need to consider carefully the merits, validity, reliability, and trustworthiness of any particular feature of a model, theory, or practice aspect in its new context before implementing it.

5.1.3 Recontextualization

This term refers to the act of implementing an approach or model developed in a certain context in a new or unfamiliar context and ensuring its applicability. Say, for instance, researchers apply self- or career construction counseling or life design counseling in a typical Global South (developing country) context. To ensure the trustworthiness of the intervention in the "foreign" context, careful piloting followed by more extensive research on the intervention (including rigorous examination of the implementation itself as well as of the outcomes of the pilot and follow-up studies) is needed to ensure that future application of the intervention will meet its intended purpose (The American Heritage Dictionary of the English language, 2016). According to the Oxford Reference Dictionary (n.d.), too, recontextualization means taking a model or strategy developed in a given context, at a given time, and in a given space or location and resituating or using such a model or strategy in a different context, with a different group of assessees, or under a new set of circumstances ("making the familiar strange and the strange familiar") (Novalis, in Oxford Reference Dictionary, n.d., n.p.). This strategy is mostly followed when interventions developed in Global North contexts are used in Global South contexts. Such interventions are typically reframed or expressed in a different way in new contexts, often by altering or changing the original intervention, approach, or model in a respectful and considered manner.

Implementing a positivist ("test-and-tell"/person-environment fit) model to deal with people's/assessees' career indecision is an example of inadequate contextualization (Savickas, 1995). Doing so is tantamount to the decontextualization and objectification of assessees, which can, of course, lead to poor outcomes. Assessees' subjective indecision- and indecisiveness-related experiences are often largely disregarded in the process. In such instances, their indecision or indecisiveness instead of themselves as persons with indecision or undecidedness are foregrounded (an eventuality that is purposely pre-empted whenever self- and career construction as well as life design approaches are implemented). Savickas (1995) emphasizes the importance of recontextualizing assessees' career indecision or undecidedness appropriately by eliciting and promoting understanding of their subjective career-stories first. Recontextualizing assessees' stories involves objectifying of these stories with a view to opening new perspectives for assessees and positioning or situating challenging ('problematic') aspects in new stories during the process of life design counseling. These stories are co-contextualized (see below) when career counselors and assessees collaboratively plan action steps and strategies to deal with "problems" and enact ("actualize" or realize) assessees' career identities (they jointly agree on activities that can be carried out to represent these new identities).

5.1.4 Co-Contextualization

Co-contextualization is the ultimate step in contextualizing 'models', assessment instruments, and interventions. This is accomplished when researchers consult assessees in any project with a view to contextualizing a model developed in a context different to the one in which it is currently applied. Consider, for instance, the introduction of career construction theory in a typical developing country and asking assessees about their role models. In many parts of Africa, assessees will list their parents and refuse to list other role models. Failing to consider the emotionally significant influence of fathers (also mothers and other family members) on their children's career decision in collectivist African contexts is not consistent with sound theory or helpful. Asking for clarification of responses at all stages is crucial. Also, failing to consider the deep sense of respect that pervades African societies when questions are posed and responded to can be extremely limiting. Many African learners, for example, instead of responding 'openly', will provide an answer they believe or hope will please the researcher-counselor. Such answers will, of course, negatively impact the validity and reliability of responses. The first question in the *CCI* ("How can I be useful to you?") respectfully deals with power-related issues. I agree with Reid (2018) that even in those instances where these experiences turn out to be extremely hurtful, painful, or upsetting, the technique works well. This is because the person remains in control of what is happening, has herself or himself chosen these "micro-stories", and proposes her or his own interpretation of them. However, it cannot be posed without first asking how the question will be understood by assessees. Even where assessees provide seemingly lucid and clear responses, it is essential to ask them to clarify what their responses mean before drawing any conclusions.

Whatever you observe about your clients when you first meet them (including their hand movements, questions, comments, clothing) should be noted carefully. Thibault (2004) adds to the discussion on co-contextualization by stating that people's spoken language is generally accompanied by manual-brachial gestures, poses, looks, bodily movements, and facial expressions. These signs and symbols co-contextualize each other in shaping conversations. Co-contextualization does not imply that some modalities are merely linearly added to others because they cannot be regarded as entirely separate and independent of each other. Rather, they are diverse "semiotic modalities co-evolved with each other on the phylogenetic timescale and co-developed and co-individuated on the ontogenetic scale. They also co-contextualize each other on the timescale of particular discursive activities and the textual productions that derive from these" (Thibault, 2004, p. 192).

From a practical point of view, therefore, accepting and advancing the notion and importance of adopting a not-knowing position (Anderson & Goolishian, 1992) substantially enhances co-contextualization. It is crucial always to make a conscious attempt to carefully observe, listen to, and refrain from "advising" people. Offering advice seems to be especially rewarding for some counselors themselves. Schaerer et al.'s (2018) research, for instance, revealed that people who display a desire to be in control show an increased need to have power and are more likely to advise others on different matters. Offering advice enhances their feelings of being in control, and if the advice is accepted, their feelings of being powerful and in control are increased. It may be that ways and styles of counseling in which "advice" is dispensed may enhance some counselors' and therapists' feelings of being powerful (Cardoso, 2016). Seemingly, these kinds of professions sometimes attract people that have a need for power (Schaerer, Tost, Huang, Gino, & Larrick, 2018; Thomas & Sosin, 2011).

Below, I elaborate on a valuable lesson on the importance of co-contextualization and abandoning preconceived ideas in indigenous contexts especially.

5.2 The Importance of Co-Contextualizing and Abandoning Preconceived Ideas: A Lesson Within a Lesson

The importance of abandoning pre-conceived ideas and adopting a not-knowing position (Anderson & Goolishian, 1992) was often brought home to me during my research at, for instance, the Good Work Foundation (GWF, 2019; see Chap. 7). Below, I discuss one such instance.

During my second visit to the GWF in 2018, I was offered a cup of the best cappuccino I had ever tasted anywhere in the world and subsequently asked to meet the local barista ('Jabu') who had prepared the drink. It turned out that he hailed from a desperately poor area, had been raised by his grandmother, and had been taken in and trained by the GWF at her request. I was moved by his poignant life story, which I hope will one day be published by a publisher such as Amazon (representatives of the company are regularly invited to the GWF to share in some of the life stories of the assessees and publish them). This invitation comprises a creative and uplifting endeavor that speaks volumes of the way colleagues at the GWF are practicing self- and career construction. I later invited Jabu to send me an e-mail on his story. In it, he revealed that he had dropped out of school early in his life because he struggled with reading and writing and had no access to any kind of support. The GWF then gave him a life-changing opportunity (see their website for these and other stories: goodworkfoundation.org) to train as a coffee barista. On completing his training, he was employed by the GWF and began to see his future in a totally different light. He had hope again and experienced a sense of purpose in his life. He now serves as a role model to many others. His own his role model was Dritan Alsela.[2]

[2]Dritan Alsela is a famous German barista in the world of coffee. He was a role model who inspired Jabu to be a barista.

His story was also a timely lesson within a lesson for me. I discussed the possibility of trying to help him by adding his life story to my website, but the GWF executive said that this would not be useful in their context as their policy was to subsume the needs of the individual in the needs of the collective. Helping one person among many others who were equally needy would likely embarrass him and even lead to ostracism. Once again, I was reminded of the need to ensure that psychosocial understanding is enhanced in these contexts and of the importance of abandoning preconceived ideas about communities and how to "advise" them. I was again reminded to focus on trying to understand the context first before taking any steps to 'help', especially in contexts that differed from my own.

5.3 Using Different Career Counseling Paradigms in a "Typical" Global South (Developing Country) Context: Multilevel Contextualization to Address Diversity Needs

The economies of many Global North countries are post-industrial in nature. Conversely, the economies of most Global South countries have a predominantly industrial character. Some of these countries, such as South Africa, have first world and third world socioeconomic characteristics. In these countries, career counseling theory and practice should provide for both present-day and traditional career counseling intervention styles (respectively drawing on contemporary but also on more traditional theoretical and conceptual paradigms). Depending on the kind of context in which career counseling is requested, career counselors may draw either on a trait-and-factor approach (e.g. in contexts where brief career counseling is sought for hundreds of learners and where life design has not been administered previously). Conversely, in a private school context, where individual career counseling is sought for individual learners, where the life design approach has been introduced, and where career counselors trained in the newer paradigms are available to intervene, it would be acceptable to implement a life design-based approach.

These kinds of matters should be planned, implemented, and regulated at national education policy-making level. Regrettably, in developing countries, there is often a lack of planning and implementation (or insight into these matters) at a national level.

Models for cultural adaptation of career counseling are not readily available to researchers and practitioners interested in adapting constructs developed in different cultures. I am in favor of an approach that considers the cultural differences that define clients' realities and promotes culturally-sensitive and -appropriate intervention (Sue, Ivey, & Pederson, 1996). Therefore, I tend to follow an emic-etic (culture-specific but at the same time cross-culturally applicable) approach to career counseling (Berry, Poortinga, Segall, & Dasen, 1992). This approach "[integrates] the insider's deep understanding with the outsider's critique" (Whiteman, p. 3). It examines culture-specific behaviors, traits, and measures from within a culture to provide insight into indigenous phenomena from insiders' perspective (emic approach; an inductive process that allows data to speak for themselves). However, it also considers whether behaviors, traits, and measures apply across cultures (universally and independent of one or more cultures) (etic approach).

In summary: career counseling approaches that are used and questions that are asked should at least to some extent extend beyond cultural borders. If this is not the case, questionnaires, measuring instruments, and intervention strategies will lack equivalence (uniformity). In such a scenario, questions, measures, and interventions cannot be compared practically because they cannot be claimed to measure the same constructs cross-culturally (in different cultures) (Pedersen, 1991; Pedersen et al., 1989). Below, I demonstrate what I mean.

5.4 Contextualizing Different Kinds of Requests for Career Counseling

The following four career counseling-related requests are largely representative of the different kinds of career counseling that are most often sought from career counseling practitioners. When approached for career counseling, I generally encounter the following categories of requests and caveats.

a. Requests for the assessment of a large group of learners[3] (mostly indigent learners from disadvantaged rural areas or township or inner-city schools). Often the entity soliciting career counseling services for learners operates on a shoestring budget and has person-environment fit (positivist/objective) assessment in mind. As many learners as possible must be assessed in a short period of time.
b. Requests for career counseling for poor learners (virtually) without charge. Such requests often stipulate that learners' marks should be used together with the results of an interest test.
c. Requests for integrative qualitative and quantitative career counseling in groups. Typically, this kind of request is made by people attached to affluent private schools where most of the parents of the learners can afford to pay for this more expensive service.
d. Requests for a complete assessment that includes personality (including interest) tests, study orientation questionnaires, and aptitude tests. In most instances, either individual learners themselves or their parents (on their behalf) make such appointments with career counselors. In these cases, time and funding are not a problem, and the services are mainly offered in large urban centers.

[3]For the purposes of this book, the word "learners" refers to either learners still at school or to students at tertiary institutions.

It should be clear from the preceding that indigent learners are at a major disadvantage with regard to career counseling. It is also clear that an innovative approach is needed to career counseling that meets the following criteria: It is already provided early in schools in the form of enjoyable activities, it does not take up too much time, it does not cost too much, many learners can be assessed simultaneously, it should be fun, and the strategy is rigorous and consistent with best practice in career counseling intervention (meets minimum quality assurance criteria).

5.5 Contextualization of Career Counseling Theory and Assessment

Three levels of contextualization. As has been pointed out so far in this chapter, four phases of contextualization can be distinguished. Contextualization can also be classified as "internal" (contextualization that occurs in the original context in which a theory or model was conceptualized) or as "external" (contextualization that occurs in a context different to the one in which the model was developed). The "different" context or the so-called "target" context is the one where the contextualized theory or intervention will be applied. Table 5.1 shows the contours of integrating the three phases associated with contextualization and the different levels at which they occur (Butler 1997, 2005; Thibault, 2004).

Table 5.1 is explained below.

a. Kind of paradigm. As discussed in Chaps. 2 and 3, the following successive career counseling paradigms have held sway since the beginning of the previous century: Vocational guidance, career guidance or education, self- and career construction, and life design. It should again be emphasized that much depends on the specific context in which career counseling is administered. For example, in Global North countries, the life design model has yielded excellent outcomes, while in many Global South countries (underdeveloped countries where the economies are by and large still structured the way they were in the early part of the previous century), the vocational guidance paradigm still serves a useful purpose, and most local career counselors consider it unnecessary to reconsider the way they practice.
b. Perspective or viewpoint. In an innovative contextualization model, perspectives can be reframed and/or merged or blended to update an existing model. Whereas, for example, in a psychodynamic model, people's subconscious motives are foregrounded and regarded as determining a person's future, from a career construction perspective, people's earliest memories are elicited to identify their key life themes.[4] Drawing on the person-environment fit approach then enables career counselors to help clients find suitable work environments where they can enact these themes, heal others and, in doing so, also heal themselves.

---

[4]Career counselors who are uncomfortable in dealing with the pain in talking with clients should not enquire about earliest recollections.

Table 5.1 Contours of integrating the phases (Butler 1997, 2005; Thibault, 2004) and levels of contextualization

Original model, approach, and associated intervention	Four levels of contextualization		Three contextualization phases			Contextualized model, approach, and associated intervention (styles and techniques)
			Decontextualize	Recontextualize	Co-contextualize	
		a. Paradigmatic				
		b. Perspectival				
		c. Content				
		d. Implementation				

c. Content. Permission can be obtained from the developers of tests to restandardize any given assessment instrument and/or its associated intervention strategies and techniques. This can be achieved by, for instance, adding, omitting, or rephrasing or changing questions in questionnaires so that they are appropriate for use in the new contexts in which they will be used.
d. Implementation. How career counseling is implemented (administered) depends on the context in which it is provided. While one-to-one counseling may be better suited to individualist cultures, group-based counseling will be more appropriate in collective cultures. Similarly, depending on how the economy of a given country is structured, using a traditional approach may be more or less appropriate than using a narrative approach.

5.6 The South African Case: Crafting a Competency Framework for Career Development Practitioners in South Africa (FCDPSA) (DHET, 2016)

Currently, in South Africa, three related (and somewhat overlapping) types of career development practitioners (CDPs) are being instituted by the FCDPSA based on rigorous examination of available competency frameworks internationally. The FCDPSA demonstrates how best practice internationally can be drawn on and contextualized for application in a Global South local context. The FCDPSA document distinguishes between three levels of practitioners.

a. Entry level career development practitioners (ELCDPs). These practitioners are allowed to provide information at basic level regarding, for instance, fields of study, careers, financial aid, education institutions, etc.
b. Advanced level career development practitioners (ALCDPs). These practitioners demonstrate the knowledge and skills needed to administer career choice information and guidance (applying career development theories and decision-making models at a more advanced level). They are, for instance, allowed to administer non-standardized assessments and provide people with career and study options in individual and group contexts.
c. Specialist career development practitioners (SCDPs). These practitioners are qualified to deliver professional, specialist services in career development areas that include career counseling, executive coaching, career development research, psychometric assessment, and outplacement center development. They are generally registered with professional bodies.

Table 5.2 shows the overlap between these three classification levels and the intervention levels relating to vocational guidance, career education, and life design.

As can be seen from Table 5.2, the framework provides space for vocational guidance, career and educational guidance, career counseling, and life design. The type and level of intervention depends on the context in which any given service is provided.

Table 5.2 Intersection between CDP interventions and career counseling intervention models

Career counseling model	Related intervention	Career development practitioner level
Vocational guidance	Provide general information	1 (Entry)
Career guidance/education	Provide psychoeducational and psychosocial information	2 (Advanced)
Career counseling and life design	Enhance people's sense of meaning, purpose, and hope	3 (Specialist)

Sharf (2013) describes life design as a contextually and culturally sensitive innovation in career counseling, contending that it demonstrates the deconstruction of "grand" career counseling theories in favor of localized, contextualized, and more cultural theoretical approaches (Watson, 2006). Life design intervention is consistent with the narrative turn and the general acceptance that qualitative approaches to career counseling have received over the past three or more decades. The next section discusses why contextualization of life design intervention in developing country contexts in particular is important and how such contextualization can be achieved.

5.7 Contextualizing the Implementation of Counseling for Self- and Career Construction in Developing Country Contexts

As mentioned earlier, the South African career counseling scenario is unique largely because South Africa accommodates many different socioeconomic contexts and strata. While, at the one end of the socioeconomic continuum, many contexts have a seriously deprived or disadvantaged nature, at the other end, some contexts display a spectacularly prosperous character. However, the traditional person-environment fit model of vocational guidance still prevails in most contexts. The situation is exacerbated by the fact that very few career counselors are trained in contemporary career counseling paradigms. Life design counseling, for instance, is still largely unknown in Africa and is practiced only in a very small number of contexts. Maree (2017a, 2017b, 2017c), Maree, Cook, and Fletcher (2018), Sethlare, Wood, and Meyer (2017), Watson (2013), Wessels and Diale (2017), and a few others, have demonstrated the value of resituating and modifying life design counseling to enhance its usefulness in South African and African contexts as a whole and then applying it successfully in individual African contexts. Maree (2017a), in particular, has shown how life design counseling can be adapted for use in group-based African contexts. There are, however, several caveats in this regard.

Individual contexts. There can be little doubt about the theoretical rigor (validity, reliability, and trustworthiness) as well as the practical value of self- and career construction theories in Global North countries in particular. This is evident from the numerous articles and books on the subject that have appeared during the past few decades (Maree, 2013, 2019c). However, this is not the case in Global South countries. More research is needed to assess the value of the approach in these countries. Some authors have raised questions about what they refer to as "untested assumptions" in regard to self- and career construction intervention. More particularly, the applicability of some of the five *CCI* questions (Savickas, 2011) and, especially, the interpretation of the responses to these questions in developing countries have been questioned (Reid, 2018; Watson, 2013). Similarly, some career counselors have expressed uncertainty about how people's responses to some of the questions should be related to the practice of career counseling.

In my experience, innovating career counseling is not high on the agenda of national education departments. Likewise, very little attention is given to newer approaches such as career construction and life design, especially in countries with a collectivist culture. My research (Maree, 2017a, 2019b, 2019c) on the implementation of self- and career construction intervention in disadvantaged, predominantly black, communities has highlighted the need to examine the value and validity of the approach. Below, I discuss some of the challenges associated with some of the questions in the *CCI* when asked in developing country contexts especially.

a. The introductory question ("How can I be useful to you?") is rarely answered satisfactorily in local indigenous (group) contexts. My research suggests that in many areas the word "useful" has a negative connotation and seems to be associated with the word "abuse". Over time, I have therefore changed the question to "How can I be useful, valuable, or helpful to you?" While I share the concerns expressed by many that the word "help(ful)" may imply that the career counselor remains the sole expert on the assessee, feedback suggests that this is, in fact, not how most assessees interpret the word.
b. Role models (heroes and heroines): The ultimate career counseling question.
   Many years of research in diverse contexts has convinced me of the value of enquiring about assessees' role models. It has also taught me much about the importance of contextualizing assessees' responses in research settings. Asking assessees to list their role models will often yield unsatisfactory results. In hierarchical societies especially, adaptation of such key concepts is critical. Direct translation of the term "role model" often does not provide the desired information. Sensoy-Briddick (H. Sensoy-Briddick, personal communication, October 19, 2019) recommends that counselors ask assessees to list the people or fictitious characters they admired the most as a way of identifying the assessees' ideal selves. Moreover, they are taught and expected to respect their parents and obey their wishes, with the result that parents are often listed as primary role models. According to Watson (2013), parental roles are particularly problematic. In a sense, children become a captive audience and will obey the wishes (including the career wishes) their parents have for them. Parents' knowledge about the world of work in these contexts is often limited, outdated, and inaccurate, thus severely limiting the value of parents being listed as role models.
   Since individuals take in their parents so directly, Savickas (M. L. Savickas, personal communication, October 3, 2019a, 2019b) mentions that career counselors can ask clients for three adjectives that describe each parent. If time permits,

clients can be asked for three stories, one for each adjective for each parent (six stories in all if career counselors need them). In this way, the direct influence of what assessees have taken in can be assessed. They can be asked about role models to see what they have taken on from their role models.

c. Asking assessees about their favorite magazines, too, generally yields very little usable information. In disadvantaged communities, the parents of assessees can rarely afford magazines. Consequently, it serves little purpose to enquire about assessees' favorite magazines. Asking this question thus amounts to decontextualization.
d. Similarly, enquiring about assessees' favorite books (particularly in disadvantaged contexts) often yields unsatisfactory results. Most assessees are not able to name a favorite book or story. Here, it is necessary to contextualize the question by, for instance, asking assessees what their favorite story is from the Bible or other religious source. Alternatively, they can be asked to name or share with the counselor their favorite folk story told to them by the elders in their family.
e. In disadvantaged areas such as those in South Africa, it is advisable not to assume anything and not to try to interpret assessees' responses on the basis of any assumption. Instead, assessees should be asked to explain and clarify the meaning of their responses carefully, which can often be time-consuming. This should be done to avoid misunderstanding and is even more important in contexts where the career counselor is unfamiliar with assessees' vernacular. It is also important to clarify idiosyncratic cultural connotations associated with assessees' answers. The sense of modesty and respect for others (people in positions of authority in particular) that characterizes African culture in general often means that assessees may be hesitant or scared to say anything that may be construed as disrespectful or arrogant, thus inhibiting their natural responses. Lastly, assessees' body language should be interpreted with extreme caution, and any interpretation of such "language" should be clarified with people familiar with its cultural connotations—such as understanding that assessees who do not make eye contact are not being disrespectful. Quite the opposite: Not making eye contact with older people is regarded as a token of respect in most African cultures.

Group-based contexts (also see Chap. 10). The sections below should be read bearing the following in mind: The *CCI* was not designed for use in group-based contexts. It was first and foremost devised for use with individual people in one-to-one, private contexts. This includes meeting the career counseling needs of a person struggling to choose between competing career trajectories or journeys (formerly referred to as "paths"[5]) such as

a. enrolling full time for a master's degree or rather entering the world of work and studying part time;
b. choosing between two competing fields of study;

---

[5]The word "path" suggests a linear, straightforward trajectory towards choosing and constructing a career—a notion that no longer holds true today.

c. deciding whether to stay on in a given work context or accept a meaningful job opportunity in a different organization; and
d. deciding to continue working in a chosen work environment that no longer meets the person's expectations or enrolling in a different field of study altogether in order to meet her or his deep-seated but unmet need to experience a sense of purpose in her or his career.

As mentioned earlier, I have found the *CCI* an invaluable interview and intervention-enhancing instrument that can be used to address people's career concerns effectively, irrespective of the cultural context in which it is used. However, research on the use of the *CCI* (Savickas, 2011) in group-based contexts in several projects has not yielded satisfactory results. First, it seems that the unstructured approach does not elicit sufficient usable information to ensure rigorous career counseling. Second, the small number of questions do not yield sufficiently rich data on which to base career counseling regarding assessees' choice of a certain type of school, their choice of subjects, or their choice of a field of study. Third, the majority of learners in disadvantaged contexts in particular may not be familiar with some of the questions. Fourth, many learners cite their parents as their primary role models (see my earlier comments in this regard). Fifth, a virtually insurmountable challenge when using the *CCI* in group contexts is the fifth question (What are your earliest recollections?). After considering thousands of responses, and comparing the answers of assessees who were asked the original fifth question in the *CCI*, as well as different variations of Question 5, eventually it emerged that questions such as "What were your three biggest challenges when you were young?" or "What were the three most hurtful experiences in your youth that you do not want others to go through as well?" (the second last question (Part 2, *CIP*))[6] yielded themes very similar to those obtained by asking Question 5 (*CCI*) in individual contexts. In 2009, during his visit to South Africa to receive an honorary doctorate from the University of Pretoria, I discussed this research finding with Mark Savickas: In group contexts, when time is at a premium, it is impossible to elicit all assessees' three earliest recollections (let alone clarify their responses with them individually). I therefore always replace the question about the three earliest recollections with the question about assessees' three biggest challenges when they were young. Whereas it takes approximately 45 min to elicit satisfactory responses to the three earliest recollections question, it takes a few minutes only to elicit equally satisfactory responses to this question (the last question in Part 4, *CIP*).[7]

[6]When I accepted a full-time appointment at the University of Pretoria many years ago, I began to design a narrative questionnaire that could be used to facilitate "career guidance" in group contexts especially (see Chap. 8, Aim of the *CIP*).

[7]Since this question may cause severe abreaction by highly sensitive and/or traumatized assessees, I removed it from the *CIP* because the questionnaire is also used by people with suitable qualifications in education but without postgraduate training in psychology. These colleagues, while doing a sterling job in general, are not qualified to deal with traumatized assessees.

The use of some postmodern career assessment and counseling techniques appear not to be conducive to promoting career counseling in group-based contexts. The use of collages, for instance, often does not yield satisfactory outcomes in group-based, resource-scarce contexts. Many learners never or very rarely have access to and struggle to use magazines to create collages largely because magazines generally are a luxury in these contexts. In many instances, people are "trapped" at the lowest rung of the Maslowian ladder. For them, attaining the level of authentic self-expression and progressing to higher rungs is daunting. Consequently, the use of such techniques does not meaningfully advance the writing of their life stories.

Life design counseling. Life design counseling can be described as a pioneering, avant garde, and highly innovative addition to the field of career counseling (Nota & Rossier, 2015). However, while this exciting intervention is used in some Global North contexts (North American and a few Western European countries in particular) and is well reported on, its applicability and value in Global South (developing country) contexts is still a legitimate question. Applying life design counseling on a number of occasions during the past few years, jointly with my students and colleagues (2018) and also on my own in a private practice setup (2018), has convinced me of the value and power of the approach. A recent project of mine at the GWF (Maree, 2019a), the so-called JuniorTukkie Project (Maree, 2018) and the SACDA Project (Taylor & Beukes, 2019), provided compelling evidence of the value of life design counseling in contexts similar to this one. Granted, we did have to make a number of changes to the original life design intervention schedule (Maree, 2018).

A caveat is appropriate at this stage: While the approach seemed to work satisfactorily in the context referred to here, it should be mentioned that women's subservient position in this male-dominated community adversely influenced the impact of the intervention on the women. I soon realized that changing the contextual situation of women is a prerequisite for satisfactory life design intervention. This includes changing the low status of women in these types of communities (Ribeiro & Gama de Almeida, 2019). Furthermore, my research in townships as well as in seriously disadvantaged urban and rural areas uncovered a degree of unwillingness to engage in interventions designed to advance self- and career construction. Sadly, the prevailing discourse in these communities reflected an overwhelming desire merely to find work that would enable people to earn a living. Such an attitude, shaped largely by pre-industrial socioeconomic influences, is an indictment of society's reluctance and failure to provide sustainable, decent work for all people (Kossen & McIlveen, 2018), despite the fact that policy makers often make a plea for "solidarity" with unemployed and underemployed people. My research also confirms Watson's view (2013) that career adaptability should be interpreted contextually in contexts that differ from typical European and North American contexts.

5.8 Summary

Sharf (2013, p. 17) asserts that "[n]o career theories of development have been formulated to apply specifically to one culture or another. However, research has been done on the applicability of particular career development theories to specific cultural groups." This assertion is somewhat problematic according to Watson (2013). Even though it probably was not the intention of theorists that career counseling theories should apply to specific cultures (or contexts), this is what happened. It also goes without saying that what works in one part of the world may not work in other parts, mainly because of significant socioeconomic and cultural disparities. In many parts of South Africa, and Africa generally, unemployment is rife, poverty is endemic, and occupational opportunities are almost non-existent. Terms such as "adaptability" and "adaptive behavior" have a different connotation to that in "typical" Global North countries. As a result, state-of-the-art interventions such as self- and career construction and life design of necessity need to be altered somewhat to ensure their usefulness in Global South contexts. This is why I often prefer the phrase "life design-based" (or "-related") intervention instead of just "life design" intervention. What we are actually trying to achieve is to "postmodernize" career counseling intervention in local contexts.

Fundamental changes such as "globalization, migration, and population diversity around the world" (Suchy, 2016, p. 973) have taken place over the past few decades, impelled by global trends such as mass migration. Suchy (2016, p. 973) rightly argues that "[d]efining a population by country borders only makes sense to the extent that countries are characterized by a single language and a unified educational context". Today, however, only a small and ever-shrinking number of countries have only one language and an integrated educational context. Shuttleworth (2018) agrees with Suchy and asks whether population-based norms have become obsolete. Thinking innovatively is key to addressing these issues. This includes not only constantly updating, innovating, and further developing theories, interventions, and associated career counseling instruments but also contextualizing theories and interventions for use in contexts different to those in which they were initially developed. Sharf's assertion cited above would therefore make more sense if tweaked a little to read, "career theories of development [**can no longer be conceptualised as if they**] should be formulated to apply specifically to one culture [**or context**] or another (Sharf, 2013, p. 17)" (my own emphasis added). Working in silos to develop "local" theories and interventions is out of step with global trends. In matters related to theory development and the development of assessment techniques and strategies, it would therefore be wise to adopt a broader, open-minded, and innovative global approach.

Lastly: In this book, I discuss several examples of how different people managed to overcome poverty and advance their careers. However, even though the majority of examples relate to people who were given an opportunity to study that enabled them to progress in their career-lives, it should be emphasized (as some of the case studies illustrate) that I do not regard studying as the "only" mechanism for achieving social and work-related advancement. A versatile integrative career counseling model opens up a variety of ways to help people overcome poverty, design themselves, and construct their careers (Savickas, 2019b).

Chapter 6 covers innovating the language of the career counseling discourse.

References

Anderson, H., & Goolishian, H. (1992). Human systems as linguistic systems: Evolving ideas about the implications for theory and practice. *Family Process, 27,* 371–393.

Berry, J. W., Poortinga, Y. H., Segall, M. H., & Dasen, P. R. (1992). *Cross-cultural psychology: Research and applications.* Cambridge: Cambridge University Press.

Collins dictionary. (n.d.). *Definition of 'decontextualize'.* Retrieved from https://www.collinsdictionary.com/dictionary/english/decontextualize.

Cardoso, P. (2016). Integrating life-design counseling and psychotherapy: Possibilities and practices. *Career Development Quarterly, 64,* 49–63. https://doi.org/10.1002/cdq.12040.

Cranford, P. (1999). Julius Nyerere: Reflections on the legacy of his socialism. *Canadian Journal of African Studies, 33*(1), 137–152.

Department of Higher Education and Training (DHET). (2016). *Competency framework for career development practitioners in South Africa.* Pretoria, South Africa: Government Printers.

Good Work Foundation (GWF). (2019). *Good Work Foundation: 2019 prospectus.* (Unpublished document.) Hazyview, South Africa: The Good Work Foundation. Retrieved from https://www.goodworkfoundation.org/wp-content/uploads/2019/09/TTA-Prospectus-2019_redux-.pdf.

Ibdawoh, B., & Dibua, J. I. (2003). Deconstructing *Ujamaa*: The legacy of Julius Nyerere in the quest for social and economic development in Africa. *African Journal of Political Science, 8*(1), 59–83.

Kossen, C., & McIlveen, P. (2018). Unemployment from the perspective of the psychology of working. *Journal of Career Development, 45,* 474–488.

Macmillan Dictionary. (n.d.). *Contextualise.* Retrieved from http://www.macmillandictionary.com/thesaurus-category/british/to-study-check-or-examine-something.

Maree, J. G. (2013). *Counseling for career construction: Connecting life themes to construct life portraits: Turning pain into hope.* Rotterdam, The Netherlands: Sense.

Maree, J. G. (2017a). Life design counselling. In Stead, G. & Watson, M. (Eds.), *Career psychology* (3rd ed.) (pp. 105-118). Pretoria, South Africa: Van Schaik.

Maree, J. G. (2017b). Utilizing career adaptability and career resilience to promote employability and decent work and alleviate poverty. In J. G. Maree (Ed.), *Handbook of career adaptability, employability, and resilience* (pp. 349-373). New York, NY: Springer.

Maree, J. G. (Ed.). (2017c). *Handbook of career adaptability, employability, and resilience.* New York, NY: Springer.

Maree, J. G. (2018). Using life design counseling for career construction to facilitate sustainable employability and decent work in a developing country context. In V. Cohen-Scali, J. Pouyaud, M. Podgórny, V. Drabik-Podgórny, G. Aisenson, J-L. Bernaud, I. Moumoula., J. Guichard (Eds.). *Interventions in career design and education* (pp. 195–214). New York, NY: Springer.

Maree, J. G. (2019a, June). *Career Development in Africa: Decent work for all: Brief photomontage.* Keynote Address at the Annual Career Development Practitioner Congress, Emperors Palace Conference Centre, Kempton Park, South Africa.

Maree, J. G. (2019b). Postmodernising career counseling in a deep rural context. In J. G. Maree (Ed.), *Handbook of innovative career counseling* (pp. 577-596). New York, NY: Springer.

Maree, J. G. (2019c). Innovative career construction counselling for a creative adolescent. *British Journal of Guidance and Counselling.* https://doi.org/10.1080/03069885.2018.1504202.

Maree, J. G., Cook, A. V., & Fletcher, L. (2018). Assessment of the value of group-based counselling for career construction. *International Journal of Adolescence and Youth, 23*(1), 118–132. https://doi.org/10.1080/02673843.2017.1309324.
Nota, L., & Rossier, J. (Eds.). (2015). *Handbook of the life design paradigm: From practice to theory and from theory to practice*. Boston, MA: Hogrefe.
Ntinda, K., Maree, J. G., Mpofu, E., & Seeco, E. (2014). In-school psychosocial support services for safeguarding children's rights: Results and implications of a Botswana study. *School Psychology International, 35*(3), 280–293.
Nussbaum, B., Palsule, S., & Mkhize, V. (2010). *Personal growth African style*. Johannesburg, South Africa: Penguin.
Oxford Reference Dictionary. (n.d.) *Recontextualization*. Retrieved from http://www.oxfordreference.com/view/10.1093/oi/authority.20110803100408361.
Pedersen, P. B. (1991). Multiculturalism as a generic approach to counselling. *Journal of Counseling and Development, 70*(1), 6–12.
Pedersen, P. B., Draguns, J. G., Lonner, W. J., & Trimble, J. E. (1989). *Counseling across cultures*. Honolulu, HI: University of Hawaii Press.
Psychology dictionary. (n.d.) *What is decontextualization*? Retrieved from https://psychologydictionary.org/decontextualization/.
Reid, H. (2018, July). Prompting reflection and learning in career construction counseling: Three research studies evaluating process and practice in the UK. In P. J. Hartung (Chair), *Reflexivity and change in life designing: Perspectives from process research*. 29th International Congress of Applied Psychology (ICAP 2018) conducted at the Palais des Congrès, Montréal, Québec, Canada.
Ribeiro, M. A., & Gama de Almeida, M. C. C. (2019). A socio-constructionist career counseling grounded on intersectionality of gender, class and race/ethnicity. In J. G. Maree (Ed.), *Handbook of innovative career counseling)* (pp. 597–614). New York, NY: Springer.
Savickas, M. L. (1995). Examining the personal meaning of inventoried interests during career counseling. *Journal of Career Assessment, 3*(2), 188–201.
Savickas, M. L. (2011). Reshaping the story of career counseling. In K. Maree (Ed.), *Shaping the story—A guide to facilitate narrative counseling* (pp. 1–3). Boston/Rotterdam, The Netherlands: Sense.
Savickas, M. L. (2015). Career counseling paradigms: Guiding, developing, and designing. In P. Hartung, M. Savickas, & W. Walsh (Eds.), *The APA handbook of career intervention* (Vol. 1, pp. 129–143). Washington, DC: APA Books.
Savickas, M. L. (2019a). *Theories of psychotherapy series. Career counseling* (2nd ed.). Washington, DC: American Psychological Association.
Savickas, M. L. (2019b, September). *Designing a self and constructing a career in post-traditional societies*. Keynote address at the 43rd international association for educational and vocational guidance Conference, Bratislava, Slovakia.
Schaerer, M., Tost, L. P., Huang, L., Gino, F., & Larrick, R. (2018). Advice Giving: A Subtle Pathway to Power. *Personality and Social Psychology Bulletin, 44*(5), 746–761.
Sethlare, R., Wood, L., & Meyer, L. (2017). Exploring Group Life Design with teachers in the context of poverty related psychosocial challenges. *South African Journal of Education, 37*(4): Art. # 1493, 8 pages. https://doi.org/10.15700/saje.v37n4a1493.
Sharf, R. S. (2013). Advances in theories of career development. In W. B. Walsh, M. L. Savickas, & P. J. Hartung (Eds.), *Handbook of vocational psychology: Theory, research, and practice* (pp. 2–32). New York: Routledge.
Shuttleworth-Edwards, A. B. (2018). Response to Taylor and de Beer (2018) on population-based norms and IQ testing. *South African Journal of Psychology, 48*(2), 175–178.
Suchy, Y. (2016). Population-based norms in crisis. *The Clinical Neuropsychologist, 30,* 97–974.
Sue, D. W. E., Ivey, A. E. E., & Pedersen, P. B. E. (1996). *A theory of multicultural counseling and therapy*. Pacific Grove, CA: Brooks/Cole Publishing.

Taylor, N., & & Beukes, C. (2019). A life design-related career development intervention for working adults in the manufacturing, engineering and related sectors. *African Journal of Career Development, 1*(1). Retrieved from https://ajcd.africa/index.php/ajcd/article/view/2.

The American Heritage Dictionary of the English language. (2016). *Recontextualize.* Retrieved from http://www.yourdictionary.com/recontextualize.

Thibault, P. J. (2004). *Brain, mind, and the signifying body: An ecosocial semiotic theory.* London, England: Continuum.

Thomas, J. C., & Sosin, L. (2011). *Therapeutic expedition: Equipping the Christian counselor for the journey.* Nashville, TN: Broadman & Holman.

Watson, M. B. (2006). Career counselling theory, culture and constructivism. In M. McMahon & W. Patton (Eds.), *Career counselling: Constructivist approaches* (pp. 45–56). Abingdon, Oxon: Routledge.

Watson, M. B. (2013). Deconstruction, reconstruction, co-construction: Career construction theory in a developing world context. *Indian Journal of Career and Livelihood Planning, 2*(1), 3–14.

Watson, M., Nota, L., & McMahon, M. (2015). Childhood career development [Special issue]. *International Journal for Educational and Vocational Guidance, 15*(2), 95–97.

Wessels, C. J. J., & Diale, B. M. (2017). Facebook as an instrument to enhance the career construction journeys of adolescent learners. *South African Journal of Education, 37*(4): Art. # 1470, 12 pages. https://doi.org/10.15700/saje.v37n4a1470.

Winnicott, D. W. (1965). *The family and individual development.* London, England: Tavistock.

Winnicott, D. W. (1969). *The use of an object and relating through identifications in playing and reality.* London, England: Routledge.

Winnicott, D. W. (1987). *The maturational processes and the facilitating environment.* London, England: Hogarth Press.

Chapter 6
Innovating the Language of the Career Counseling Discourse

> *Do not fear to be eccentric in opinion, for every opinion now accepted was once eccentric.* (Bertrand Russell)

Abstract In this chapter, I discuss the extent and effect of some of the changes in the world of work that have taken place globally in the past few decades. I then show how these changes are reflected in the changing language of the career counseling discourse and manifest in the language of business (the world of work today). I explain also how change is demonstrated by the changing language of business and economics. Some shop window names and signage designs (from cities across the world) are discussed briefly to shed light on the career psychology theory behind avant garde shop names that relates directly or indirectly to recent trends in the language of the career counseling discourse.

6.1 Extent and Effect of Some of the Changes in the World of Work

As mentioned earlier, discontinuity currently characterizes numerous occupational contexts. Major changes have taken place in the world economy over the past few decades, driven by the fourth economic wave (Schwab, 2017), the Fourth Industrial Revolution (Work 4.0), and the fifth information wave (Gurri, 2013). Hartung (2013) maintains that the following three waves of theory and intervention today characterize the career counseling discipline.

> The first wave concerned matching people to jobs. The second wave concentrated on managing worker and other life roles over the life span. The third wave involves contemporary models and methods focused on making meaning through work and relationships (p. 16).

More than anything, these changes have changed views on how career counseling decisions should be taken and managed. Krumboltz and Chan (2005) accordingly argue:

J. G. (Kobus) Maree, *Innovating Counseling for Self- and Career Construction*,
https://doi.org/10.1007/978-3-030-48648-8_6

> Expecting people to decide on a lifetime career and commit to that choice is a formula for personal disaster. Circumstances change, economic cycles have their booms and busts, technology advances, and people's interests change over time. Remaining ever open-minded is the smartest way to adapt to change (p. 351).

Against this background, I now elaborate on innovation in the language of the career counseling discourse.

6.2 Innovating the Language of the Career Counseling Discourse

The open-minded way in which the language of the career counseling discourse has developed and articulated new terminology to capture the essence of change and to redefine occurrences in the occupational world to reclaim a sense of control over the ever-changing work situation (described by some as already out of control) deserves some consideration. More specifically, many new terms and expressions have been coined to indicate changes in the workplace.

Examples of the new terminology that describes what is happening currently in the occupational world globally are shown in Table 6.1.

Individually and collectively, these terms point to growing occupational insecurity and uncertainty and reflect five trends in particular:

a. Many workers are endeavoring to manage their own careers in preference to finding employment in an environment controlled by forces beyond themselves. Career adaptability has become essential.
b. Becoming employable is far more important than trying only to find a lifetime job in one organization. In fact, some authors argue that the notion of "employment counseling" (Busque, 1995, n.p.) has become more urgent than career counseling in Global South contexts in particular (Maree, 2016).
c. By engaging in meaningful work, people tend to experience a sense of belonging somewhere and being connected to others (Blustein, 2013). Today, however, fewer people are experiencing a sense of connection with their occupational environment as can be seen in the growing incidence of work-related trauma and attempts to deal with it.
d. Contemporary workers growing belief that work has little meaning and purpose has stimulated their desire to rekindle a sense of hope and purpose in their career-lives.
e. Wolfe (2016) argues that currently, and also in the immediate future, it will be essential to acquire skills and proficiencies that will not be easily replaceable by robots and artificial intelligence. He contends that the so-called five C's are skills that cannot easily be acquired by robots: collaboration, creativity, conscientiousness, critical thinking, and curiosity

Table 6.1 Examples of new terminology in career counseling

	New terms to describe careers	Meaning of term
1	Customized careers	Climbing the corporate ladder is less important today. Workers prefer to focus on meeting their own unique needs and often refuse to sacrifice private time to satisfy the needs of employers. Occupational portfolios are customized to suit their personal needs in the first place and not the needs of their employers (Benko & Weisberg, 2007)
2	Kaleidoscopic careers	Workers create careers on their own terms, which are defined by a multilayered and constantly shifting construction of their own values, choices, and preferences (Mainiero & Sullivan, 2005)
3	Post-industrial careers	The idea of "stable work identities" is disappearing. Many workers today have to re-invent themselves continuously in different work-related contexts (Gershuny, 1993)
4	Boundaryless careers	Many workers demonstrate an increased desire to be independent. Consequently, "traditional" work agreements with organizations are decreasing rapidly in favor of self-directed and self-managed careers: "A common factor in the occurrence of all [the different meanings of boundaryless] is one of independence from, rather than dependence on, traditional career arrangements" (Arthur, 1994; Arthur & Rousseau, 1996, p. 6)
5	Post-corporate careers	Many workers are losing their jobs in the 21st century, particularly in corporate environments. They therefore have to move from trying to find permanent "jobs" in one (large) organization to undertaking temporary "projects" with smaller, flexible firms; and from finding "jobs" to finding a conduit for their unique talents, identifying market-related opportunities", and identifying their personal "competitive advantage" (Pharaoh, 2009, p. 5)
6	Protean careers	Many workers show a preference for self-employment and consequently contract their skills out in different fields (Fenwick, 2004). Career resilience has become essential to deal with occupational changes brought about by technological advances (Baruch, 2004; Hall, 1996a, 1996b)
7	Portfolio careers	Workers are increasingly marketing and contracting and leasing out their occupational skills in diverse contexts and negotiating agreements that promote self-employment (Handy, 1995)
8	Hourglass economy careers	The future global economy will be marked by an increase in high-skilled and well-paid workers juxtaposed with large numbers of low-skilled/unskilled and poorly paid workers (Applebaum, Bernhardt, & Murnane, 2003; Keep & Brown, 2005). The economy will consequently increasingly take on an hourglass shape (Campbell et al., 2001; Moynagh & Worsley, 2005)

(continued)

Table 6.1 (continued)

	New terms to describe careers	Meaning of term
9	Dejobbing	Successive global economic meltdowns and downturns have caused sweeping changes in the world of work, leading to large numbers of people seeking work and unemployed and "insecure" workers. Terms such as self-entrepreneurs, gig economy, temporary, full time, non-permanent, contingent, casual, (temporary) contract, freelance, outsourced, part time, external, atypical, adjunct, consultant, project-based, agency, non-standard, marginal, subcontracted, undeclared, and self-employed are used to describe work and these workers (Robertson, 2017; Savickas, 2012)
10	Gig economy	This term refers to an insecure economic environment in which permanent jobs are replaced by contract and short(er) term jobs (Graham & Wood, 2016; Graham, Hjorth, & Lehdonvirta, 2017)
11	Pivoting	Kirtley (in Cameron, 2019) describes pivoting as "the ability of an entrepreneur to dramatically adapt strategy to avoid failure and get onto a positive path towards success" (p. 1). According to Kirtley (in Cameron, 2019), "A pivot is, 'I've changed and redirected my strategy. I was a game company, and now I am a photo-sharing website'. That kind of change is actually an accumulation of adds and exits" (p. 7)
12	Wirk	This term refers to full- and part-time internet work. Any person who has access to the internet is capable of carrying out "wirk" to earn an income (Reverso dictionary, 2019)

The advent of the narrative approach to career counseling and counseling for self- and career construction in particular has led to many new terms[1] that are referred to and used in this book.

6.3 Graphical Depiction of the Changing Language of Economics

Savickas (2005) argues that all meaning is concentrated in words (language), and he uses social constructionism as a metatheory for the essence of knowledge construction. Savickas (2011) emphasizes also the importance of work contexts as holding environments (Winnicott, 1964). Flum concurs by stating that "to work is to relate" (2015, p. 148). Savickas (2016a, 2016b) adds, however, that feelings of loneliness (and even hopelessness) in the workplace are increasing because good interpersonal relationships at work seem to be less and less valued. These sentiments are reflected in the names of some shops and other points of sale in the postmodern era. However,

[1]For a complete glossary of these terms, see Savickas (2019).

on the other hand, many shop names reflect a sense of positivity, inspiration, and encouragement in these turbulent times.

Below I briefly discuss some shop window names and signage designs that convey messages to their audiences to explain what I mean.

Shop window names and signage designs depicting the changing language of business (the world of work today). The language of business (the world of work) is extremely sensitive and quick to respond to and exploit changes in the world of work but also to changes in the psychology of consumers' attitudes and buying habits.

The shop window names and signage designs relate directly or indirectly to recent trends in the language of the career counseling discourse. Interested readers will note that all these names have been chosen carefully and in accordance with standard guidelines for naming businesses such as brevity, easy to spell, descriptive of the business, consistent with the brand, searchable, easy to remember, not overspecific, uniqueness, the business's vision, values, passions, and goals ("16 tips for naming your startup", 2019; 5 steps to name your creative business successfully, n.d.; Dimitrijevic, 2019; Haskins, 2019; Henriques, 2011; Rūmī & Barks, 1996; The Staff of Entrepreneur Media, 2018).

Each of the shop window names and signage designs discussed below speaks to a concept that represents a new idea in the field of career counseling. In the words of Deliry-Antheaume (2003), they are "based on impressions drawn from qualitative data gathered during … journey[s]" (p. 1) to various parts of the world. They represent innovations in the fields of career counseling and business (the economy). There is, of course, often a discrepancy between the abstract concepts and ideals conveyed implicitly by these shop names and the realities that people face in the 21st century. Here, I draw on these shop window names and signage designs as spaces for a creative experience and especially for foregrounding the power of visual designing to explain key aspects of life designing graphically.

The real story. People share a common desire not only to share their own stories but also to listen to and understand the stories of others.

Our story. *Live it (Narratability and (auto)biographicity*[2]). Sharing our stories is one aspect of (auto)biographicity; enacting our life stories is the second.

Forever new (innovating and redesigning). Much has already been written in this book about the importance of promoting our career-life story by constantly renovating, redesigning, and innovating ourselves.

Choice (right to choose instead of being advised and told what to choose). Being allowed to exercise one's own choice, albeit a choice that is based partly on information provided by others, is integral to postmodern career counseling.

Oh my! (creativity). Being creative and able to conceptualize new ideas and link them to actions is widely regarded as a good way to promote one's employability.

Diverse (diversity). Our postmodern world is increasingly becoming a "global village", a phenomenon promoted by mass migration. Embracing diversity is also a key feature of employability.

---

[2]Interpretations of the deeper meaning of shop window names and signage designs appear between brackets.

Photograph 6.1 Loving one's job

***Inspiracja* (*inspiring others*).** As essential as it is to do so already, it is speculated that inspiring clients (and remaining inspired ourselves) will become a central career counseling goal in the Fifth Industrial Revolution.

Signature (self-and career identity). People's deep need to uncover their unique identity (the "glue" or adhesive that will hold their storyline together in a changing world) is key to helping them experience a sense of purpose in their career-lives.

I love my job (need to belong). Although not a photograph of a shop window name or signage design, this photograph demonstrates an employee's wish to experience a sense of belonging, which is pivotal to enhancing job satisfaction (Photograph 6.1).

Identity (personal identity). Drawing on a storied approach is a powerful way of helping people establish who they are, where they belong, and how they can experience a sense of meaning and purpose in their career-lives.

No one (Seems incomplete.) ***(feeling alienated and isolated in a workplace that no longer really cares about its workers)***. People's sense of isolation, alienation, and of being left "behind" in rapidly changing occupational contexts is considered a serious problem by career counselors.

Contempo (postmodernizing expectations). The importance of accepting and embracing new developments in our rapidly changing society is a central feature of postmodern career counseling.

I am (being acknowledged and recognized). Promoting clients' narratability and identity, eliciting their life stories, and helping them draw on these stories to manage repeated career transitions is our ultimate gift to them and also their ultimate gift to themselves.

6.4 Summary

Against the background of fundamental changes in the world of work, career counseling theorists, researchers, and practitioners need to advance the language of career counseling while reconsidering, renovating, and innovating existing paradigms in career counseling itself. Likewise, it is essential at the same time to devise and implement new career counseling interventions, approaches, methods, and assessment instruments. This chapter focused on a number of new terms and constructs that have been put forward to capture the essence of change and to reclaim a sense of control over the continually changing work situation. It is interesting to see how these new terms and expressions have been graphically captured in the changing language of business and the economy. The shop window names and signage designs (from cities across the globe) all show avant garde shop window names and signage designs that relate directly or indirectly to recent trends in the language of the career counseling discourse. Shop window names and signage designs (carefully selected by business people to convey the essence of their brand) reflect broader global trends in the world of business and the economy (M. A. Ribeiro, personal communication, October 02, 2019). They also reflect, especially from the perspective of this book, trends in career counseling. Closer inspection of these names reveals a curious overlap between what the world of business is achieving (constantly updating and innovating itself) and the kind of response to global changes the career counseling profession is advocating.

In Chap. 7, the focus shifts to a discussion of how social justice (advocacy) and sustainable decent work for all can be promoted.

References

16 tips for naming your startup. (2019). Retrieved from https://www.quicksprout.com/tips-for-naming-your-startup/.

5 steps to name your creative business successfully. (n.d.) Retrieved from https://www.thedesigntrust.co.uk/name-your-creative-business/.

Applebaum, E., Bernhardt, A., & Murnane, R. J. (Eds.). (2003). *Low wage America—How employers are reshaping opportunity in the workplace*. New York, NY: SAGE.

Arthur, M. B. (1994). The boundaryless career: A new perspective for organizational inquiry. *Journal of Organizational Behavior, 15,* 295–306. https://doi.org/10.1002/job.4030150402.

Arthur, M. B., & Rousseau, D. M. (1996). *The boundaryless career: A new employment principle for a new organizational era*. New York, NY: Oxford University Press.

Baruch, Y. (2004). Transforming careers: From linear to multidirectional career paths. *Career Development International, 9,* 58–73.

Benko, C., & Weisberg, A. (2007). *Mass career customization*. Boston, MA: Harvard Business School Press.

Blustein, D. L. (2013). The psychology of working: A new perspective for a new era. In D. L. Blustein (Ed.), *The Oxford handbook of the psychology of working* (pp. 3–18). Oxford, England: Oxford University Press.

Busque, G. (1995). *Measurement model for employment counselling*. ERIC Digest. Retrieved from https://www.ericdigests.org/1998-2/model.htm.
Cameron, D. (2019). *Most entrepreneurs fail. Entrepreneurial heroes know how to "pivot"*. Retrieved from https://www.biznews.com/entrepreneur/2019/06/14/most-entrepreneurs-fail-entrepreneurial-heroes-know-how-to-pivot?utm_source=Biznews.com+Main&utm_campaign=bc5466da10-dailyinsider&utm_medium=email&utm_term=0_b56abc3f25-bc5466da10-101338097.
Campbell, M., Baldwin, S., Johnson, S., Chapman, R., Upton, A., & Watson, F. (2001). *Skills in England 2001—The research report*. Nottingham, England: DFES Publications.
Deliry-Antheaume, E. (2003). Readings from the walls: Art and education. *Perspectives in Education, 21*(2), 1–14.
Dimitrijevic, I. (2019). *The psychology behind business names: 6 important factors to consider*. Retrieved from https://medium.com/@IvanDSEO/the-psychology-behind-business-names-6-important-factors-to-consider-57f047febdef.
Fenwick, T. J. (2004). Learning in portfolio work: Anchored innovation and mobile identities. *Studies in Continuing Education, 26,* 229–241.
Gershuny, J. (1993). Post-industrial career structures in Britain. In G. Esping-Andersen (Ed.), *Changing classes* (pp. 136–170). London, England: SAGE.
Graham, M., & Wood, A. (2016). Why the digital gig economy needs co-ops and unions. *openDemocracy*, September 15.
Graham, M., Hjorth, I., & Lehdonvirta, V. (2017). Digital labour and development: Impacts of global digital labour platforms and the gig economy on worker livelihoods. *Transfer, 23*(2), 135–162. https://doi.org/10.1177/1024258916687250.
Gurri, M. (2013). *The revolt of the public and the crisis of authority in the new millennium*. [Kindle DX version]. Retrieved from Amazon.com.
Hall, D. T. (1996a). Protean careers of the 21st century. *Academy of Management Executive, 10,* 8–16.
Hall, D. T. (1996b). *The career is dead—Long live the career*. San Francisco, CA.: Jossey Bass.
Handy, C. (1995). *The age of unreason*. London, United Kingdom: Arrow books.
Hartung, P. J. (2013). Career construction counselling. In A. Di Fabio & J. G. Maree (Eds.), *Psychology of career counseling: New challenges for a new era* (pp. 15–28). Hauppauge, New York: Nova Science.
Haskins, J. (2019). 7 tips for choosing a business name. Retrieved from https://www.legalzoom.com/articles/7-tips-for-choosing-a-business-name.
Henriques, G. (2011). *A new unified theory of psychology* (11th ed.). New York, NY: Springer.
Keep, E., & Brown, A. (2005). Moving beyond discussions about paradigm shifts—Creating space for multiple meanings and narratives on changing patterns of employment and careers. *Career Research and Development, 13,* 11–19.
Krumboltz, J. D., & Chan, A. (2005). Professional issues in vocational psychology. In W. Walsh & M. L. Savickas (Eds.), *Handbook of vocational psychology* (3rd ed., pp. 347–370). Mahwah, NJ: Lawrence Erlbaum Associates.
Mainiero, L. A., & Sullivan, S. E. (2005). Kaleidoscope careers: An alternative explanation for the opt-out revolution. *Academy of Management Executive, 19,* 106–123.
Maree, J. G. (2016). *Maree Career Matrix (MCM)*. Randburg, South Africa: JvR Psychometrics.
Moynagh, M., & Worsley, R. (2005). *Working in the twenty-first century*. Leeds, England: ESRC Future of Work Programme and King's Lynn, The Tomorrow Project.
Pharaoh, A. (2009). *Preparing for your post corporate career*. Retrieved from www.pharoah.pro/docs/post-corporate-career.pdf.
Reverso dictionary. (2019). *Wirk*. Retrieved from https://dictionary.reverso.net/english-definition/Wirk.
Robertson, P. (2017, September 08). Not lovin' it: How insecure work creates insecure lifestyles for the poorest in society. *The Conversation, Africa Edition*. Retrieved from https://theconversation.com/not-lovin-it-how-insecure-work-creates-insecure-lifestyles-for-the-poorest-in-society-82726.

Rūmī, J. M., & Barks, C. (1996). *The essential Rumi.* (1st HarperCollins paperback ed.). San Francisco, CA: Harper.

Savickas, M. L. (2005). The theory and practice of career construction. In S. Brown & R. W. Lent (Eds.), *Career development and counseling: Putting theory and research to work* (pp. 42–70). New York, NY: John Wiley.

Savickas, M. L. (2011). Reshaping the story of career counseling. In K. Maree (Ed.), *Shaping the story—A guide to facilitate narrative counseling* (pp. 1–3). Boston/Rotterdam, The Netherlands: Sense.

Savickas, M. L. (2012). Life design: A paradigm for career intervention in the 21st century. *Journal of Counseling & Development, 90,* 13–19.

Savickas, M. L. (2016a, July). *Meaning at work: Work at meaning.* Closing keynote presentation, National Career Development Association Conference, Chicago, United States of America.

Savickas, M. L. (2016b). Reflection and reflexivity during life-design interventions: Comments on Career Construction Counseling. *Journal of Vocational Behavior, 97,* 84–89.

Savickas, M. L. (2019). *Theories of psychotherapy series. Career counseling* (2nd ed.). Washington, DC: American Psychological Association.

Schwab, K. (2017). *The fourth industrial revolution.* New York, NY: Crown Business.

The Staff of Entrepreneur Media, Inc. (2018). *Start your own business* (7th ed.). Irvine, CA: Entrepreneur Press.

Winnicott, D. W. (1964). *The child, the family and the outside world.* Cambridge, MA: Perseus.

Wolfe (2016). Are jobseekers better @ job search than recruiters are @ finding talent? Retrieved from https://www.successperformancesolutions.com/.

Chapter 7
Innovating Career Counseling by Promoting Social Justice (Advocacy) and Decent Work for All: Helping People Make Social Contributions and Heal Themselves

Everyone can rise above their circumstances and achieve success if they are dedicated to and passionate about what they do (Nelson Mandela)

Abstract This chapter covers the emotional effect of changes in the world of work that have taken place globally over the past few decades on people. The discussion then moves to the need for and importance of career counseling as a means to help people interpret and deal with these changes. Also discussed is the idiosyncratic situation and needs of people in disadvantaged areas, as well as the importance of attending to their career counseling needs. A case study showing how career counseling can be postmodernized in a seriously disadvantaged environment is presented before the chapter is concluded.

7.1 Orientation

Since the current socioeconomic disruption is at its worst among the most disadvantaged and vulnerable populations (such as those in rural regions, informal settlements, and townships), I believe that innovation in career counseling should first and foremost target and be guided by the unique needs of these populations. The impact of occupational changes on disadvantaged people especially is devastating. In many previous publications, over the past two decades in particular, my colleagues and I (Maree, 2018, 2019a, 2019d) have elaborated on the horrendous influence of occupational changes on the career-lives of people in general but on disadvantaged people in particular. Workers often experience their work as lacking meaning and alien and subsequently struggle to come to terms with all the changes that enforce numerous work transitions on them (Maree, 2015). Deprived of the former safe occupational spaces (Winnicott, 1964) work used to provide for them, many workers have lost their jobs, struggle to find employment elsewhere, experience a sense of loss of control over key facets of their career-lives, and, eventually, their sense of meaning, purpose, and hope. In a sense, one can therefore argue that many people's biggest

J. G. (Kobus) Maree, *Innovating Counseling for Self- and Career Construction*,
https://doi.org/10.1007/978-3-030-48648-8_7

career counseling need today is no longer "vocational guidance", "career education", or even "career counseling" but rather "employability counseling" (Fugate & Kinicki, 2008; Guilbert et al., 2016). Because career adaptability is a key prerequisite for employability, promoting such adaptability lies at the heart of helping people become employable.

Unemployment poses a far greater challenge in Global South countries, for instance in Africa, than in Global North countries. According to the International Labor Organization (ILO, 2019, p. 1): "In 2017, extreme working poverty remained widespread, with more than 300 million workers in emerging and developing countries having a per capita household income or consumption of less than US$1.90 (PPP) [1.65 Euro] per day. Overall, progress in reducing working poverty is too slow to keep pace with the growing labor force in developing countries, where the number of people in extreme working poverty is expected to exceed 114 million in 2018, or 40 per cent of all employed people." In addition (ILO, 2019, p. 1), "the number of workers in vulnerable forms of employment (own-account workers and contributing family workers) is likely to increase in the years to come". Seemingly, there is very little chance of global poverty being eradicated, as specified in the United Nations Sustainable Development Goals (UN, 2019). One of my greatest concerns is that resources-related structural inequalities have an extremely adverse emotional influence on people, and the impact is most destructive on young people. We therefore need to focus on disadvantaged people and the promotion of social justice or advocacy in our efforts to innovate and renovate career counseling. Seen from this perspective, the link between career counseling and social justice (advocacy) is clear.

I have witnessed first-hand during many research projects and outplacement workshops the daunting hardships people living in these conditions have to endure. Hearing them express their sense of hopelessness, desperation, marginalization, and pain has touched me deeply. Worryingly, young people are increasingly venting their anger and frustration about their dire work situation. They are aware that most of them will not realize their dream of finding sustainable, decent work, irrespective of how hard they try or their level of training. Consequently, the future looks bleak, with little chance that spiraling unemployment will decline. This also means that crime and lawlessness (often resulting from the inability to find sustainable work) are likely to become even worse in the future.

In their desperate quest for some kind of work, disadvantaged people generally have no one to turn to for career counseling. Even when they do receive vocational guidance, the need to uncover their initial, deep-rooted (often subconscious) "pain" (driving motives) is not attended to. There is insufficient evidence of active self- and career construction (Maree, 2014a, 2014b; Savickas, 2011a, 2011b). This matter will be discussed next.

7.2 Importance of Attending to the Self- and Career Construction Counseling Needs of Disadvantaged People Especially

Many children leave school without completing Grade 12 and/or achieving adequate marks in Grade 12, and also without having acquired important life skills or acquired some knowledge of business. Naidoo, Pretorius, and Nicholas (2017) state that career counseling is available to wealthy people in Global South countries such as South Africa but that indigent people simply cannot afford this often expensive service, which is deplorable as lack of such counseling exacerbates the already high unemployment among these people. The situation is made worse by the high level of student non-achievement' or 'poor achievement' in tertiary education (Maree, 2010a, 2019a). Making career counseling available to the millions of people who currently do not have access to this service can help reduce the high failure rate at tertiary institutions and thus contribute to economic growth and political stability. However, to achieve this aim, more is needed that mere expressions of intention, camaraderie, and empathy.

Below, I explain why eliciting subjective and objective career counseling information career counseling can best serve the needs of disadvantaged people.

7.3 Significance of Eliciting Subjective and Objective Career Counseling Information from Disadvantaged People

Previous research on people in disadvantaged contexts confirmed the importance of obtaining subjective, qualitative information on careers in addition to objective career-related information for such people (Maree, 2014a, 2014b, 2014c, 2014d, 2018) to help them choose appropriate careers and succeed in them. Not only do they generally display a serious lack of knowledge about careers (Brown, 2002), they are especially unsure about their career identities. In interventions in disadvantaged contexts, assessees' life stories should be elicited and interpreted circumspectly by professionals adequately acquainted with their contexts and skilled in administering career counseling in diverse contexts. Assessees should also be furnished with sufficient information about the world of work, and their scores in tests and at school should be interpreted dynamically. Even in cases where their perceptions appear unrealistic, it should be remembered that people are guided largely by their own perceptions of their skills and by their confidence in achieving success in a given field of study and its associated career.

The storied approach is fully compatible with Global South (such as African) contexts. In fact, this approach has been "practiced" across Africa for millennia. Stevens, Duncan, and Sonn (2010) contend that "black history … has been passed on through the art of storytelling" (p. 18). Underlying this approach is the social constructionism paradigm, which advocates identity formation rather than personality traits, career adaptability rather than "maturity", the use of "stories" (narratives) along with "scores" (numbers), forward movement that culminates in action rather than passivity and mere intention, and becoming **employable rather than merely looking for a job.** Ultimately, the aim of this approach is to help people manage repeated career-related transitions in their work-lives and convert career counseling into an intervention (instead of an "assessment") that promotes reflexive, dialogical meaning co-construction by career counselors and their clients (Blustein, Palladino Schultheiss, & Flum, 2004; Cardoso, Silva, Gonçalves, & Duarte, 2014; McIlveen, Ford, & Dun, 2005).

A case study showing how career counseling can be postmodernized in a seriously disadvantaged environment is presented below.

7.4 Case Study: Life Design-Related Intervention in a Seriously Disadvantaged Context

7.4.1 My Experiences at the Good Work Foundation

Below, I draw on my research-related experiences at the Good Work Foundation (GWF), which is under Kate, GWF's CEO, and Mo Groch's inspiring leadership. In a deep rural part of South Africa, the GWF is exemplifying the practical implementation of self- and career construction and life design theory. Of the adult learners, 90^{+}% recently left school, are unemployed, and could not succeed in enrolling at a tertiary training institution. They lack the skills needed to become employable, and their possibilities of finding sustainable work are gloomy. With the support of key partners, the GWF presents fundamental literacy training and career education to school-aged and adult learners (visit http://www.goodworkfoundation.org for more information). In addition to running learning academies, the GWF offers English, mathematics, digital literacy, and life skills training courses for those learners still at school, while the GWF's career guidance academies offer digital literacy courses for adult learners.

A bridging year is offered to adult, unemployed school-leavers as a second chance to upskill themselves and enhance their chances of acceptance into fields of study they did not previously qualify for, thus improving their employability, career resilience, and career agility. After having acquired a sound English and digital literacy foundation, adult learners not only attend career academies (located at the digital learning centers) but also start serving the local economy. Specialized modules in wine, coffee, and front-of-house management can be completed or students can further their education by studying at the GWF's Information Communication Technology (ICT) Academy. Once they have successfully completed their training, they are employed locally, find employment elsewhere, or continue studying either online or at tertiary training institutions.

What about the GWF approach is innovative? First, in a remote corner of Africa, they offer education and training that compares well with the best analogous training globally. Second, Kate and Mo Groch's realization of the importance of training their students in a way that promotes their career "adaptability" and "the proficiency to find employment" (employability) instead of merely helping them "find employment". Third, their emphasis on advancing their students' twin survival [thriving] skills of information communication technology (ICT) literacy and proficiency in English (the language of business globally). This insight and practice are consistent with Ross' (2016) view that becoming proficient in (a) English and (in certain instances) also in other foreign languages and in (b) the language of computers will help people communicate (connect, network) better—communication competency can arguably be regarded as **the** key skill that advances career adaptability and employability in today's occupational world. Fourth, their awareness of the importance of providing life- and career construction-based counseling for each student and offering training that is on a par with life design-based training anywhere else in the world.

Using the *CIP* and the *MCM*, GWF colleagues could offer the latest qualitative (narrative, storied) career counseling to those learners who had completed their bridging year. This was a considerable achievement in a resource-scarce, deep rural region, dotted with informal settlements (informally known as squatter camps).

7.4.2 Life Design-Based Intervention Research at the GWF

During 2016, 2017, 2018, and 2019, GWF colleagues and I collaborated on three life design-based projects (see Table 7.1) aimed at demonstrating how life- and career construction (using the *CIP* and the *MCM*) could assist students to choose fields of study, construct themselves and their careers, and eventually design successful lives and make social contributions (Maree, 2019a, 2019b).

The students' positive feedback and exciting progress indicated the success and validity of the intervention strategy (see Table 7.1 below for details), which is also easily replicable in other rural contexts.

7.4.3 Brief Discussion of the Outcomes of the Intervention (Maree, 2019a, 2019b)

Some of the trends that emerged from analyzing the data obtained through the projects warrant mention.

First, while the participants' overall career adaptability showed improvement, important differences were noted between the men's and women's pretest and post-test scores in the *Career Adapt-Abilities Scale* (*CAAS*; Maree, 2012a). Second, the main finding was that only the women's Curiosity improved significantly (as opposed

Table 7.1 The life design intervention plan

Steps	Intervention objective (Savickas et al., 2009)	Activities and techniques to achieve intervention outcomes
General	Help participants grow psychologically and promote their wellbeing	Uncover themes and patterns in participants' observations, life stories, and beliefs
Step 1	Establish a satisfactory working relationship	Conduct group discussions to help participants get to know each other better. Complete Part 1 (biographical details) of the *CIP* and the *MCM*
Step 2	Examine participants' (subjective) sense of self and encourage self-reflection and reflexivity	Complete Parts 2 and 3 of the *CIP*. Participants reflect on their answers
Step 3	Objectify participants' stories and open up new perspectives on these stories	Participants craft their power, value, or identity statements and life story titles and headings. Life stories are (re)constructed in terms of past and present chapters
Step 4	Contextualize challenges or challenging areas in new stories Reconfirm participants' capacity to construct their career identities	Review challenges ("problems") and consider them as opportunities for growth Identify and confirm strengths and problem-solving capacities
Step 5	Construct participants' identities Jointly design plans to help participants overcome barriers Share "new" stories with a compassionate audience	Revisit power, value, or identity statements. Juxtapose painful or hurtful (past) and hope-filled (future) stories and "faulty" beliefs and inspiring decisions. Complete mission and vision statements. Participants elicit advice from within themselves by revisiting their favorite quotations
Step 6	Conduct regular follow-ups	Counselor conducts regular follow-ups and decides on possible further intervention

to the improvement in the men's Concern, Control, and Curiosity scores). Third, scrutiny of the women's narratives (qualitative outcomes) confirmed the lowly status of women in this male-dominated, deep rural region where women are generally still expected to be submissive to men, to raise the children, and occupy themselves with household chores. As a result, the female participants seemed more curious about job opportunities, but their depressing circumstances largely precluded their actually converting opportunities into realities. Some of their comments are given below.

> "I can only become happy when I leave this place forever" (Sarah, a 22-year-year woman).
>
> "There is no support for my dreams in our township" (Angie, 23 years old).
>
> "My greatest area for development is being unable to stand up for myself" (Pearl, 25 years old).

Above all, considering factors such as the cost and time to complete projects, the GWF projects (essentially narrative, qualitative, group-based life design interventions in resource-constrained rural environments) are easily replicable in similar contexts. The innovative nature of the approach is lauded and enthusiastically embraced by all concerned. In addition to the positive research outcomes, the projects have already reduced the likelihood of the students discontinuing their participation, dropping out of the projects, ending up on the streets with a bleak future, and swelling the ranks of the unemployed in the region.

Previously (Maree, 2018), I identified some key factors that both individually and collectively promote poverty alleviation, sustainable development, and decent work. First, a keen sense of innovation, goal-setting, planning and implementing rolling plans, flexibility, careful prior planning, willingness to become involved, as well as the capacity to adapt pre-planned schedules, strategies, and interventions as and when needed. Second, accepting the inevitability of change and exhibiting a willingness to embrace a protean change orientation (adapting schedules and making changes when needed). Third, a capacity to renovate old-fashioned ideas and engender new and contextually appropriate ones. Fourth, a sense of actionality (being able and willing to move forward enthusiastically) and the belief that positive developments are about to happen. Fifth, taking the lead and ensuring project sustainability. Sixth, accepting that these kinds of projects almost always occur in uncontrolled conditions (Savickas et al. 2009). Seventh, researchers and practitioners should understand and accept that human behavior can best be comprehended and appreciated only in those contexts where such behavior happens (Brown & Brooks, 1996). It is therefore essential to abandon predetermined and often biased assumptions about groups of people and how to "help them". Instead, encouraging personal and collective agency and personal authorship should be prioritized. Lastly, unselfishness and a genuine desire to change the lives of vulnerable and marginalized groups of people are prerequisites for the success of any intervention in disadvantaged contexts.

7.5 Summary

This chapter covered innovating career counseling to promote social justice (advocacy) and sustainable decent work for all. Sadly, though, despite our best efforts, attempts to implement education, training, and counseling assessment instruments to prepare everyone for a rapidly changing world have been less than successful. In many instances, these efforts may have had unintended adverse effects. For example, it was recently announced that the South Africa education authorities had decided to introduce coding and robotics into schools at Grade 9 level through a subject called "digital learning" to prepare learners for the changed and changing world of work. While this is a laudable idea, only the more affluent schools will be able to afford the state-of-the-art equipment (including computer laboratories) and appoint qualified teachers to teach and train the learners. Most learners in resource-constrained contexts will not have access to this kind of training. Rivett (2019) points out that large numbers of properly trained teachers will be needed to execute the plan: "Computers have to be available on the school premises together with the relevant IT infrastructure and internet connectivity" (p. 2). Stringent safety measures will also be needed to prevent equipment from disappearing. The chances of successfully introducing these measures across the continent at present are virtually non-existent. Since "the risk of not being able to attain the skill of coding will be a risk of not attaining a job" (p. 2), these developments will in all likelihood serve only to widen the already huge gap between affluent and indigent people. Rivett righty asks the question: "Will the country end up with another subject that creates 'have and have-nots'?" (p. 2).

On a more positive note: The successful implementation of the career counseling approach advocated in this book in a typical Global South (in this case, African) context is promising and bodes well for the future. I believe that replicating this model across Africa can advance the adaptability and employability of large numbers of impoverished people. Judging by the qualitative feedback of the participants in our own projects, the intervention promoted the welfare of the participants facing extreme hardship and large-scale unemployment. The intervention also reinforced their career resilience and agility, enhanced their career adaptability, promoted their sense of occupational, personal, and self-identity, employability, and improved their chances of finding sustainable decent work (many of them actually succeeded in finding sustainable work[1]). The approach therefore holds much promise as a conduit for promoting Goal 8 of the UN Agenda (UN, 2016, p. 1): "Promote sustained, inclusive, and sustainable economic growth, full and productive employment and decent work for all."

In conclusion: The effect of technological advances on the nature of work is felt by many workers across the world currently. Occupational inequality[2] highlight the ever-growing division in the current workplace. The following is just one example: Remote engagement is bound to become the 'new normal' in work contexts. For various reasons (including the threat posed by the coronavirus pandemic), a large and ever-growing number of people are allowed or even compelled to work remotely. Whereas the majority of more privileged workers are allowed and able to stay (and work from) home, the less privileged still have to travel to the workplace and run the risk of contracting the coronavirus.

I can add also that I agree with Bar-On's (2007) view that conditions in which people are deprived of the opportunity to blossom can hide and perhaps even destroy their self- and career construction. This sad situation compounds the human tragedy stemming from disadvantage, joblessness, and inequality. He rightly asks how many great leaders we have lost/are losing, such as Nelson Mandela, Mother Teresa of Calcutta, Marx, Freud, and Einstein … people who may have contributed significantly to improving the lives of millions of people. Also, bearing in mind that unemployment is considered a major cause of the Arab Spring, the current situation in Global South countries especially poses a real threat to world peace. I believe that adopting the

[1]Colleagues from the GWF regularly update me on the extent to which participants are succeeding in finding sustainable decent work.

[2]See Chap. 7.

twofold Mandela response to counter adversity and its associated challenges will boost our individual and collective efforts to achieve sustainable decent work for all, especially those with economic and other kinds of disadvantage. This response to challenges relates to overcoming major challenges while also taking advantage of the multiple opportunities embedded in change (including the opportunity to make social contributions). This response is well aligned with "[t]he 21st-century perspective on career counseling [that] moves from the empiricism of objective vocational guiding and the humanism of subjective career developing to the social constructionism of projective life designing" (Savickas, 2015, p. 136).

In Chap. 8, I discuss how the *CIP* can be used to elicit the life stories of people innovatively and qualitatively.

References

Bar-On, R. (2007). The relationship between emotional intelligence and giftedness. *Gifted Education International, 23,* 136–150.

Blustein, D. L., Palladino Schulteiss, D. E., & Flum, H. (2004). Toward a relational perspective of the psychology of careers and working: A social constructionist analysis. *Journal of Vocational Behavior, 6,* 423–440.

Brown, D. (2002). Status of theories of career choice and development. In D. Brown, & Associates (Eds.), *Career choice and development* (4th ed., pp. 510–515). San Francisco, CA: Jossey-Bass.

Brown, D., & Brooks, L. (Eds.). (1996). *Career choice and development.* San Francisco, CA: Jossey-Bass.

Cardoso, P., Silva, J. R., Gonçalves, M. M., & Duarte, M. E. (2014). Narrative innovation in life design counseling: The case of Ryan. *Journal of Vocational Behavior, 85,* 276–286. https://doi.org/10.1016/j.jvb.2014.08.001.

Fugate, M., & Kinicki, A. M. (2008). A dispositional approach to employability: Development of a measure and test of implications for employee reactions to organizational change. *Journal of Occupational and Organizational Psychology, 81*(3), 503–527.

Guilbert, R., Bernaud, J., Gouvernet, B., & Rossier, J. (2016). Employability: Review and research prospects. *International Journal for Educational and Vocational Guidance, 16*(1), 69 89.

International Labor Organization. (2019). *World employment and social outlook: Trends 2019.* Retrieved from: https://www.ilo.org/global/research/global-reports/weso/2019/lang–en/index.htm.

Maree, J. G. (2010). Brief overview of the advancement of postmodern approaches to career counseling. *Journal of Psychology in Africa, 20,* 361–369.

Maree, J. G. (2012). *Two DVD set: A guide to reflective career counselling—with Prof Maree.* Randburg, South Africa: JvR Psychometrics.

Maree, J. G. (2014a). Poverty and life designing. In L. Nota & J. Rossier (Eds.), *Handbook of the life design paradigm: From practice to theory* (pp. 233–248). Boston, MA: Hogrefe.

Maree, J. G. (2014b). Creating a sense of hope: The essence of career construction for life designing in a developing country context. In M. Pope, L. Y. Flores, & J. Rottinghaus (Eds.), *The role of values in careers* (pp. 213–232). Charlotte, NC: Information Age.

Maree, J. G. (2014c, May). *Psychology for all: Examining the merits of a brief, simultaneous, quantitative + qualitative (career) counselling strategy.* Keynote address, 5th World Conference on Psychology, Counseling and Guidance, Dubrovnik, Croatia.

Maree, J. G. (2014d, July). *Educing life themes to co-construct life portraits and turn decision into movement*. Keynote address (Division 16), 28th International Congress of Applied Psychology. Palais Des Congrès, Paris, France.
Maree, J. G. (2015, September 6). *DVD trailer: A guide to reflective career counselling*. Retrieved from https://www.youtube.com/watch?v=3Rb8oIJTd6Y.
Maree, J. G. (2018). Using life design counseling for career construction to facilitate sustainable employability and decent work in a developing country context. In V. Cohen-Scali, J. Pouyaud, M. Podgórny, V. Drabik-Podgórny, G. Aisenson, J-L. Bernaud, I. Moumoula., J. Guichard (Eds.), *Interventions in career design and education* (pp. 195–214). New York, NY: Springer.
Maree, J. G. (2019a, June). *Career Development in Africa: Decent work for all: Brief photomontage*. Keynote Address at the Annual Career Development Practitioner Congress, Emperors Palace Conference Centre, Kempton Park, South Africa.
Maree, J. G. (2019b). Innovative career construction counselling for a creative adolescent. *British Journal of Guidance and Counselling*. https://doi.org/10.1080/03069885.2018.1504202.
Maree, J. G. (2019c). Postmodernising career counseling in a deep rural context. In J. G. Maree (Ed.), *Handbook of innovative career counseling* (pp. 577–596). New York, NY: Springer.
McIlveen, P., Ford, T., & Dun, K. (2005). A narrative sentence-completion process for systems career assessment. *Australian Journal of Career Development, 14,* 30–38.
Naidoo, A. V., Pretorius, T. B., & Nicholas, L. (2017). The emergence of career psychology in South Africa: A socio-historical perspective. In G. B. Stead & M. B. Watson (Eds.), *Career psychology in the South African context* (3rd ed., pp. 1–20). Pretoria, South Africa: Van Schaik.
Rivett, U. (2019). Coding in South African schools: What needs to happen to make it work. *The Conversation*. Retrieved from https://www.moneyweb.co.za/news/tech/coding-in-sa-schools-what-needs-to-happen-to-make-it-work/.
Ross, A. (2016). *The industries of the future*. New York: NY: Simon & Schuster.
Savickas, M. L. (2011a). Reshaping the story of career counseling. In K. Maree (Ed.), *Shaping the story—A guide to facilitate narrative counseling* (pp. 1–3). Boston/Rotterdam, The Netherlands: Sense.
Savickas, M. L. (2011b). *Career counseling*. Washington, DC: American Psychological Association.
Savickas, M. L. (2015). Career counseling paradigms: Guiding, developing, and designing. In P. Hartung, M. Savickas, & W. Walsh (Eds.), *The APA handbook of career intervention* (Vol. 1, pp. 129–143). Washington, DC: APA Books.
Savickas, M. L., Nota, L., Rossier, J., & Dauwalder, J. P., Duarte, M. E., Guichard, J., … Van Vianen, A. E. M. (2009). Life designing: A paradigm for career construction in the 21st century. *Journal of Vocational Behavior, 75*, 239–250.
Stevens, G., Duncan, N., & Sonn, C. (2010). The apartheid archive: Memory, voice and narrative as liberatory praxis. *Psychology in Society, 40,* 8–28.
United Nations (UN) (2016). *Transforming our world: The 2030 Agenda for sustainable development*. Retrieved from https://sustainabledevelopment.un.org/post2015/transformingourworld.
United Nations (UN). (2019). *Sustainable development goals: 17 goals to transform our world*. Retrieved from https://www.un.org/sustainabledevelopment/development-agenda/.
Winnicott, D. W. (1964). *The child, the family and the outside world*. Cambridge, MA: Perseus.

Part III
Practical Implementation: How the MCM and the CIP can be Used to Facilitate Career Counseling

Chapter 8
Eliciting Life Stories Innovatively and Qualitatively: Using the *CIP* in Career Counseling

The universe is not made up of atoms; it's made up of tiny stories (Joseph Gordon-Levitt)

Abstract This chapter begins by explaining why the *CIP* was developed as a questionnaire to promote counseling self- and career construction as well as life design intervention. This is followed by a discussion of factors related to the theoretical and conceptual framework of the *CIP*. Next, I deal with the nature of the questionnaire and discuss briefly its aim and four-part layout before focusing on some requirements for administering the *CIP*. The importance of focusing on the *CIP* as a unit, the issue of how feedback to assessees should be given, and how qualitative analysis should be explained are then discussed. Information is provided to guide practitioners in their interpretation of responses to *CIP* questions. The chapter concludes with an explanation of how rigorous interpretation can be promoted, the key issue of choosing a career and linking this choice to writing mission and vision statements, crafting a career plan, and forward movement (including job analysis).

8.1 Orientation

Acceptance of the value and effectiveness of qualitative, subjective, or "storied" approaches in conjunction with objective or quantitative approaches has increased markedly over the past few decades.[1] This is due largely to the pioneering work of Mark Savickas (2019a), and a number of other scholars. Savickas' *CCI* has become arguably the most used and most written about (quantitative or qualitative) career counseling assessment instrument, which also includes an invaluable intervention strategy. Many other qualitative instruments can be distinguished (Arthur, Neault, & McMahon, 2019), each related to a particular theory. Many of these instruments also

[1]For the purposes of this book, the term "job analysis" refers to both job analysis and career exploration.

J. G. (Kobus) Maree, *Innovating Counseling for Self- and Career Construction*,
https://doi.org/10.1007/978-3-030-48648-8_8

have links with the techniques and interventions designed and developed by Savickas and Guichard.

Crisp (2002) argues that if one could compress all facets of a particular language, something would probably come about "emerging out of an immense history, an amalgamation of all human experience, constantly shifting" (p. 25). It would probably enable one to form an idea of the nature of the human 'story', characterized by emotions such as pain, hatred, fear, joy, love, and a sense of accomplishment; "general" facets of human life. Using a similar lens, career counselors conduct research to design brief questionnaires to help them elicit a small, yet reliable and trustworthy samples of responses from their clients. Analyzing these responses can help clients identify key career-life themes and thereby understand themselves better, elicit advice from within, and regain hope and purpose in their lives. The *CCI* probably comes as close to achieving these aims as any other similar questionnaire. The *CIP* is especially useful in group contexts.

Interested readers are referred also to a DVD (Maree, 2012) that JvR (the only Sub-Saharan test distributor approved by Multi-Health Systems (MHS)) and I produced a few years ago. In the meantime, interested readers are encouraged to visit YouTube and watch the following clips.

- DVD trailer: A guide to reflective career counseling (Maree 2013, 2012)
- Trailer: *Die windpomp* (Jacaranda, 2015)

They will immediately be able to make the connection between the two clips and discover the power of the new approach to career counseling.[2]

Below, I discuss aspects of the theoretical and conceptual framework of the *CIP* and clarify a number of important terms.

8.2 Aspects of the Conceptual Framework of the *CIP*

8.2.1 What Is Career Interest?

Holland (1997) argues that choosing a career is an expression of a person's personality, while Super (1972) maintains that a career is the implementation of a person's self-concept. However, interest alone is no guarantee for success in a given career. Maree (2013) states that personal traits such as perseverance, self-discipline, resoluteness, conscientiousness, determination, and temperament are crucially important in assessing whether a career choice is feasible or not. Aptitude, intelligence, and interest on their own provide no guarantee of success.

Savickas (2019a) more recently defined interest as "a psychosocial tensional state between an individual's needs and social opportunities to attain goals that satisfy those needs" (p. 163). Also, Savickas' (2005) career construction theory holds that

[2]See the section titled "Notes" at the end of this book for more details.

"individuals construct their careers by imposing meaning on their vocational behavior and occupational experiences" (p. 43) and that "occupation provides a mechanism for social integration" (p. 48) and for making social contributions. This book should be read with these two definitions/perspectives in mind.

8.2.2 Stability and Role of Career Interest Profiles

Based on the responses of seven leading international experts to the question, "When do people's interest profiles begin to stabilize?", Maree (2016) concluded as follows:

> There is thus general agreement that, even at a relatively young age, interests appear to be moderately steady or stable. However, generally speaking, interests only stabilize at some time between Grades 11 and 12. That said, interest profiles can continue to stabilize until a person's mid-twenties. Lastly, acquiring additional (new) information regarding other contextual conditions and influences (including people's knowledge and perception of their abilities, work, and employment opportunities, employability, as well as other aspects of the occupational world) keep on influencing their interest profiles throughout life (p. 14).

8.2.3 Techniques for Assessing People's Career Interests

The *CIP* merges a number of methods typically used to assess people's career interests, for instance interviewing (asking people directly about their interests and interest category patterns), observing (observing them execute certain activities in natural environments), and administering informal questionnaires (three methods grounded in narrative theory).

8.3 Developing the *CIP*

8.3.1 Brief Background

Maree (2019a, 2019b) and Maree and Beck (2004) have highlighted the challenges associated with relying solely on the results and profiles of "traditional" career counseling assessment and intervention in Global South contexts especially. Stead and Watson (1998, 2017), too, have highlighted the challenges associated with the use of "proven" assessment methods (namely that these procedures as well as their underlying assumptions are often almost exclusively Western culture orientated and not sufficiently applicable to other cultures). There is a dearth of psychometric tests and trustworthy, scientifically based qualitative assessment instruments specifically designed for local contexts as well as uncertainty in regard to theoretical models that may best suit the idiosyncratic cultural contexts of local people (Savickas,

1993). Savickas (2015a) states that career counseling is inextricably interwoven with people's cultural contexts—people can best be understood by trying to understand them in terms of their unique cultural roots. General agreement exists that psychometric assessment in isolation will not adequately assess subjective aspects of people's lived experiences.

8.3.2 Theoretical and Conceptual Framework of the CIP

Grounded primarily in self- and career construction theory (Guichard, 2009; Savickas, 2011a), *CIP* questions are used to elicit information that relates to the differential, developmental, and psychodynamic (storied) traditions.[3] It was developed to provide some of the information generated by the *Career Construction Interview* (*CCI*) (formerly known as the *Career Style Interview* or the *Career Story Interview*) (Savickas, 1989, 1998; 2019a), which, in turn, provides information generated by career- and life style assessment and counseling (Adler, 1958, 1998; Sweeney & Myers, 1986; Taber & Briddick, 2011). This include questions about role models and earliest recollections (Adler, 1998) and questions that draw on narrative career counseling theory and practice (Cochran, 1997). *CIP* intervention emphasizes the importance of helping people accept authorship of their own life stories, reflect on their answers, and listen to (and actually hear) and advise themselves. This approach holds that micro-life stories and successive chapters of people's life stories are closely interwoven and build on previous chapters but is also related to and influences future chapters as life experiences (Maree, 2013). Including the psychodynamic approach (in which the narrative paradigm is embedded) facilitates the elicitation of questions about people's earliest memories and biggest 'challenges' when they were young in the narration process. In addition, the *CIP* is premised on elements of psychosocial, self-concept, and self-efficacy development in adolescence. The framework discussed above is informed by the belief that what people know, who they are (their identities), and who they become develop through their lived experiences and during social discourse with others (Savickas et al., 2009). As discussed earlier, the belief that people are shaped by their environments (and vice versa) (a reciprocal process) is central to the storied approach. An interactionist perspective, which also contains elements of relational theory, is thus advanced.

8.3.3 Conceptual Framework of the CIP

Figure 8.1 shows the conceptual framework of the *CIP*.

[3]Self-construction theory (Guichard, 2009, 2016), career construction theory (Savickas, 2005), and life design counseling (Savickas et al., 2009) are discussed in Chap. 2.

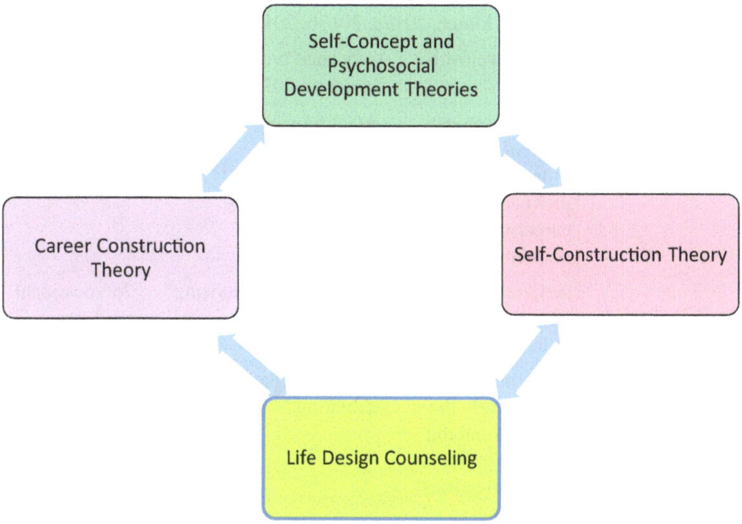

Fig. 8.1 CIP's conceptual framework

In terms of psychosocial and self-concept development frameworks, people are required to confront and deal with challenges throughout their lives, many of which are often not resolved and recur later in their career-lives. It goes without saying that the extent to which people deal with these challenges influences their identity formation. Self- and career construction can be facilitated at any stage in people's lives to enable them to narrate their autobiographies or life stories (narratability). Most importantly, career counselors should emphasize clients' *personal agency* and promote the acceptance of personal authorship of their life stories.

8.3.4 Using the CIP *to Promote Postmodern (Narrative, Qualitative, or Storied) Career Counseling*

The *Career Interest Profile* (*CIP)* is itself a unique assessment instrument that facilitates and promotes counseling for self- and career construction intervention. It is not an interest "test". Rather, it is used to elicit career-story-related information qualitatively (Table 8.1). Its small quantitative part (Part 2) has demonstrated satisfactory test-retest reliability and content and criterion-related validity (Maree & Sommerville, 2008). It can be administered individually and in group contexts. Carefully and purposefully structured, the *CIP* questions promote reflection and, ultimately, reflexivity to develop narratability and biographicity and facilitate the clarification and construction of career-life stories (Maree, 2013).

Table 8.1 Description of the CIP (Maree, 2017a, 2017b, 2017c)

Part	Number of questions	Questions involve …	Associated practices (Savickas, 2011a, 2019a)	Paradigm (Savickas, 2019a).
1	1b Four questions and subquestions	1c Biographical particulars, family influences, and provisional career-related pointers	1d Guiding and advising	1e Vocational guidance
2	2b Four questions and subquestions	2c Qualitative career choice indicators	2d Guiding and advising	2e Vocational guidance
3	3b Two extended questions	3c Identifying qualitatively the six most and the six least preferred career categories (from a list of 19)	3d Educating and facilitating	3e Vocational guidance/Career development
4	4b Fourteen questions and subquestions	4c Small or micro-life story narratives	4d Designing and healing	4e Career counseling and Life design

8.4 Aim of the *CIP*

The *CIP* was conceptualized in 1985 and developed further gradually over time to achieve the outcomes discussed below (see Table 8.1) (Maree, 1986, 1996, 2006, 2008, 2009; 2010a, 2010b, 2010c, 2010d, 2017a, 2017b). At the time, I began to develop a 60^{+}-page qualitative (narrative) workbook entitled *Individual workbook for career guidance investigation* (actually a series of questions and subquestions on a wide variety of career counseling topics aimed at eliciting career choice information in addition to the "usual" quantitative information typically obtained in the late 20th century) to facilitate "career guidance".[4] Over time, the "*workbook*" went through various iterations and became shorter and shorter. Learning about the pioneering work of Mark Savickas in 1993 marked the turning point in the development of the questionnaire. I subsequently endeavored to adapt the questionnaire to facilitate career- (and later self- and life design-) based career counseling in individual and (especially) group contexts. I changed the name of the instrument to the *Career Interest Profile* (*CIP*) and increasingly adopted a social constructionist perspective. Over three decades, drawing on a large number of publications on the qualitative,

[4]At the time, I was also writing my first teenage novel (*Trial match*) (Maree, 1996) in which the main character presents for career counseling and is introduced to my first attempt at devising a qualitative (storied) intervention and assessment strategy. This was followed by another teenage novel entitled *Zweepi, the spinning game* in 2005 (Maree, 2005). I started writing both books to deal with my own pain at the time, and doing so enabled me to experience first-hand the power of the storied approach to career counseling.

postmodern (narrative) approach to career counseling, feedback from thousands of research participants and global scholars such as Savickas, Hartung, Briddick, Sensoy-Briddick, Patton, Watson, McMahon, McIlveen, and Amundson, I updated the *CIP* to reflect Mark Savickas' (and others') ground-breaking work in the field. I endeavored also to ensure that it promoted the elicitation of concise yet sufficiently "rich" and interpretable data in both individual and group contexts.

The *CIP* (see Table 8.1) was designed to help people uncover and interpret their interests, potential, career values and, especially, their key life themes and, in so doing, design a career plan or life theme. Moreover, it is based on the belief that people can construct personal meaning and purpose from their numerous life encounters or happenstances (chance encounters) (Krumboltz, 2003, 2015; Vecchio, 2013). The *CIP* advocates a flexible and open-minded approach to data construction. Following a postmodern approach, the *CIP* structure is there to serve career counselors and their clients and not vice versa. In addition, the *CIP* is premised on the belief that objective and subjective information is needed to help people make theoretically grounded, informed, and appropriate career decisions. The *CIP* assumes also that the more comprehensive the objective and subjective information that can be elicited and used to compile preliminary information on which career choice-related decisions can be made, the better. Lastly, the *CIP* adheres to the view that career counseling should be based on the analysis of autobiographies and carefully assembled and coherent meanings, rather than on questionnaires that, for instance, test aptitude alone.

Above all, the *CIP* helps career counselors listen **for** instead of **to** their clients' life stories and storylines (Savickas, 2016, Welty, 1998).

8.4.1 Rationale for Parts 1, 2, and 4

Parts 1, 2, and 4 of the *CIP* were designed to obtain, qualitatively, a profile of people's life themes and interests. The ultimate aim is to promote people's career counseling capacity by empowering them to make informed decisions about their career journeys, design successful lives, make social contributions, and, ultimately, live purposeful lives. The *CIP* confirms the value of an autobiographical approach to career counseling—embedded in social constructionism—and shows that narrating and drawing on their autobiographies is important in counseling people of all ages. It also acknowledges that the primary allegiance in career counseling should not be to specific theoretical approaches or techniques but, rather, to the best ways of serving clients.

8.4.2 Rationale for Part 3: Career Stereotypes

Hall, Halstead, and Taylor (1986b) state that "[i]n most cultures generally accepted ideas ('stereotypes') are held regarding the activities, responsibilities and the role of a particular job; that occupations can be grouped according to activities, demands and roles, and that these groups are synonymous with fields of occupational interest" (p. 1).

Based on the view discussed above (i.e. that people's configuration of interests can be split into different, often overlapping, career categories), I, in turn, based the number of different career categories on Holland's (1985, 1997) sixfold conceptualization of the continuum of interests and associated careers, the *South African Vocational Interest Inventory's* (*SAVII*) (Du Toit, Prinsloo, Gevers, & Harilall, 1993) 18-fold distinction, Kuder's (1977) 10-fold conceptualization of different stereotypical career interest categories, and Rothwell and Miller's (Miller, 1968) hypothesizing of 12 stereotypical career categories or preferences.

8.4.3 Rationale for Using an Integrative QUALITATIVE-Quantitative Approach in Career Counseling

Based on an integrative QUALITATIVE-quantitative approach, the *CIP* can be used together with the *Maree Career Matrix (MCM)* (see the next chapter) to promote integrative qualitative-quantitative career counseling (Maree & Taylor, 2016a, 2016b) and understanding of the multiple unique and distinguishing experiences of people and subsequently advance the construction, deconstruction, reconstruction, co-construction, and, ultimately, the rewriting of their career and life stories. Using the two instruments together, career counselors can help clients navigate repeated crossroads in their career-lives, enhance their sense of self-respect, regain their sense of self, and rediscover a sense of purpose in their lives. This can be achieved by uncovering and enacting their key life themes to enable them to "hold" themselves in uncertain and changing times of transitions (Neault & Pickerell, 2019), to transform hurt into hope, and to convert areas for development ("weaknesses") into strengths, and non-successes ("failures") into triumph. Intervention using these two instruments also supports Krumboltz's (1993) view (Patterson-Mills, 2014) that "[t]here is no division between personal and career counseling … personal and career counseling are one and the same" (p. 24) and demonstrates the folly of attempting to distinguish between these two forms of intervention.

8.4.4 Brief Description of the Four Parts of the CIP

It should be emphasized up front that the administration of the *CIP* is premised on the belief that the small number of carefully selected questions contained in the questionnaire collectively constitute a satisfactory "microcosm" of questions to obtain sufficient information to elicit people's "grand life story" (to the extent that this is possible).

Part 1. In Part 1 of the *CIP*, assessees are requested to provide biographical details and family influences.

Part 2. Part 2 contains questions on career choice (e.g. "Tell me which three specific careers (e.g. teacher) you think you would like most and least at this stage and, for each career, give the single most important reason why this is the case").

Part 3. In Part 3 ("career category preferences/dislikes"), assessees are required to

a. from a total of 19 broad, encompassing career categories, identify and rank their five or six most preferred career categories in order of preference;
b. likewise, identify and rank their five or six least liked career categories in order of dislike;
c. underline approximately 10–15 specific occupations that they are most interested in **green**, and
d. underline approximately 10–15 specific occupations that they are least interested in **red**.

The most preferred and most disliked career categories provide career counselors with a starting point for examining clients' career profiles in greater depth (Maree, 2010a).

Part 4. Lastly, Part 4 comprises a number of micro-life story questions.

8.5 The *CIP* Online

The *CIP* is available on the JvR Psychometrics Online Platform.

8.5.1 Prerequisites for Administering the CIP

Even though no specific additional training (regarding the use of the questionnaire) is required, users of the questionnaire are advised to attend continuing professional development (CPD) workshops to learn about the latest developments in career counseling and test development before starting to use the *CIP* in, for instance, private practice, at schools, at further education and training colleges, or at universities, for either research or career counseling. As stated previously, administrators should self-administer the questionnaire before administering it to clients.

8.6 Interpreting Life Stories ("Profiles") Elicited by the *CIP*: General Guidelines

8.6.1 The CIP *as a Unit*

All questions have been structured in such a way that a coherent and logical flow is evident. Beginning from an "on the edge of flow in career counseling" perspective, with straightforward, easy-to-answer questions, the questionnaire moves gradually to deeper and more profound questions to promote and actually achieve "flow" in the career story and intervention. Towards the second part of Part 4 in particular, assessees respond to questions that tap into the subconscious to elicit key life themes and inner advice. All questions correlate positively on multiple levels. Stated differently: Questions are repeated in various ways to facilitate response consistency (creating a qualitative consistency index). Inconsistent responses are generally indicative of assessees being in a hurry, overly anxious, tired, unresponsive, unenthusiastic, uncooperative, or oppositional defiant. Compare, for example, Rose's response to Statement 3(b) ("I do not enjoy doing"), namely, "Meeting and socializing with people" to her response to Instruction 1a (Part 2) ("Write down the names of the five specific careers you think you would like most"), namely, "Teacher because I love working with people." James, on the other hand, indicated a strong preference for social, caregiving, and community services, yet he indicated a strong dislike for becoming a teacher. Questioned about his seemingly inconsistent responses, he explained that "My father says teachers are disrespected by others, and I see how my own teachers struggle to maintain discipline in their classrooms and get through their work". As mentioned earlier, it is essential to examine seemingly inconsistent answers carefully and clarify such responses with assessees.

8.6.2 Importance of the Second Last Question in Part 4

The last question before assessees are asked to reflect on how they experienced the intervention (i.e. "What were your three biggest challenges ("problems") when you were young?") should at all times be asked only once a "safe" or "sacred" space (a trusting space) has been created (Savickas, 2011c; Winnicott, 1969, 1987). Otherwise, counselors will most likely encounter resistance ("I do not want to talk about these") or avoidance ("I cannot remember"). Responses to these questions are extremely important and correlate positively with responses to the question about assessees' earliest recollections.

8.6.3 Case Vignettes

Case vignette 1. Below, I discuss the responses of a 16-year-old learner from a seriously disadvantaged environment (where most of the roads are impassable in rainy weather). His biggest challenges (or main memories) when he was very young were:[5]

a. "I watched while many of my friends were hit by cars."
b. "Many of these children subsequently died. The nearest hospital was far away."
c. "Being unable to help any of them."

In his response to the first instruction in Part 2 of the *CIP* ("List your three favorite careers and provide the single most important reason for your choices"), he wrote:

i. "A mechanical engineer so that I can design motor cars that can be handled more easily."
ii. "A paramedic so that I can attend to the victims of motor car accidents."
iii. "A teacher so that I can teach drivers and learners how to use the roads."

This young man, with his knack for mechanical things, is a qualified mechanical engineering technologist today (having completed his studies at a university of technology). He is passionate about the medical side of his job (referred to above) and often works in provincial hospitals over weekends. He also gives road safety lessons at rural schools in particular.

People use various ways to express and deal with their feelings of hurt or pain. While some write songs, poems, or stories, others prefer, for instance, to master music instruments and express their emotions in that way, participate in sport, or study hard. As career counselors, it is our job to help clients channel their actions in a constructive and positive manner and make their hurt a gift to others. The following is just one example from the Global South, South African context: In the early 1960s, Toinette, a fan of the vocal group Johnny Kongos and the G-men, was killed in a motorcar accident while on her way to one of the group's concerts. The group was touched by her untimely passing and later wrote the song *Tulips for Toinette* (Samson, 2017), which soon became a big hit in South Africa and inspired many people. Also listen to the song *Go rest high on that mountain* for a moving and enlightening explanation of how writing and singing can be harnessed to convert hurt into hope, purpose, and a social contribution (Ronald, 2014).

Case vignette 2. Consider the following responses of a 16-year-old girl to the question about her greatest challenges and her earliest recollections.

Biggest challenge: "Having to smile and act (pretend) that it did not hurt when I was mocked by my friends because my father left my mother for a black woman. Our small community was still very "conservative."

Earliest recollection: Background: "I was always an insecure child. At the age of seven, I was chosen to play the role of a fairy in our school play. Initially, I felt very

[5]The responses of the participants are verbatim with only very light editing in order to preserve the authenticity of the responses.

nervous and scared. However, we practiced a lot, and, over time, I began to enjoy the experience of acting (I loved wearing my pink dress and my crown!)." (SMILES) "On the night the actual show took place, my fear returned. I cried while mommy and teacher put on my dress, fitted my wings, and put on my make-up. When they were done, teacher held a small mirror in front of me ... one of those that enlarges faces, and asked me whether I thought the audience would be able to recognize me. I said 'no'. I still remember her reply: 'So what is there to be scared of?' Somehow that put me at ease because I understood that I had actually become a different person for the time being. In the end, I enjoyed the show and felt proud of myself."

Joey (the young girl) and I then together came up with the following headline for her first recollection: "Acting and entertaining alleviates insecurity".

Joey is currently enrolled for a degree in drama and plans to combine her studies with a degree in educational psychology.

Case vignette 3. Shaun, a 17-year-old learner from a broken family, confided in me that he used to be a shy, uncertain, and insecure young child. Moreover, he experienced rejection at various levels during his early years and always felt marginalized and unwelcome in his peer group. His earliest recollection was being mocked in front of his friends because of his "effeminate" behavior.

Today, he is a magician. In his own words: "Now most people accept me, admire me, and want to be in my presence to see how I perform 'magic'."

8.6.4 Commencing Feedback

This depends on the counselor's personal preferences.

Career counselors can commence feedback by asking Questions a-d below (assessees generally know what the appropriate answers are—if not, keep on probing until appropriate responses are given).

a. "Who knows you better than anybody else?"
b. "I will now be reading your career-life story narrative back to you. However, whose voice will you really be hearing?"
c. "One should ideally listen to one voice; follow one person's advice only ... that is also the person that one can then blame if things do not turn out the way one would want them to. Whose voice is that?"

By this time, almost all assessees should have identified the following pattern: "I know myself better than anybody else"; "I should listen carefully to others' 'advice', but only I can make my own, important life decisions: in the final instance, I should follow my own advice."

d. "If you drive away from my rooms today, and you are stopped by someone who asks for directions, what will your reply be?" Assessees almost always respond, "Where do you want to go to?" or "What is your destination?"

These questions are used to convey the message that matters such as fields of study, careers, or occupations can be likened to signboards people encounter as they journey through life in their search for meaning and purposefulness. What constitutes meaning and purpose in the lives of individual people is revealed by key themes in their lives (including the need and desire to help others, defending defenseless people against bullying, giving a voice to the "unvoiced", breaking down artificial barriers between people, and so on).

If the question about the three earliest recollections is included, I first discuss the assessee's earliest recollections (her or his "deepest secrets"). Otherwise, feedback commences with a discussion of responses to the questions about the three biggest challenges or most hurtful experiences in the assessee's youth. The counselor explains that the experiences reflect the assessee's key life themes and the major challenges she is facing (Maree, 2017b), but, more importantly, they reflect her own advice on how the challenges can be resolved.

8.6.5 Dealing with the Mistaken Idea that Career Counselors Can or Will "Tell" Assessees What to Do

The approach advocated in this book works particularly well with adolescents who frequently respond as follows: "I do not take kindly to being told what to do." This is, in fact, how I recently handled a similar kind of response from Susan (an assessee):

"How can I be of use or of help to you?"

Susan: "Tell me what to study and in which careers I will be successful and happy."

"What do you value most?"

Susan: "Not being told to do things."

I drew on this response to explain that I agreed that no one should tell someone else what to do and that that was the reason why I could not "tell" her what to study but, instead, guide her towards taking that decision by herself.

In response to the question: "What were your three biggest challenges ('problems') when you were young?", Susan replied: "I was left with no choice but to relocate to England with my parents at the age of eight after our family had been brutally attacked in our house." After some prompting, she admitted that, a few years later, she was glad that the family had had to relocate because it turned out that the move was for the best. She has made many friends and is doing well at school. Almost as an afterthought, she added: "Above all, our house does not even have burglar bars."

I helped her to connect the dots still further by stating: "You are right; no person should decide on your behalf. However, when life imposes changes on us that we have no control over, it is useful to realize that while we cannot control certain occurrences in life, we can still control our reactions to what happens to us."

8.6.6 Explaining the Concept of Qualitative Information Analysis to Assessees: Enabling People to Identify Their Key Life Themes

I use the following example to illustrate how qualitative information analysis can be conducted to help people identify their key life themes.

Recently, in an effort to obtain information about a certain client, I asked five of her acquaintances to write brief notes about her. This is what they wrote:

a. "You will always find her working in the townships on Saturdays, trying to make a difference in the lives of less privileged children."
b. "When a friend of hers was recently accused unfairly of cheating in a test by a lecturer, she made an appointment with the lecturer and insisted that he apologize to the friend in front of the class."
c. "Her favorite saying when she sees that one of her classmates is depressed is: 'I'm a listener. You are welcome to tell me what is wrong.' And she never shares others' secrets with anyone."
d. "She is the chairperson of the school's outreach project in an informal settlement."
e. "Thanks to her initiative, every teacher regularly receives a flower and a brief 'thank you' signed by all the learners to show their appreciation for the teacher's dedication and commitment."

Assessees generally experience little trouble in identifying the main themes and subthemes in such comments.

Similarly, I ask assessees to identify key themes and subthemes in their own life stories. They are generally able to mention themes such as "I love working with people" or "I am an active, outdoors person", as well as corresponding subthemes such as "I care about young children especially" and "I love participating in sport". I then help them fine-tune their key life themes and subthemes with minimal prompting. This goes on until, jointly, we arrive at what appear to be their authentic themes and subthemes. We read and reread and meta-reflect on these themes and subthemes until they authorize or approve their themes. In our final step, we link these themes and subthemes with specific fields of study and careers. Noting repeated phrases (which shed light on the themes and subthemes) is especially helpful (see Table 20). The idea of "data saturation" or arriving at a point where no more themes and subthemes emerge is also explained to them. The large number of questions in the *CIP* promotes the aim of arriving at a point of data saturation.

8.6.7 Integrative Qualitative-Quantitative Career Counseling: Where to Start the Analysis

When quantitative and qualitative career counseling methods are integrated, career counselors can begin by either analyzing the quantitative or the qualitative information first. Inductive analysis is done to uncover life themes. Personally, I score tests after the inductive process has taken place so as not to confuse the process but also to ensure that analysis of the quantitative information does not become more of a deductive process. However, because I am advocating the postmodernizing of career counseling, I take trouble to emphasize the following once again: Career counselors may, of course, choose whatever style they prefer because the style of analysis and intervention is not a matter of right or wrong. However, it is essential to read assessees' responses (reflections) back to them verbatim. They should also be advised that they should identify their central life themes before deciding on specific careers (this will serve as a means to enact their life themes). Likewise, it is important to remind them repeatedly to "reflect on their reflections" and share their insights with the counselor. Offering minimal interpretation promotes assessees' creative critical thinking and enables them to listen to and also hear what they are essentially telling themselves.

After having analyzed and clarified the life stories (consisting of the outcomes of the qualitative assessment), the outcomes (results) of the quantitative assessment are communicated to those concerned. What I have found particularly helpful is the creation of a table to establish a crosswalk between the "stories" and "scores". In practice, there is always a significant overlap between the two sets of information. Table 20 reveals that the quantitative information did not add meaningfully to the information obtained qualitatively.

Some key aspects of the interpretation of assessees' answers to questions in the *CIP* are discussed below.

8.7 Key Aspects of the Interpretation of Assessees' Answers to Questions in the *CIP*: Specific Guidelines

The following guidelines help in the use and interpretation of the *CIP*.

i. Feedback on *CIP* outcomes should be given on a one-to-one basis.
   Outcomes should always be interpreted against the background of the "presenting problem" (the reason why assessment was sought), which is revealed by assessees' response to the first question in Part 4: "How can I be of use, value, or help to you?" or "What are you hoping to gain from the intervention?"
ii. Career counselors should ensure that children in particular were not compelled to present for career counseling against their will.

iii. People generally consult career counselors at a time when they have already decided to make a change in their career-lives. They also usually have an idea of what the answer is to their "presenting problem".
iv. Responses to the question referred to above should be entered verbatim in the counselor's career counseling report, under the heading "Presenting problem", "Reason for referral", or "Reason for consulting the psychologist" to promote the authenticity of the report.
v. Feedback on outcomes should be linked to a longer-term change (development) strategy to help assessees move forward actively.
vi. Assessees' progress and how they experienced the intervention should be traced.
vii. The outcomes should be integrated with the outcomes obtained from other information sources. Counseling for self- and career construction principles should form the basis of interpretation.
viii. The *CIP* should be seen as part of a broader strategy to counsel assessees. The information should always be interpreted in the context of an assessee's total functioning and should be related to other information about the assessee such as his or her early development and information provided by family members, teachers, and friends. Other questionnaire information can include the assessee's personality, aptitudes, general intelligence, emotional-social intelligence, (career) adaptability, academic achievement, and understanding of the language in which the questionnaire was administered.
ix. Coherent as well as less coherent life stories should be interpreted as unique stories that can have a significant effect on the interpretation of a specific assessee's profile and his or her eventual career decisions. While some assessees may demonstrate a well-developed sense of self and career-related identity, others may not.
x. Discrepancies between responses to questions that are expected to yield consistent answers should be examined carefully. If, for instance, a female assessee lists "teacher" and "psychologist" as her two favorite careers, yet lists "social, caregiving, and community service" as her least preferred career category, she should be asked to explain her answers.
xi. Assessees should be requested to answer the questions on career choice in Part 2 of the *CIP* **before** estimating and ranking their five most preferred career choices, and also their five or six least preferred career choices from the *CIP* list of 19 career categories in Part 3 of the *CIP*. Moreover, they should respond to the questions posed in Part 2 and 3 before their *MCM* scores are revealed to prevent contamination of the outcomes (i.e. to prevent *MCM* scores from influencing assessees' responses to the questions posed in Part 2 and 3 of the *CIP*). Focusing on the similarities and differences between the 'test results' and assessees' own estimates of interests and confidence can help career counselors initiate discussions on assessees' results.
xii. Assessees should, of course, be observed carefully and observations recorded meticulously, including all body language-related responses.

xiii. At the end of the career counseling intervention, career counselors should revert to the reason for requesting career counseling to determine whether the intervention sufficiently addressed their goal for the counseling.
xiv. The intervention should be concluded by establishing qualitatively the usefulness of the intervention.

The rationale for some of the *CIP* questions is given in Table 8.2 below to guide practitioners in their interpretation of "stories" and "scores".

Table 8.2 Rationale for some of the questions in the CIP (see also Adler, 1929, 1933; Cochran, 1997; Guichard, 2009; Jung, 1977; Savickas, 2011a, 2011b, 2011c; 2015b, 2019a)

	Question	Rationale
1.	How can I be of help, use, or value to you? Or: What are you hoping to gain from this intervention?	Invites assessees to communicate their goals for the counseling and to convey the message that they are the sole experts on themselves and that they are capable of helping themselves (guided by the counselor)
2.	What are or were your favorite subjects?	These subjects often reveal or confirm assessees' interest patterns
3.	What is/are your dream career(s)?	Many assessees are "unvoiced" (have never been allowed to say what they really want to do as a career). This question enables them to be open and honest
4.	What are a. your seven greatest strengths? b. your areas for growth?	Provides assessees with a "voice" to tell the counselor who they really believe they are and to enable them to hear what they are actually telling themselves
5.	What do you value most?	Enables assessees to share their deepest values with the counselor
6.	What were your (three) biggest challenges ("problems") when you were young? (I allow assessees also to answer the following question: "What were the three most hurtful experiences in your youth? Experiences that you don't want others to go through?")	Enables assessees to share their "deepest secrets" with the counselor and to reveal what they had to suffer passively in early life as well as what they want to do most in life (to actively undo what they had to suffer passively)
7.	a. Whom did you admire or who were your three role models when you were young, and why?	Role models represent assessees' sense of who they are; the building blocks they use to construct themselves
	b. Whom do you admire today, and why?	Many assessees' role models change over time as and when they discover more appropriate people they can identify with (C. Briddick, personal communication, September 27, 2019)
8.	What are your three favorite mottos (quotations)?	Indicates assessees' advice to themselves at that moment

8.7.1 *Interpreting the* CIP-*Elicited Life Story Responses and Reflections*

I recommend that career counselors use the following table to interpret responses to a number of key *CIP* questions.

8.7.2 *Analyzing Assessees' Three Earliest Recollections*

(This question does not appear in the published version of the *CIP* as I believe it should be asked only by psychologists because it sometimes elicits extreme emotions (and even abreaction) that are best dealt with by a suitably qualified person. Should this happen, and you do not feel equipped to handle the challenge, you should refer the assessee to an appropriately qualified professional.)

The four steps listed below are followed in analyzing the three earliest recollections (Maree, 2013, 2017b).

a. The assessee's own words are carefully noted and written down verbatim by the counselor. The first verb the assessee used in the first recollection is carefully noted because it generally indicates how people connect with the world.
b. Words, phrases, and expressions that can possibly shed light on the assessees' central life themes are noted.
c. The assessee is asked to recount the feelings or emotions she associates with each of the three events portrayed in the stories. Once again, her responses are carefully written down.
d. Next, the assessee is asked if she regularly reads newspaper articles. She is then requested to imagine that all three stories will appear in a newspaper the following day and to write a heading for each story. In addition, she is asked to ensure that each heading contains a subject, a verb, and an object (e.g. "Enthusiastic audience appreciates actor's fine performance"). She is then told that the counselor and she will collaborate to put the finishing touches to the headings. However, the counselor can collaborate only once she has told him what she believes the essence of the three stories is as revealed by the three headings. Lastly, once they have finalized the three headings, she is asked to assume that the three stories will appear in an omnibus of three stories and that she has to write an encompassing heading for this omnibus edition. (Counselors are strongly discouraged from volunteering examples of earliest recollections. In the majority of instances when examples are given, assessees attempt to recount recollections that are similar in nature and structure to these examples.)

Many assessees spontaneously include their earliest recollections in the "My life story" narrative that I ask all assessees to write and bring along on the day of the assessment.

Three questions that I often encounter that relate to the use of the earliest recollections technique are discussed briefly below.

8.7.3 *What Do I Do When Assessees Refuse to Share Their Earliest Recollections?*

While most assessees will be willing and able to share their earliest recollections with their counselors, some may refuse to do so. In such instances, there is insufficient trust between the two parties or it may just be a case of the assessees being unable to recall something that they regard as sufficiently important to share with their counselors. In the majority of cases, assessees are generally willing to share later memories, which should be accepted by counselors.[6]

8.7.4 *What if These Memories Are "Untrue"?*

It does not really matter whether the memories are true or not true. Assessees will share those memories that they need to share on a given occasion—not merely because they want to share them but also because they use them "for crucial things like creating a sense of personal identity" (Nash, 2018, p. 3), which is of particular interest to counselors.

8.7.5 *How Far Back Can People Remember?*

According to Justice, Convey, and Akthar (2018), people, on average, are able to report memories that occurred during the first half of the third year of their lives (3.24 years to be precise)" (p. 3).

8.7.6 *Noting Repeated Words or Phrases*

As mentioned earlier, it is essential to note repeated words, expressions, or phrases. These repetitions are then read back verbatim to the assessees concerned to authenticate what they have said. They are encouraged to listen carefully to their spoken

[6]If clients insist on sharing later recollections, I of course respect their wishes. Irrespective of clients' preferences, it is important to consider the possible value and impact of such recollections on the career counseling process. Anecdotal evidence may be meaningful.

words. By urging assessees to repeat these words and expressions out loud, they experience them as genuine.

8.7.7 Observing the Assessee

The counselor observes the assessee carefully and records her body movements in detail. The counselor later integrates these observations into the counseling phases and sessions (Savickas, 2009).

8.7.8 Key Life Themes

Key life themes (or patterns) can be identified through careful analysis of assessees' responses to a number of carefully chosen narrative questions and observation of their behavior. Consider Rose's (pseudonym; Grade 11 learner) responses to some of the questions in the *CIP*:

Counselor (C):	"What are you hoping to gain from the intervention?"
Rose (R):	"Help me narrow down my options. I have always been interested in the human body and in helping others. Some teachers have said that I should become a nurse, for instance, but I need more clarity."
C:	"What are your areas for growth?"
R:	"I find it hard to see people or animals suffer emotionally or physically."
C:	"What do other people say about you?"
R:	"She really cares about others."
C:	"What is your favorite subject?"
R:	"Life sciences."
C:	"What are your favorite quotations?"
R:	"Make the difference you want to see in life." "Don't wait for others to do things."
C:	"Who is your role model?"
R:	"Sister Tlale. She is a nurse who works in the community I come from. I have always admired her and wanted to be like her and to have the knowledge to help sick people get well again."
C:	"What was your biggest challenge when you were young?"
R:	"Seeing so many people suffer from illnesses" (See also the section on the notion of tuning pain into hope.)
C:	"What is your earliest recollection?"
R:	"At the age of six, on my way home after school, one of my friends was driven over by a taxi. We waited next to her until helped arrived. I wanted to help her but did not know what to do. I felt so helpless"

The themes of "wanting to help others" and of "working in a medical-related environment" are clear from the above responses.

With the necessary training, career counselors should not find it difficult to identify assessees' major life themes. However, this technique should not be used by counselors until they have received sufficient training from an experienced counselor.

8.7.9 Using Triangulation and Crystallization to Promote Quality Assurance

I frequently ask assessees to reflect on the crosswalk (or crossover) between their responses to different questions in the *CIP* (crystallization) and also between the two "sets" of outcomes (stories and scores) (triangulation) (see Table 11.3: Linking life themes, interests, and possible fields of study/careers). We then co-construct a list of fields of study they can analyze to arrive at an informed choice. For instance, Mary (pseudonym) notes that she has listed Mathematics and/or accounting industry as her first most preferred career category, Accountant as her second most preferred career, Accountancy as her first most preferred subject (crystallization) and then says that solving mathematical problems is her greatest strength (triangulation). She achieves 78% in mathematics and 83% in stanines of 8, 8, and 7 respectively in the subtests Problem solving, Comparison, and Price Controlling of the *Standard Aptitude Tests* (Owen, 2000). In this instance, the overall patterns are clear. (Mary's parents insisted on the administration of aptitude tests in addition to non-cognitive assessment.)

In my experience, analysis of quantitative results seldom enhances the list of fields of study that assessees may choose to "job analyze" after gaining access to the qualitative outcomes. Employing a qualitative and an integrative approach together, on the other hand, enables assessees to uncover major life themes and decide on appropriate fields of study and associated careers. It enables them to construct themselves and use their careers as a means to fit work into their lives, make-meaning, and live purposeful lives (Hartung, 2010a, 2010b; Savickas, 2005).[7]

8.7.10 Developing Mission and Vision Statements

Near the end of the feedback phase, as recommended by Savickas (2019a), the following instruction is given to assessees: "Now combine your strongest points with your areas for growth in one value, power, or identity sentence that communicates your uniqueness. Begin with the words "*I am* ..." Next, career counselors and assessees together extract sufficient appropriate words and phrases from assessees'

---

[7] I believe that the qualitative approach not only helps assessees uncover their interest patterns but also yields sufficient information to facilitate trustworthy career counseling. However, much will depend on the experience and level of expertise of individual career counselors.

reflections on the *CIP* questions to write a summative sentence that encapsulates the essence of their career-life story narrative and signifies their future intention. The sentence should relate directly to assessees' character arc, which is defined as an "aspect of a theme that portrays where an individual started, is now, and wants to end up on some internal issue" (Savickas, 2019a, p. 162). The sentence should therefore capture as accurately as possible assessees' **mission and vision statements.** It should reveal what they want to **do in a career** to achieve **personal meaning** in their career-lives [**mission statement**], make a **social contribution,** and experience a **sense of purpose** in their lives [**vision statement**]. While counselors serve as "editors" of assessees' narratives, key "messages" and advice should be elicited, emerge from, and be found within assesses themselves.

Such statements can be used to formulate assessees' fundamental intention, help them make meaning, identify a sense of purpose in their lives, and include courses of action and specific goals in line with their central purpose. These statements are usually positive, uplifting, and inspiring and are aimed at helping assessees identify the goals they need to achieve in order to meet their life and career purpose (their vision). These statements should be brief, clear, accurate, and powerful. Moreover, to ensure that the statements are authentic, assessees (in collaboration with career counselors) should quote verbatim their own words (responses) in the statements. In addition, the statements should be written in a way that reflects assessees' key life themes in terms of their future intention. The future scenario that is spelled out should be linked directly to assessees' initially expressed reason for seeking career counseling.

Below I provide examples of mission and vision statements.

8.7.11 Examples of Mission and Vision Statements

(A *preliminary* combined mission and vision statement may read something like this: "I will be happy and experience a sense of purpose in my career-life when I work in an environment where my work and I are respected and where I can earn a decent living, support my family, and help people that struggle financially." Or "I will be happy and experience a sense of meaning and purpose when I work in an environment where I can experience fulfillment in my work, earn enough money to live comfortably, provide for my loved ones, plan for the future, help others, and believe that my career-life is purposeful." However, it is not essential always to craft preliminary vision and mission statements.)

Example 1 Below is an example of the link between a career choice and vision and mission statements.

a. "I want to become a … (**career or occupational choice**) (for instance, "a lawyer"), b. so that I can … (**personal meaning; mission statement)** (for instance, "defend people in a court of law and use my talent to debate matters, draw on my language skills, and demonstrate my ability to remain calm under pressure"), and, c. in the process, … (**social meaning; make a social contribution; vision statement**) (for instance, "fulfil my desire to help people who have suffered or are suffering injustice deal with those who bully or hurt them, restore their dignity, and teach them how to stand up for themselves").

Example 2 "I will become a medical doctor (**career choice**) so that I can build on my interest in medicine, my achievements in life sciences, and my ability to identify trends in people's physical conditions (**personal meaning**), help those in physical pain get better and, in the process, deal with my deep regret at not having been able to help my little brother after a serious motorcycle accident many years ago. That will make my life purposeful (**social meaning**)."

During the crafting of mission and vision statements, the focus is on reflections on how assessees can transform challenges (previously referred to as "problems") experienced in their early years (such as having struggled to concentrate, having stuttered, or not having had friends) into hopeful and purpose-filled themes, inspiring and healing others and, at the same time, healing themselves. This future scenario should relate to assessees' stated reasons for seeking career counseling.

A client (a rape survivor) reported some 17 years ago:

"I have pasted my mission and vision statements on the mirror that I use in the mornings for combing my hair and on my study table where they are easily visible. The statements read as follows: 'First, I want to attain a good mark in my next mathematics test and exam (micro- or short-term statement). Second, I will try to get an A in mathematics at the end of Grade 12 to improve my chances of selection for medical studies (meso- or medium-term statement). In the long run, I want to work in a rural region as a medical doctor and provide much needed medical care to highly vulnerable of people" (a major life theme—the "glue" that holds her career-life story together) (macro- or long-term statement).

Today, she is a medical doctor, specializing in cases that involve sexual assault and posttraumatic stress disorder.

8.7.12 Discussion of "Standard" Questions from Career Counseling Practitioners

How Many Phases and Sessions Are Needed for Career Counseling? Career counseling is a flexible matter that should be discussed and contracted before the counseling commences. While three phases should generally suffice, career counselors should decide on the number of sessions depending on circumstances and on the smoothness of the client-counselor relationship (Cardoso, Savickas, & Gonçalves, 2019). Moreover, they may wish to use only certain questions in the *CIP* or emphasize only some of them, depending on a number of factors such as the idiosyncratic needs of those who present for career counseling, their experience, level of self-insight, cognitions, motivations, and strivings. Clients' reflections on and responses to the opening question will generally help counselors decide which factors should be foregrounded and emphasized. Lastly: Career counselors' personal style will influence and co-determine how the outcomes of the intervention should be presented orally and in written form.

Does Every Life Story Necessarily Start with Pain? Some people struggle to understand or accept that every person's life story starts with "pain". This is understandable. They generally ask, "What about people who did not "suffer" in childhood—do memories of pleasure/joy not inform their first recollections/stories?" Hartung (P. J. Hartung, personal communication, October 23, 2012) maintains that career construction counseling commences with recollections or memories of stories (preoccupations) that could possibly also comprise happy and pleasant memories. There are also those key moments in childhood when children are made to feel special and moments when we marvel at their resilience. Savickas (M. L. Savickas, personal communication, October 3, 2019) maintains that all children need one person who shows genuine concern, care, and love for them—irrespective of whether that person is a parent, a grandparent, or anyone else. The most striking and easy to comprehend examples of earliest recollections point to preoccupations that are cheerful and pleasant are generally those of top-achieving people. The more people experience pain or hurt and struggle, the more they feel they have to 'prove' themselves. Pleasant or happy memories often point to a preoccupation with attaining happiness. The career story emerges now as an earliest recollection to remind people of that preoccupation (in times of transition and difficulty). In summary: It should be noted that "pain" or "hurt" or "suffering" does not always imply suffering and trauma in the "normal" sense. Instead, it should be interpreted through the lens and sense of "troubling", "disconcerting", and "concerning" but also "displaying resilience" or "feeling happy or special" (C. Briddick, personal communication, September 27, 2019).

Explaining/Interpreting Responses that Yield Unsatisfactory Outcomes. In most cases, assessees and counselors will be able to identify patterns in assessees' micro-life stories. However, in a small number of instances, these stories may lack coherence, may appear inconsistent, or may be incomplete. On completion of the *CIP*, these assessees should be given access to a safe or "sacred" place where they can openly discuss their views on the questionnaire. They should then be asked to elaborate on how they experienced the intervention and explain why their experiences were positive or negative. The reasons could include:

i. They did not answer the questionnaire accurately or honestly because they might have been trying to compensate for real or imagined deficiencies in their personalities or behavior, and/or presented themselves differently from whom they really were. Even though it is unlikely that assessees would be dishonest in this kind of questionnaire, some might have felt that they lacked the freedom to give honest answers if, for instance, their study/career preferences differed from those of their parents or other significant others.
ii. They might have felt depressed (or were emotionally unstable) and inadvertently provided inaccurate information.

iii. They might have not fully understood the language in the questionnaire or might not have expressed themselves clearly.
iv. They might have not known themselves sufficiently well to provide unreliable answers.
v. They might have not been motivated to complete the questionnaire; for instance, they might have not wanted to be assessed and might have believed they were being assessed against their will.
vi. They might have been overly anxious and not able to provide reliable responses.
vii. They might have felt uncomfortable with or did not trust the counselor sufficiently, making it difficult to share their deepest emotions or feelings ("secrets") with the counselor.
viii. They might have been very poor and have had limited exposure to the world of work.
ix. In some instances, displacement or transference and/or countertransference might have impacted the dialogue between counselor and assessee negatively and prevented the elicitation of reliable career-life stories.

8.8 Summary

Savickas (2016) states that career counselors should listen for a pattern of language and develop a technique for listening for clients' stories. He adds that career counselors should decide on and implement a strategy for identifying how clients' "hearts" edit their own stories: "Use my strategy or use your own but you need to have some way to listen for valid stories; not veracity" (Savickas, 2016, n.p.). Taking my cue from him, I constantly try to ensure that the *CIP* (in conjunction with the *MCM*) advances the elicitation of concise but sufficiently 'rich' and interpretable 'stories' in both individual and group contexts. This strategy yields excellent results (see, for instance, Cook & Maree, 2016; Di Fabio & Maree, 2013a, 2013b; Maree, 2018a, 2018b, 2018c). Regarding the *CIP* as a dynamic instrument and updating it regularly through the years has enabled me to stay abreast of the latest developments in the world of work. By making many changes on a bi-yearly basis, repeated recontextualization and co-contextualization have been advanced consistently. To this end, the inputs of research participants, private clients, assessees, colleagues, and numerous other stakeholders from often widely different socioeconomic backgrounds are obtained and scrutinized whenever the instrument is updated. At a conceptual level, the ongoing research and publications of Savickas (2019a), Guichard (2018), and other colleagues working in the field of self- and career construction and life design are carefully considered to ensure that the *CIP*'s its content and language remain relevant despite ongoing changes in occupational and other contexts (Borchard, 1995). These colleagues' insights help me make timely changes to the wording of some questions and even reorganize the content in a few instances to reflect the *CIP*'s underlying paradigmatic and conceptual framework. Great care is taken to ensure that its value is not exaggerated and that the career counselor is not regarded as the sole expert whose "advice" (recommendations) should be accepted without questioning. This is (a) to prevent the "un-voicing" of assessees and (b) excluding them from the process of making key career choice decisions and denying them the opportunity to advise themselves regarding their own choices about a career, to enable and empower them instead of just helping them fit into certain careers "optimally" and labelling or categorizing them (Friedman, 2016; Savickas, 1993, 2004).

In conclusion: The *CIP* integrates qualitative and quantitative assessment approaches to advance people's reflections on their life stories as well as reflexivity and, consequently, narratability, and autobiographicity.

Chapter 9 discusses the development and implementation of the *MCM*.

References

Adler, A. (1929). *The science of living*. New York, NY: Greenberg.

Adler, A. (1933). *What life should mean to you*. Shropshire, England: Unwin Books.

Adler, A. (1958). *What life should mean to you*. New York, NY: Capricorn Books.

Adler, A. (1998). Understanding children with emotional problems. *The Journal of Humanistic Psychology, 38*(1), 121–127.

Arthur, N., Neault, R., & McMahon, M. (Eds.). (2019). *Career theories and models at work: Ideas for practice*. Toronto, ON: CERIC.

Borchard, D. C. (1995). Planning for career and life: Job surfing on the tidal waves of change. *The Futurist, 29,* 8–12.

Cardoso, P., Savickas, M. L., & Gonçalves, M. M. (2019). Career Construction Counseling: Proposal for an Integrative Model. *Career Development Quarterly, 67,* 188–204.

Cochran, L. R. (1997). *Career counseling: A narrative approach*. Pacific Grove, CA: Thousand Oaks.

Cook, A., & Maree, J. G. (2016). Efficacy of using career and self-construction to help learners manage career-related transitions. *South African Journal of Education, 36*(1), 1–11.

Crisp, T. (2002). *Dream dictionary*. New York, NY: Random House.

Di Fabio, A., & Maree, J. G. (2013a). Career counseling: The usefulness of the *Career Interest* Profile (*CIP*). *Journal for Psychology in Africa, 23*(1), 41–51.

Di Fabio, A., & Maree, J. G. (2013b). The effectiveness of the *Career Interest Profile* (*CIP*). *Journal of Employment Counseling, 50,* 110–123.

Du Toit, R., Prinsloo, W. B. J., Gevers, J., & Harilall, R. (1993). *Manual for the South African Vocational Interest Inventory (SAVII)*. Pretoria, South Africa: HSRC.

Friedman, T. L. (2016). *Thank you for being late: An optimist's guide to thriving in the age of accelerations*. New York, NY: Farrar, Straus, & Giraux.

Guichard, J. (2009). Self-constructing. *Journal of Vocational Behavior, 75,* 251–258.

Guichard, J. (2016). Reflexivity in life design interventions: Comments on life and career design dialogues. *Journal of Vocational Behavior, 97,* 78–83.

Guichard, J. (2018). Final purposes for life-and-career design interventions in the anthropocene era. In V. Cohen-Scali, L. Nota, & J. Rossier (Eds.), *New perspectives on career guidance and counseling in Europe. Building careers in changing and diverse societies* (pp. 189–204). New York, NY: Springer.

Hall, B. A., Halstead, M. E., & Taylor, T. R. (1986). *Test administrator's manual for the Rothwell-Miller Interest Blank*. Pretoria, South Africa: HSRC.

Hartung, P. J. (2010a). Career assessment: Using scores and stories in life designing. In J. G. Maree (Ed.), *Career counselling: Methods that work* (pp. 1–10). Cape Town, South Africa: Juta & Company Ltd.

Hartung, P. J. (2010b). Identifying life-career themes with the career story interview. In J. G. Maree (Ed.), *Career counselling: Techniques that work* (pp. 161–166). Cape Town, South Africa: Juta & Company Ltd.

Holland, J. L. (1985). *Making vocational choices: A theory of vocational personalities and work environments* (2nd ed.). Upper Saddle River, NJ: Prentice Hall.

Holland, J. L. (1997). *Making vocational choices: A theory of vocational personalities and work environments* (3rd ed.). Lutz, FL: Psychological Assessment Resources.

Jacaranda FM. (2015, February 27). *Die windpomp trailer*. Retrieved from https://www.youtube.com/watch?v=GC68LxWK9J4.

Jung, C. G. (1977). *Two essays on analytical psychology*. Princeton, NJ: Princeton University Press.

Justice, L. V, Convey, M., & Akthar. S. (2018). *What is your first memory – and did it ever really happen*? Retrieved from https://theconversation.com/what-is-your-first-memory-and-did-it-ever-really-happen-95953?utm_medium=email&utm_campaign=Latest%20from%E2%80%A6.

Krumboltz, J. D. (2003). Creating and capitalizing on happenstance in educational and vocational guidance. In R. Kunz, J. P. Dauwalder, & J. Renz (Eds.), *Quality development in vocational counselling and training* (pp. 30–32). Zürich, Switzerland: SVB.

Krumboltz, J. D. (1993). Integrating career and personal counseling. *The Career Development Quarterly, 42,* 143–148.

Krumboltz, J. D. (2015). The purpose of career counseling. *Career Convergence Magazine*, April, 3–4.

Kuder, G. F. (1977). *Activity interests and occupational choice*. Chicago, IL: Science Research Associates.

Maree, J. G. (1986). *Individual workbook for career guidance investigation*. Pretoria, South Africa: University of Pretoria.

Maree, J. G. (1996). *Individual workbook for career guidance investigation (Shortened version)*. Pretoria, South Africa: University of Pretoria.

Maree, J. G. (2005). The torn learning sprockets: Stars in the ascendant. *Gifted Education International, 20,* 380–390.

Maree, J. G. (2006). *The Career Interest Profile (Version 1)*. Randburg, South Africa: JvR Psychometrics.

Maree, J. G. (2008). *Career Interest Profile (Version 2)*. Randburg, South Africa: JvR Psychometrics.

Maree, J. G. (2009). Career counseling in the 21st century: South African institutions of higher education at the crossroads. *South African Journal of Higher Education, 23,* 429–435.

Maree, J. G. (2010a). Brief overview of the advancement of postmodern approaches to career counseling. *Journal of Psychology in Africa, 20,* 361–369.

Maree, J. G. (2010b). Using early memories in career-story interviewing. In J. G. Maree (Ed.), *Career counseling: Methods that work* (pp. 167–199). Cape Town, South Africa: Juta Academic.

Maree, J. G. (2010c). *The Career Interest Profile* (Version 3). Randburg, South Africa: JvR Psychometrics.

Maree, J. G. (2010d). Critical appraisal of the system of education and prospects of meeting the manpower and developmental needs of South Africa. *Africa Insight*, *40*, 85–108.

Maree, J. G. (2012). *Two DVD set: A guide to reflective career counselling – with Prof Maree*. Randburg, South Africa: JvR Psychometrics.

Maree, J. G. (2013). *Counseling for career construction: Connecting life themes to construct life portraits: Turning pain into hope*. Rotterdam, The Netherlands: Sense.

Maree, J. G. (2016). *Maree Career Matrix (MCM)*. Randburg, South Africa: JvR Psychometrics.

Maree, J. G. (2017a). *The Career Interest Profile (Version 6)*. Randburg, SA: JvR Psychometrics.

Maree, J. G. (2017b). *The Career Interest Profile (CIP) (version 6): Obtaining, qualitatively, a profile of personal career-life themes and interests*. Randburg: JvR Psychometrics.

Maree, J. G. (2017c). Life design counselling. In G. Stead & M. Watson (Eds.), *Career psychology* (3rd ed., pp. 105–118). Pretoria, South Africa: Van Schaik.

Maree, J. G. (2018a). Perspective: Promoting career development in the early years of people's lives through self- and career construction counselling to promote their career resilience and career adaptability. *Early Child Development and Care, 188*(4), 421–424. https://doi.org/10.1080/03004430.2018.1438748.

Maree, J. G. (2018b). Promoting career development and life design in the early years of a person's life. *Early Child Development and Care, 188*(4), 425–436. https://doi.org/10.1080/03004430.2017.1345892.

Maree, J. G. (2018c). Advancing career counselling research and practice using a new quantitative + qualitative approach to elicit clients' advice from within. *South African Journal of Higher Education, 32*(4), 149–170.

Maree, J. G. (2019a, June). *Career Development in Africa: Decent work for all: Brief photomontage.* Keynote Address at the Annual Career Development Practitioner Congress, Emperors Palace Conference Centre, Kempton Park, South Africa.

Maree, J. G. (2019b). Postmodernising career counseling in a deep rural context. In J. G. Maree (Ed.), *Handbook of innovative career counseling* (pp. 577–596). New York, NY: Springer.

Maree, J. G., & Beck, G. (2004). Using various approaches in career counselling for traditionally disadvantaged (and other) clients: Some limitations of a new frontier. *South African Journal of Education, 24*(1), 80–87.

Maree, J. G., & Sommerville, J. (2008). Development of a post-modern career interest questionnaire. *Journal of Psychology in Africa, 17,* 125–130.

Maree, J. G., & Taylor, N. (2016a). *Manual for the Maree Career Matrix (MCM).* Randburg, SA: JvR Psychometrics.

Maree, J. G., & Taylor, N. (2016b). Development of the *Maree Career Matrix*: A new interest inventory. *South African Journal of Psychology, 46*(4), 462–476. https://doi.org/10.1177/0081246316641558.

Miller, K. M. (1968). *Manual for the Rothwell-Miller Interest Blank.* Windsor, England: NFER.

Nash, R. (2018). *Are memories reliable? Expert explains how they change more than we realize.* Retrieved from https://theconversation.com/are-memories-reliable-expert-explains-how-they-change-more-than-we-realise-106461?utm_medium=email&utm_ca....

Neault, R., & Pickerell. (2019). Maximizing career engagement across a lifetime of transitions. In J. G. Maree (Ed.), *Handbook of innovative career counseling* (pp. 195–212). New York, NY: Springer.

Owen, K. (2000). *Manual for the Differential Aptitude Tests (SAT-L).* Pretoria, South Africa: HSRC.

Patterson-Mills, S. (2014). Ethics in a nutshell. *NCDA Career Developments, 30*(2), 24.

Ronald, V. (2014, May 11). Vince Gill: *Go rest high on that mountain.* Retrieved from https://www.youtube.com/watch?v=xA9M3MpFPQY.

Samson, J. (2017). *1001 South African songs you must hear.* Retrieved from https://1001sasongs.wordpress.com/2017/04/21/tulips-for-toinette-johnny-kongos-the-g-men/.

Savickas, M. L. (1989). Career-style assessment and counseling. In T. Sweeney (Ed.), *Adlerian counseling: A practical approach for a new decade* (3rd ed., pp. 289–320). Muncie, IN: Accelerated Development Press.

Savickas, M. L. (1993). Career counseling in the postmodern era. *Journal of Cognitive Psychotherapy: An International Quarterly, 7,* 205–215.

Savickas, M. L. (1998). Career style assessment and counseling. In T. Sweeney (Ed.), *Adlerian counseling: A practitioner's approach* (4th ed., pp. 329–359). Philadelphia, PA: Accelerated Development.

Savickas, M. L. (2004). Vocational psychology, overview. In C. Spielberger (Ed.), *Encyclopedia of applied psychology* (pp. 655–667). Amsterdam, the Netherlands: Elsevier.

Savickas, M. L. (2005). The theory and practice of career construction. In S. Brown & R. W. Lent (Eds.), *Career development and counseling: Putting theory and research to work* (pp. 42–70). New York, NY: John Wiley.

Savickas, M. L. (2011a). Reshaping the story of career counseling. In K. Maree (Ed.), *Shaping the story – a guide to facilitate narrative counseling* (pp. 1–3). Boston/Rotterdam, The Netherlands: Sense.

Savickas, M. L. (2011b). *Career counseling.* Washington, DC: American Psychological Association.

Savickas, M. L. (2011c). *Career counseling [DVD].* Washington, DC: American Psychological Association.
Savickas, M. L. (2015a). Career counseling paradigms: Guiding, developing, and designing. In P. Hartung, M. Savickas, & W. Walsh (Eds.), *The APA handbook of career intervention* (Vol. 1) (pp. 129-143). Washington, DC: APA Books.
Savickas, M. L. (2015b). *Life-design counseling manual.* Rootstown, OH: Author.
Savickas, M. L. (2016, July). *Meaning at work: Work at meaning.* Closing keynote presentation, National Career Development Association Conference, Chicago, United States of America.
Savickas, M. L. (2019). *Theories of psychotherapy series. Career counseling* (2nd ed.). Washington, DC: American Psychological Association.
Savickas, M. L., Nota, L., Rossier, J., & Dauwalder, J. P., Duarte, M. E., Guichard, J., ... Van Vianen, A. E. M. (2009). Life designing: A paradigm for career construction in the 21st century. *Journal of Vocational Behavior, 75,* 239-250.
Stead, G. B., & Watson, M. B. (1998). Career research in South Africa: Challenges for the future. *Journal of Vocational Behavior, 52*(3), 289–299. https://doi.org/10.1006/jvbe.19.
Stead, G. B., & Watson, M. B. (Eds.). (2017). *Career psychology in the South African context* (3rd ed.). Pretoria: Van Schaik Publishers.
Super, D. E. (1972). Vocational development theory: Persons, positions, processes. In J. M. Whiteley & A. Resnikoff (Eds.), *Perspectives on vocational development* (pp. 13–33). Washington, DC: American Personnel and Guidance Association.
Sweeney, T. J., & Myers, J. E. (1986). Early Recollections: An Adlerian technique with older people. *The Clinical Gerontologist, 4*(4), 3–12.
Taber, B. J., & Briddick, W. C. (2011). Adlerian based career counseling in the age of Protean Careers. *Journal of Individual Psychology, 67*(2), 107–121.
Vecchio, C. A. (2013). Happenstance. In M. L. Savickas (Ed.), *Ten ideas that changed career development* (p. 12). Broken Arrow, OK: NCDA.
Welty, E. (1998). *One writer's beginnings.* Cambridge, MA: Harvard University Press.
Winnicott, D. W. (1969). *The use of an object and relating through identifications in playing and reality.* London, England: Routledge.
Winnicott, D. W. (1987). *The maturational processes and the facilitating environment.* London, England: Hogarth Press.

Chapter 9
The Development and Implementation of the *MCM*

> *Choose a job you love, and you will never have to work a day in your life* (Confucius)

Abstract This chapter begins by discussing the continued use of test scores in career counseling in conjunction with people's "stories". It examines the value of drawing on self-estimates of interests and confidence about aptitude for certain careers. It stresses the importance of using a combination of factors to predict career success and elaborates on various factors in the development and standardization of the *MCM*. The conceptual framework of the instrument and some aspects of its psychometric properties are dealt with in the final section of the chapter.

9.1 Orientation

As stated earlier, in many parts of the world (in Global South contexts especially), the positivist ("test-and-tell") approach to career counseling still predominates in career counseling. This is largely because of the idiosyncratic way in which the economies of individual countries are structured, the lack of training for career counselors in contemporary assessment and intervention modes, and the belief among some career counseling practitioners that there is insufficient evidence to confirm the trustworthiness, reliability, and/or validity of contemporary approaches and interventions. That said, to survive in the new world of work, career counselors, need to become adaptable and flexible, think innovatively, and rise above negative and outdated discourses on career choice and execution. They need to

a. be aware of the past and use what worked well in the past;
b. stay grounded in the prevailing reality and use current insights and research findings to adapt and improve their practice; and
c. anticipate the future and design a style of career counseling that will equip themselves and their clients with the skills needed to succeed in a future that will bear increasingly less resemblance to the present.

J. G. (Kobus) Maree, *Innovating Counseling for Self- and Career Construction*,
https://doi.org/10.1007/978-3-030-48648-8_9

9.2 Using a Combination of Factors to Predict Career Success

Even in the 21st century, predicting accurately who will achieve success in their chosen careers and go on to design and live purposeful lives is extremely difficult (Pretorius & Morgan, 2010). An intricate combination of interrelated factors that include career interests, sense of self, self-efficacy, self-worth, and academic achievement can influence people's choice of, and achievement in, different study fields and careers (Patrick, Care, & Ainley, 2011). It is therefore necessary to investigate the influence of factors other than the self-reported results obtained through interest inventories on the ultimate choice of a career. Emotional stability, emotional-social intelligence, a mindset of recognizing and also creating opportunities as opposed to merely trying to solve problems, the capacity to postpone meeting short-term needs in favor of longer-term needs, perseverance, self-discipline, and related personality traits all contribute to successful self- and life construction (Guichard, 2009, 2013a, 2013b) or enactment (actualization) of potential (Maslow, 1987).

Next, I explain my reasons for obtaining people's self-estimates of interests and confidence about aptitude for certain careers.

9.2.1 Self-estimates of Interests and Confidence About Aptitude for Certain Careers

The *MCM*'s qualitative predecessor, the *CIP*, was designed first, after which the focus switched to the development of a quantitative instrument that could be used in conjunction with the narrative strategy. The *MCM* was developed against the background of

a. the belief that the results of all tests should be triangulated with the results of other inventories and with qualitative data obtained from a narrative or storied perspective especially, considering the numerous factors that co-determine success in the world of work, and
b. the demand for new, up-to-date interest questionnaires globally. More specifically, the *MCM* was designed against the backdrop of the following comment (Gottfredson, 2002).

> A reader familiar with Holland's developmental views who did not know that the following sentence was written by Bandura (1991), might guess that Holland wrote it: 'People's beliefs in their [self-] efficacy influence the choices they make, their aspirations, how much effort they mobilize in a given endeavor, how long they persevere in the face of difficulties and setbacks, whether their thought patterns are self-hindering or self-aiding, the amount of stress they experience in coping with taxing environmental demands' (p. 257).

My own research supports this comment (Maree & Taylor, 2016b). Most researchers agree that a healthy sense of self-efficacy contributes to people's career-life success (Rossier, 2015). There is also general agreement on the need to obtain an indication of people's measured (yielded by career interest inventories) and self-estimated (obtained qualitatively) interests as well as their (qualitatively) estimated career confidence levels for purposes of administering career counseling. This is because people's confidence (about whether they have the aptitude to be successful in a given career) helps them develop the competencies they need to succeed in given careers (Gottfredson, 2002; Holland, 1997). They participate in activities they believe they can execute successfully, which increases their interest in such activities. Conversely, people who believe they are deficient in the skills needed to achieve success in certain activities are likely to avoid such activities and, consequently, do not develop the competencies needed to succeed in the particular activities.

9.2.2 *Self-efficacy and Prediction of Career Success*

Self-efficacy, defined by Bandura (1986) as "people's judgements of their capabilities to organize and execute courses of action required to attain designated types of performances" (p. 391) refers not only to people's management and control of their thoughts, emotions, deeds, and their perceived capacity to achieve certain goals (Savickas, 1994) but also to their perception of their ability to perform certain kinds of actions proficiently. According to Bandura (1986, 1997), people's self-efficacy substantially influences what they do, their sense of who they are, their control over matters, and their self-agency. Swanson (2002) believes that a strong "sense of self-efficacy is an important contributor to the attainment of occupational success" (p. 522). He goes on to say that "[r]esearch suggests that a solid sense of self-efficacy is an integral factor in the attainment of further competencies and success" (p. 525). He also contends that people's observed self-efficacy can co-determine the acquisition of those essential cognitive, self-management, and interpersonal skills needed for a successful career and can therefore influence whether they will succeed in their chosen careers. After reviewing research on the topic, Hackett and Betz (1992, 1995) and Taylor and Betz (1983), too, concluded that career self-efficacy can indeed predict choice of field of study and career.

9.2.3 *Importance of Obtaining Self-estimates of Interests in Addition to Measured Interests*

Even though Athanasou and Cooksey (1993) maintain that terms such as "stated interests", "self-evaluations", "professed interests", and "expressed interests" correlate positively with the term "self-estimates", for the purposes of this book, I will use the term "self-estimates" only. Athanasou and Cooksey (1993) have demonstrated that assessees are very capable of providing accurate estimates of their interests. Moreover, these estimates are mostly consistent with their measured scores on standardized interest inventories. These authors accordingly stress the importance of evaluating the outcomes of interest inventories against the outcomes of self-estimates of interest. They agree with Mischel (1977, p. 248) that "what the person tells us directly turns out to be as valuable an index as any other indirect sign" and Burisch (1984), who cautions people against the use of "unreliable" inventories and questionnaires. Hansen (2005), Hirschi, and Läge (2008) and Zytowski (1999), too, propose that assessees should be invited to predict their interest inventory scores to determine the degree and direction of the correlation between predicted and measured scores. The two sets of outcomes or scores should subsequently be compared, after which similarities and differences should be examined and clarified by career counselors and assessees. This examination should provide an indication of assessees' grasp of their authentic interests. Healy and Mourton (1984) also found that self-estimates of career interests accurately predict assessees' career choice readiness. Based on their research, Hirschi and Läge (2008) argue that asking assessees to self-estimate their interest types before revealing their measured scores can help career counselors talk to them more meaningfully about the outcomes of assessments.

The next section focuses on the link between people's abilities, self-estimates of abilities, and career choice.

9.2.4 Abilities, Self-estimates of Abilities, and Career Choice

Predictive value of IQ, abilities, and competencies. Intelligence tests (which are, in essence, little more than achievement tests) (Van Eeden, 1991) and aptitude tests more likely indicate what people have already learnt than predict what they can learn. Without denying the value of intelligence and aptitude tests as a means of establishing a person's ability, it should be kept in mind that behavior is influenced by numerous factors. The result of any IQ or aptitude test is largely dependent on what someone has already learnt through formal life experiences, the intellectual skills gained through good education, and a background conducive to attaining those skills measurable by IQ and aptitude tests. Gati (2013) and Prediger (1999) express their reservations about "standard" practice in career counseling, namely that assessed abilities are often considered a predictive factor in the career counseling process. They contend that formal and informal self-estimates of ability can be particularly useful, especially when combined with the results of objective tests and/or school marks. These self-estimates can shed light on many factors such as under- or overestimation of ability (Ryan-Krane & Tirre, 2005).

Gati and Asher (2001a, 2001b) and Gottfredson (2005) also refer to Prediger (1999) who found that self-estimates of abilities can be as valid as the results of ability assessments. Prediger (1999) argues that aptitude tests cannot measure more than six actual abilities and therefore recommends the use of self-reports of perceived abilities in addition to the actual results of aptitude tests during career counseling. He adds that assessees' self-estimates of their ability can yield more useful information on predicting educational and career accomplishment than traditional measures of ability.

Correlations between occupational preferences and aspirations and choice of a successful career. Holland, Gottfredson, and Baker (1990) contend that career predictive effectiveness can be greatly improved by (a) asking assesses for two or more occupational aspirations, and (b) using aspiration and interest questionnaires concurrently. Levin and Gati (2014) emphasize the usefulness of including assessment of a person's career preferences in career counseling rather than basing the recommendation of possible careers on a "holistic" list of careers. Miller, Springer, Tobacyk, and Wells (2004) maintain that "career counselors should at least consider asking clients about their occupational daydreams early in the counseling process" (p. 59).

Research by Holland and Gottfredson (1975) indicates that people's current career aspirations are significantly linked to their previous career aspirations: "In nearly every instance [of our research], vocational aspirations were at least as efficient as inventory scales and were often substantially more efficient" (p. 359). Porfeli, Lee, and Vondracek (2013) argue that career aspirations become increasingly more stable as children advance into adolescence and adulthood.

The comparative value of perceived and measured aptitude in predicting success in a career is discussed below.

The predictive value of self-estimates of career and aptitude (confidence about aptitude). Gottfredson (2002) maintains that sufficient evidence exists to demonstrate the predictive value of categorized aspirations and self-estimates in addition to measured interests (using a standardized questionnaire) and that self-estimates or self-ratings can be construed as (Holland)-type-specific self-efficacy expectations. Gati, Fishman-Nadav, and Shiloh (2006) established positive correlations between people's measured abilities, their self-estimates of abilities, and their preferences for using their measured abilities in their future careers. The lowest correlation they found was between measured abilities and career preferences. Betz and Hackett (1986) and Lent and Hackett (1987) contend that self-estimates of abilities impact a wide variety of career choice actions, the degree of interest shown in careers, and, especially, the actual careers that are chosen and engaged in. Campbell, Hyne, and Nilson (1992, p. 39), too, assert that "self-perceptions about skills—that is, an individual's beliefs about how well he or she can perform different occupational activities–already play an important role in career choices". My own research over two decades (Maree, 2005, 2012a, 2012b, 2014) supports these views as well as the view that people's self-concept co-determines what careers they will be interested in. I also concur with Campbell, Hyne, and Nilson's (1992) view that test-takers' own informal assessment of their skill or confidence mostly indicates satisfactorily their actual skill in a given area.

Gati, Fishman-Nadav, and Shiloh (2006) highlight three aspects of abilities that appear to be related to career decision-making and career counseling, namely measured abilities, self-estimations of abilities, and readiness and willingness to use abilities. They list a number of leading theorists and practitioners who stress the importance of reflecting on people's perceptions of their abilities (to be successful in certain careers) in the career counseling situation.

The theories underpinning the conceptual framework of the *MCM* are discussed next.

9.3 Theoretical and Conceptual Framework of the *MCM*

Figure 9.1 shows the theoretical and conceptual framework of the *MCM*. The three theories referred to in this figure are discussed below.

The *MCM*'s theoretical and conceptual framework blends three theories proposed by Osipow (1990), Osipow and Fitzgerald (1996), and elaborated on by Ackerman and Beier (2003). More specifically, the *MCM* extends and implements Holland's interest theory and model with links to (a) trait-and-factor theory, (b) developmental theory, and (c) the social learning theory (and its application to career decision making) within social cognitive career theory) (Lent, Brown, & Hackett, 1994) framework (informed by Bandura's (1986) views on self-efficacy).

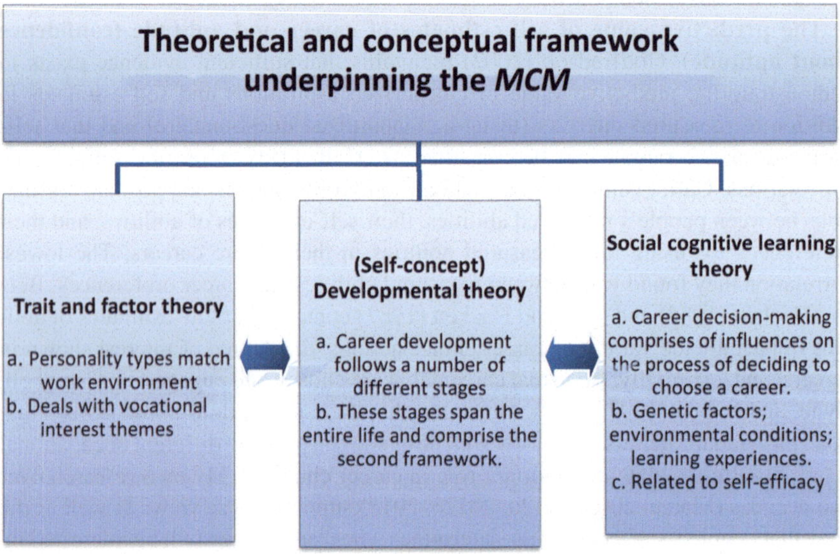

Fig. 9.1 Theoretical and conceptual framework underpinning the *MCM*

9.3.1 Trait and Factor Theory

The first theoretical framework, namely the psychology of occupations (Holland, 1997; Hartung, 2013a, 2013b; Parsons, 1909), comprises trait and factor approaches. This framework reflects Holland's (1985, 1997) theory by dealing with vocational interest themes and implying that personality types match work environments. It also reflects Dawis and Lofquist's (1984) theory of work adjustment.

9.3.2 (Self-concept) Developmental Theory

In terms of the (self-concept) developmental theoretical framework (also referred to as the psychology of careers, cf. Hartung, 2013a, 2013b; Super, 1980), a number of different stages spanning people's lives constitute career development. These stages constitute the second framework, which reflects Super's (1963, 1972, 1990) life span, life-space theory (formerly referred to as his career development theory and then as his developmental self-concept theory). Super (1963) identified five consecutive career development stages, namely growth (birth to 14 years), exploration (15–24 years), establishment (25–44 years), maintenance (45–64 years), and decline (65-).[1] Super (1963, 1990) stresses the significance of people's personality (including their self-concept), interests, abilities, and career choice as extensions of their self-concept. Maddux (1995) defines self-concept as the totality of people's beliefs about themselves, and self-esteem as the totality of their appraisal of these beliefs. People's self-concept, in particular, is emphasized inasmuch as it is woven into their interests (or career preferences) and abilities (or career competencies) (Osipow, 1983). Holland and Gottfredson (1975, p. 361) maintain that "[v]ocational choices involve an implementation of one's self-concept". Holland (1997) adds that the degree of congruence between people's personalities and their work environment will determine their career satisfaction, stability, and achievement.

9.3.3 Social-Cognitive Learning Theory

The third encompassing theoretical framework is based on theories of social learning, including those of Krumboltz (1993) and Krumboltz, Mitchell, and Jones (1976). These influences include genetic factors, the environmental conditions in which people live, and also their learning experiences. Social-cognitive learning theory has close links with notions of self-efficacy (Bandura, 1986, 1991, 1997; Hackett & Betz, 1992; Lent, Brown, & Hackett, 1994) and work volition. Self-efficacy differs from, for instance, sense of self, self-esteem, and self-concept in that it relates to

[1] I believe that these stages and the time frames associated with each reflect an outdated view on career development. However, an elaboration on the matter falls outside the scope of this book.

a particular assignment or task (Tschannen-Moran, Woolfolk Hoy, & Hoy, 1998). It can be defined as people's unique beliefs regarding the degree to which they can control events that influence them and shape their lives. Put differently: Self-efficacy can be described as "future orientation" (Swanson, 2002) as it deals with the degree of competence people expect they will demonstrate in given situations. It also relates to the control people exercise over their thoughts, emotions, actions, and accomplishments, and their perceived ability to achieve certain goals (Savickas, 1994). Darcy and Tracey (2003) contend that self-efficacy includes people's estimation of their capacity to execute a certain kind of behavior effectively. Work volition (Blustein, 2006), on the other hand, is defined as people's belief that they can make career-related decisions without restrictions despite the existence of possible constraints (Duffy, Bott, Torrey, & Webster, 2013; Duffy, Diemer, Perry, Laurenzi, & Torrey, 2012). Both self-efficacy and work volition are shaped by social learning (Duffy et al., 2012; Duffy, Diemer, & Jadidian, 2012; Savickas, 2013).

Given its significance in the *MCM*, I will now elaborate on Holland's theory and model of career choice by first discussing career stereotypes or typecasts, which form the basis of Holland's (1985, 1997) person(-ality) (interests)-work environment (world of work) hexagon.

9.3.4 Career Stereotypes

Holland's (1985, 1997) career choice theory and accompanying model of occupational (vocational) choices and work environments in terms of personality types is essentially a personality theory that holds that personality types match work environments (Savickas, 1994) and that people's personalities can consequently be classified in terms of a hexagonal model that also represents occupational environments.[2] Holland (1985, 1997) argues that the world of interests, but also the world of careers, can be described as comprising six interest categories: Realistic (R), Investigative (I), Artistic (A), Social (S), Enterprising (E), and Conventional (C). This model supports Hall, Halstead, and Taylor's (1986, p. 1) view that "in most cultures generally accepted ideas are held regarding the activities, responsibilities and the role of a particular job". Furthermore, people base their career choices on these stereotypes, irrespective of whether they are truthful or inaccurate.[3]

Kuder (1977) and Low, Mijung, Roberts, and Rounds (2005), too, argue that an "optimal fit" is sought between people's personality profiles in terms of their preferences expressed in their responses to questions about career stereotypes. Kuder worked from the premise that there are 10 distinguishable stereotype career interest categories: Artistic, Clerical, Computational, Literary, Mechanical, Musical,

---

[2]The word "stereotype" may have a negative connotation for some people. It is used in this book as it is commonly used by authors in this context.

[3]It should be noted that Holland neither suggested that there are only (these) six types of people in the world, nor that any given person fits into only one of the six types (Swanson, 2002).

Outdoor, Persuasive, and Scientific, and Social services. He differentiated more finely between interest categories by expanding Holland's typology in the following manner: Realistic was separated into Outdoor and Mechanical preferences; Artistic was separated into Artistic, Literary, and Musical preferences; and Conventional was separated into Clerical and Computational preferences. Rothwell and Miller (Miller, 1968), designers of the *RMIB*, in turn, worked from the premise that 12 stereotypical career preferences could be identified: Computational, Esthetical, Clerical, Literary, Mechanical, Medical, Musical, Outdoor, Persuasive, Practical, Scientific, and Social service. Prediger (1982) proposed that Holland's sixfold set of interest "themes" could be condensed into only two encompassing dimensions, namely (a) things and ideas, and (b) data and people. I, too, believe that people's configuration of interests can be split into a number of different (often overlapping) career categories.

Hall, Halstead, and Taylor (1986) and Miller (1968) list the following three assumptions that underpin a number of widely used career inventories, including questionnaires based on the Holland model (e.g. the *Self-Directed Search* (*SDS*) (Gevers, Du Toit, & Harilall, 1997), the *South African Vocational Interest Inventory* (*SAVII*) (Du Toit, 1992), the *Rothwell-Miller Interest Blank* (*RMIB*) (used with the *MCM* to determine concurrent validity), and questionnaires based on the Kuder model (Kuder, 1977).

a. Careers, occupations, and jobs can be classified into an arbitrary number of stereotypical, generally accepted work environments or work categories on the basis of factors such as people's perceptions of work roles, job demands, work characteristics, and types of activities in those categories.
b. These stereotypical career categories correspond positively with people's interest fields and preferences. In other words, work environments match personality types.
c. People's responses to questions about stereotypical, generally accepted work environments or work categories yield important information about their interests in or preferences for these stereotypes.

Holland's theory and model of career choice is touched on below, after which the number of fields in the *MCM* is discussed.

9.3.5 Holland's Theory and Model of Career Choice

Holland (1997) maintains that consistency is sought between vocational environments and interest fields. A relationship exists between career categories in the sense that adjacent career categories (e.g. Enterprising and Clerical) are similar, categories separated by another category (e.g. Investigative and Social) are fairly similar, and opposite categories (e.g. Realistic and Clerical) are dissimilar. According to Holland's theory and model, behavior(al) style or personality type is the predominant factor influencing career choice development (Holland, 1985, 1997; Savickas, 1994).

9.3.6 Why 19 Career Categories?

As mentioned earlier, I, like many researchers and practitioners before me, believe that a person's configuration of interests can be split up into a number of different and yet often overlapping career categories. I therefore tried out various options—10, 12, 15, 16, and 19 categories—because most occupations encompass more than one interest category. Whereas it would have been much easier to work with a smaller number of career categories, I eventually decided on 19 categories, which can all be regarded as subfields of the sixfold Holland (1997) RIASEC hexagon. Below, I explain my reasons for working with 19 career categories.[4]

First, over the past few decades, fundamental changes have taken place in the world of work. Today, old careers disappear as quickly as new careers appear. A glance at career interest inventories currently in use globally reveals radical changes in the stereotypical view of careers. The categories proposed by Holland (1973) (six), Kuder (1975) (10), and Miller (1968) (12) do not satisfactorily reflect careers such as those in the evolving field of information communication technology (ICT), the field of sport, and the hospitality, travel, and tourism industry. I agree with Campbell, Hyne, and Nilson (1992) (developers of the *Campbell Interest and Skill Survey* (*CISS*)), who proposed a larger number of refined "pairs of basic scales" (p. 85) (in essence, subscales of their sevenfold orientation scale), and Du Toit et al. (1993), who proposed 18 subfields of Holland's (1973, 1997) model, that it is useful to refine broader categories or orientations into a larger number of subcategories.

Second, career counselors and their clients repeatedly say that job analysis is extremely difficult if too many different careers are associated with only a few, overly broad, encompassing career categories. I wanted to design an inventory that would help career counselors guide clients in analyzing careers in a well-structured manner.

Third, I was aware that some people might think that working in this way would create the impression that the career counselor was acting as the sole "expert" on the client, but nothing could be further from the truth. In this book, I explain the importance of implementing an integrative strategy during career counseling and contend that listing a number of careers for analysis is a useful starting point for conducting thorough job analysis, which introduces people to the much wider world of careers on offer.

9.4 Developing the *MCM*

It should be clear from what has been written above that people's sense of self, their self-efficacy and self-worth, their career identity, and their self-estimates of their career interests and confidence in their aptitude for certain careers are crucial in

[4]There is a strong overlap between these 19 career categories and Holland's RIASEC model. For more details, see Ferreira and Morgan (2019) and Maree (2016).

predicting career choice as well as success. It is against this background that I decided in 2002 to design an interest questionnaire that could be used to determine people's articulated career interests in addition to their self-estimates of their confidence in their ability to succeed in given careers. No other African-developed questionnaire was available at the time. However, my primary goal was to design a "quantitative" version of the *CIP* (which was into its 17th year of development at that stage) to promote triangulation in career counseling in African contexts.

9.5 Rationale for the Development of the *Maree Career Matrix (MCM)*

Many authors have criticized the continued use of career counseling theoretical models and interventions developed in Global North (North American and European) as well as in Global South (developing) countries. Consequently, there have been repeated calls for research on the development of approaches that are more compatible with conditions in these latter countries (Lopez, Levers, May, & Vogel, 2011). Cultural, educational, and socioeconomic factors need also to be considered to ensure that career counseling is useful and relevant in these countries (Alika & Egbochuku, 2009; Metz & Guichard, 2009). It is disconcerting that only a small number of psychometric tests have been designed for diverse developing contexts (Maree, 2013a). While I believe that some models, strategies, questionnaires, and tests developed in North American and European contexts can be adapted, standardized, and successfully implemented in third world (developing country) contexts, I believe also that research should simultaneously be conducted on the design, development, and production of local models, strategies, interventions, questionnaires, and tests. The design, development, and standardization of the *MCM* was therefore based on the view that it was better to construct updated interest-related questionnaires in developing countries (South Africa in particular) than to uncritically accept questionnaires developed elsewhere in the world. My aim was consistent with the sentiments expressed by the Health Professions Council of South Africa:

> The history of development and use of psychometric measuring devices, instruments, methods and techniques in South Africa has been tainted by the legacy of segregation which influenced certain stereotypical attitudes and culturally insensitive and inappropriate interventions. As a result, very few tests are available that have been developed and applied with the necessary appreciation of cultural and other diversity concerns with a view to standardizing same for all South Africans (HPCSA, 2010, p. 1).

I also agree with Oakland (2004) that test design and development should form part of countries' broader socioeconomic aims. Maree (2013a) argues that South Africa (and, indeed, all developing countries) needs an indigenous theory base for and approach to test design and development. South African psychologists[5] should

[5]The term "psychologist" is used to refer to psychologists, registered counselors, and psychometrists alike and is used interchangeably with the term "career counselor".

consider whether the tests they use, and also their assessment-related activities in general, help prepare their clients for changing global contexts. The feasibilities of the 21st century labor market economics should co-determine assessment strategies while theory development should be based on career-related concepts such as internationalization, globalization, diversification of the workforce, labor shortages and surpluses, continuous or lifelong training, multiskilling, and Work 4.0 demands (such as the acquisition of information communication technology skills and robotization) (Maree, 2009; 2019a, 2019b).

All the above highlights the need for the development of innovative approaches to career counseling and career choice decisions (Amundson, Niles, & Harris-Bowlsbey, 2004; Hartung, 2018, 2019; Sharf, 2013; Savickas, 2019a, 2019b). Career counseling has to meet the unique needs of individual people across the diversity spectrum while also catering for the needs of large groups of people. Savickas (1993) reminds us that counseling approaches should "fit the spirit of the age, if clients are to accept them as useful" (p. 207).

9.5.1 Aim of the MCM

Developed in South Africa, the *Maree Career Matrix* (*MCM*) is a measure of (a) career interests and (b) self-estimates of confidence about aptitude to follow certain careers. The research project of which the *MCM* forms part was initiated in response to the global shift towards acceptance of the importance of incorporating qualitative assessment strategies and techniques during career counseling. However, it was also an attempt to respond to the local need for career counseling for the vast majority of the population who currently do not have access to any career counseling whatsoever. The *MCM* is thus a response to calls for contextualizing and indigenizing approaches developed in Global North countries in Global South countries. It also forms part of ongoing research aimed at devising brief, narrative strategies to administer career counseling that will entail integrating qualitative and quantitative assessment strategies and techniques to help people realize that they are the architects of their own lives and the authors of their own career-life stories.

As mentioned earlier, career counselors should make use of counseling techniques that include a perusal and analysis of autobiographies and carefully assembled and intelligible meanings in conjunction with the interpretation of questionnaire/inventory results or tests that assess various facets of personality such as aptitude and interest.

9.5.2 How Were the Different Careers Selected?

During the development of the questionnaire and, more specifically, when it was decided which careers should be included in the different career categories, consideration was given to various factors (see below). Extensive research has revealed a paucity of reliable information on which careers are mainly followed by the various cultural groups in (South) Africa (Maree & Molepo, 2007, 2016). However, it was always my intention to assess "new" careers as well as those already represented across the population. Video/Animation games developer, Robotics engineer, Brand manager, and Computer systems analyst, for example, were included in the questionnaire. They are not common careers for members of the majority of cultural groups in South Africa (this can be verified by contacting the various professional bodies), but this does not mean that all learners should not be introduced to such careers. I also included descriptions of all the careers listed in the *MCM* so that the assessees could know what each of the careers entailed.

9.5.3 Self-reporting Interest Levels and Skills (or Confidence) Levels

Self-reporting interest levels. The *MCM* statements concern assessees' feelings and views regarding 152 different careers. They are requested to assess these careers according to how they feel about them. They are first asked to rate the extent to which they believe they are interested in each of these careers, irrespective of whether they believe they have the capacity to execute the kind of work required in these careers successfully. They have to use the following three-point Likert rating scale.

2 = I am definitely interested in this career
1 = I am unsure (maybe interested)
0 = I am definitely not interested in this career

Self-Reporting Skills (or Confidence) Levels. Assessees are then requested to specify how confident they feel that they will be able to do the work required by each different career. Put differently: They are asked to indicate how sure they believe they are that they have adequate aptitude to execute a particular career successfully. They are reminded to disregard the matter of whether they are actually interested in doing the kind of work required by a particular career and to indicate only their confidence about being able to do the work required by that career successfully. They have to use the following rating scale.

2 = I will definitely be able to do the work
1 = I am unsure (perhaps)
0 = I will definitely not be able to do the work

All test-takers should be given copies of the list of career definitions, and most of them should be able to complete the questionnaire within 25–35 min.

Scoring the Questionnaire. The questionnaire can either be completed in hard copy format and hand-scored or completed (and scored electronically) online. (As already mentioned, both the *MCM* and the *CIP* are available online as well, and lengthy reports are written on completion of the instruments. The reports are structured to facilitate individual as well as group administration, interpretation, and integration of outcomes along the lines recommended in Sect. 10.3).

9.6 Plotting the Final Scores on the Career Matrix

Assessees' final scores are plotted (see Fig. 9.2) on the career matrix using the letters **A - S**. Scores are plotted in one of four quadrants and give test-takers an informative career interests and confidence map divided into four areas:

1. "Go for it!"
2. "Upskill yourself".
3. "Use it, don't lose it".
4. "Bottom of the pile".

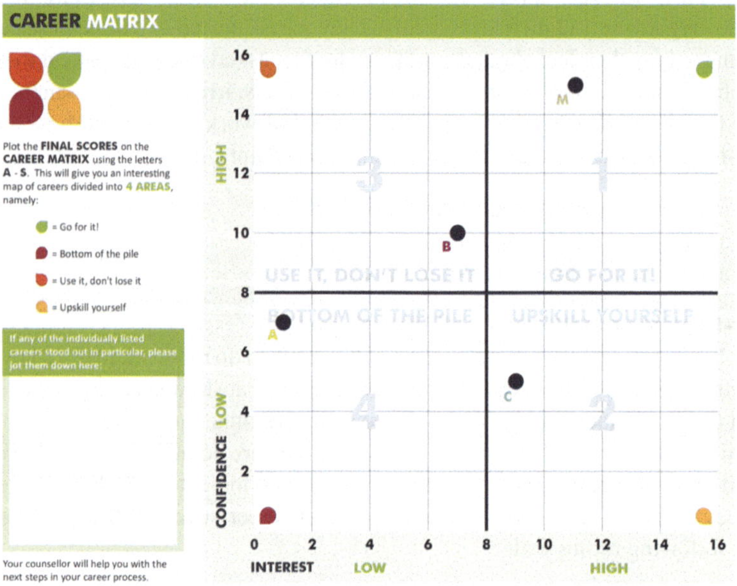

Fig. 9.2 Plotting the *MCM* scores

See the example (plotted scores in the matrix) below: The assessee achieves the following raw scores: Category 1 (Practical-technical) (A): Interest: 1, Confidence: 7; Category 2 (B) (Practical-creative): Interest: 7, Confidence: 10; Category 3 (C) (Musical): Interest: 9, Confidence: 5; Category 13 (M) (Sport): Interest: 11, Confidence: 15. The four scores (A, B, C, and M) are plotted on the matrix below.

(Stanines (standardized scores) are available and can, of course, also be used to create the career matrix. However, personally, I prefer to use raw scores because postmodern counseling is far more interested in examining assessees' idiosyncratic stories and scores than in comparing their scores and stories with those of others.)

9.6.1 Prerequisites for Administering the MCM

All psychologists, registered counselors, and psychometrists may administer and interpret the *MCM* without additional training. However, test administrators should self-administer the questionnaire before administering it to assessees.

9.6.2 Using and Interpreting the MCM

i Ideally, feedback on the *MCM* results should be given on a one-to-one basis.

ii Results should always be interpreted against the background of the "presenting problem" (the reason why assessment was sought).

iii Feedback could be given in a single session, but outcomes should be linked to a longer-term change (development) strategy.

iv Assessees should be followed up to trace their progress and the success of the intervention.

v When interpreting the *MCM* for an individual assessee, the profile should never be interpreted either in isolation or as an "absolute" measurement. The results should be integrated with the results obtained from other data sources, that is, other questionnaires and qualitative data sources (see below). Given the movement towards general acceptance of an integrated approach to career counseling globally, career construction counseling principles should be considered during career counseling.

vi The *MCM* should always be used as part of a broader strategy to counsel assessees. The data should always be interpreted in the context of assessees' total functioning and should be related to other data about them. Such other data include salient information on their early development, and information provided by family members, teachers, and friends. Other questionnaire information can include their personality, aptitudes, intelligence, emotional-social intelligence, (career) adaptability, academic achievement, and understanding of the language in which the questionnaire was administered.

vii Clear preferences and confidence levels as well as low preferences and confidence levels should be interpreted carefully as idiosyncratic interest and confidence configurations can have a powerful effect on the interpretation of a specific assessee's profile and his or her eventual career decisions. While some assessees may have many strong (or weak) preferences and confidence levels, others may have only a few.

viii Noticeable differences between self-estimates of interest and self-estimates of confidence levels should be attended to carefully. All instances where these differences exceed four points should be clarified in order to determine assessees' reasons for the differences.

ix Assessees should be asked to estimate and rank their five to seven most preferred career choices and also their five to seven least preferred career choices from the list of 19 career categories before their scores are revealed. Focusing on similarities and differences between the test outcomes and assessees' own estimates of interests and confidence can help career counselors facilitate discussions on assessees' results.

9.6.3 Interpreting the Interest and Confidence Scores

A clear distinction should be drawn between interest and confidence scores. Clear or high interest scores indicate strong interests in given categories, and clear or high confidence scores indicate assessees' strong belief that they are capable of successfully executing careers listed in or related to those career categories. Likewise, low interest scores indicate weak interests in given categories, and low confidence scores indicate assessees' belief that they are not capable of successfully executing careers listed in or related to those career categories. I recommend the use of the following guidelines to distinguish between interest and confidence scores (when considered separately).

Stanine scores between 7 and 9 should be considered high.

Stanine scores between 4 and 6 should be considered average.

Stanine scores between 1 and 3 should be considered low.

The following two, broad integrated interest and confidence response categories can be identified.

i Well-differentiated response sets (see Fig. 9.3). These assessees display clearly differentiated interest and confidence profiles with a fair distribution of high, average, and low interest and confidence levels across Quadrants 1, 2, 3, and 4. Assessees with well-differentiated profiles are typically sure about what they want to and can do, have a healthy sense of self-efficacy and sense of self, and should have less difficulty in choosing appropriate fields of study and careers.

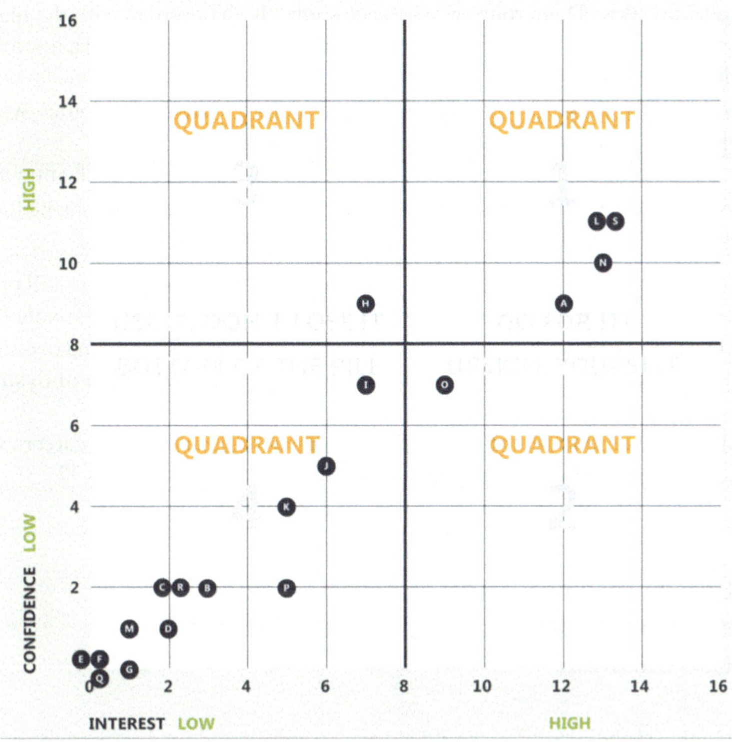

Fig. 9.3 Well-differentiated profile

ii Undifferentiated response sets. These assessees show little differentiation between scores, which are clustered together. Assessees with undifferentiated profiles are often unsure about what they want to do, have a weak self-concept and/or sense of self and may experience trouble in choosing appropriate fields of study and careers. They frequently have inadequate exposure to the world of careers, are depressed, or did not understand what most of the careers entailed.

My own research has revealed that practitioners will very rarely come across this kind of profile.

9.7 Interpreting the Career Matrix

The following three broad types of interest and confidence profiles can be distinguished.

i "High" profiles: This group of assessees show "high" profiles with the majority of scores high or relatively high (located mainly in Quadrant 1) and a few average and/or low scores.
ii "Average" profiles: This group of assessees show "average" profiles with the majority of scores average, some high and some low.
iii "Low" profiles: These assessees show overall "low" profiles with the majority of scores being low or relatively low and a few relatively high. Even in such cases, assessees often feel quite sure about what they want to do.

It should be noted that overall "high", "average", or "low" profiles can still provide career counselors with useful information on individual assessees' relatively higher and lower scores or their idiosyncratic strongest and weakest interests and confidence. It should also be noted that "low" profiles can also give an indication of dysthymia or depression.

Lastly: it is useful to return to the *MCM* items and focus on those careers where the assessees rated either or both their interest and their confidence as '2'.

9.8 Importance of Identifying Highest Interest and Confidence Scores Irrespective of Profile Classification

Overall highest relative scores should always be considered for career analysis. In all instances, irrespective of whether assessees have clear preferences and confidence levels as well as low preferences and confidence levels or not, it remains important to identify their five, six, or seven combined "most relevant" interest and confidence scores.

Scores in the four quadrants should be interpreted as follows (examples of scores that fall predominantly in each quadrant appear below the discussion of each of the four categories):

1. "Go for it!" (Fig. 9.4). Scores in this quadrant indicate strong or definite, clearly defined levels of interests and confidence (i.e. assessees believe that they will succeed in corresponding career categories). Corresponding career categories should be considered for job analysis by assessees with a view to possibly pursuing careers associated with these categories.
2. "Upskill yourself". Scores in this quadrant indicate high interests in specific fields and equivalent low(er) confidence levels. Assessees need to establish why they believe they do not have the capabilities or competencies needed to succeed in the career categories they definitely prefer. They should carefully consider possible reasons for not believing that they will succeed in these careers. They may have been negatively influenced by people who led them to believe they could not succeed in these careers without really knowing them (the assessees) well enough to draw this conclusion. They should also consider (for instance)

Fig. 9.4 Most scores falling in the "Go for it!" quadrant (1)

their school marks, the results of personality (including aptitude) tests, and entrance requirements for corresponding career categories and talk to people already studying or working in these fields to find out more about these categories. Where possible, they should improve their skills levels in this quadrant by developing these competencies. It is easier to develop a skill than an interest. Here, too, my own research has revealed that practitioners will very rarely come across this kind of profile.

3. "Use it, don't lose it". Scores in this quadrant indicate high confidence levels in certain fields and corresponding low(er) interest levels. Assessees should be advised to find out why they are not interested in these fields despite believing that they possess the competencies needed to succeed in the career categories indicated. They should be advised to investigate related careers (through thorough job analysis) to determine if their negative feelings about these careers are perhaps caused by matters that have little to do with the actual careers. This may include a dislike for teachers teaching certain subjects or incorrect information about these careers. Or, they may simply not know enough about the careers to take an interest in them. They may also be negatively influenced by typecasts or

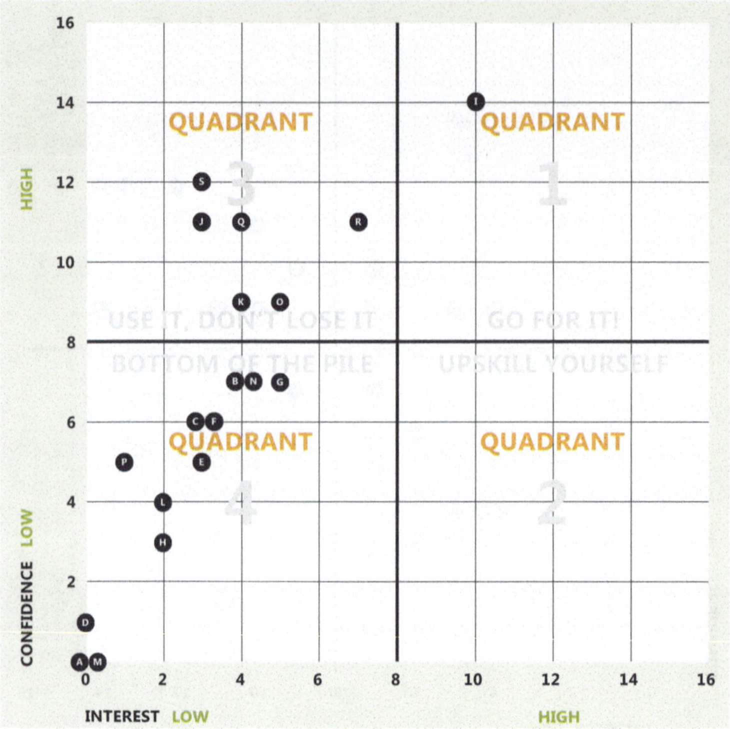

Fig. 9.5 Most scores fall in either the "Use it, don't lose it" quadrant (3) or the "Bottom of the pile" quadrant (4)

stereotypes (general ideas held by people about certain careers). Where possible, they should use their skills in areas that interest them more (Fig. 9.5).

4. "Bottom of the pile". Scores in this quadrant indicate low interest and confidence levels. Assessees are free to disregard these career categories, which is often a relief for them. Some people find it easier to identify what they do not want rather than what they do want. In this way, they can, through a process of elimination, get closer to what they do want. However, some assessees consistently display low interest and confidence profiles, in which case the categories in which they achieved the relative highest scores should be investigated.

Even though this is an exceptionally low profile, the combined highest interest and confidence scores are clear.

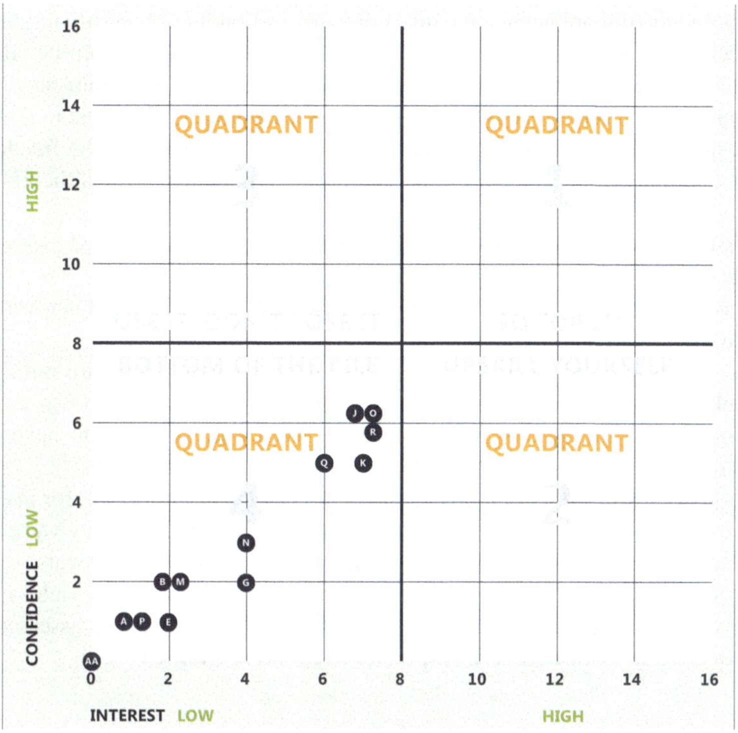

Fig. 9.6 Extremely low profile (all scores fall in the "Bottom of the pile" quadrant (4))

9.9 Important General Comment

In all instances, irrespective of whether assessees have clear preferences and confidence levels as well as low preferences and confidence levels or not, it remains key to identify assessees' five, six, or seven combined "most relevant" interest and confidence scores. **Even if all the combined interest and confidence categories profiles fall in the "Bottom of the pile" quadrant** (see, for instance, Fig. 9.6), the five to seven categories in which they achieved the relative highest scores should be identified and further investigated.

9.10 Diagnosing Profiles

On completing the *MCM*, assessees should be placed in an environment where they can openly discuss their experience of the questionnaire. They should then be asked to explain their reasons for their explicit preferences or confidence levels or lack thereof. These reasons may include:

i. Those who did not answer the questionnaire accurately or honestly might have been trying to compensate for real or imagined deficiencies in their personality or behavior and/or presented themselves differently from whom they really were. Even though it is unlikely that assessees would be dishonest in this kind of questionnaire, some might have felt that they did not have the freedom to give honest answers if, for instance, their preferences and those of their parents clashed.
ii. Assessees from impoverished backgrounds might have had limited exposure to the world of work.
iii. Assessees who felt depressed or were emotionally unstable might inadvertently have provided inaccurate information.
iv. Assessees who did not understand the language of the questionnaire sufficiently well might not have expressed themselves appropriately.
v. Assessees who did not know themselves sufficiently well might have given unreliable answers.
vi. Assessees who were not motivated to complete the questionnaire, for instance, those who did not want to be assessed and who believed that they were being assessed against their will might may not have given reliable answers.
vii. Assessees who believed (incorrectly) that higher scores would yield a more favorable impression of themselves. This is one of the reasons assessees are requested to **limit their 2-2 responses to no more than 20**.

9.11 Job Analysis as a Key Goal of Career Counseling Intervention

I agree with Krumboltz's (2015, p. 3) sentiments:

> I no longer think that making a career decision is the goal. Instead the goal should be to launch the client on an exploratory task of talking with lots of people, helping other people with whatever tasks they faced at the moment, reading interesting articles about future occupational trends, applying to whatever jobs happen to be open now, interviewing people who are happy with the work they are doing now, and never making a permanent occupational choice.

A list of possible fields of study for job analysis is agreed upon, information is provided on possible training institutions, and possible areas for development are dealt with by the provision of psychoeducational and psychosocial information. This step is concluded by the spelling out of action steps (including ways of conducting job analyses and reaching agreement on short-, medium-, and long-term steps). Once assessees have an idea of what careers they would like to pursue, they should actively explore and monitor their provisional choices through job analysis, which includes the following:

a. Discussing their findings and options with an "audience" (e.g. their parents, friends, teachers, employers, and employees).

b. Networking with as many entities as possible to obtain work-related information. Seeking interviews with people (or companies) specializing in their preferred career options and with people already established in the field. Assessees should be encouraged to persevere and write reports on the quality of interviews and the extent to which they were helpful. They need to prepare themselves for each interview by, for example, making a list of questions to ask the interviewer. They should also be advised on how to conduct themselves in an interview. Assessees still at school could ask their language or life orientation[6] teachers to arrange mock interviews in class. Such techniques should stand assessees in good stead when they conduct job analysis or job interviews.
c. Seeking vacation employment.
d. Asking tertiary training institutions for details of, for example, their fees and courses. Often this kind of information can be accessed over the internet and will enable assessees to compare the courses and facilities offered by different institutions.
e. Visiting various locations where different careers are followed in order to observe employees and ask questions.
f. Using social media, libraries, and the internet to research career options related to their key life themes. They should also seek opportunities for internships, learnerships, mentoring, temporary or vacation employment, site visits, interviews, volunteer work, and work shadowing to understand the realities of the careers they have identified.
g. Enquiring about the possibility of "work shadowing", temporary employment, and volunteer work.
h. Obtaining and studying literature on careers.
i. Using the internet to peruse relevant websites.
j. Organizing mentorship and engaging in vicarious learning. They should actively make use of other sources of information on careers such as books, videos, podcasts, brochures, and vacation schools.

To help them in their job analysis activities, they are provided with a list of relevant websites and contact details of training institutions and individuals. It should be emphasized, though, that these steps are broad guidelines only. Career counselors are free to adapt the suggested structure and emphasize micro- and macro-outcomes as they think fit. Assessees' actions should ultimately be converted into constructive behavior that helps shape their character and promote their sense of purpose.

Assessees need to be reminded of the importance of qualifications. While this does not mean that they need the highest qualifications to enjoy a rewarding career, they should obtain qualifications that are in line with their aspirations and, ideally, enhance their employability. Most posts correspond with formal qualifications of some kind. If assessees do not have the qualifications required by employers for advertised posts, they will probably not even be interviewed for the position, no matter how talented they may be in the particular field.

[6]In South Africa, "career guidance" is offered within the context of life orientation (which forms part of the life skills program in schools).

Using the *MCM* as a discussion document to facilitate intervention. Despite the fact that the *MCM* is a quantitative instrument, an integrative approach to data analysis during the career counseling process with assessees who have completed the questionnaire should be followed because such an approach

i. gets assessees to take an active role in obtaining and interpreting data;
ii. sees the individual holistically rather than as an "object" to be pinned down by "precise" measurements of elements of interest;
iii. reduces the artificial distinction between career counseling, counseling, therapy, and assessment;
iv. is more informal and allows for more flexibility and initiative on the part of the career counselor than do standardized tests (Hoare, McIlveen, & Hamilton, 2012);
v. facilitates open-ended, divergent, and holistic interpretations and discussions; and
vi. is especially useful when there is significant diversity among assessees (Goldman, 1990).

The 19 career categories in the *MCM* give career counselors a starting point for clarifying and discussing career profiles in greater depth. Anyone with a working knowledge of possible careers and categories of work should be able to understand the terminology in the questionnaire sufficiently well to make informed decisions when completing the questionnaire. However, if assessees have had only limited exposure to the world of work, they should be exposed to this world in some or other way before they attempt to answer the questionnaire.

Using the outcomes of the *MCM* in career counseling intervention. Below I elaborate on a possible strategy a career counselor could use to implement *MCM* results.

i. Assessees should be reminded that the process of choosing and following an appropriate career is a lifelong, continuous process that starts at birth and carries on even after "retirement",[7] that very few people choose one career and remain in that career for the remainder of their lives in the 21st century, and that most people will have an increasing number of jobs in a lifetime (jobs that are often very different from one another).
ii. Assessees should be reminded that, instead of arguing in terms of "right" or "wrong" occupations, they should think rather in terms of more or less appropriate occupations. There are numerous identifiable occupations (and careers), and any given person may choose and be successful in many of these possible occupations and careers.

No instrument is so sophisticated that it can predict with 100% accuracy which career or careers assessees should follow. Assessees should be told this. When a

[7]Perspectives on 'retirement' and retirement activities are changing rapidly and include starting one's own (new) business, doing part-time work, taking up a new work role, or working in a changed or different capacity.

person asks, "Tell me what I must do", the answer should be: "I will do my best to be useful, helpful, or of value to you. However, in career counseling contexts, you should note that it is not useful or correct to think in terms of 'right' or 'wrong' answers or in terms of what you 'must' do. Only you can tell yourself what to do. At best, career counselors can provide you with sufficient information elicited from you (the only expert there will ever be on you) to enable you to make appropriate and informed choices.

9.12 Psychometric Properties of the *MCM*

Without going into detail (interested readers are referred to those sources listed in the list of references at the end of this book for more details), it can be stated that the *MCM* is a rigorous measure of interest and confidence, is easy to use, and has excellent psychometric qualities (see, for instance, Maree and Taylor (2016a, 2016b for more details). Moreover, it takes comparatively little time to administer, score, and interpret, yields reliable and valid results, and is standardized. It can be administered to individuals or large groups of people with little difficulty. While the questionnaire was originally standardized on a sample of high school learners, Ferreira and Morgan's (2019) research recently confirmed the structural validity and reliability of the *MCM* when used to assess the career interests and confidence (about aptitude) of adults. Data are regularly gathered on assessees' profiles in different age brackets and cultural groups, and their progress is traced to investigate further and enhance the predictive value of the questionnaire.

9.13 Summary

The development of the *MCM* is well aligned with the counseling for self- and career construction theoretical framework espoused in this book. Drawing on trait and factor theory, self-concept development theory, and social cognitive learning theory, the questionnaire yields quantitative outcomes that can be triangulated with *CIP* outcomes to promote self- and career construction counseling. The questionnaire is easy to use, does not take much time to administer, and has excellent psychometric properties. Using the *MCM* in the way described in this book should enable career counselors to help their clients to make meaning of work during their career journeys and to choose and construct careers that will help them design themselves, and live purposeful lives in which they can make meaningful social contributions (Savickas, 2019b). Ultimately, such intervention should contribute to people's search to uncover or rediscover the "magic" in their life stories

In Chapter 10, I discuss the integrative use of stories and scores to promote innovative career counseling in individual and group contexts.

References

Ackerman, P. L., & Beier, M. E. (2003). Intelligence, personality, and interests in the career choice process. *Journal of Career Assessment, 11,* 205–218.

Alika, H. I., & Egbochuku, E. O. (2009). Vocational interest, counselling, socio-economic status and age as correlated of re-entry of girls into schools in Edo state. *Edo Journal of Counselling, 2*(1), 9–16.

Amundson, N., Niles, S., & Harris-Bowlsbey, J. (2004). *Essential elements of career counselling.* Vancouver, Canada: Merrill Prentice-Hall.

Athanasou, J. A., & Cooksey, R. W. (1993). Self-estimates of vocational interests. *Australian Psychologist, 28,* 118–127.

Bandura, A. (1986). *Social foundations of thought and action: A social cognitive theory.* Englewood Cliffs, NJ: Prentice Hall.

Bandura, A. (1991). Social cognitive theory of self-regulation. *Organizational Behavior and Human Decision Processes, 50,* 248–287.

Bandura, A. (1997). *Self-efficacy: The exercise of control.* New York, NY: Freeman.

Betz, N. E., & Hackett, G. (1986). Applications of self-efficacy theory to understanding career choice behavior. *Journal of Social and Clinical Psychology, 4,* 279–289.

Blustein, D. L. (2006). *The psychology of working: A new perspective for career development, counseling, and public policy.* New York, NY: Routledge.

Burisch, M. (1984). Approaches to personality inventory construction: A comparison of merits. *American Psychologist, 39,* 214–227.

Campbell, D. P., Hyne, S. A., & Nilsen, D. L. (1992). *Manual for the Campbell interest and skill survey.* Colorado Springs, CL: Pearson.

Darcy, M., & Tracey, T. J. (2003). Integrating abilities and interests in career choice: Maximal versus typical assessment. *Journal of Career Assessment, 11,* 219–237.

Dawis, R. V., & Lofquist, L. (1984). *A psychological theory of work adjustment.* Minneapolis, MN: University of Minnesota Press.

Du Toit, R. (1992). *South African Vocational Interest Inventory.* Pretoria, South Africa: HSRC.

Du Toit, R., Prinsloo, W. B. J., Gevers, J., & Harilall, R. (1993). *Manual for the South African Vocational Interest Inventory (SAVII).* Pretoria, South Africa: HSRC.

Duffy, R. D., Diemer, M. A., & Jadidian, A. (2012). The development and initial validation of the work volition scale-student version. *The Counseling Psychologist, 40,* 291–319.

Duffy, R. D., Diemer, M. A., Perry, J. C., Laurenzi, C., & Torrey, C. L. (2012). The construction and initial validation of the Work Volition Scale. *Journal of Vocational Behavior, 80,* 400-411.

Duffy, R. D., Bott, E. M., Torrey, C. L., & Webster, G. D. (2013). Work volition as a critical moderator in the prediction of job satisfaction. *Journal of Career Assessment, 21*(1), 20–31.

Ferreira, J. C., & Morgan, B. (2019). An investigation of the psychometric properties of the *Maree Career Matrix. South African Journal of Psychology, 49*(2), 206–218.

Gati, I. (2013). Advances in career decision making. In B. W. Walsh, M. L. Savickas, & P. J. Hartung (Eds.), *Handbook of vocational psychology* (pp. 183–215). New York, NY: Routledge.

Gati, I., & Asher, I. (2001a). The PIC model for career decision making: Prescreening, in-depth exploration, and choice. In F. T. L. Leong & A. Barak (Eds.), *Contemporary models in vocational psychology* (pp. 7–54). Mahwah, NJ: Erlbaum.

Gati, I., & Asher, I. (2001b). Prescreening, in-depth exploration, and choice: From decision theory to career counseling practice. *Career Development Quarterly, 50,* 140–157.

Gati, I., Fishman-Nadav, Y., & Shiloh, S. (2006). The relations between preferences for using abilities, self-estimated abilities, and measured abilities among career counseling clients. *Journal of Vocational Behavior, 68,* 24–38.

Gevers, J., Du Toit, R., & Harilall, R. (1997). *Manual for the Self-Directed Search (SDS).* Pretoria, South Africa: HSRC.

Goldman, L. (1990). Qualitative assessment. *The Counseling Psychologist, 18,* 205–213.

Gottfredson, G. D. (2002). Interests, aspirations, self-estimates, and the Self-Directed search. *Journal of Career Assessment, 10,* 200–208.

Gottfredson, L. S. (2005). Applying Gottfredson's theory of circumscription and compromise in career guidance and counseling. In S. D. Brown & R. W. Lent (Eds.), *Career development and counseling: Putting theory and research to work* (pp. 71–100). Hoboken, NJ: Wiley.

Guichard, J. (2009). Self-constructing. *Journal of Vocational Behavior, 75,* 251–258.

Guichard, J. (2013a, November). *Career guidance, education, and dialogues for a fair and sustainable human development*. Inaugural conference of the UNESCO chair of Lifelong guidance and counselling, University of Wroclaw, Poland.

Guichard, J. (2013b). What competencies need people living in liquid societies to design their lives and direct their careers? In A. Di Fabio & J. G. Maree (Eds.), *Psychology of career counseling: New challenges for a new era* (pp. 41–60). New York, NY: Nova.

Hackett, G., & Betz, N. E. (1992). Self-efficacy perceptions and the career-related choices of college students. In D. H. Schunk & J. L. Meece (Eds.), *Student perceptions in the classroom* (pp. 229–246). Hillsdale, NJ: Lawrence Erlbaum.

Hackett, G., & Betz, N. E. (1995). Self-efficacy and career choice and development. In J. E. Maddux (Ed.), *Self-efficacy, adaptation, and adjustment: Theory, research and application* (pp. 249–280). New York, NY: Plenum Press.

Hall, B. A., Halstead, M. E., & Taylor, T. R. (1986). *Test administrator's manual for the Rothwell-Miller Interest Blank*. Pretoria, South Africa: HSRC.

Hansen, J. I. C. (2005). Assessment of interests. In S. D. Brown & R. W. Lent (Eds.), *Career development and counseling* (pp. 281–314). New York, NY: John Wiley.

Hartung, P. J. (2013a). The life-span, life-space theory of careers. In S. D. Brown & R. W. Lent (Eds.), *Career development and counseling: Putting theory and research to work* (2nd ed., pp. 83–113). Hoboken, NJ: John Wiley & Sons.

Hartung, P. J. (2013b). Career construction counselling. A. Di Fabio & J. G. Maree (Eds.), *Psychology of career counseling: New challenges for a new era* (pp. 15–28). Hauppauge, New York: Nova Science.

Hartung, P. J. (2018, July). Life design: *A unifying paradigm for international Counseling Psychology. Paper prepared for Division 16*. Presidential Address at the 29th International Congress of Applied Psychology. Montréal, Quebec, Canada.

Hartung, P. J. (2019). Life design: A paradigm for innovating career counselling in global context. In J. G. Maree (Ed.), *Handbook of innovative career counseling* (pp. 3–18). New York, NY: Springer.

Health Professions Council of South Africa (HPCSA). (2010). *Policy on the classification of psychometric measuring devices, methods and techniques*. Pretoria, South Africa: HPCSA.

Healy, C. C., & Mourton, D. L. (1984). The effects of an abbreviated self-directed Search on the career decision competencies of community college students. *The Vocational Guidance Quarterly, 33,* 55–62.

Hirschi, A., & Läge, D. (2008). Holland's secondary constructs of vocational interests and career choice readiness of secondary students. *Journal of Individual Differences, 28,* 205–218.

Hoare, P. N., McIlveen, P., & Hamilton, N. (2012). Acceptance and commitment therapy (ACT) as a career counselling strategy. *International Journal for Educational and Vocational Guidance, 12*(3), 171–187.

Holland, J. L. (1973). *Making vocational choices: A theory of careers*. Upper Saddle River, NJ: Prentice-Hall.

Holland, J. L. (1985). *Making vocational choices: A theory of vocational personalities and work environments* (2nd ed.). Upper Saddle River, NJ: Prentice Hall.

Holland, J. L. (1997). *Making vocational choices: A theory of vocational personalities and work environments* (3rd ed.). Lutz, FL: Psychological Assessment Resources.

Holland, J. H., & Gottfredson, G. D. (1975). Predictive value and psychological meaning of vocational aspirations. *Journal of Vocational Behavior, 6,* 349–363.

Holland, J. L., Gottfredson, G. D., & Baker, H. G. (1990). The validity of vocational aspirations and interest inventories: Extended, replicated and reinterpreted. *Journal of Counseling Psychology, 37,* 337–342.

Krumboltz, J. D. (1993). Integrating career and personal counseling. *The Career Development Quarterly, 42,* 143–148.

Krumboltz, J. D. (2015). The purpose of career counseling. *Career Convergence Magazine*, April, 3–4.

Krumboltz, J. D., Mitchell, A. M., & Jones, G. B. (1976). A social learning theory of career selection. *The Counseling Psychologist, 6*(1), 71–81.

Kuder, G. F. (1975). *Kuder General Interest Survey manual.* Chicago, IL: Science Research Associates.

Kuder, G. F. (1977). *Activity interests and occupational choice.* Chicago, IL: Science Research Associates.

Lent, R. W., & Hackett, G. (1987). Career self-efficacy: Empirical status and future directions. *Journal of Vocational Behavior, 30,* 347–382.

Lent, R. W., Brown, S. D., & Hackett, G. (1994). Toward a unifying social cognitive theory of career and academic interest, choice, and performance. *Journal of Vocational Behavior, 45,* 79–122.

Levin, N., & Gati, I. (2014). Facilitating the transition from school to work with a career decision-making approach: Process-related assessments and the PIC model. *Career Planning and Adult Development Journal, 30,* 127–143.

Lopez Levers, L. L., May, M., & Vogel, G. (2011). Research on counseling in African settings. In E. Mpofu (Ed.), *Counseling people of African ancestry* (pp. 57–74). New York, NY: Cambridge University Press.

Low, K. S. D., Mijung, Y., Roberts, B. W., & Rounds, J. (2005). Stability of vocational interests from early adolescence to middle adulthood: A quantitative review of longitudinal studies. *Psychological Bulletin, 131,* 713–737.

Maddux, J. E. (1995). Self-efficacy theory: An introduction. In J. E. Maddux (Ed.), *Self-efficacy, adaptation, and adjustment* (pp. 3–33). New York, NY: Plenum Press.

Maree, J. G. (2005). The torn learning sprockets: Stars in the ascendant. *Gifted Education International, 20,* 380–390.

Maree, J. G. (2009). Career counseling in the 21st century: South African institutions of higher education at the crossroads. *South African Journal of Higher Education, 23,* 429–435.

Maree, J. G. (2012a). *Career Adapt-Abilities Scale*—South African form: Psychometric properties and construct validity. *Journal of Vocational Behaviour, 80*(3), 730–733. https://doi.org/10.1016/j.jvb.2012.01.005.

Maree, J. G. (2012b). *Two DVD set: A guide to reflective career counselling—with Prof Maree.* Randburg, South Africa: JvR Psychometrics.

Maree, J. G. (2013). *Counseling for career construction: Connecting life themes to construct life portraits: Turning pain into hope.* Rotterdam, The Netherlands: Sense.

Maree, J. G. (2014, July). *Educing life themes to co-construct life portraits and turn decision into movement.* Keynote address (Division 16), 28th International Congress of Applied Psychology. Palais Des Congrès, Paris, France.

Maree, J. G. (2016). Using interpersonal process during career construction counseling to promote reflexivity and expedite change. *Journal of Vocational Behaviour, 96,* 22–30.

Maree, J. G. (2019a, June). *Career development in Africa: Decent work for all: Brief photomontage.* Keynote Address at the Annual Career Development Practitioner Congress, Emperors Palace Conference Centre, Kempton Park, South Africa.

Maree, J. G. (2019b). Postmodernising career counseling in a deep rural context. In J. G. Maree (Ed.), *Handbook of innovative career counseling* (pp. 577–596). New York, NY: Springer.

Maree, J. G., & Molepo, J. M. (2007). Facilitating postmodern career counseling in the Limpopo Province of South Africa: A rocky ride to hope. *Australian Journal of Career Counseling, 16,* 62–70.

Maree, J. G., & Molepo, M. (2016). Implementing a qualitative (narrative) approach in cross-cultural career counselling. In M. McMahon (Ed.), *Career counselling: Constructivist approaches* (2nd ed., pp. 65–78). Rotterdam, The Netherlands: Sense.

Maree, J. G., & Taylor, N. (2016a). *Manual for the Maree Career Matrix (MCM)*. Randburg, SA: JvR Psychometrics.

Maree, J. G., & Taylor, N. (2016b). Development of the *Maree Career Matrix*: A new interest inventory. *South African Journal of Psychology, 46*(4), 462–476. https://doi.org/10.1177/0081246316641558.

Maslow, A. H. (1987). *Motivation and personality* (2nd ed.). New York, NY: Addison-Wesley.

Metz, A. J., & Guichard, J. (2009). Vocational psychology and new challenges. *The Career Development Quarterly, 57,* 310–318.

Miller, K. M. (1968). *Manual for the Rothwell-Miller Interest Blank*. Windsor, England: NFER.

Miller, M. J., Springer, T. P., Tobacyk, J., & Wells, D. (2004). Congruency between occupational daydreams and *SDS* scores among college students. *College Student Journal, 38*(1), 57–59.

Mischel, W. (1977). On the future of personality assessment. *American Psychologist, 32,* 246–654.

Oakland, T. (2004). Use of educational and psychological tests internationally. *Applied Psychology: An International Review, 53,* 157–172.

Osipow, S. H. (1983). *Theories of career development* (3rd ed.). Englewood Cliffs, NJ: Prentice-Hall.

Osipow, S. H. (1990). Convergence in theories of career choice and development: Review and prospect. *Journal of Vocational Behavior, 36,* 122–131.

Osipow, S. H., & Fitzgerald, L. F. (1996). *Theories of career development* (4th ed.). Boston, MA: Allyn & Bacon.

Parsons, F. (1909). *Choosing a vocation*. Boston, MA: Houghton Mifflin.

Patrick, L., Care, E., & Ainley, M. (2011). The relationship between vocational interests, self-efficacy, and achievement in the prediction of educational pathways. *Journal of Career Assessment, 19*(1), 61–74.

Porfeli, E., Lee, B., & Vondracek, F. W. (2013). Identity development and careers in adolescents and emerging adults: Content, process, and structure. In B. W. Walsh, M. L. Savickas, & P. J. Hartung (Eds.), *Handbook of vocational psychology: Theory, research and practice* (4th ed., pp. 133–154). New York, NY: Routledge.

Prediger, D. J. (1982). Dimensions underlying Holland's hexagon: Missing link between interests and occupations. *Journal of Vocational Behavior, 21,* 259–287.

Prediger, D. J. (1999). Integrating interests and abilities for career exploration: General considerations. In M. L. Savickas & A. R. Spokane (Eds.), *Vocational interests: Meaning, measurement, and counseling use* (pp. 295–325). Palo Alto, CA: Davies-Black.

Pretorius, H. G., & Morgan, B. (2010). Can tests 'predict' success or help you find a career. In K. Maree (Ed.), *Career counselling: Methods that work* (pp. 45–52). Cape Town, South Africa: Juta.

Rossier, J. (2015). Career adaptability and life designing. In L. Nota & J. Rossier (Eds.), *Handbook of the life design paradigm: From practice to theory and from theory to practice* (pp. 154–164). Boston, MA: Hogrefe.

Ryan-Krane, N. E., & Tirre, W. C. (2005). Ability assessment in career counseling. In S. D. Brown & R. W. Lent (Eds.), *Career development and counseling* (pp. 330–352). Hoboken, NJ: John Wiley.

Savickas, M. L. (1993). Career counseling in the postmodern era. *Journal of Cognitive Psychotherapy: An International Quarterly, 7,* 205–215.

Savickas, M. L. (1994). Overview of career development. In M. L. Savickas & R. W. Lent (Eds.), *Convergence in career development theories* (pp. 139–154). Palo Alto, CA: CPP Books.

Savickas, M. L. (2013). Career construction theory and practice. In R. W. Lent & S. D. Brown (Eds.), *Career development and counseling: Putting theory and research into work* (2nd ed., pp. 147–183). Hoboken, NJ: Wiley.

Savickas, M. L. (2019a). *Theories of psychotherapy series. Career counseling* (2nd ed.). Washington, DC: American Psychological Association.

Savickas, M. L. (2019b, September). *Designing a self and constructing a career in post-traditional societies*. Keynote address at the 43rd international association for educational and vocational guidance Conference, Bratislava, Slovakia.
Sharf, R. S. (2013). Advances in theories of career development. In W. B. Walsh, M. L. Savickas, & P. J. Hartung (Eds.), *Handbook of vocational psychology: Theory, research, and practice* (pp. 2–32). New York: Routledge.
Super, D. E. (1963). Self-concepts in vocational development. In D. Super, R. Starishevsky, N. Matlin, & J. P. Jordaan (Eds.), *Career development: Self-concept theory* (pp. 1–26). New York, NY: College Entrance Examination Board.
Super, D. E. (1972). Vocational development theory: Persons, positions, processes. In J. M. Whiteley & A. Resnikoff (Eds.), *Perspectives on vocational development* (pp. 13–33). Washington, DC: American Personnel and Guidance Association.
Super, D. E. (1980). A life-span, life-space approach to career development. *Journal of Vocational Behavior, 16,* 282–298.
Super, D. E. (1990). Career and life development. In D. Brown & L. Brooks (Eds.), *Career choice and development* (2nd ed., pp. 192–234). San Francisco, CA: Jossey-Bass.
Swanson, J. (2002). Understanding the complexity of clients' lives: Infusing a truly integrative career-personal perspective into graduate training. *The Counseling Psychologist, 30,* 815–832.
Taylor, K. M., & Betz, N. E. (1983). Applications of self-efficacy theory to the understanding and treatment of career indecision. *Journal of Vocational Behavior, 22,* 63–81.
Tschannen-Moran, M., Woolfolk Hoy, A., & Hoy, A. (1998). Teacher efficacy: Its meaning and measure. *Review of Educational Research, 68,* 202–248.
Van Eeden, R. (1991). *Manual for the Senior South African Individual Scale—Revised (SSAIS-R), (Part 1)*. Pretoria, South Africa: Human Sciences Research Council.
Zytowski, D. G. (1999). How to talk to people about their interest inventory results. In M. L. Savickas, M. L., & Spokane, A. R. (Eds.). *Vocational interests: Meaning, measurement, and counseling use* (pp. 277–293). Palo Alto, CA: Davies-Black.

Chapter 10
Integrating Stories and Scores to Promote Innovative Career Counseling in Individual and Group Contexts

You can't connect the dots looking forward; you can only connect them looking backwards (Steve Jobs)

Abstract This chapter begins with a theoretical overview of Savickas' thoughts on how the many different "dots" can be connected in career counseling once assessees' stories have been elicited qualitatively (using the *CCI*) to craft their "life portraits". Next, I explain briefly what is meant by a career-life story narrative and then discuss the value of eliciting stories and scores integratively to enable career counselors to help assessees use and synthesize their responses and reflections. I then summarize the importance and essence of integrative QUALITATIVE-quantitative group career counseling and discuss practical aspects of using the career choice and construction conversation template in individual and group contexts to enhance assessees' reflections on their stories and scores and to connect what they consciously know or are aware of with subconscious advice. The overall aim of career counseling is to deal with people's authentic reason for seeking counseling—this and a few general issues are discussed before the chapter is concluded.

10.1 Enhancing Reflection, Reflexivity, Narratability, and Autobiographicity: General Overview

Today, career counselors have access to a broad array of strategies[1] and techniques they can employ to **elicit** assessees' career stories and scores, which are then integrated and used to facilitate critical self-reflection and promote reflexivity and, in doing so, enhance assessees' narratability and autobiographicity (Briddick & Sensoy-Briddick, 2013). This involves (in one-to-one contexts) primarily the *Career*

[1]For the purposes of this book, the term "strategies" refers to a broad array of information-generating or -constructing methods (predominantly qualitative but also quantitative), depending on the particular preferences of individual career counselors.

J. G. (Kobus) Maree, *Innovating Counseling for Self- and Career Construction*,
https://doi.org/10.1007/978-3-030-48648-8_10

Construction Interview but also adjunct career counseling techniques and instruments such as the *My Career Story* (*MCS*) (Savickas & Hartung, 2012) and the *Career Interest Profile* (*CIP*) (in group contexts, too) (Di Fabio & Maree, 2013a, 2013b; Maree, 2017). Individually and collectively, these strategies enhance narratability and autobiographicity. Self-reflection and reflexivity are promoted by career counselors in the following manner: Assessees' answers to questions are read back to them verbatim while career counselors repeatedly enquire whether what they (assessees) are saying and thinking is consistent with what they are trying to say. Career counselors also repeatedly ask assessees whether what they (counselors) think they are hearing is what the assessees are trying to say ("Is this what you are trying to say? Am I hearing you correctly?"). This promotes **authorization** (validation or, in certain instances, invalidation of counselors' understanding of assessees' oral and/or written comments or responses). The aim is to enhance triangulation and crystallization (Richardson, 2002) to establish the trustworthiness, validity, and credibility of assessees' responses and reflections. These reflections on answers to questions asked in qualitative career counseling instruments such as the *CIP* help career counselors advance communication on micro-, meso-, and macro-levels. Assessees are thus helped to reflect on a micro-level (by, for instance, responding to questions that relate to their interests, strengths, and areas for development), on a meso-level (by, for instance, linking the abovementioned information with specific careers and associated fields of study), and on a macro-level (by, for instance, establishing the initial pain or hurt in their lives (unfinished stories) and what their key life themes are). This strategy stands in stark contrast to the former strategy of obtaining information on assessees' personality traits and the requirements for specific jobs and then informing them which fields of study and careers are the "right" ones for them. As other authors have also cautioned (Anderson & Goolishian, 1992; Hartung 2013a, 2013b), the authorization phase should be managed with appropriate circumspection and respect. Adopting a "not-knowing" position and role (Anderson & Goolishian, 1992) is key in this regard. Once **authorization** has taken place, **action steps** and **forward movement** are needed to help assessees crystallize (Cochran, 1997) their career decisions.

Integrating or synthesizing the outcomes of counseling for self- and career construction in a coherent, concise, and user-friendly manner comprises a key aspect of this kind of intervention. This matter is addressed next.

10.1.1 Helping Assessees Integrate (Synthesize) Their Responses and Reflections

"Testing" people to obtain their scores on inventories and assessing them to elicit their personal stories is a valuable starting point for career counseling. However, interpreting assessees' stories and scores professionally is both a science and an art that takes a great deal of training and exercise. In addition, without compassionate and professional integration, these scores and stories mean little.

10.1.2 Determining the Effectiveness of Interventions

Determining the effectiveness of interventions is essential. (Depending on the context, I use brief qualitative questionnaires as well as (in group contexts) quantitative measures such as the *CAAS* (Maree, 2012b; Savickas & Porfeli, 2012) and/or the *Career Decision-making Difficulties Questionnaire* (*CDDQ*) (Gati, 2011a, 2011b) for purposes of pre- and post-test assessment.).

10.1.3 General Principles Guiding Life Portraits

In an earlier publication, *Counseling for career construction* (Maree, 2013a), I dealt almost exclusively with the use of qualitative assessment and intervention as well as the integration of qualitative outcomes. The publication was based largely on and promoted the use of the *Career Construction Interview* (*CCI*) and integrating its outcomes with the outcomes of adjunct questionnaires (Hartung, 2010a, 2010b; Savickas, 2009a, 2009b, 2011). The success of the *CCI* and the associated intervention in eliciting assessees' life stories and in drawing on these stories to advance their career choice, career- and self-construction, and life design enactment has been pointed out in numerous articles. Savickas (2019) explains that when only the *CCI* is used to facilitate intervention, after the first phase, career counselors and assessees jointly connect the often seemingly unconnected or unrelated dots in assessees' responses to the *CCI*. This is achieved by integrating assessees' micro-stories (comprising their responses and reflections) into a coherent and comprehensive narrative (macro-story or life portrait).[2] This narrative is read back to them in the second phase, and they are asked to correct any "errors" and clarify any misunderstandings until they feel comfortable to approve the narrative. Counselors and assessees then work together to enhance co-construction and fine-tuning of the narrative, and, in the concluding phase, they jointly devise a plan of action to promote forward movement.

Savickas (2019) states that life portraits should be guided by the following general principles. They should

a. provide an accurate, authentic, and realistic reflection of who assessees are at that stage;
b. indicate opportunities for self-development and self- and career construction;

[2]See Sect. 10.1.4. These narratives can take many forms, depending of the preferences of individual career counselors.

c. focus on identified life themes that can advance assessees' career storylines (career plots);
d. be authentic and coherent; and
e. address the twin aspects of meaning and purpose in assessees' storylines.

Once assessees have authorized their career story narratives, expressed intentions and aims should be converted into action steps. Assessees are expected to carry out these action steps and report back to their career counselors regularly on their progress. Many of the principles in the *CCI* analysis strategy can be adapted and included in a strategy to interpret and integrate "stories" and/or "scores" (connect the dots, so to speak) in instances where the *CCI* itself is not used during the facilitation of career counseling. This view is confirmed by Cochran (1997) who states that: "The task of career counseling is to construct narratives a person can enact … at stake, then, is whether or not a person's career is shaped by a personal vision of life at best" (p. 151).

Another caveat is appropriate at this point: While I believe that experienced career counselors have the capacity to draw on "stories" to facilitate career counseling in individual intervention with emotionally well-functioning assessees, less experienced career counselors will need more information to enable them to administer career counseling successfully. Moreover, in group contexts, the *CCI* does not suffice for purposes of eliciting adequate information to ensure satisfactory career counseling. It is essential to elicit and draw on "stories" and "scores" to ensure the rigor of the intervention. In this chapter, I will therefore focus on the integration or synthesis of the outcomes of an integrative QUALITATIVE-quantitative approach to career counseling (using the *CIP* with or without the *MCM*).

The following points need re-emphasis.

a. There is no one right or wrong way to facilitate career counseling. Different styles can be distinguished and used.
b. The style of career counseling that is chosen should suit the preferred style of the career counselor involved and, of course, address assessees' needs and not the other way round.

These points are discussed below.

10.1.4 General Principles Guiding the Crafting of Career-Life Story Narratives

The crafting of career-life story narratives can be handled in different ways, depending on the orientation and preference of individual career counselors.

First, there is no right or wrong way to craft the narrative (see, for instance, Addendum B for a postmodern narrative that one of my former students wrote under my supervision and Addendum C for an example of the Career-life story narrative that I prefer). Nor, as I have explained, is there a right or wrong title for the narrative.

Second, counselors may wish to take their cue from Savickas (2019) (who refers to such a narrative as a "Life portrait") for one way of handling narrative crafting. For more examples of life portraits, see, for instance, Maree (2013a, 2013b, 2015a, 2015b, 2016), Savickas (2019), and Taber (2013).

Third, counselors—who let assessees complete the *CIP* and the *MCM* online—can download the "electronic reports" and reflect on one or both reports. Sufficient space is available on these "electronic reports" for all reflections to be noted. (Assessees share all reflections on the micro-stories with their counselor.).

Fourth, assessees can take home either the entire electronic online *CIP* (and *MCM*) report(s) or only the actual **career-life story narrative** that comprises the

a. identity, power, or value statement;
b. occupational statement (that covers the tentatively chosen fields of study);
c. mission statement;
d. vision statement; and
e. "way forward" (job analysis and guidelines) narratives.

Fifth, alternatively, counselors can collate relevant information from electronic reports and devise their own version of the **career-life story narrative**.

Sixth, assessees can complete the *CIP* and *MCM* in hard copy format and use the **"Integrative career choice and construction conversation" template** to craft their **career-life story narrative in collaboration with a career counselor** and take this document home.

Seventh, assessees who work in group-based contexts, too, can use the **"Integrative career choice and construction conversation" template** (Addendum A) to craft their **career-life story narrative** and take this document home. (Many career counselors have reported this template to be extremely useful in group contexts).

Some career counselors have asked whether it is preferable to allow assessees to take only the Integrated career choice and construction conversation home. In my opinion—and I have discussed this matter with Dr. Jopie van Rooyen: CEO, JvR Psychometrics) (J. de Beer, personal communication, July 22, 2019)—this decision depends on the personal judgment of the individual counselor responsible for the assessment. In certain instances, a brief summary may be enough. This is especially the case when reflection and feedback on the "Career-life story narrative" is handled with individual assessees in a thorough manner and when the counselor is satisfied that assessees have grasped matters well enough to make additional information unnecessary.

10.2 Integrating QUALITATIVE and Quantitative Group Career Counseling Outcomes in Individual and Group Contexts

10.2.1 Introduction

First, facilitating and expediting integrative career counseling research and practice require the development and use of appropriate assessment instruments to reflect the progress from using test scores in (relative) isolation to using and integrating assessees' scores and stories (McMahon & Patton, 2002). Consistent with the aims of career construction counseling, such assessment instruments should be used also to encourage and enable assessees to narrate their autobiographies in such a way that counselors and they themselves are prompted to listen to and actually hear (construct), "uncode" (unpack or deconstruct), shed light on, and eventually revise (reconstruct) these stories together (co-construct) as the need arises.

Second, a persistent storyline in integrative approaches to career counseling is the importance of helping assessees uncover key life themes and integrate them in their career-lives. Research (Hartung & Cadaret, 2017; Maree, 2019) has confirmed the effectiveness of this kind of career counseling with late primary and secondary school learners, emerging adults (Arnett, 2007), as well as with older people because of its power to enhance their adaptability, resilience, and employability (and, accordingly, their prospects of finding and accessing sustainable decent work (Hartung & Cadaret, 2017)). Key to the success of the newer approach is its emphasis on managing volatility in the current job market in respect of assessees' career identities. This approach promotes and inspires the exploration of diverse work and career selves (Oyserman, Bybee, & Terry, 2006). Life design counseling in particular uses this approach (Savickas, 2015a, 2015b) to promote critical self- and meta-reflection and reflexivity to bring about change, forward movement, and progress (Hartung, 2013; Maree, 2013a; Savickas, 2016a, 2016b).

Third, as mentioned earlier, while drawing on the twin paradigms of career construction theory and self-construction theory, and promoting Savickas' *CCI*, I focus on group-based intervention in particular and on using the *MCM* and the *CIP* to create and promote a platform for initiating action and forward movement. This approach endorses Duffy and Dik's (2009, p. 441) view that "[o]nce clients have addressed the broad level of life purpose or meaning, a next step is for counselors to help clients connect what they view as their life purpose or role in the larger society with their activity within the work role".

Fourth, irrespective of whether I work in individual or group contexts, I prefer to elicit clients' "stories" and "scores" simultaneously and subsequently analyze and integrate them. Aware of Bernard & Ryan's (2010, p. 107) comment that "[n]o matter how hard we try there are no purely inductive studies", I prefer an inductive-deductive style for purposes of analyzing and interpreting the information obtained from clients.

Fifth, in line with standard ethical guidelines, all aspects of an assessment should be contracted with assessees in writing up front.

10.2.2 Ground Rules

The following "ground rules" apply (Maree, 2013a).

a. The theoretical underpinnings that researchers use to conceptualize their main ideas and analyze the outcomes of their intervention should be sound and clearly explained.
b. The outcomes and aims of their intervention should be obvious and unambiguous.
c. The intended outcomes should be easily measurable and clearly stated up front.
d. Special care should be taken to explain the procedure that will be followed to obtain sufficient information (put differently: to generate or construct data) to provide adequate career counseling and ensure that the intervention can be replicated.
e. A number of reflective questions should always be asked at the end of any career counseling intervention. I prefer to end the intervention by asking assessees to respond to the following questions: (a) How did you experience the intervention? (b) What else is there that I should know about you that did not come out during the intervention? (c) What changes did you experience during the intervention? (d) What prompted these changes?

10.2.3 Structure of Career Counseling Phases and Sessions

Although this is flexible, the following guidelines govern career counseling in general.

In phase 1, an intake interview is conducted, after which assessment commences.

In phase 2, the stories and scores obtained during the first phase are analyzed jointly by career counselor and assessees from a career construction perspective.

In phase 3, an action plan is agreed upon by counselor and assessees to facilitate forward movement. If assessees wish it, follow-up meetings can be scheduled. Lastly, short-, medium-, and long-term feedback is provided by the assessees.

Practitioners and researchers should adapt the sequence proposed above in any way they think fit. Factors that may influence the number and duration of the phases and sessions, such as the following, need to be taken into account and will co-determine the number of sessions as well as the number of hours devoted to, for instance, sessions and individual or group discussions.

a. Whether individual or group assessment is taking place.
b. The relevant individual or institution's schedule as well as the schedule of the career counselor.

c. The availability of the assessees.
d. The size of groups (in the case of group assessment).
e. The facilities available (in the case of group assessment). I am, for instance, often requested to administer the *CIP* and the *MCM* online when only a handful of computers are available. This is almost always the case during research projects, especially when the research is done in rural or township schools.
f. The time available and other possible time constraints.
g. Issues such as the time it takes assessees to complete assessments and their fatigue levels.

Inexperienced practitioners and researchers should clarify these matters beforehand with experienced colleagues.

10.3 Making Sense of People's Life Stories and Scores: Some Guidelines and Suggestions for Facilitating "Best Practice" in Group Career Counseling

10.3.1 Some General Guidelines

To begin with: As mentioned above, group-based career counseling intervention can be done in various ways, depending on a number of factors such as the number of assessees, the context in which the assessment takes place, the time and resources available, and the general dynamics of the group (e.g. private school or rural school context). I prefer a three-phase intervention strategy that runs over a number of weeks, bearing in mind the schedule of the institution where the intervention is conducted and the "contract" with the institution that requested the intervention.

After the nature and aim of the assessment have been explained, I provide details of the procedures that will be followed and the assessment instruments that will be used. The *MCM* is completed first and then the *CIP* (or vice versa, if preferred). Assessments can include the use of hard copies of the instruments or the completion of both questionnaires online. Thereafter, during as many sessions as the counselor thinks necessary, the stories and scores (or the stories on their own) are systematically analyzed, and **an integrated career-life story narrative comprising an account of the person's career-life story at the time of the assessment** is crafted.

10.3.2 Some Methodological Guidelines

a. Individual assessees reflect on their responses in groups.
b. Different subgroups should first be constituted, after which the assessees should be given the opportunity to decide on and join particular groups (Maree, Cook,

& Fletcher, 2018). Where possible, I establish different subgroups (four, five, or six participants per subgroup).

c. The interaction between career counselor and assessees then commences, using the "drawing on the input of the audience" methodology (Briddick & Sensoy-Briddick, 2013; Di Fabio & Maree, 2013a, 2013b).
d. During the intervention, the assessees (sitting in a circle or working in groups) interact with the career counselor one at a time.
e. The counselor provides career counseling by carefully integrating and discussing an individual assessee's *CIP* and *MCM* (see Appendix A) outcomes with him or her, while the other assessees (the audience) respond to prompts by the career counselor and the assessee alike (without addressing the assessee directly but simultaneously self-reflecting on the counselor's comments, prompts, and questions to the assessee). In other words, the group members are considered participants in an individual counseling session while simultaneously self-reflecting on the questions put to the assessee who is being counseled.
f. The career counselor helps the assessee (a) identify central life themes that are evident from the responses to Parts 1, 2, and 4 in particular, (b) identify his or her main career-related interests, issues, and concerns from the responses to Part 4 of the *CIP* in particular, and (c) elicit advice from within, regarding how she or he can enhance his or her sense of self and self-awareness, shed light on his or her career identities, and turn pain-related issues and concerns into themes of hope and inspiration that can advance his or her individual life projects (Di Fabio & Maree, 2013a, 2013b). Cochran (1992) alludes to life projects by stating that one's "unique and general life tasks become integrated about a personal theme to define a career project" (p. 196) (see Tables 10.1 and 10.2).
g. She or he is subsequently encouraged (directly and indirectly) to share advice from within to achieve greater self-awareness as well as awareness of his or her career-life projects (e.g. by asking what his or her favorite quotations mean to him or her and even requesting more favorite quotations). All the group members are thus afforded an opportunity to receive individual career counseling and also to form part of the audience.

A sufficient number of suitably qualified assistants should also attend the session to assist the counselor.

10.3.3 Exemplifying the Practical Implementation of Group Career Counseling

As mentioned earlier, the number of phases and sessions is flexible and open to negotiation. In the case of the so-called Junior Tukkies (see photographs below), for instance, they are brought to the University of Pretoria for six days in the middle of the year only. They participate in a number of activities of various kinds, including career counseling. I am allocated the first day to complete the assessment and then allowed a

Table 10.1 Summarized explanation of how hard copy *MCM* and *CIP* responses can be integrated (using the "Integrative Career Choice and Construction Conversation" Template (Addendum A))

Phase	Step	Detailed explanation
One: Eliciting the life story		Biographical information is obtained, and the assessment is conducted. In other words, assessees complete the *CIP* and the *MCM* and have their *CIP* stories and their *MCM* reports ready
Two: Authorizing (validating) the life story		Once assessees' stories have been elicited and their scores obtained, they are asked to complete the **"Integrative career choice and construction conversation" template**. This phase consists of the following five-step strategy to assist assessees in integrating the career-related information into a tangible career map or plan
	1	Steps are taken to **craft an identity, value, or power statement**
	2	Assessees are asked to transfer additional information (for more details, see Addendum A) from their *CIP* answer sheet, their *MCM* report, and their school marks to the **"Integrative career choice and construction conversation" template**
	3	Assessees are guided in identifying their integrated main interest categories/patterns based on the information provided in the table compiled in **Step 2**
	4	Assessees are requested to indicate the fields of study in which they want to study and where they want to study after completing school (some useful websites are provided to help them obtain information about careers and tertiary training institutions)
	5	Assessees are assisted to draw up their own personal career plan by integrating the information from all the above steps. To achieve this important aim, they are helped to complete the following sentence: a. I want to study (**field(s) of study**) so that I can b. (**here they allude to the personal meaning they want to derive from executing the associated job(s) (mission statement)** and in the process c. (here they allude to **the social meaning and sense of purpose they want to derive from executing these jobs (vision statement)**
Three: Devising action plans to bring about action and forward movement	1	After assessees' life themes have been connected jointly by the assessees and the career counselor, their field of study and career choice suggestions are concluded by helping them plan a thorough job analysis strategy. Assessees are expected to make a conscious effort to think about the **psychosocial** and **psychoeducational** issues that were brought to light
Four: Obtaining feedback	1	Assessees are allowed to return home and requested to reflect on their reflections, write down how they experienced the intervention, and report back to the career counselor regularly. This feedback helps the career counsellor evaluate assessees' progress and adapt his or her practice to better meet their needs

Table 10.2 Summarized explanation of how *MCM* and *CIP* online responses ("reports") can be integrated

Phase	Step	Detailed explanation
One: Eliciting the life story		Biographical information is obtained, and the assessment is conducted online. In other words, assessees complete the *CIP* and the *MCM* and have their *CIP MCM* online reports ready
Two: Authorizing (validating) the life story)		Analysis and synthesis of *CIP* and *MCM* online "reports" is done according to a number of broad guidelines that facilitate reflection and reflexivity. This phase consists of the following three-step strategy to assist assessees in integrating the career-related information into a tangible career map or plan
	1	Presenting and reflecting on assessees' responses
	2	Making sense of the reflections by "connecting the dots"
	3	Formulating assessees' personal mission and vision statements
Three: Devising action plans to bring about action and forward movement	1	**Action steps: Conducting job analysis to facilitate forward movement by assessees**
Four: Obtaining feedback	1	Assessees are allowed to return home and requested to reflect on their reflections, write down how they experienced the intervention, and report back to the career counselor regularly. This is because we really care about our clients, because the information they provide enables us to check on their progress and promote their chances of designing themselves successfully, and because their feedback provides useful information that we can use to and\just our practice to fit clients' needs more adequately

number of hours a few days later to conclude my intervention. In this instance, I have to complete the assessment and intervention in two sessions. Notwithstanding that, all assessees are requested to provide feedback to me electronically (Photographs 10.1 and 10.2).

Below, I discuss how assessees can be helped to integrate (synthesize) their responses and reflections to craft their power, value, or identity statements, help them identify possible careers and associated fields of study, articulate their mission and vision statements, as well as devise their plan of action to help them move forward.

Photograph 10.1 Day 1: Junior Tukkies completing the MCM and CIP

I first explain how hard copy responses can be integrated (using the "Integrative Career Choice and Construction Conversation" Template (Addendum A)), after which the focus shifts to an explanation of how the *CIP* and *MCM* online "reports" can be constructed and integrated (using the *CIP* and *MCM* online "reports").

10.4 Constructing, Analyzing, and Integrating the *CIP* and *MCM* Hard Copy "Reports"

Table 10.1 provides a summarized explanation of how hard copy *MCM* and *CIP* responses can be integrated (using the "Integrative Career Choice and Construction Conversation" Template (Addendum A)).

Photograph 10.2 Day 2: Junior Tukkies integrating (synthesizing) their responses and reflections

10.4.1 Group Career Counseling: Helping Assessees to Integrate (Synthesize) Their Responses and Reflections

Phase 1. Biographical information is obtained, and the assessment is conducted. In other words, assessees complete the *CIP* and the *MCM* and have their *CIP* stories and their *MCM* reports ready. (They can also include other information that is available.)

Phase 2. Once assessees' stories have been elicited and their scores obtained, they are asked to complete the **"Integrative career choice and construction conversation" template** (Addendum A). This phase consists of the following five-step strategy to assist assessees in integrating the career-related information into a tangible career map or plan.

In **Step 1**, steps are taken to **craft an identity, value, or power statement.** The aim of the statement is to enable assessees to integrate the two sets of outcomes by summarizing some main patterns from their life stories and by focusing on their areas for development, values, key life themes, and interest patterns. First, they list their seven greatest strengths, then their seven areas for growth, followed by their highest, strongest, or core values (their North Star or personal mission and vision statement) and their central life themes. Next, they are helped to integrate all of the above (their strengths, areas for growth, values, and key life themes) by writing a sentence that summarizes their identity (their identity, value, or power statement) as a precursor to formulating their mission and vision statements. (One, two, or three sentences are written down to indicate their uniqueness.) They are asked to begin with the words "I am …" This narrative consists of a sentence such as the following: "I am a kindhearted, principled, dedicated, compassionate and strong-willed person. I am articulate and very good at languages. I care about people and animals in general and about those that have suffered injustice or abuse in particular. I become despondent from time to time and am impatient with lazy people. I worry a little too much, and I sometimes overreact. I tend to neglect my own needs, I work too hard, and I get irritated easily when people make a lot of noise. Having experienced injustice and bullying when I was young, and having witnessed people close to me suffer the same fate, I feel passionate about helping people and animals who have suffered or are suffering deal with their suffering."

It is essential to repeat verbatim assessees' words in these statements as often as possible, as well as those in the vision and mission statements, and, in fact, in every kind of "report" or narrative that is written after assessments. I agree with Savickas (2019); Savickas and Hartung (2012) who explain to assessees that the more often they tell their stories, the more authentic these stories become. At the same time, assessees gain more confidence in these stories and become more comfortable about enacting or living the stories. Savickas (2019) puts it this way: "The more people tell their life story, the more real it becomes, and consequently the more real they become" (p. 40).

In **Step 2**, assessees are asked to transfer additional information (for more details, see Addendum A) from their *CIP* answer sheet, their *MCM* report, and their school marks to the "**Integrative career choice and construction conversation" template.** They are also allowed to include other related information if they have access to such information.

In **Step 3**, assessees are guided in identifying their integrated main interest categories/patterns based on the information provided in the table compiled in **Step 2**.

In **Step 4**, assessees are requested to indicate where they want to study after completing school (some useful websites are provided to help them obtain information about careers and tertiary training institutions).

In **Step 5**, assessees are assisted to draw up their own personal career plan by integrating the information from all the above steps. To achieve this important aim, they are helped to complete the following sentence):

I a. want to study ([**field(s) of study**)] so that I can b. (**here they allude to the personal meaning they want to derive from executing the job(s) associated with these fields of study [mission statement]**) and in the process c. (here they allude to **the social meaning and sense of purpose they want to derive from executing these jobs (listed below) [vision statement]**).

Phase 3. **Step 1**: **Action steps: Conducting job analysis to facilitate forward movement by assessees** After assessees' life themes have been connected jointly by the assessees and the career counselor, their field of study and career choice suggestions are concluded by helping them plan a thorough job analysis strategy. The aim is to expedite forward movement and progress by taking a number of action steps. They are also provided with **general career choice information**, and aspects of **psychoeducational** information (e.g. time management strategies) as well as **psychosocial** information (e.g. how to enhance their sense of self and improve their interpersonal relationships) are discussed. Assessees are expected to make a conscious effort to think about the **psychosocial** and **psychoeducational** issues that were brought to light. Lastly, they are allowed to return home and requested to reflect on their reflections, write down how they experienced the intervention, and report back to the career counselor regularly. It is particularly important to feedback on whether they believe the intervention bolstered their belief that they were on their way to experiencing **a sense of personal meaning and purpose** in their future career-lives (the core aim of career counseling).

Step 2: Follow-up: Obtaining short-, medium-, and long-term feedback.

10.4.2 Constructing, Analyzing, and Integrating the CIP *and* MCM *Online "Reports"*

Table 10.2 provides a summarized explanation of how *MCM* and *CIP* online responses ("reports") can be integrated.

***Phase 1*. First, the *MCM* and the *CIP* are completed online.**

***Phase 2*.** Analysis of *CIP* and *MCM* online "reports" is done according to a number of broad guidelines that facilitate reflection and reflexivity. These online "reports" (used together or individually) enable counselors and assessees to identify or uncover assessees' key life themes, patterns, or trends and arrive at their "career-life story narratives". The following three steps are recommended.

Step 1: Presenting and Reflecting on Assessees' Responses

This step comprises the presentation of and reflection on assessees' responses (previously referred to as "results") as well as guidelines on how outcomes should be interpreted. These guidelines are interspersed throughout the "report" at key points in the narrative.[3]

Section 1: Reflecting on assessees' expectations about the process.
Section 2: Gaining perspective by establishing assessees' career identity.
Section 3: Reflecting on the meaning of career influences on assessees' career-lives.
Section 4: Reflecting on assessees' most preferred and least preferred career category options, on their preferred and least preferred careers, and on their "dream" careers. Here, *MCM* outcomes (if available) are triangulated against *CIP* outcomes and a provisional list of fields and associated careers is compiled.
Section 5: Reflecting on assessees' experience of the assessment.

Step 2: **Making sense of the reflections by "connecting the dots"**.
First, strengths, areas for development, personality attributes, and values are reflected on. *Next*, themes, patterns, and trends are identified and connected to a number of possible careers and fields of study. This step is *concluded* with the crafting of the assessee's power, value, or identity statement.

Step 3: **Formulating assessees' personal mission and vision statements**. Here, counselors and assessees try make sense of all the reflections and associated insights (themes) identified in the previous step to help assessees make meaning **of** and find a sense of purpose **in** their career-lives.

***Phase 3*. Step 1**: **Action steps: Conducting job analysis to facilitate forward movement by assessees.**

Step 2: Follow-up: Obtaining short-, medium-, and long-term feedback.

10.4.3 Addressing Assessees' Authentic Reason for Consulting Career Counselors

As mentioned earlier, at the conclusion of every assessment, all assessees should be given an opportunity to reflect on whether the assessment had satisfactorily addressed their reason for seeking career counseling in the first place. A simple "yes" or "no" answer will not suffice. Readers are reminded of the value of asking questions such as the following to clarify assessees' questions or comments: "I am just wondering if anything has happened to prompt this visit/your question/your comment/observation." They are also reminded of the key importance of the "five golden minutes" at the end of each phase or session—a time when assesses are likely to raise issues that are particularly germane to their career-life stories.

[3]Obtaining copies of actual online reports by completing the *MCM* and the *CIP* online will make it easy for readers to understand this section and apply the guidelines presented here.

10.5 Differences Between Individual and Group Assessment

The difference between individual, small group, or large group assessment lies in the process of intervention itself and not in the contents that are covered. In the case of individual assessments, I am sometimes asked to administer and wrap up career counseling in the space of one day (occasionally a person flies to South Africa to consult me, and I am given only one day to complete the assessment). In such cases, I often proceed with telecounseling. I am more frequently being requested to counsel local or international clients electronically. In such instances, the *CIP* and *MCM* are completed online (under my supervision) and feedback is conducted via Skype. Tertiary training institutions also often ask me to complete the assessment within the space of three days, two days, or even a day and a half, depending on their own program and schedule.

Table 10.3 summarizes some of the differences and similarities between individual and group assessment.

10.5.1 Some Important Additional Suggestions

Obtaining regular feedback from assesses helps career counselors assess the short-, medium, and long-term usefulness and sustainability of their interventions. It is also important to report on research done with small, medium, and larger groups of people in diverse contexts in order to improve the applicability of new instruments and strategies and advance the generalizability of interventions and instruments. Similarly, I advocate the development and "standardization" of innovative techniques and instruments in addition to the ones discussed here.

Lastly: Over time, I have learned to regard every single expression of people as very useful in helping them decide on and "construct" their future careers. Below are some examples of what I mean.

Example 1: Paying special attention to **sketches or other forms of doodling** during breaks in the assessment.

Steve drew the following sketch during his break (Fig. 10.1).

Consistent with his earliest recollections (two of his recollections alluded to being involved in (a) helping his father design a shed on their farm and (b) helping his teacher build a duck pond at school) and other aspects of his life story, Steve displayed a propensity for working in the engineering and the built environment. He is currently studying architecture.

Example 2: Asking **whether there is anything else an assessee wishes to add to what she or he has already shared with me**

At the conclusion of his assessment, Geoff was asked whether there was anything else he wished to add to what he had already shared with me. He confirmed his wish to become a chef, but his father had said that he would not pay for his studies unless

Table 10.3 Summarized explanation of some of the differences and similarities between individual and group assessment

	Facet	Individual counseling	Group counseling (How does group counseling differ from individual counseling?, n.d.; Maree, Cook, & Fletcher, 2018; Pyle & Hayden, 2015)
Theoretical			
1	Theoretical underpinnings	Interest in and drawing on qualitative (storied) approaches, either alone or together with quantitative (objective) approaches, has increased substantially in recent times	Traditional approaches still prevail
2	Content of the intervention	Content is by and large the same Existential counseling is promoted	Content is by and large the same. The storied approach (including the use of the earliest recollections strategy, where applicable) is more time-consuming than a predominantly quantitative approach
3	Research	Much research has been done on the viability of self- and career construction and life design intervention (increasingly, too, in developing countries)	Little research has been done on the viability of group-based, integrative career counseling intervention, self- and career construction, and life design intervention (in developing countries in particular)
Logistics			
1	Number of counselors	Usually only one counselor is involved	Multiple counselors and assistants may be involved
2	Time (and efficiency)	Time is not a major factor	Time is a major factor. Efficiency is enhanced because more than one client's needs can be addressed
3	Costs	Cost per client is often relatively high	Relative cost per client is lower
4	Process of intervention	Easy to arrange with individual client	Organization is more challenging. The needs, idiosyncratic preferences, and programs of multiple stakeholders (e.g. clients, schools, corporations, and universities) have to be considered

(continued)

Table 10.3 (continued)

	Facet	Individual counseling	**Group counseling** (How does group counseling differ from individual counseling?, n.d.; Maree, Cook, & Fletcher, 2018; Pyle & Hayden, 2015)
5	Phases and sessions	Three phases and sessions normally suffice, depending on circumstances and the quality of the client-counselor relationship	The number of phases and sessions is determined by the preferences and needs of multiple stakeholders (a somewhat more complex exercise in group contexts)
Quality assurance			
1	Maintaining order	Easy to maintain order	Can be challenging—involving appropriate support staff is crucial
2	Rigor	Easy to ensure	More difficult to ensure in larger groups
3	Feedback is enhanced	More time can be devoted to individual clients. The discussion of more sensitive topics is facilitated	Providing richer feedback is facilitated, and a wider variety of diverse views can be obtained
Interpersonal benefits			
1	Audience	Counselor becomes the audience	Group provides a broader audience. Career counseling is "normalized" because clients embrace the fact that they are not "the only ones" with career counseling needs and questions
2	Network	Counselor may refer clients to other entities to broaden their networks	Group members also form part of a broader network
3	Client perspective	Counselor and client together shape the client's perspective	Group members' contributions help to shape individual clients' perspectives further. Interpersonal learning is enhanced
4	Holding environment	Counselor provides holding environment	Group members become part of the broader holding environment.
5	Training	High level of training in working with individual clients is needed	The ability to manage a group, solve problems, and communicate well is essential in addition to the skills needed to administer individual counseling
Obtaining metainformation			

(continued)

Table 10.3 (continued)

	Facet	Individual counseling	Group counseling (How does group counseling differ from individual counseling?, n.d.; Maree, Cook, & Fletcher, 2018; Pyle & Hayden, 2015)
1	Observation	Noting carefully and later integrating observations into the counseling sessions is easily achievable	Noting carefully and later integrating observations into the counseling sessions can be challenging

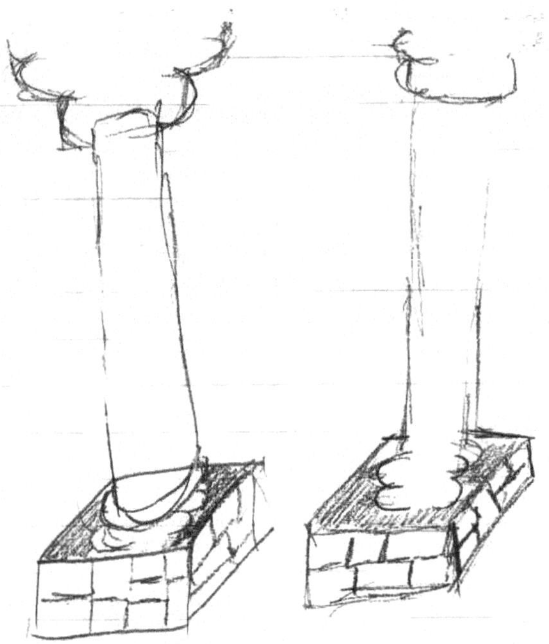

Fig. 10.1 Value of doodle sketch

he chose a "worthwhile" field of study. Geoff subsequently completed his studies in law after which he signed up with a hotel group, received appropriate training, and today is a highly successful international chef.

Example 3: **Clarifying seemingly inconsistentinformation or inappropriate responses**

After Shaun's assessment, during the feedback discussion between him, his parents, and me, we decided that he would do thorough job analysis of a number of fields of study. He seemed distant, though, and merely confirmed that "today's assessment has confirmed my belief that I should study to become a civil engineer". I then said that he should try to find a way to express his love for music (his responses to a number of *CIP* questions revealed a strong interest in music). He looked at me in a puzzled way and then asked his mother why she had told me about his "musical activities". She smiled and said she had in fact not told me about them. She then asked him whether he perhaps did not wish to discuss the matter with me, upon which he produced his cell phone and played me a beautiful song that he had composed. Shaun hesitantly confirmed that he had not wanted to disappoint his father (who wanted him to become a civil engineer), otherwise he would have entered the field of music. His parents and I agreed that he should do a thorough job analysis and make up his own mind as to what he really wanted to study. He subsequently enrolled on a course in civil engineering but also attended a number of short courses on singing, song-writing, and music production during his studies. Today, he is practicing engineer but also a popular singer-songwriter in his own right.

10.6 Summary

Career counselors have access to a broad array of strategies and techniques for eliciting people's career stories and their scores to promote critical self-reflection and reflexivity and, in doing so, enhance narratability and autobiographicity (Briddick, Sensoy-Briddick, & Savickas, 2018). This chapter focused on how an integrative QUALITATIVE-quantitative approach to career counseling using instruments such as the *CIP* (qualitative) with or without the *MCM* (quantitative) can be used to facilitate career counseling in individual as well as in group contexts. Following the kind of structured approach advocated in this chapter, career counselors should be able to help assessees formulate their identity, value, or power statements, decide on possible careers and associated fields of study, and, eventually, draft their mission and vision statements. A suitable course of action can then be devised to enable assessees to move forward. Ensuring that intervention aims are consistent with the reasons people sought career counseling in the first place should at all times be our priority. Likewise, conducting follow-up is essential.

The integrative approach espoused here is described by Laher, Fynn, and Kramer (2019) as "interesting also in [its] diverse applications of narrative research that do not necessarily conform to the method as explicated in methods textbooks" (p. 11). The authors go on to state that this style of research blurs the researcher-practitioner boundaries and provides an "excellent example of socially relevant research in contexts of practice" (p. 11). A recent intervention research project conducted at correctional facilities confirmed the truth of these statements and provided further evidence of the power of the approach outlined here. The project also confirmed the need of inmates (to me, the word "convicts" is an inappropriate term that has no place in a postmodern society) for support to convert their idiosyncratic kind of hurt into hope, social contributions, and a sense of purpose (Taylor & Beukes, 2019). I believe career counselors should also occasionally conduct this kind of intervention research in contexts that are off the beaten career counseling track.

Chapter 11 discusses a number of cases studies in diverse contexts to demonstrate the implementation of the strategy advocated in this chapter.

References

Anderson, H., & Goolishian, H. (1992). Human systems as linguistic systems: Evolving ideas about the implications for theory and practice. *Family Process, 27,* 371–393.

Arnett, J. J. (2007). Emerging adulthood: What is it and what is it good for? *Society for Research in Child Development, 1*(2), 68–73.

Bernard, H. R, & Ryan, G. W. (2010). *Analyzing qualitative data: Systematic approaches.* Beverly Hills, CA: Sage.

Briddick, W. C., & Sensoy-Briddick, H. (2013). The role of audience in life design. In A. Di Fabio & J. G. Maree (Eds.), *Psychology of career counseling: New challenges for a new era* (pp. 69–83). New York, NY: Nova Science.

Briddick, W., Sensoy-Briddick, H., & Savickas, S. (2018). Career construction materials: The story of a career development curriculum in a Turkish school. *Early Child Development and Care, 188*(4), 478–489. https://doi.org/10.1080/03004430.2017.1423483.

Cochran, L. R. (1992). The career project. *Journal of Career Development, 18*(3), 187–197.

Cochran, L. R. (1997). *Career counseling: A narrative approach.* Pacific Grove, CA: Thousand Oaks.

Di Fabio, A., & Maree, J. G. (2013a). Career counseling: The usefulness of the *Career Interest* Profile (*CIP*). *Journal for Psychology in Africa, 23*(1), 41–51.

Di Fabio, A., & Maree, J. G. (2013b). The effectiveness of the *Career Interest Profile* (*CIP*). *Journal of Employment Counseling, 50,* 110–123.

Duffy, R. D., & Dik, B. J. (2009). Beyond the self: External influences in the career development process. *The Career Development Quarterly, 58,* 29–43.

Gati, I. (2011a). *Abridged professional manual for the Career Decision-making Difficulties Questionnaire* (*CDDQ*). Author.

Gati, I. (2011b). *Career Decision-making Difficulties Questionnaire (CDDQ): Abridged Professional Manual.* Retrieved from http://kivunim.huji.ac.il/cddq/CDDQ-Manual-3-2011.doc.

Hartung, P. J. (2010a). Career assessment: Using scores and stories in life designing. In J. G. Maree (Ed.), *Career counselling: Methods that work* (pp. 1–10). Cape Town, South Africa: Juta & Company, Ltd.

Hartung, P. J. (2010b). Identifying life-career themes with the career story interview. In J. G. Maree (Ed.) *Career counselling: Techniques that work* (pp. 161–166). Cape Town, South Africa: Juta & Company, Ltd.

Hartung, P. J. (2013). The life-span, life-space theory of careers. In S. D. Brown, & R. W. Lent (Eds.), *Career development and counseling: Putting theory and research to work* (2nd ed., pp. 83–113). Hoboken, NJ: John Wiley & Sons.

Hartung, P. J. (2013a). The life-span, life-space theory of careers. In S. D. Brown, & R. W. Lent (Eds.), *Career development and counseling: Putting theory and research to work* (2nd ed., pp. 83–113). Hoboken, NJ: John Wiley & Sons.

Hartung, P. J. (2013b). Career construction counselling. A. Di Fabio & J. G. Maree (Eds.), *Psychology of career counseling: New challenges for a new era* (pp. 15–28). Hauppauge, New York: Nova Science.

Hartung, P. J., & Cadaret, M. J. (2017). Career adaptability: Changing self and situation for satisfaction and success. In J. G. Maree (Ed.), *Psychology of career adaptability, employability, and resilience* (pp. 15–28). New York, NY: Springer.

How does group counseling differ from individual counseling? (n.d.) Retrieved from https://onlinedegrees.bradley.edu/blog/how-does-group-counseling-differ-from-individual-counseling/.

Laher, S., Fynn, A., & Kramer, S. (Eds.). (2019). Research as practice: Contextualising applied research in the South African context. In S. Laher, A., Fynn, & S. Kramer (Eds.), *Transforming research methods in the social sciences. Case studies from South Africa.* (pp. 1–18). Johannesburg, South Africa: Wits University Press.

Maree, J. G. (2012b). Using "informal" hypnotherapy in career counselling: Blending Savickas and Erickson to "free the angel". *South African Journal of Psychology, 42*(2), 156–168. Retrieved from https://journals.sagepub.com.uplib.idm.oclc.org/doi/pdf/10.1177/008124631204200203.
Maree, J. G. (2013a). *Counseling for career construction: Connecting life themes to construct life portraits: Turning pain into hope.* Rotterdam, The Netherlands: Sense.
Maree, J. G. (2013b). Latest developments in career counselling in South Africa: Towards a positive approach. *South African Journal of Psychology, 43*(4), 409–421.
Maree, J. G. (2015a, September 6). *DVD trailer: A guide to reflective career counselling.* Retrieved from https://www.youtube.com/watch?v=3Rb8oIJTd6Y.
Maree, J. G. (2015b). Research on life design in (South) Africa: A qualitative analysis. *South African Journal of Psychology, 45*, 332–348.
Maree, J. G. (2016). Using interpersonal process during career construction counseling to promote reflexivity and expedite change. *Journal of Vocational Behaviour, 96*, 22–30.
Maree, J. G. (2017). *The Career Interest Profile (CIP) (version 6): Obtaining, qualitatively, a profile of personal career-life themes and interests.* Randburg: JvR Psychometrics.
Maree, J. G. (2019, June). *Career development in Africa: Decent work for all: Brief photomontage.* Keynote Address at the Annual Career Development Practitioner Congress, Emperors Palace Conference Centre, Kempton Park, South Africa.
Maree, J. G., Cook, A. V., & Fletcher, L. (2018). Assessment of the value of group-based counselling for career construction. *International Journal of Adolescence and Youth, 23*(1), 118–132. https://doi.org/10.1080/02673843.2017.1309324.
McMahon, M., & Patton, W. (2002). Using qualitative assessment in career counseling. *International Journal for Educational and Vocational Guidance, 2,* 51–66.
Oyserman, D., Bybee, D., & Terry, K. (2006). Possible selves and academic outcomes: How and when possible selves impel action. *Journal of Personality and Social Psychology, 91,* 188–204.
Pyle, K. R., & Hayden, S. C. (2015). *Group career counseling: Practices and principles* (2nd ed.). Broken Arrow, OK: National Career Development Association.
Richardson, G. (2002). The metatheory of resilience and resiliency. *Journal of Clinical Psychology, 58*(3), 307–321.
Savickas, M. L. (2009a, April). *The essentials of life design counseling.* Invited public lecture, the University of Pretoria, Pretoria, South Africa.
Savickas, M. L. (2009b, April). *Utilizing early anecdotes in counseling in the 21st century.* Keynote presentation, SA Society for Clinical Hypnosis. Pretoria, South Africa.
Savickas, M. L. (2011). Reshaping the story of career counseling. In K. Maree (Ed.), Shaping the story—A guide to facilitate narrative counseling (pp. 1–3). Boston/Rotterdam, The Netherlands: Sense.
Savickas, M. L. (2015a). Career counseling paradigms: Guiding, developing, and designing. In P. Hartung, M. Savickas, & W. Walsh (Eds.), *The APA handbook of career intervention* (Vol. 1, pp. 129–143). Washington, DC: APA Books.
Savickas, M. L. (2015b). *Life-design counseling manual.* Rootstown, OH: Author.
Savickas, M. L. (2016a, July). *Meaning at work: Work at meaning.* Closing keynote presentation, National Career Development Association Conference, Chicago, United States of America.
Savickas, M. L. (2016b). Reflection and reflexivity during life-design interventions: Comments on career construction counseling. *Journal of Vocational Behavior, 97,* 84–89.
Savickas, M. L. (2019). *Theories of psychotherapy series. Career counseling* (2nd ed.). Washington, DC: American Psychological Association.
Savickas, M. L., & Hartung, P. J. (2012, June). *My career story: An autobiographical workbook for life-career success.* Retrieved from www.vocopher.com.
Savickas, M. L., & Porfeli, E. J. (2012). *Career Adapt-Abilities Scale*: Construction, reliability, and measurement equivalence across 13 countries. *Journal of Vocational Behavior, 80,* 661–673. https://doi.org/10.1016/j.jvb.2012.01.011.

Taber, B. J. (2013). The career construction interview and its use in career counseling. In A. Di Fabio & J. G. Maree (Eds.), *Psychology of career counseling: New challenges for a new era* (pp. 149–160). Hauppauge, NY: Nova Science.

Taylor, N., & Beukes, C. (2019). A life design-related career development intervention for working adults in the manufacturing, engineering and related sectors. *African Journal of Career Development*, *1*(1). Retrieved from https://ajcd.africa/index.php/ajcd/article/view/2.

Part IV
From Theory to Practice: Case Studies

Chapter 11
Case Studies Demonstrating the Use of Integrative QUALITATIVE-Quantitative Career Counseling Intervention to Promote Innovation in Career Counseling Across the Life Span

"The value of an idea lies in the using of it." (Thomas Edison).

Abstract This chapter reports on the practical implementation of the theoretical and conceptual framework outlined and discussed in the first 10 chapters of the book. Examples of the implementation of the *CIP* (either on its own or together with the *MCM*), in individual and in group-based contexts, are provided. By including narratives in the form of case studies, I hope to demonstrate how theory can be converted into practice and vice versa. Hopefully, the case study narratives will be illuminating for career counselors and indicate how they can partner with clients to enhance their self- and career construction. First, the implementation of the *CIP* in conjunction with the *MCM* and connecting the dots to confirm a career choice in an "uncomplicated case" is discussed. The focus then shifts to a discussion of a number of purposely selected case studies in more or less detail before the chapter is concluded.

11.1 Orientation

A basic ethical principle in psychology is that no person should be allowed to administer any assessment or facilitate an associated intervention with any instrument(s) unless and until she or he has self-administered it. The same rule applies here. Irrespective of how experienced career counselors are, completing the *CIP* and the *MCM* first and, if at all possible, receiving basic training in its administration and the interpretation of its outcomes is crucial. As mentioned earlier, the *CIP* is an extremely versatile instrument that enables career counselors to help people examine, reflect on, and draw on the myriad of influences that have individually and collectively shaped, inspired, and contributed to their career choice decision-making. This also applies to the analysis of its outcomes. For the most part, I draw on the *CIP* narrative

J. G. (Kobus) Maree, *Innovating Counseling for Self- and Career Construction*,
https://doi.org/10.1007/978-3-030-48648-8_11

structure and include relevant information from the *MCM* that can also be obtained by administering the *MCM* in either hard copy or online format.

11.2 Uncovering Assessees' Advice to Themselves

The implicit advice embedded in assessees' favorite quotations can be drawn on when the counselor thinks this appropriate. Consider, for instance, the advice implicit in the following quotations proffered by Joan whose marks had dropped unexpectedly during her previous examination.

"Smile, it's going to be alright."

"Never give up."

"The sun is always shining brightly somewhere."

When one considers that Joan's boyfriend of three years had decided to terminate their relationship three months prior to the assessment, which left her inconsolable and no longer motivated to study, her advice to herself from within on how to face the future with renewed hope is clear. Likewise, John's[1] advice to himself is clear from the following quotation: "Failure is the opportunity to rethink, begin and try again." (John had unsuccessfully applied for acceptance into a school of medicine and was very depressed when he consulted me.) Also consider the following quotation by Teresa who was angry with her teachers because she believed they were responsible for her not having been elected to the school's representative student council.

"Holding on to anger is like drinking poison and expecting the other person to die."

"Kill them with kindness."

Teresa's implicit advice to herself is evident in these quotations.

In the next section, I discuss case studies on the implementation of the *CIP* in conjunction with the *MCM* or on its own.

11.3 Implementation of the *CIP* in Conjunction with the *MCM*

The first case study demonstrates how *CIP* and *MCM* outcomes **yielded by the online *CIP* and *MCM* reports** can be integrated. This is an example of an "uncomplicated" assessment, which should be the case with most assessees. In other words, counselors with adequate training and experience should experience little difficulty in

i. uncovering assessees' interests, values, strongest points, areas for growth, and key life themes;

---

[1] Pseudonyms are used in all the case studies. Written informed consent and assent (where applicable) was obtained from all stakeholders, confidentiality was guaranteed, and participants were invited to authorize or de-authorise all the information obtained during the intervention.

ii. jointly with them,

a. identifying the main patterns, themes, and subthemes in their life stories, and
b. integrating or weaving together these themes **within** but also **between** the two paradigms (qualitative and quantitative) in such a way that assessees can find "answers" to their reason for seeking counseling.

Next, the focus shifts to a discussion of a few cases that can be described as "less uncomplicated".

Lastly, a number of very brief "case studies" are considered where the responses to a few select questions enable assessees to explain their reason for consulting a career counselor (formerly referred to as the "presenting problem"). Depending on assessees' level of development, unique situation, and the information available on them, career counselors may decide to use either all or only a few questions.

It should again be emphasized that each "case" is unique and should be treated as such. Gone are the days when career counselors were interested almost exclusively in how their clients differed from or resembled others. What we are interested in today is each individual assessee's idiosyncratic life story. Not how she or he compares with others.

11.4 Selected Case Studies

Below, a number of purposely selected case studies are discussed in more or less detail (see Table 11.1 for a summary of the case studies).

11.5 Case Study 1: Connecting the Dots to "Confirm" a Career Choice: "Uncomplicated Case"

This case study was chosen purposely to demonstrate how *CIP* and *MCM* online outcomes can be integrated and used to facilitate integrative counseling for self- and career construction for a person with a moratorium career choice status (a person in a state of transition that normally involves enhanced work role commitment) (Marcia, 1983; Porfeli et al., 2011; Rottinghaus & Miller, 2013; Sharf, 2013).

Participant and context. Candice (pseudonym; a 17-year-old Indian woman) was selected randomly from a group of learners who had participated in a group-based career counseling research project in 2019. She completed the *CIP* and the *MCM* online.

Her responses to some of the questions in the *CIP* (Parts 1, 2, and 4) are given and discussed briefly below.

Table 11.1 Summary of case studies

No	Biographical details	Type of career counseling challenge or insecurity experienced (Career indecision. n.d.; Di Fabio & Kenny, 2011; Gati & Saka, 2011a, b; Gati & Asher, 2001a, b; Gati, Krausz, & Osipow, 1996; Kelly & Lee, 2005; Maree, 2016b; 2019a, b; Morgan & Ness, 2003; Wanberg & Muchinsky, 1992)	Career choice identity status (Erikson, 1982; Gati, Krausz, & Osipow, 1996; Marcia, 1964, 1966, 1980, 1983; Morgan & Ness, 2011; Porfeli, Vondracek, & Weigold, 2011; Rottinghaus & Miller, 2013; Sharf, 2013; Sweitzer, 2011)	Assessments completed	Style of analysis In all instances, assessees' mission and vision statements were completed and included in their career-life story narratives
1.	Candice, a 17-year-old Indian woman)	Insecurity that sets in when people encounter "natural" points of transition or crossroads during their academic careers (such as transitioning from one school phase to another and having to choose between certain subjects)	Moratorium/"Developmental" indecision (1): "uncomplicated" case	*CIP* and *MCM* (online)	Using the *CIP* and *MCM* online report templates
2.	Nkepile, 22-year- old black, Pedi-speaking woman	Decision further stalled by lack of access to resources	Moratorium/"Developmental" indecision (2): "more challenging" case	*CIP* and *MCM* (hard copy format)	Using the integrative career choice and construction conversation template

(continued)

Table 11.1 (continued)

No	Biographical details	Type of career counseling challenge or insecurity experienced (Career indecision. n.d.; Di Fabio & Kenny, 2011; Gati & Saka, 2011a, b; Gati & Asher, 2001a, b; Gati, Krausz, & Osipow, 1996; Kelly & Lee, 2005; Maree, 2016b; 2019a, b; Morgan & Ness, 2003; Wanberg & Muchinsky, 1992)	Career choice identity status (Erikson, 1982; Gati, Krausz, & Osipow, 1996; Marcia, 1964, 1966, 1980, 1983; Morgan & Ness, 2011; Porfeli, Vondracek, & Weigold, 2011; Rottinghaus & Miller, 2013; Sharf, 2013; Sweitzer, 2011)	Assessments completed	Style of analysis In all instances, assessees' mission and vision statements were completed and included in their career-life story narratives
3.	Violet, a 35-year-old Afrikaans- speaking woman	Choice anxiety (being anxious about making or taking career-decision choice)	Foreclosure (client's sense of creativity stifled by undue parental influence)	*CIP* and *MCM* (hard copy format)	Brief qualitative analysis of assessee's responses Key life themes and interests linked with and related to specific study fields and associated work environments
4.	Fikani, a 20-year-old black, Sotho-speaking man	Insecurity that sets in when people encounter "natural" points of transition or crossroads during their academic careers; decision further stalled by lack of access to resources	Undifferentiated (1) (decision stalled by lack of access to resources)	*CIP* and *MCM* (hard copy format)	Brief qualitative analysis of assessee's responses Key life themes and interests linked with and related to specific study fields and associated work environments

(continued)

Table 11.1 (continued)

No	Biographical details	Type of career counseling challenge or insecurity experienced (Career indecision. n.d.; Di Fabio & Kenny, 2011; Gati & Saka, 2011a, b; Gati & Asher, 2001a, b; Gati, Krausz, & Osipow, 1996; Kelly & Lee, 2005; Maree, 2016b; 2019a, b; Morgan & Ness, 2003; Wanberg & Muchinsky, 1992)	Career choice identity status (Erikson, 1982; Gati, Krausz, & Osipow, 1996; Marcia, 1964, 1966, 1980, 1983; Morgan & Ness, 2011; Porfeli, Vondracek, & Weigold, 2011; Rottinghaus & Miller, 2013; Sharf, 2013; Sweitzer, 2011)	Assessments completed	Style of analysis In all instances, assessees' mission and vision statements were completed and included in their career-life story narratives
5.	Michael, a 25-year-old English-speaking man	Career decision-making difficulties of a more pervasive and "pathological" nature	Undifferentiated (2) (decision further stalled by difficulties of a more pervasive and "pathological" nature)	*CIP* and *MCM* (hard copy format)	Brief qualitative analysis of assessee's responses Key life themes and interests linked with and related to specific study fields and associated work environments
6.	Jeannie, a 67-year-old white, English-speaking woman in an executive position	Seeking increased self-awareness and further development	Achieved identity status	*CIP* and *MCM* (online)	Using the *CIP* and *MCM* online report template
7.	Wayde, a 20-year-old German mother-tongue speaking man	Insecurity that sets in when people encounter "natural" points of transition or crossroads during their academic careers (such as transitioning from one school phase to another or from school to tertiary training institutions)	Undifferentiated career status	*CIP* and *MCM* (hard copy format)	Brief qualitative analysis of assessee's responses Key life themes and interests linked with and related to specific study fields and associated work environments

(continued)

Table 11.1 (continued)

No	Biographical details	Type of career counseling challenge or insecurity experienced (Career indecision. n.d.; Di Fabio & Kenny, 2011; Gati & Saka, 2011a, b; Gati & Asher, 2001a, b; Gati, Krausz, & Osipow, 1996; Kelly & Lee, 2005; Maree, 2016b; 2019a, b; Morgan & Ness, 2003; Wanberg & Muchinsky, 1992)	Career choice identity status (Erikson, 1982; Gati, Krausz, & Osipow, 1996; Marcia, 1964, 1966, 1980, 1983; Morgan & Ness, 2011; Porfeli, Vondracek, & Weigold, 2011; Rottinghaus & Miller, 2013; Sharf, 2013; Sweitzer, 2011)	Assessments completed	Style of analysis In all instances, assessees' mission and vision statements were completed and included in their career-life story narratives
8.	Marie, a 19-year-old first-year Indian student	Career indecision due to discrepancy between assessee's own views and the views of significant others about career decision choices (perceiving either objectively or subjectively disagreement with or disapproval of significant others about career choices)	Moratorium status: Parental preferences adversely influence client decisions	*CIP* and *MCM* (hard copy format)	Brief qualitative analysis of assessee's responses Key life themes and interests linked with and related to specific study fields and associated work environments

Step 1: Reflecting on Candice's responses[2,3]

Section 11.1: Candice's expectations about the intervention

In response to the question "How can I be of use, of help, or of value to you today?" (This question can also be changed to, for instance, "What are you hoping to gain from the intervention?"), Candice replied:

"I am interested in a number of fields, and people believe I should become an accountant. I am hoping you will be able to tell me which career choice will be the "right" one for me."

Reflection: Candice was tactfully reminded first that it was inappropriate to use words such as "right", "wrong", or "best" in career counseling contexts. Instead, she was advised that it would be more appropriate to use words such as "(more) appropriate", "(less) appropriate", or even "inappropriate" choices (depending on assessees' unique circumstances and contexts).

Candice confirmed that she felt quite sure about her general field of study. However, she needed help regarding which field of study might be the "best" or "right" for her. She also sought clarity on which other fields of study she could conduct job analysis on.

Section 11.2: Gaining perspective: Establishing Candice's career identity

My seven greatest strengths are the following: "I am …
resilient, and I will keep persisting and rise above the knocks in life;
organized and very busy, so I need to be organized to handle my life;
grounded in reality—I believe everything happens for a reason;
patient and happy to wait and keep trying until something happens;
inquisitive and curious about our world and want to learn more;
an outdoors person, and
good with people and animals and love taking care of animals in particular."

My seven areas for development or growth[4]. "I …
need to learn to say no to certain things and accept that I cannot do everything in life;
must accept that I cannot control/determine the outcome of everything;
need to listen to other people more;
need to consider others more;
want to become even better at motivating people and helping animals; and
want to become even kinder to people and animals, as well as even more humble and selfless."

[2]Due to space constraints, only a limited number of responses are given here. Also see Chap. 8, Sect. 8.7.12, where the question regarding how many and which questions suffice to facilitate triangulation and crystallization and ensure reliable, valid, and trustworthy career counseling is discussed in more detail.

[3]As mentioned earlier, career counselors may of course use any word they prefer to refer to what was earlier referred to as the "results".

[4]Career counselors should ensure that assessees understand what is meant by "areas for development". Some assessees incorrectly assume that it refers to areas where they are educated such as primary school, high school, and university.

I admired the following three people, sport stars, or animation characters when I was young (or they were my role models when I was young) (Candice could list only three role models that dated back to when she was 13 or 14 years old):

"Nelson Mandela because he was able to forgive and see what needed to be done. He fought for what was right and has always inspired me to stand up for what I believe in. He has inspired me to live by the concept of Ubuntu and always try to be the best person I can possibly be. He fought for his rights and brought peace to a country during a time when it was needed most."

"Lawrence Anthony because he inspired me to try to form connections with animals. I admired his determination and his longing to make a difference, which paid off. I also admired what he did for nature conservation. What he did for conservation and for many animals still inspires me today. He put their lives over his own and continued to fight for what he believed in and to save the lives of those who do not have a voice of their own. I want to make a difference like he did."

"Helen, a female sheep farmer. She used to run the dairy while her husband managed the farm, but a few years ago he passed away. Since then she has taken over the whole farm and runs it at the highest standard. She is capable of making the most of difficult situations; her strength and courage inspire me."

My three mottos or favorite quotations:

"Hard work beats talent when talent fails to work hard."

"Failing to plan is planning to fail."

"Everything happens for a reason."

I enjoy:

"Finding out/discovering information about the biological world. Life sciences is one of my favorite subjects as a result. I love exercise and participate in multiple sports, such as netball, swimming, basketball and recreational running. I love reading. I enjoy being outdoors/in nature and my favorite place to be is in a game reserve."

My favorite

Magazine:	"National Geographic"
TV Program:	"Grey's Anatomy"
Website:	"NatGeo Your Shot"

What do you regard as your major themes/patterns?

"My growth and development as a person. I have grown from being extremely shy with low self-esteem to a confident, determined person. The theme of rising up from disappointments, the theme for fighting for what you believe in, and hard work. The theme of being comforted by my pets … of loving to take care of people and animals in need."

My three biggest challenges ("problems"[5]) when I was young

"My parents got divorced and I felt deserted."

"I was unsure of myself."

"I did not believe in myself and had no friends except for my beloved pets."

Reflection: Write down the main themes, patterns, or trends you identified from your answers to these questions

"Discovering information about the biological world, adventure-related activities, working with animals, being outdoors, being in nature, being active, having experienced and dealing effectively from disappointments. Life sciences is one of my favorite subjects as a result. Connecting with animals, standing up for what is right, defending entities that cannot defend themselves. I want to become the best person I can be, fight for the rights of "unvoiced" people, connect with animals, make a difference by taking care of animals and promoting nature conservation. I want to make the most of challenging situations and inspire others to do likewise."

Try to link these themes to possible work environments/careers

"Veterinary sciences, medicine, nature conservation, nursing, and law."

Section 11.3: Reflect on the meaning of career influences in your life

Parental advice

"My parents are both working in the field of accounting, and they love doing what they are doing. I am often told by them that I take after them and that I should become an accountant or actuary. However, I have always believed in my right to choose what I want to do with my life. They are therefore willing to support me in the career I wish to study."

Teachers' advice

"Something in the mathematical, accountancy, or biological field."

Reflection: Write down the main themes, patterns, or trends you identified from your answers to these questions.

"Similar to what I have already mentioned, but also that others also believe I should follow in the footsteps of my parents."

Section 11.4: Choosing preferred career category options from the list of 19 of your most and least preferred career categories

According to the *CIP* (Version 6) (Maree, 2017), Candice's preferred interest categories were the following:

Adventure, plants, animals, and the environment

Medical and/or paramedical services

Research

---

[5]From a positive career counseling perspective, words such as "problems" and "failures" have no place in postmodern career counseling; hence the use of double inverted commas.

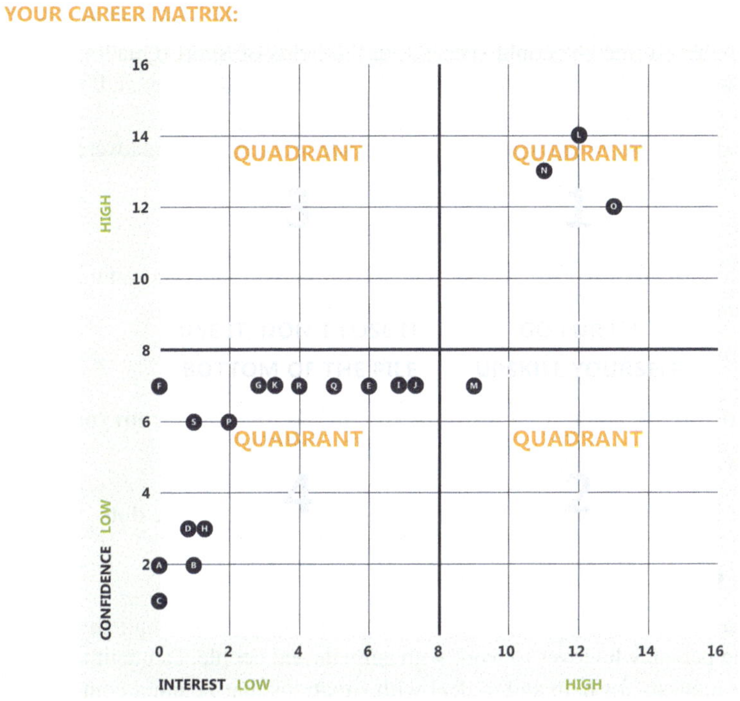

Fig. 11.1 Candice's *MCM* profile

Mathematics and/or accounting industry
Social, caregiving, and/or community services
Executive and management practice.

Career matrix

Candice's career matrix is shown below (Fig. 11.1).

Reflection

Three career categories fell in Quadrant 1, namely:

1. Adventure activities, nature, and outdoor life
2. Research
3. Medical and or paramedical services

These scores indicate definite (strong), clearly defined interest and confidence levels. In other words, Candice believed that she would succeed in corresponding career categories (which should be considered for job analysis) and possibly pursuing careers associated with these categories.

Furthermore, Candice's matrix reveals that she was also interested, and to a certain extent believed that she could succeed, in the fields of Sport (Quadrant 2), Mathematics and/or accounting industry, as well as Social, caregiving, and/or community services (Quadrant 4).

The overlap between the interest and confidence categories uncovered by the *CIP* and the *MCM* is thus clear.

Section 11.5: Additional comments

"I am a hard-working, diligent person. I love both people and animals, but I am particularly protective when it comes to animals."

Reflection

Write down the themes, patterns, or trends you identified from your answers.

"I am particularly protective of animals."

Step 2: Making sense of the information and connecting the dots

Power, value, or identity statement

"I am a resilient, persistent, organized, optimistic, patient, inquisitive, and hard-working person who loves to work with animals and people. I sometimes struggle to decline requests for help and to deal with situations that I cannot control. I want to improve my listening skills, be even more considerate, motivating, and helpful, and be (even more) modest and selfless."

Possible fields of study

"Veterinary science, nursing, dentistry, agriculture, biological sciences in general, nature conservation, and medicine."

Step 3: Formulating personal mission and vision statements (to help you make meaning of and experience a sense of purpose in your career-life)

Mission statement (personal meaning)

"I will be happy and experience a sense of meaning when I work in an environment where I can work with and enact my ability to work with animals in need, construct and develop my caring side, display my dedication, and actualize my given talents."

Vision statement (social meaning)

"I want to make enough money to take care of my family's needs but especially the needs of stray animals and poor people and travel the world to learn from how others in my field. I want to take care of the medical and emotional needs of animals but also their owners' emotional needs. Hopefully I can one day establish a foundation that will help me take care of stray animals and protect the environment. That will make my life purposeful."

This future scenario directly covers Candice's stated reasons for seeking career counseling.

Step 4: Moving forward

Action steps: Conducting job analysis

Candice was requested to do a thorough job analysis comprising the following steps.

i. Discuss your findings and options with an "audience" (e.g. your parents, friends, teachers and, of course, employers and employees).
ii. Using the career options suggested by the *CIP* process, obtain, study, and analyze information from training institutions.
iii. Network with as many individuals and institutions as possible to obtain current, realistic, work-related information. Make sure that the costs, admission requirements, and information on the subjects are in line with your life realities and self-knowledge.
iv. Use social media, libraries, and the internet to research career options related to your *CIP* themes.
v. Seek opportunities for internships, learnerships, mentoring, vacation employment, site visits, interviews, and "work shadowing" to understand the realities of the careers you have identified.
vi. Visit locations where different careers are pursued (observe employees and ask questions).
vii. Organize mentorship and engage in vicarious learning. Actively analyze other sources of information on careers such as books (read), videos (watch), brochures (inspect), and vacation schools (attend).
viii. Enquire about the possibility of "work shadowing", temporary employment, and volunteer work.

Planning Candice's next steps

Together, we decided on the following action plans.

"Today I will reflect on what we have done so far and record my reflections."

"This week I will discuss the "outcomes" and my reflections with as many people as possible to obtain more clarity and find out how others respond to my decisions."

"This month I will begin to set up appointments with relevant institutions and individuals."

"This year I will conduct thorough job analyses and strive to attain the best marks I can to increase my chances of being accepted into veterinary science."

"In five years' time I will hopefully be almost done with my studies and celebrate not only my success but also the wonderful position I am in by already helping animals and reaching out to their owners."

Sequel

Candice applied successfully for acceptance into the veterinary science program and is currently enrolled on a five-year degree course to become a veterinary surgeon.

The second case study demonstrates how *CIP* and *MCM* outcomes **yielded by the online *CIP* and *MCM* reports** can be integrated by using the **"Integrative career choice and construction conversation" template**.

11.6 Case Study 2: Nkepile: Dealing with Moratorium/"Developmental" Indecision

Case Study 2 was chosen purposely to demonstrate how *CIP* and *MCM* outcomes (hard copy format) can be integrated and used to facilitate integrative counseling for self- and career construction for a person with a moratorium career choice status (a person who has committed herself or himself to meticulously examined work roles yet shows high levels of career self-doubt and flexibility) (Marcia, 1983; Porfeli et al., 2011).

Participant and context

Nkepile (a pseudonym; a 22-year-old black, Pedi-speaking woman, the fourth of five children) was selected purposely from a group of black women who had participated in group-based life counseling for self- and career construction at a rural training institution in 2018. She was unable to find sustainable employment and consequently struggled to secure a stable income and take care of her own needs and those of her child. Asked what she was hoping to gain from the intervention, she replied: "I am totally clueless about what I would like to do. Assist me and help me find out what my "true" passion is and what careers will suit this passion. What careers will I do best in? Which career is the "right"[6] one for me?"

After I had explained to the group what the intervention entailed, they agreed to our following an integrative QUALITATIVE-quantitative approach.

Procedure

It was agreed with the training institution that the intervention would be concluded in three phases. The first intervention lasted about six hours (09:00 to roughly 15:00) and included a few breaks. After a brief introductory discussion, the assessees/participants completed the Career Adapt-Abilities Scale (CAAS; Maree, 2012b; Savickas & Porfeli, 2012), then the *MCM*, followed by the *CIP*. Both questionnaires were completed in hard copy format.

On Day 2, the assessees completed the "Integrative career choice and construction conversation" template (Table 11.2) in groups of five. Reflexivity (meta-reflection) was facilitated by requesting the assessees to reflect repeatedly on their reflections (comprising their responses to questions in the *MCM* and the *CIP* in particular). I offered generalized information, psychosocial information, and psychoeducational information, as well as career counseling (see Table 6), but I stressed that I would not

[6]Whenever careers were labelled as "right" or "wrong", the participants were informed that it is more correct to refer to careers as inappropriate, less appropriate, or appropriate.

Table 11.2 "Integrative career choice and construction conversation": Nkepile

Step 1: Summarize some main patterns from your career story narratives (career interest profile)						
Strengths	"I am respectful, work well under pressure and work hard, love working with people, am a listener, am courageous, can be strong when I have to be, love sharing ideas"					
Areas for growth	"I am not good at working with my hands, hate seeing people (children especially) suffer, have not found a good job, have not yet secured a spot at university, "fell" but regained control over my life [for ethical reasons, the nature of her "fall" will not be elaborated on here]					
Values	"I respect others, achieve academically, love to comfort sad people, and I am honest"					
Central life themes	"Helping people that suffer or that have "fallen" rise again" "Getting up after a fall" "Touching the lives of others that have suffered"					
Now combine all of the above (your strengths, areas for growth, values and central life themes) into two or three sentences that communicate your uniqueness. Begin with the words "I am …						
"I am academically ambitious and respectful; I am a structured person who works well under pressure and works hard; I love working with people; I never give up; I am courageous; I can be strong when I have to be, and I love sharing ideas. However, I am not good at working with my hands; I cannot tolerate seeing people (children especially) suffer without trying to do something. Like my role models, I want to work with and uplift people that suffer; I come from a very poor family; I aim to improve myself and touch people; and I want them get up after challenges like I myself did"						
Step 2: Please complete the following table by referring to your *CIP* answer sheet, *MCM* report, and school marks (you may also include your personality type information if you have access to it)						
Career interest profile (*CIP*)			Maree Career Matrix (*MCM*)		School marks by subject at the end of last year	
Seven preferred interest categories	Five preferred careers	Seven careers underlined in green	Preferred (Interest And Confidence) career categories	Specific careers you scored both high interest (2) and confidence (2)	Subject	Mark (%)
1. Social, caregiving, and community services	1. Social worker	Social worker	1. Office work (administrative and clerical activities)	1. Social worker	1. History	64

(continued)

Table 11.2 (continued)

Step 2: Please complete the following table by referring to your *CIP* answer sheet, *MCM* report, and school marks (you may also include your personality type information if you have access to it)						
Career interest profile (*CIP*)			Maree Career Matrix (*MCM*)		School marks by subject at the end of last year	
Seven preferred interest categories	Five preferred careers	Seven careers underlined in green	Preferred (Interest And Confidence) career categories	Specific careers you scored both high interest (2) and confidence (2)	Subject	Mark (%)
2. Office-based work (administrative, clerical, and organizational activities)	2. Clerk/Office administrator	Administrator	2. Social, caregiving, and community services	2. Secretary	2. Mathematical literacy	62
3. Entrepreneurship; running a personal business	3. Teacher	Psychologist	3. Tourism and the hospitality industry	3. Teacher	3. Tourism management	55
4. Word artistry	4. Receptionist	Communication specialist	4. Entrepreneurship; running a personal business	4. Call center operator	4. Business studies	51
5. Tourism and the hospitality industry	5. Safety officer	Computer programmer	5. Information and communication technology	5. Bank teller	5. Geography	53
6. Information and communication technology	6. Airhostess	Receptionist	6.	6. Data capturer	6. English	54
7.	7. Psychologist	Air hostess	7.	7. Hotel clerk	7. Pedi	61
8.	8.		8.	8. Small business owner	8.	

(continued)

Table 11.2 (continued)

Step 3: Identify your integrated main interest categories/patterns (based on the information provided in the table above)				
Interest category or field				
1		Social, caregiving, and community services		
2		Office-based work (administrative, clerical, and organizational activities)		
3		Entrepreneurship; running a personal business		
4		Tourism and the hospitality industry		
5		Word artistry		
6		Information and communication technology		
Step 4: Where do you want to study after having completed grade 12?				
Summarized possible career choices		University	University of technology	Tvet College/Private Training
1	Social worker	Nkepile would prefer to study at a university. However, she would be willing to study at any institution that would be prepared to take her in		
2	Teacher			
3	Office administrator			
4	Educational psychologist			
5	Nurse			
6	Hairdresser			

be dispensing "advice". Instead, we used the career choice and construction conversation template to help them uncover, interpret, and integrate key life themes that emerged from the *CIP* responses ("stories") in particular (the qualitative assessment). On the basis of their themes, and integrating them with the interest-related outcomes yielded by the *MCM* outcomes ("scores"), the assessees were helped to advise themselves on their career choices and on how to make meaning of and uncover a sense of purpose and hope in their career-lives.

In line with Cardoso's (2016) recommendation that people should be educated about their career counseling goals and the associated actions (to strengthen our "working alliance"), I repeated my first question to the assessees ("Who knows you better than anyone else?") whenever an assessee explicitly or implicitly asked me for "advice". Instead of my dispensing advice, they were repeatedly encouraged to reflect on their initial answers to questions in the questionnaires in their groups. The test (*MCM*) was scored manually, and the life themes were uncovered jointly with the assessees. The information was coded by external coders to ensure that the identified themes corresponded to the assessees' answers ("data") to promote the rigor of the deductive process.

Step 1: Reflecting on Nkepile's responses

To save space, only a selected number of responses are given below. As the reader will see, these responses were sufficient for administering career counseling.

My greatest strengths: "I am respectful, work well under pressure, work hard, love working with people, am a listener, am courageous, can be strong when I have to be, and love sharing ideas."

My areas for development: "I am not good at working with my hands, hate seeing people (children especially) suffer, have not found a good job, have not yet secured a spot at university, "fell" but regained control over my life [for ethical reasons, the nature of her "fall" will not be elaborated on here].

My values: "I respect others, do well academically, love to comfort sad people, and I am honest."

People I admired when I was young: "Felicia Mabusa. She was a social worker who had her own TV show, cared for, and was always uplifting people."

"Brenda Fassie. She came from a very poor family and lost her father when she was two but still managed to become a star and touched people with her music."

"Later in my life, when [former State President] Mandela was released, I learned to admire him greatly, especially because of his respectful attitude and his strong love for children."

Events that influenced me most in life: "My granny and I attended a graduation party for a member of our extended family. Since that day I also wanted to graduate with a certificate, diploma, or degree."

"The day I had to give my baby away."

My mottos (the meaning she attached to these mottos appears in square brackets):

"Never give up." [Always keep on trying, no matter how tough things are.]

"What you give out is what you get back." [Never blame your circumstances for your own 'failure'.]

"If you do not want to, you won't." [A person's attitude influences the degree of success she will achieve in life.]

My biggest successes: "I passed Grade 12, obtained an Occupational Health and Safety Certificate (OHSC), obtained my driver's license, and I am the one that is always there for abused friends. I stood up again after I had fallen, and I managed to deal with abuse."

My biggest non-successes ("failures")[7]: "I am currently not studying and developing myself further, which means that I am not improving myself and equipping myself with the knowledge that is needed to help others properly. I 'fell' (emotionally) and almost 'faded' [her elaboration on the matter falls outside the scope of this book]. I was abused and I barely escaped from a burning house."

Title of my life story: "The bumpy ride from poverty and abuse to being given an opportunity."

Chapter titles

"Being poor and hungry"

"Abuse and heartbreak"

"Rescued by angels"

"Rising again, achieving success, and hoping to realize my dreams"

"Fearing that I may lose hope and "fade" again"

(When asked if she would like to explain what the word "fade" meant to her, she replied: "It means that I suffer emotional pain that causes me to "fail" from doing what I can and should be doing or achieving.")

Step 2: Making overall sense of the information: Connecting the dots

We drew on Table 11.2 to facilitate our discussion.

Section 11.1: Reflecting **on Nkepile's expectations about the intervention.**

Facing a "standard" crossroads in her career-life, Nkepile felt uncertain about a future career and field of study and needed "help" regarding what her "true" passion and associated careers were. Believing in the reality of terms such as "best" and "right" or "wrong" careers, she was expecting the counselor to "tell" her which career to choose (a common phenomenon in disadvantaged but also more affluent areas in Africa, even today).

Section 11.2: Gaining perspective by establishing Nkepile's career identity

Together with her friends (under my supervision), and with the support of experienced group leaders, Nkepile reflected carefully on her responses to the *CIP* questions.

"I can work with all people, I love working with abused and other children, and I would love to be involved in helping others, young women that have "fallen"

[7] I always explain that the word "failure" is a misleading term in career counseling contexts because, today, we regard non-successes as opportunities for development and not as "failures".

especially. I enjoy listening to others, and it is important to me to develop myself. I am a structured person."

Section 11.3: Reflecting on the meaning of career influences in Nkepile's life

"I come from a very poor family. My mother is unemployed, and my father is a temporary construction worker. Our entire family struggles, and there is no career trend in the family. We do whatever we can just to earn a living. My parents want me to study information technology because they believe that doing so will help me find employment."

Section 11.4: Reflecting on Nkepile's preferred career category options, on her most and least preferred careers, and on her dream career. The *MCM* outcomes were triangulated against the *CIP* outcomes.

According to the *CIP*, Nkepile's preferred interest categories were:

Social, caregiving, and community services
Office-based (administrative, clerical, and organizational activities) work
Entrepreneurship; running a personal business
Word artistry
Tourism and the hospitality industry

Her highest preferred interest categories according to the Maree Career Matrix are listed below:

Office work (administrative and clerical activities)
Social, caregiving, and community services
Tourism and the hospitality industry
Entrepreneurship; running a personal business
Word artistry

Three career categories fell in Quadrant 1, namely:

Office work (administrative and clerical activities)
Social, caregiving, and community services
Tourism and the hospitality industry

Reflection

Here, too, the overlap between the interest categories uncovered by the *CIP* and the *MCM* was clear.

Section 11.5

Reflecting on her experience of the assessment, Nkepile commented: "I got an opportunity to state and experience my strengths, areas for growth, "weaknesses", and painful moments in my life. I never thought I would want and be able to talk about my abuse in front of others. This somehow made me feel'cleaner'."

Step 3: Making sense of all the themes identified

We jointly identified the following themes: "I can work with all people, I love working with abused (and other) children, and I would love to be involved in helping others; I enjoy listening to others, it is important to me to develop myself, and I am a structured person."

Next, themes, patterns, and trends were identified and connected to a number of possible careers and fields of study. Nkepile and I together decided that she should do a thorough job analysis on (for instance) the following fields of study: social work, teaching (specializing in educational psychology), office administration, nursing, and hairdressing.

This step was concluded with the crafting of her power, value, or identity statement. This is what Nkepile wrote: "I am academically ambitious and respectful; I am a structured person who works well under pressure and works hard; I love working with people; I never give up; I am courageous and can be strong when I have to be; I love sharing ideas. However, I am not good at working with my hands; I cannot tolerate seeing people (children especially) suffer without trying to do something. Like my role models, I come from a very poor family, I aim to improve myself and uplift people that suffer, and I want them to get up after challenges like I myself did."

Next, we formulated Nkepile's personal mission and vision statements. She was clear about her decision: "I want to become a social worker

so that I can (personal meaning)

draw on my ability and meet my need to work with people; realize my capacity to function and serve them in a structured environment; actualize and show my inner strength, courage, and resilience; and improve myself

and in the process make social contributions (social meaning) and experience a sense of purpose in my work-life. I want to work with and uplift people that suffer (children especially) and use my position to improve the lives of young women especially by helping them get up again after challenges. I am hoping to establish an orphanage for children in the region where I grew up and inspire people to assist me and contribute to our community."

Step 4: Action steps: Conducting job analysis to facilitate forward movement by Nkepile

Next, I recommended that she apply for help from the National Student Financial Aid Scheme (NSFAS) (the government-sponsored student bursary and loan scheme). She was awarded a bursary, which, enabled her to resolve the financial challenges that were preventing her from realizing her dreams. I also provided her and the group with the website addresses of tertiary training institutions where she could obtain more information on the courses she was interested in (**general information**). I then recommended that she conduct a thorough job analysis on each of the identified fields of study and visit websites where she could find more information on how to study at university (**psychoeducational information**). She was also referred to websites like my own (www.kobus.maree.org) where she could obtain information on how to deal with stress and anxiety. It was suggested that she speak to teachers and a local educational psychologist about her tendency to become overly stressed and anxious, and also see a local social worker or psychologist about her unresolved feelings regarding events that had happened early in her life, including the loss and trauma she had experienced (**career counseling**).

Some Useful Websites and Phone Numbers

www.onetonline.org/find/

www.careers24.com

www.gostudy.net

www.jobspace.co.za

www.careersunlimimited.co.za

www.labour.gov.za/DOL/legislation/acts/how-tos/skill-development/how-to-join-a-learnership-if-you-are-unemployed;

www.interns24.co.za/list-available-learnerships-south-africa/?gclid=EAIaIQobChMI__XiraT-2gIVg7DtCh0LgwBzEAAYASAAEgIgB_D_BwE

www.careersportal.co.za;

www.careerplanet.co.za;

www.saqa.org.za (for critical skills career list);

www.careerexpo.co.za;

www.careers.co.za;

http://www.careerjunction.co.za/;

www.pacecareers.com/;

www.skillsportal.co.za;

www.pacegostudy.mobi;

http://www.nqf.org.za/;

http://ncap.careerhelp.org.za/occupations;

DHET Helpline 0800 8722 222; DHET Career Development Services: 0860 35 66 35 or careerhelp@dhet.gov.za; http://www.careerhelp.org.za

Step 5: My Personal Career Plan

Integrate all the Information From all the Above Steps and Complete the Following Sentence.

I want to study (field(s) of study) to become

"a social worker, teacher, office administrator, nurse, hairdresser, or educational psychologist

so that I can (personal meaning)

draw on my ability and meet my need to work with people and realize my capacity to function and serve them in a structured environment; actualize and show my inner strength, courage, and resilience, and improve myself

and in the process (social meaning)

work with and uplift people that suffer (children especially); use my position to improve the lives of young women especially; touch people's lives by helping them get up again after challenges. I am hoping to establish an orphanage for children in the region where I grew up and inspire people to assist me and contribute to our community."

Step 6: Thorough Job Analysis

Step 7: Providing Feedback

My very best wishes for a bright future accompany you.

Experience of the Intervention

Asked how she had experienced the intervention, Nkepile replied: "I liked how the different themes and career choices were linked. We got to realize our values, strengths, and "weaknesses", and we got to see the light as to what careers would best address our themes personality in a way that would help us to help others in our careers. Everyone got enough time to speak and get the input of others. I told you my story as best I could, and the last few questions especially hurt me. Allowing us to talk about ourselves and our experiences and feelings uncovered deep pain but also revealed qualities in me that I never thought I had. Getting to listen to myself and to tell my stories to others, too, who understand, was comforting and soothing."

Asked what had changed during the intervention and why, she wrote: "I now understand myself and my emotions better, and I have enough information about possible careers to help me decide. My true passion is now clear to me, and the career that I am interested in pursuing will help me do the things that I feel passionately about."

Follow-Up

Six months after the intervention, Nkepile confirmed that she had decided to study social work. She also confirmed that she was accepted into a degree course in social work.

The third study format differs from that of the previous case studies. **This is because the previous case studies drew on electronic reports of the *CIP* and *MCM* while this one draws on hard copy versions of the two questionnaires.**

11.7 Case Study 3: Violet: A Case of Foreclosure Career Choice Identity Status: From Basing the Choice of a Career on Parental Advice to a Choice Based on a Person's Key Life Themes

This case study was chosen purposely to demonstrate how *CIP* and *MCM* outcomes (hard copy format) outcomes can be integrated and used to facilitate integrative counseling for self- and career construction for a student with a foreclosure career choice identity status (while she has committed herself to distinct career, occupational, and ideological choices, these are choices that have been made on her behalf by her parents (and other significant others) instead of by herself) (Marcia, 1966, 1980, 1983).

Participant and context

Violet, a 35-year-old, Afrikaans-speaking accountant and lecturer in statistics, requested career counseling in 2018. The repetitive nature of her work was frustrating her. She had provisionally decided to take a sabbatical year in 2019 to further her master's degree studies in statistics. She dreaded the idea of conducting research and reporting on matters that she was not interested in. She feared that she was continuing on a career trajectory that would allow her little time to participate in creative activities. She could not see her current career ever allowing her to meet her creative needs satisfactorily. Prior to the assessment, we agreed on the implementation of an integrative QUALITATIVE-quantitative assessment (using the *CIP* and the *MCM*[8]).

Outcomes ("results")

What are you hoping to gain from the assessment?

Violet stated that she had found herself "at a crossroads" in her career. She was seeking "guidelines" on possible alternative careers that might be more in tune with her "style of functioning".

Violet's responses to selected questions appear below.[9] The assessment was done in English. She was requested to prepare a brief, written autobiographical narrative of her life (titled "My life story"), including a story title and illustrative subheadings, and to bring the narrative (her brief "autobiography") along on the assessment day or, alternatively, email it to me. In her "My life story", she described herself as an intelligent, creative, organized, stylish, dedicated, and punctual person who had the ability to work with people. However, she did not enjoy working under pressure. She enjoyed and thrived on change and being allowed to do new things. She expected expectations of her to be clear, and she hated being disrespected. She sometimes struggled to navigate her way in "uncharted territory". Inner harmony was important to her.

i. What are your

a. greatest strengths?

"I am intelligent, creative, organised, stylish, diligent, punctual, and I can work with people."

b. areas for growth? "I dislike working under pressure and unexpected change; I do not function well when expectations are unclear; I dread uncharted waters; and I am afraid to venture into something new."

ii. What do you value most?

---

[8]The rule of thumb in career counseling assessment is that people who attended an English school (and worked in an English environment) should preferably be assessed in English, irrespective of what their mother tongue was.

[9]Due to space constraints and the need to demonstrate the resourcefulness of the *CIP*, only selected responses are provided in the case studies.

"Inner harmony, aesthetics, creativity, family, and financial stability together with generosity."

iii. What do you enjoy doing?

"Working with words and writing, of course. Blogging, working at my own pace, being allowed to be creative, painting, doing ballet. When I was five years old, my friend and I enjoyed playing journalist-journalist. I loved pretending that we were writing articles!"

iv. What did your parents or teachers advise you to study?

"Accountancy because 'it is an excellent career for a woman' and 'you will always be assured of a job'. I never enjoyed my studies and cried endlessly during my final study year. The three years during which I did my articles were the unhappiest years of my life."

v. Whom did you admire or who were your role models when you were young, and why? (Her sense of who she wants to be or become.)

"My ballet teacher at school. She was stylish and always looked pretty, and she danced beautifully and worked so well with all her learners."

"My mother.[10] We are very different. She can do everything I cannot do, ha-ha. She is the best example of 'blossom where you are planted'. She studied computer science but developed herself from a farmer's wife into a wedding venue owner, a sheep farmer, and a tourism expert, and she is always, always there for me, even though she is extremely busy."

"My father who studied marketing. He reads widely and has a wide taste in music. Although he has been farming for a long time, he does not fit into the traditional picture of a farmer. I admire him for not allowing himself to be put in a box He taught me to treat all people with respect and dignity, which is demonstrated so well by how he deals with his farm workers."

vi. a. What are your favourite quotations?

"Live beautiful." (Approach life in a beautiful way.)

"The truth will set you free." (Although it sometimes seems easier to hide from the truth, it is always the most liberating option to face the truth.)

"That's okay." (Take life as it comes and make the best of everything.)

b. What is your own motto? ("How do you want others to quote you in the future?")

"Do not wake up one day, only to realise that your soul has stagnated and that you are no longer capable of finding a job."

vii. What were the three most hurtful experiences in your youth?

---

[10]I am that parents are regarded as guiding lines rather than role models. However, Violet insisted on citing them here.

"I was terribly scared when I made a mistake because I was humiliated when I did."

"I was afraid of not meeting people's expectations of me or, rather, what I thought they were expecting from me."

"I received hidings because I was terribly shy and afraid of the unknown."

"I could not handle conflict because I did not want to hurt others; yet, they would hurt me needlessly and often for no reason. I was 'smart' and humble, and some friends did not like that." (She chose to list more than three experiences.)

The following recurring themes emerged from her responses: a sense of insecurity, anxiety, and uncertainty; being reserved; a sense of creativity; feeling unfilled and bullied; desiring to write; not being allowed to make important choices herself.

An overlap was evident between her responses to the question, "What were the three most hurtful experiences in your youth that you do not want others to go through as well?" and her earliest recollections, which were

a. her deep fear of making mistakes,
b. not living up to or meeting (what she believed to be) others' expectations of her,
c. her determination to do anything to avoid such disappointment, and
d. her inability to deal with conflict or any kind of rejection. More than anything, she feared doing anything that might hurt others. (These themes appear consistent with the themes that are clear from her earliest recollections and also with many of her other responses.)

Violet's three earliest recollections (Violet and I together came up with headlines for these stories).

What are the first things you remember about your life; your three earliest recollections?

Fear of 'failure' stifles young dancer's sense of creativity

"At the age of six, I was selected to participate in a ballet performance. I was so happy. My mother helped me to dress and change into a number of outfits while my friend's mother did likewise. Since I kept on drifting into my world of fantasy, my mother told me to focus on the task at hand. She insisted that unless I focus, I would fall behind in my school work and be unable to do the things that were expected of me and consequently struggle at school. Her words made me think and feel that it was not okay for me to 'dream'. Instead, it seemed to be essential to stay in the 'real' instead of in my 'dream' world, even if school work and related activities did not interest me."

As an afterthought, Violet reflected that, lately, she had begun to struggle to focus on certain aspects of her work that she was not interested in. "Today, I struggle to negotiate unchartered waters." Here, Violet spontaneously reflects on her reflections—in other words, meta-reflection occurs. This happens when participants 'step out' of their stories as it were and uncover key life themes without any intervention from the counselor. This kind of occurrence is quite rare and typically provides strong evidence of the importance of the identified themes in participants' lives.

Young girl complies with unreasonable demand to meet father's expectations

"At the age of five, we visited a well-known water resort. My father demanded that he and I enter the super tube, which was a horrible experience. Since I had nothing to hold on to, it was petrifying to slide down and my joy was immense when, finally, the terrible trip was over."

Similar to what had occurred at the end of the first recollection, she spontaneously reflected on this recollection. "Over time, I gathered that the 'forced' trip was an attempt to kick me out of the nest and expose me to the "real world. The same happened when I had to learn how to ride a bicycle. I struggled a long time to master that skill."

Struggle to balance diverse rights

"Background: My sister was born when I as two years old and immediately demanded and received most of Mommy's attention. One day, I started crying because I felt neglected but did not know how to deal with the changed situation. My mother asked me what I wanted her to do; whether I wanted her to put my baby sister in a bucket with a little lukewarm water. I agreed and was surprised and happy to hear her laughing in the water. Best of all: My mother started to attend to me again."

Once again, she added a reflective afterthought: "It was always difficult for me to 'let go'."

The first recollection uncovered the key life theme that she felt she was never allowed to express herself in an artistic, creative way. Instead, she was expected to "focus" and make sure that she did things "right". The "discovery" of this particular life theme shed light on why she decided to consult a career counselor. People often consult us when they are ready to make changes in their career-lives and to deal with key life "problems" and challenges. The first earliest recollection conveyed a readiness to take a "bold", adaptive decision, namely to express herself more creatively and let go of enforced "structures" in order to rekindle a sense of meaning and purpose in her life. Her first verb ("selected") reveals her sense of feeling that she has now been selected to play a new role and that, this time, her parents are no longer there to impose rigid structures on her.

The second earliest recollection revealed a similar theme, namely deferring to unreasonable demands so as not to hurt or disappoint (significant) others instead of following her own natural inclinations.

Violet herself interpreted the third recollection: She experienced a deep need to be reassured that she was loved.

In summary: Violet was at the time of the intervention an insecure young woman who feared rejection and doing things that might hurt others. However, her need to express herself in a creative manner had become too great to ignore any longer, which was why she consulted me. In her own words: "I did much research in search of identifying someone who would 'permit' me to listen to myself and follow my own advice instead of to others who were unwilling to let me act and do what I really wanted to in life."

Violet's integrated interest and confidence profile (based on the *CIP* and *MCM* outcomes) appears below.

Most preferred, integrated career interest and confidence profile:

Word art;

Practical-creative and consumer science;

Entrepreneurship (running a personal business);

Office work (administrative and clerical activities);

Marketing;

Engineering and the built environment (architecture was singled out in this category); and

Executive and management practice.

During the second phase of the assessment, all her responses were discussed with Violet, who had little difficulty in identifying the themes and subthemes that emerged from her reflections on the reflections discussed above. We jointly conducted a brief qualitative analysis of her responses to compile a table in which we summarized her responses and attempted to relate these to specific study fields and associated work environments that would allow her to enact (actuate or actualize) these themes and help her find purpose in her career-life (see Table 11.3 below). This table reveals a remarkable overlap between the two sets of data. Her individual agency, actorship, and authorship especially were consistently emphasized (directly and/or indirectly).

Before concluding the phase, Violet and I "co-authored" her vision and mission statements to help her make meaning of and find a sense of hope and purpose in her provisionally chosen career trajectory. In other words, to enable her to articulate a response to her deepest, existential career-life questions such as Why do I work and live? Why am I doing what I am doing in my career? What is the purpose of my career-life? Eventually, we arrived at the following narrative: "If I stay on in my field, I want to become a university professor who innovates theory and practice in the field of accountancy, collaborates with colleagues on various projects, learns from them, and contributes to their development as well. I will allow my stifled creative instincts to guide me: strive to become the editor of a scholarly journal in my field; become an avant garde kind of editor and scholar; write innovative books and move the field forward; become famous; become a person who pushes boundaries continually and extend the involvement of people in the field to 'other' areas **[personal meaning; mission statement]**."

"I want to initiate projects to enable students in my field who have 'suffered' or are still suffering like me to escape from the shackles that delay their development. Few things will please me as much as knowing that I am helping people deal with insecurity and inadequacy issues; people whose sense of creativity and desire to write is being stifled because they cannot or will not allow themselves to let go of ghosts from the past. Most importantly: I will make time to write (blogs, books, songs), to paint, to cook **[social meaning; vision statement]**."

"In short, I will honour the legacy of my parents; make them proud of me, albeit in a manner that differs slightly from what they were expecting me to do!"

We then proceeded to devise a number of strategies to promote forward movement in her career-life. First, she would proceed with her plans to go on sabbatical

Table 11.3 Linking life themes, interests, and possible fields of study/careers

Themes and subthemes	Associated field(s) of study	Data source: qualitative	Data source: quantitative.
1. Need to express her sense of creativity a. Verbal expression b. Practical-artistic expression c. Musical expression	Journalism (honors degree) Film and TV production Photography Architecture/ Interior architecture, Optometry Speech-language therapy Beauty therapy Personal appearance/Lifestyle consultant	*CIP* Self-reflection Reflexivity (overall data sources.)	*MCM*
2. Sense of insecurity and anxiety 3. Need to be held and to "hold" others 4. Concern about not meeting others' expectations	Any of the above fields (all these fields would offer Violet an opportunity to heal others and, in doing so, heal herself and master actively what she had suffered passively (Savickas, 2005)		
5. Passive acceptance of others' "advice"			
6. Feeling incompetent	Ditto	Earliest recollections	
7. Need for autonomy	Ditto	Earliest recollections	
8. ABCs			
a. Positive ABCs (strengths)		*CIP*	
b. Inadequate ABCs (areas for development)		*CIP*	
9. Need to make meaning of and experience purpose in her career-life		Reflections and reflexivity. Earliest recollections	
10. Desire to develop own career identity			

(Violet did not want us to collapse these 10 themes into a smaller number of encompassing themes.)

and continue with her master's degree studies. Second, she would follow this up by writing articles (maybe even a book) based on her research. Third, she would rethink the 'boring' topic of her master's degree and try to find an "innovative" topic for her studies. Fourth, she would conduct a thorough job analysis on specified fields of study that she could eventually enroll on. This included architecture (or interior architecture), an honors degree in journalism, optometry, speech-language therapy, and industrial psychology. Fifth, she would actively pursue part-time, creative activities such as creative writing (stories, poems, songs, blogging), listening to music she loved, and attending short courses in video production and photography to add meaning and enjoyment to her life. It was also recommended that she consult a psychologist to help her work through her sadness and lack of purpose (career therapy).

When questioned about how she had experienced the intervention and whether anything had changed during the intervention, she replied that being allowed to "speak" without reservation in a "free", yet protected environment" was cleansing and healing. In response to my question: "Is there anything else about you that I need to know?", she stated that she had always wanted to be "famous" but that she feared being "caught out" doing things that she was not really capable of doing. Asked again whether anything had changed during the intervention and what had caused the change she replied: "I received brand-new information about the world of careers. Freedom and relief because of the fact that my current career choice never made me happy." [This is because] "I was given "permission" to be who I wanted to be. And reassured that I had every right to become who I could become … hopefully even become famous! (SMILES) The thorough and respectful intervention made me feel safe and more secure." (Realizing that her tongue-in-cheek remark about "fame" was much more than a meaningless, light-hearted comment, I repeated her comments about fame to her and realized the truth in the expression, "many a true word is spoken in jest"!

Violet was reminded of the importance of transcending her own hurt and challenges and converting them into hope and purpose. She was reminded also that finding a way to heal others who had experienced challenges similar to hers would in effect mean that she would also be healing herself.

Sequel

At the end of the phase, Violet was asked to reflect on the intervention and revert to me as often as possible until she felt that she no longer wanted or needed to do so. At the time of writing this book, she was showing substantial progress on her journey towards self-healing and a purposeful life. She had relocated to a flat in a neighborhood that was more to her liking had succeeded in surrounding herself with a close-knit group of sincere, like-minded, open-minded, and creatively inclined friends. In her own words: "There have been many positive and rewarding developments; I feel happy again but I am taking things one step at a time."

When we last spoke (at the time of writing this book), Violet said: "I decided to enroll for a personal appearance consultant course, and I am so excited about the prospect! It is something that I can combine with my writing and other creative endeavors, and doing so will enable me to enter an entirely new direction without having to complete a an entirely new degree course first." She proceeded to discuss the "positive" as well as the "negative" aspects of entering this quite expensive course with me and seemed keen to take this bold step.

11.8 Case Study 4: Fikani: Undifferentiated Career Identity Status

The fourth case study was chosen purposely to demonstrate how *CIP* and *MCM* outcomes (hard copy format) can be integrated and used to facilitate integrative counseling for self- and career construction for a student with an undifferentiated career identity status (a person whose job roles and career decisions are still unclear or indistinguishable) (Marcia, 1966, 1980, 1983; Sharf, 2013).

Participant and context

Fikani (a 20-year-old black, Sotho-speaking man) was selected randomly from a group of learners who had participated in a group-based career counseling research project in 2019. His responses to some of the questions in the *CIP* (Parts 1, 2, and 4) are given below.

Outcomes

Step 1: Reflecting on Fikani's responses

Section 11.1: Your expectations about the intervention

In response to the question "How can I be of use, of help, or of value to you today?", Fikani replied: "Help me learn more about career choices and opportunities because I am very unsure about these matters. All I know is that I am quite 'technical', but I have no idea what to do or where to start. I do not have money to study, no one to help me, and I need guidance on how to access opportunities. My future does not look good to me."

Reflection

Fikani has a sound (albeit intuitive) idea of his signature strengths, but he has very little knowledge about the world of work and about how he should go about accessing study opportunities. Moreover, he feels unsure and uncertain about the future.

Section 11.2: Gaining perspective: Establishing your career identity

My seven greatest strengths are the following: "As an individual, I …

am good at and enjoy fixing computers and electrical devices and solving plumbing problems;

do my best to read although access to books is limited;

love helping others;

get on very well with people although I am a quiet person;

am hardworking;
respectful and decent; and
want to make a difference in my community."

My seven areas for development or growth. "As an individual, I …

have not been able to help my community gain access to running water, electricity, obtain a town hall, and establish a community center;

have not been able to help people in the community who struggle to survive; and

am impatient with gossiping people who do not feel for others."

Whom did you admire or who were your three role models when you were young? Why?

"I cannot remember who my role models were when I was very young. However, during high school I learned to admire the following persons:

Teaman Manzini. He advised me to follow my dream and do something technical; to work hard and focus on my goal despite our poverty.

Zodwa. It was she who convinced me of the importance of doing my schoolwork and getting a good education.

Oliver Tambo. He stood up for us during the struggle against apartheid to fight for our democracy."

What are your three mottos or favorite quotations?

"Education is the key to success."

"Unity is power."

"To share means to care."

Fikani gives evidence of a strong conviction that education will be key to his success, and he displays a strong sense of Ubuntu.

My favorite

Magazine:	"None"[11]
TV program:	"Unsure"
Website:	"Zamob.com (information about music)"
App:	"Dictionary (I can look up words that I don't understand)"

My greatest successes:

"Helping people with 'technical' problems (even their phones);
not being involved in crime like so many of my friends; and
being able to help a local farmer fix his windmills."

My three biggest challenges ("problems"):

"Not being able to receive further training;
not being able to go to a college; and
not being able to find suitable employment."

[11] See Sect. 5.7 for clarification on this matter.

Reflection

Write down the themes, patterns, or trends you identified from your answers.

"Helping other people, fixing things (phones, plugs, computers); helping people with their household problems; enjoying music; not being able to obtain worthwhile qualifications thus far."

Try to link these themes to possible work environments/careers.

"IT, electrician, plumber, cell phone technician."

Section 11.3: Reflect on the meaning of career influences in your life

Parental advice

"My parents are very poor and want me to join the police so I can have a secure income and protect the community (which is something I feel passionately about). They also say I should become a game ranger, but it is a dangerous job here; also something that I am not interested in."

Teachers' advice

"Something practical or technical."

Reflection: What themes, patterns, or trends did you identify from your answers?

"I prefer to work with my hands; to execute practical tasks."

Section 11.4: Choosing preferred career category options from the list of 19

According to the *CIP* (version 6) (Maree, 2017), Fikani's preferred interest categories were the following:

Information and communication technology
Practical-technical
Engineering and the built environment
Adventure, plants, animals, and the environment
Sport
Office-based (administrative, clerical, and organizational) activities
Musical (as a hobby only).

The *MCM* yielded the following preferred interest and confidence categories.

Information and communication technology
Practical-technical
Engineering and the built environment
Adventure, plants, animals, and the environment
Office-based (administrative, clerical, and organizational) activities
Sport
Executive and management
Tourism management

Reflection

The positive correlation between the interest categories uncovered by the *CIP* and the *MCM* was clear.

Section 11.5

Additional comments

"I grew up poor and often had to go to school without food or having eaten. I was almost killed in a violent incident when I was young, and my parents struggled hard to find a job and to make a living. I am a shy, quiet person; not talkative at all. I do not laugh a lot."

Step 2: Making sense of the information: Connecting the dots

"I am a kind-hearted, sincere, respectful, helpful human being who cherishes education and training and wants to study and better myself and make a difference in my community. Even though I am a quiet person, I get on very well with others. It makes me feel good when I help them by doing what I like most, namely fixing computers and electrical utensils, and attending to their cell phone and plumbing problems. It pains me to see so many poor people in my environment suffer, and I am determined to make a difference in my community and inspire others like my role models inspired me."

Fikani and I agreed that he would conduct job analyses on the following fields of study and associated careers: IT expert, electrician, plumber, cellphone technician, wind energy technician, and solar energy technician.

Step 3: Formulating personal mission and vision statements

Career choices associated with his key life themes: "I will be happy and experience a sense of purpose in my career-life when I work in an environment where I can fix things such as computers, cell phones, electrical appliances, and earn enough money to take care of my own and my family's needs but also the needs of my community."

"To achieve this aim, I will become an IT specialist or electrician (or maybe a cell phone technician, a wind energy technician or a solar energy technician) (occupational choice) so that I can address my own need to do practical things, fix things, help people that do not have the skills to do so **(personal meaning)**, and in the process also take care of my community's needs; deliver a much-needed service for the community. Hopefully I will be able to build a town and community hall after a while to enable frustrated youths to access constructive recreational facilities. That will make my life purposeful **(social meaning)**."

This future picture clearly reveals why he sought career counseling.

Step 4: Moving forward

Action steps: Conducting job analysis

In addition to the general steps that were indicated in the previous case studies, I alerted Fikani to various funding opportunities as well as free training and skills development opportunities offered by Skills Education and Training Authorities (SETAs). This is only one example of my colleagues' and my ongoing attempts to facilitate social justice (advocacy) and client empowerment by helping people tap into available resources (Butler, 2012; Ratts, 2009).

Sequel

Fikani is currently freelancing as an "entrepreneurial electrician" while seeking opportunities to enroll for training.

11.9 Case Study 5: Michael: Career Decision-Making Difficulties of a More Pervasive and "Pathological" Nature

The fifth case study was chosen purposely to demonstrate how *CIP* and *MCM* outcomes (hard copy format) can be integrated and used to facilitate integrative counseling for self- and career construction for a person with career decision-making difficulties of a more pervasive and "pathological" nature (Gati et al., 2011; Morgan & Ness, 2003).

Participant and context

Michael, a 25-year-old, English-speaking man, consulted me in 2016 regarding the choice of a field of study. In his own words: "I previously enrolled for a degree in law, which I completed. However, I preferred not to pursue a career in that field. I then enrolled for a degree in management, but I no longer know whether I want to study, if I want to study, and when I want to do so. Give me some guidance and direct me to a field of study that will 'suit my profile'."

My greatest strengths: "I am good at languages, musically inclined, get on well with others and establish good interpersonal relationships, good at computer skills, and a tad creative."

My favorite quotations: "All we have to decide is what to do with the time that is given to us."

"My grandfather used to say that one either has potential or doesn't when it comes to mathematics." Michael then reflected spontaneously on the matter: "It is important to me to consider everyday challenges on their own merits. Some people just manage certain things more easily than others. One just needs to be patient in every respect and success will eventually follow."

My role models: "The owner of the bookshop where I am doing part-time work. A driven human being, she is passionate about the world of books, dedicated, and she displays a sincere desire to make sure that all her employees work hard. She accepts that we all make mistakes, treats to treat all of us well, and considers our personal circumstances at all times."

According to the *CIP*, Michael's highest preferred integrated categories were Information and communication technology; Executive and management practice; Word artistry; Entrepreneurship: running and maintaining a personal business; and Social, caregiving, and community services and teaching.

The *MCM* yielded the following integrated interest and confidence categories: Word artistry; Information and communication technology; Executive and management practice; Entrepreneurship: running and maintaining a personal business; Social, caregiving, and community services and teaching; as well as Persuasive (marketing). Here, too, the overlap between the two profiles (qualitative and quantitative) was clear.

Life story title: "The tour guide"

"When I was young, we move around quite often. First, when I was born, we stayed in a men's residence (my parents were the caretakers at the time). Then we moved to a neighboring town. And another … today, we live in … it's funny, each of the places where we lived seem to represent a certain phase of my life." (HESITATES; SIGHS LIGHTLY) "I never really managed to settle down in the new environments."

Biggest challenges when you were young? "I was very shy and overweight; mocked by others, and found it difficult to talk to strangers."

"I always believed I was bad at working with numbers. I eventually passed mathematics in Grade 12, but my marks weren't good. That made me feel inferior."

Asked about his earliest recollections, he replied: "In Grade 3, I received an award for best achievement in English, which made me feel very proud and good about myself, despite my inability to do basic calculations." (Here, too, he confirms his above-average language ability).

Michael's key life themes revolved around having struggled to "take root" and settle down due to his parents moving regularly, made to feel inferior and inadequate, sadness about having been humiliated, and being withdrawn. His preferred interest and confidences categories were Word artistry; Entrepreneurship: running and maintaining a personal business; Social, caregiving, and community services and teaching; Information and communication technology; Executive and management practice; and Persuasive.

Michael and I co-constructed a few fields of study for job analysis, including journalism, tourism (management), publishing, and information sciences. He could also attend short courses in photography, creative writing, song writing, project management, and marketing. In addition, it was suggested that he consider participating in creative writing, song writing, and reading activities to add a sense of meaning and enjoyment to his life. Lastly, he was encouraged to consult a therapist to help him deal with his occasional depression.

Finally, we analyzed his own advice (contained in his favorite quotations and his reflections on it) regarding the way forward.

Sequel

Contrary to what we had agreed, Michael applied for and was accepted into a degree course in business studies. Because of his raised levels of anxiety and possibly even depression, it was suggested that he consult a psychologist for counseling. Sadly, he did not find the course to his liking and was unsuccessful in his first-year examinations—his inability to deal with modules that contained an element of mathematics and/or accountancy being the biggest stumbling block. He is currently consulting a psychologist and has been put on medication to help him deal with major depression episodes.

11.10 Case Study 6: Jeannie: Achieved Career Identity Status

This case study was chosen purposely to demonstrate how *CIP* and *MCM* (online) outcomes can be integrated to help a person with achieved identity achievement status gain enhanced self-awareness and achieve enhanced self-and career construction. (Someone who has worked through a decision-making period, has committed herself or himself to a distinct career, and has clearly identified with certain ideological perspectives.)

Participant and context

Jeannie, a 67-year-old white, English-speaking woman in an executive position, participated in a training workshop aimed at demonstrating the administration and value of the integrative approach advocated in this book. Her inspiring "story" demonstrates changing perspectives on subjects such as "retirement", continuous learning and development, and the versatility, value, and power of the integrative approach.

Eliciting Jeannie's life story

As readers will see, only a handful of responses were needed to explain Jeannie's reason for consulting a career counselor. The storylines of older, more stable people are inevitably more consistent than those of younger, less emotionally stable people.

Section 11.1: Your expectations about the intervention

"I am hoping to gain self-awareness and development."

Reflection

Jeannie was not seeking career counseling as such. A good example of a professional worker in an executive position and a continuous learner, she was constantly looking for opportunities for further development.

Section 11.2: Gaining perspective: Establishing Jeannie's career identity

My seven strengths: "I am a good listener, caring, optimistic, innovative, patient, willing to take calculated risks, and enjoy change and challenges."

My areas for development: "I find conflict situations difficult to deal with; struggle to say NO to others and to set boundaries; sometimes find focusing on routine tasks challenging; I can be stubborn, sometimes feel frustrated, and need to learn to relax more."

Role models (people I admired when I was young)

Jeannie listed family members as her early role models. Her current role models and, especially, the traits she admired in them, namely emeritus Archbishop Tutu (wisdom, positive approach to life, and spirituality), Nelson Mandela (loyalty and wisdom), and wildlife trackers (people with no formal education but inherently wise and natural "teachers") are consistent with her general storyline.

Her three mottos or favorite quotations, too, confirmed the advice that she consistently dispensed to herself, namely: "Be the change you want to see", "Gently you can change the world", and "We have rich gems beneath the ground but our greatest wealth is our people."

Jeannie's responses to questions about her favorite magazine, TV program, and book did not meaningfully clarify her life story and career identity. However, her responses to the question about her greatest successes did confirm her "story" and "identity". This is what she wrote:

"Raising my children to be respectful, committed, exceptional leaders, and caring human beings."

"My own academic and educational achievements."

"Grasping and accepting that learning is lifelong and should be celebrated; and that taking risks has vast potential for facilitating the greatest rewards—experiencing my own, ever-unfolding career journey ("path")."

My biggest challenges ("failures")

Here, her responses demonstrate how she had succeeded in mastering actively what she had suffered passively:

"As a young woman, my self-belief was less than optimal."

"Not identifying and following my North Star, my own career journey at an even earlier age."

"Learning how to deal with personal loss."

Reflection

Jeannie's key themes, patterns, or trends she identified from her answers.

"Being a genuinely caring human being; the kind of person to whom others are drawn and that people find easy to love and to identify with."

"Being respectful—respecting myself, others, and the environment."

"A desire, willingness, and ability to grow and learn from disappointments and loss—and to transform my lived experiences of loss and disappointments into supporting and encouraging others."

Section 11.4

Most preferred career categories (according to the *CIP*):

Social, caregiving, and community services

Practical-creative and consumer science

Legal practice and security services

Executive and management practice
Adventure, plants, animals, and the environment
Tourism, the hospitality, and the tourist transport industry
Research

According to the *MCM*, Jeannie's preferred career categories were as shown in her career matrix (see below) (Figure 11.2).

Most preferred interest and confidence categories:
Social, caregiving, and community services.
To a much lesser extent:
Practical creative and consumer sciences
Legal practice and security services
Executive and management practice
Adventure, plants, animals, and the environment

Again, the overlap between the qualitative and the quantitative profiles was clear.

Reflection

Only one career category fell in Quadrant 1, namely Social, caregiving, and community services. This is an example of an extremely well-differentiated ("high") interest

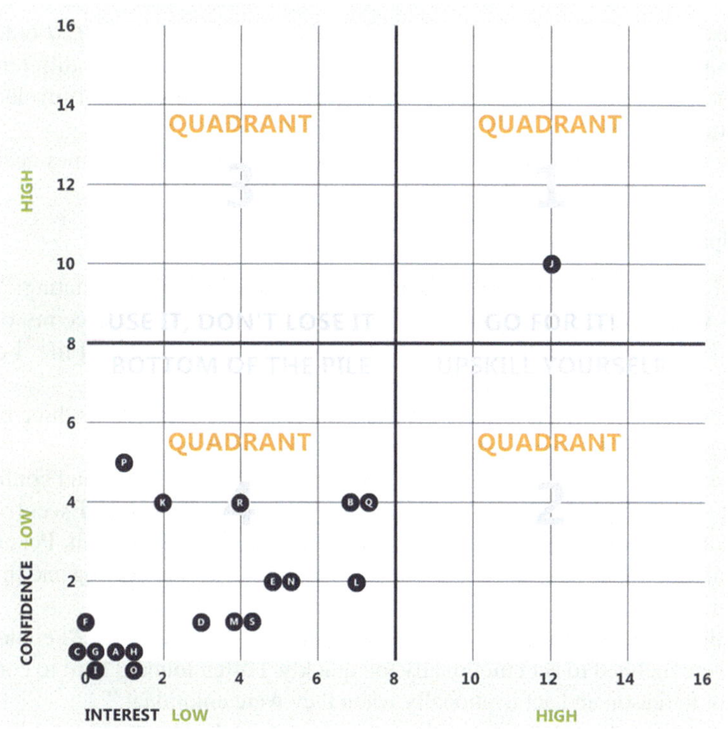

Fig. 11.2 Jeannie's *MCM* profile

and confidence score. It indicates a very well-developed profile. The overlap between the interest categories uncovered by the *CIP* and those uncovered by the *MCM* is also clear. These findings confirmed Jeannie's well-established career identity.

Section 11.5

Additional comments

"I found it difficult to focus only on myself for so long."

Reflection

This observation, too, confirmed the consistency of Jeannie's career storyline. A rare, sincere, selfless human being who loves people and strives to bring about positive change in the lives of others; those with poverty and related challenges in particular.

No wonder she experiences such a profound sense of meaning and purpose in her career-life.

11.11 Case Study 7: Wayde: A Case of Undifferentiated Career Status

This case study was chosen purposely to demonstrate how *CIP* and *MCM* outcomes (hard copy format) can be integrated in the case of a person with undifferentiated career status (a person whose job roles and career decisions are still unclear and indistinguishable)

Here is shown that only a few questions and responses are sometimes needed to facilitate a person's career choice decision.

Participant and context

Wayde (a 20-year-old, German-speaking man) consulted me in 2018, stating: "I have no idea what I should study. I have many interests and want to reduce my options so that I can study something what I will enjoy and live a successful life. I cannot identify specific things I really like and really enjoy."

Below, I focus only on his interest and confidence preferences, his three biggest challenges when he was young, and his earliest recollections.

According to the *MCM* and the *CIP*, Wayde's preferred interest and confidence categories were Legal practice and/or security services; Research; Executive and management practice; Adventure, plants, animals and the environment; Persuasive; Arts (painting, sculpture, and decorating) and culture; and Engineering and the built environment.

My three biggest challenges ("problems") when I was still young: "People close to me were inclined to act emotionally too quickly. I often found it hard to convince them not to reason and act irrationally when they were emotional."

"It was difficult to associate with many of my friends who could not be trusted when they became emotional and got angry."

"Making friends that I could trust."

Earliest recollections

Nurturing mother ensures that fairness prevails

"At the age of five, we went on holiday and camped near the seaside. Being the youngest, I did not have a bicycle. I had to run after my brother and his friends while they rode around. I then went home and cried and told my mother that I was treated unfairly. She hugged me, took me to a local shop, and asked me to choose a bicycle, which my parents bought for me the next day."

Introduction to crime story excites and scares young man

"When I was six or seven years old, my parents watched a CSI story about someone who was being murdered. I was fascinated by how the police went about to solve the mystery. That night I experienced a terrible nightmare, but my mother woke me up and assured me that everything was alright."

Young boy regrets having left little protector in the lurch

"I used to sleep with my teddy next to me in bed at night for a long while. I just felt safe with him next to me. At the age of seven, my parents and I watched the movie The golden compass. The story is somewhat vague but what I can remember clearly is that a young girl took care of a bear that later on protects her. I remember mentioning that I was so surprised to learn that real bears could be so protective and caring and saying I felt bad about not having brought him along to experience the movie with us."

Wayde was quick to point out the following key life themes that stood out for him from his answers to the questions about his three biggest challenges and his earliest recollections: The importance of remaining calm and collected in a crisis, of ensuring that fairness prevails, and of mutual trust

After having conducted job analysis on several career fields, Wayde was adamant: He, too, wanted to protect others and see that justice was done. Today, he is a fourth-year law student and "loving every minute of my studies".

11.12 Case Study 8: Marie: Dealing with a Moratorium Career Choice Status: Parental Preferences Adversely Influence Client Decisions

This case study was chosen purposely to demonstrate how *CIP* and *MCM* outcomes (hard copy format) can be integrated to counsel a person with a moratorium career choice status (a person who has committed herself or himself to meticulously examined work roles, yet gives strong evidence of (career) self-doubt and flexibility). This shows how drawing on a young woman's career interest profile and on her biggest challenge ("problem") when she was young as well as on her earliest recollection were sufficient for purposes of administering effective career counseling.

Participant and context

Marie, a 19-year-old first-year Indian student who had enrolled for a BCom (Accounting Sciences) degree, approached me for career counseling in 2016. Her stated reason for seeking my help: "I am studying to become a chartered accountant but I do not want to become one. I am only doing this because I believe my parents want me to do so. Please guide me as to which career "path" I should follow by 'honestly' judging my strengths and character."

According to the *CIP* and the *MCM*, her preferred interest and confidence categories were Medical and paramedical services; Social, care-giving, and community services and teaching; Arts (painting, sculpture, and decorating) and culture; and (to a much lesser extent) Mathematics and/or accounting industry.

Her biggest challenge ("problem") when she was young was seeing her neighbour almost drown and subsequently suffer brain damage. Her earliest recollection was the following:

Critical injury to friend traumatizes helpless young girl

"One night, when I was four or five years old, our neighbour came rushing over to our house and kept on ringing our doorbell, screaming hysterically. I remember father rushing out to her house. She was carrying her seemingly lifeless young boy in her hands. My father immediately started giving CPR to him while Mommy phoned the hospital. Soon the ambulance, medics, and paramedics were there, but I could not understand what was going on. I was terrified; the memory is one whole blur. Mother explained afterwards that the boy had fallen into the swimming pool. He survived but he was left with brain damage; he is not normal at all. I experienced feelings of sadness, fear, and confusion."

The overlap between Marie's biggest challenge and her earliest recollection was clear and constituted a key life theme. Having seen a helpless young boy in a critical medical condition, and being unable to help him, she experienced a profound need to "undo" what she had to observe passively early in life. She wanted to enter the medical field but was torn between her loyalty to her ailing father and her need to work in a medical environment where she could help people (mastering actively what she had suffered passively).

We agreed that she would carry on with her current studies while simultaneously doing a thorough job analysis on several fields of study, namely medicine, nursing, dentistry, medical sciences, pharmacy, radiography, and occupational therapy. Because of her raised levels of stress and anxiety, it was suggested that she consult a psychologist for counseling regarding management of her stress-related challenges.

Sequel

After thorough job analysis, Marie decided that she wanted to study nursing. She completed her three-year degree in accounting sciences, though, and, at the time of writing this book, she was halfway through her first year of a three-year degree in nursing. This is how she explained the situation in an email to me: "A requirement from the South African Nursing Council is that we complete a minimum of 500 h of training at a hospital during our first year of studies. I was allocated to a rural hospital. After being on my feet for 12 h on several occasions, extremely exhausted, I can say with certainty that I love what I am doing now. Helping people is the greatest joy I've ever experienced."

In a follow-up email, she wrote: "Over the weekend we attended a nursing camp at a lodge [outside the city where she was studying]. It was an enlightening experience as our lecturers gave us activities that really made us explore ourselves. For one of the activities, the facilitator made us all stand in a line and asked us a series of questions. The facilitator asked: 'If you do not have to worry about your next meal, take a step forward.' It was heart-breaking because so many of my classmates did not take a step forward. We start ward rounds at a rural hospital soon, and I am really excited."

At the time of writing this book, Marie was clearly on her way to becoming an exceptional nurse who can make a difference in the lives of many people in need.

11.13 Summary

The case studies discussed in this chapter show the usefulness and versatility of using an integrative approach in career counseling. More specifically, individually and together, they demonstrate the effectiveness of career construction counseling drawing on either the *CIP* alone or using the *CIP* in conjunction with the *MCM* to enhance innovation in career counseling. While the CCI was designed for and almost exclusively used in individual career counseling contexts, the *CIP* (as well as the *MCM*) was designed to promote both individual and group-based career construction counseling and life design. The two questionnaires can therefore be used in individual and group contexts to facilitate the choice of subjects, fields of study, careers, and, especially, meaning-making and living a purposeful life.

As these case studies have also shown, the approach advocated here can be used in both Global North and Global South contexts, and with clients with different career choice identity statuses. These carefully selected case studies also reveal the rich cultural tapestry and the diversity of our client base in South Africa. They demonstrate that there are various ways in which career counseling information can be gathered to promote rigor in career counseling. They include qualitative and quantitative, as well as a broad array of mixed methods approaches. In other words, career counselors can draw on "stories" (subjective outcomes) and/or "scores" (objective outcomes), depending on their particular preferences. That said, it should be clear from what has been written that my own preference is for an integrative approach. This approach appears to offer the best chance of generating sufficient "data" or information to help clients make well-informed decisions and advise themselves as to why they sought career counseling in the first place. The innovative manner in which seemingly unrelated information can be integrated to help clients understand and advise themselves can be mastered by all career counselors who are keen to update, innovate, and postmodernize their existing practice. The caveat is mastery of the innovative approach under the careful eye of an experienced mentor prior to applying the techniques and interventions put forward in this chapter and book.

In the penultimate chapter (Chap. 12), I draw on the inspiring career-life story of Dolly Parton who has shown the world how "negatives" can be transformed into "positives" (Freud, 1958, 1963).

References

Marcia, J. E. (1983). Some directions for the investigation of ego development in early adolescence. *Journal of Early Adolescence, 3*(3), 215–223.

Porfeli, E. J., Lee, B., Vondracek, F. W., & Weigold, I. K. (2011). A multidimensional measure of vocational identity status. *Journal of Adolescence, 34,* 853–871. https://doi.org/10.1016/j.adolescence.2011.02.001.

Rottinghaus, P. J., & Miller, A. D. (2013). Convergence of personality frameworks within vocational psychology. In W. B. Walsh, M. L. Savickas, & P. J. Hartung (Eds.), *Handbook of vocational psychology: Theory, research, and practice* (pp. 105–132). New York: Routledge.

Sharf, R. S. (2013). Advances in theories of career development. In W. B. Walsh, M. L. Savickas, & P. J. Hartung (Eds.), *Handbook of vocational psychology: Theory, research, and practice* (pp. 2–32). New York: Routledge.

Savickas, M. L., & Porfeli, E. J. (2012). Career Adapt-Abilities Scale: Construction, reliability, and measurement equivalence across 13 countries. *Journal of Vocational Behavior, 80,* 661–673. https://doi.org/10.1016/j.jvb.2012.01.011.

Cardoso, P. (2016). Integrating life-design counseling and psychotherapy: Possibilities and practices. *Career Development Quarterly, 64,* 49–63. https://doi.org/10.1002/cdq.12040.

Marcia, J. E. (1966). Development and validation of ego identity status. *Journal of Personality and Social Psychology, 3*(15), 551.

Marcia, J. E. (1980). Identity in adolescence. In J. Adelson (Ed.), *Handbook of adolescent psychology* (pp. 159–187). New York: Wiley.

Maree, J. G. (2017). *The career interest profile (Version 6).* Randburg, SA: JvR Psychometrics.

Butler, S. K. (2012). Issues of social justice and career development. *Career Planning and Adult Development Journal, 28*(1), 140–151.

Ratts, M. J. (2009). Social justice counseling: toward the development of a Fifth Force among counseling paradigms. *Journal of Humanistic Counseling, Education and Development, 48,* 160–172.

Gati, I., Gadassi, R., Saka, N., Hadadi, Y., Ansenberg, N., Friedmann, R., et al. (2011). Emotional and personality-related aspects of career decision-making difficulties: Facets of career indecisiveness. *Journal of Career Assessment, 19,* 3–20. https://doi.org/10.1177/1069072710382525.

Freud, S. (1958). On beginning the treatment: Further recommendations on the technique of psycho-analysis. In J. Strachey (Ed.), The standard edition of the complete psychological works of Sigmund Freud (vol. 12, pp. 121–144). London: Hogarth Press (Original work published in 1913).

Freud, S. (1963). *The standard edition of the complete psychological works of Sigmund Freud.* London, England: Hogarth.

Di Fabio, A., & Kenny, M. E. (2011). Promoting emotional intelligence and career decision making among Italian high school students. *Journal of Career Assessment, 19*(1), 21–34.

Gati, I., & Saka, N. (2011a). Internet-based versus paper-and-pencil assessment: Measuring career decision-making difficulties. *Journal of Career Assessment, 9,* 397–416. https://doi.org/10.1177/106907270100900406.

Gati, I., & Saka, N. (2011b). High school students' career-related decision-making difficulties. *Journal of Counseling and Development, 7*(3), 331–340.

Gati, I., & Asher, I. (2001a). The PIC model for career decision making: Prescreening, in-depth exploration, and choice. In F. T. L. Leong & A. Barak (Eds.), *Contemporary models in vocational psychology* (pp. 7–54). Mahwah, NJ: Erlbaum.

Gati, I., & Asher, I. (2001b). Prescreening, in-depth exploration, and choice: From decision theory to career counseling practice. *Career Development Quarterly, 50,* 140–157.

Gati, I., Krausz, M., & Osipow, S. H. (1996). A taxonomy of difficulties in career decision making. *Journal of Counseling Psychology, 43*(4), 510–526.

Maree, J. G. (2016). Career construction counseling with a mid-career black male. *Career Development Quarterly, 64,* 20–35.

Maree, J. G. (2019a). Career development in africa: decent work for all: brief photomontage. In Keynote address at the annual career development practitioner congress, emperors palace conference centre. South Africa: Kempton Park.

Maree, J. G. (2019b). Postmodernising career counseling in a deep rural context. In J. G. Maree (Ed.), Handbook of innovative career counseling (pp. 577–596). New York, NY: Springer.

Wanberg, C. R., & Muchinsky, P. M. (1992). A typology of career decision status: Validity extension of the vocational decision status model. *Journal of Counseling Psychology, 39,* 71–80.

Erikson, E. H. (1982). *The life cycle completed.* New York, NY: W. W. Norton.

Marcia, J. E. (1964). Determination and construct validation of ego identity status. (Unpublished doctoral dissertation.) Columbus, OH: Ohio State University.

Sweitzer, E. M. (2011). Pre- and post-secondary career selection: A process for mentorship and identity development. In J. Samide, G. T. Eliason, J. Patrick, J. Samide, G. T. Eliason, & J. Patrick (Eds.), *Career development in higher education* (pp. 75–88). Charlotte, NC: Information Age Publishing.

Savickas, M. L. (2005). The theory and practice of career construction. In S. Brown & R. W. Lent (Eds.), *Career development and counseling: Putting theory and research to work* (pp. 42–70). New York, NY: Wiley.

Kelly, K. R., & Lee, W. C. (2005). Relations of psychological type to career indecision among university students. *Journal of Psychological Type, 64,* 11–20.

Maree, J. G. (2012b). Using "informal" hypnotherapy in career counselling: Blending Savickas and Erickson to "free the angel". *South African Journal of Psychology, 42*(2), 156–168. Retrieved from https://journals.sagepub.com.uplib.idm.oclc.org/doi/pdf/10.1177/0081246312 04200203

Morgan, T., & Ness, D. (2003). Career decision-making difficulties of first-year students. *The Canadian Journal of Career Development, 2*(1), 33–39.

Part V
Examining the Link between Career Construction Theory and Practice

Chapter 12
Career Counseling as a Science, a Skill, and an Art: Drawing on the Inspiring Career-Life Story of Dolly Parton to Demonstrate How Theory Building in Career Construction Counseling is Premised on Practice

Find out who you are and do it on purpose
The way I see it, if you want the rainbow, you got to put up with the rain
Storms make trees take deeper roots (Dolly Parton)

We learned more from a three-minute record ... than we ever learned in school (Bruce Springsteen)

Abstract This chapter draws on the inspiring life story of the amazing Dolly Parton to demonstrate the remarkable overlap between multiple facets of Mark Savickas' counseling for self- and career construction theory and how this theory is practically and "naturally" enacted in numerous real-life contexts. First, a brief background to Dolly Parton's life is presented, and the overlap between her career-life story and the theory of career construction counseling is outlined. A truncated biography of Dolly Parton follows, after which the focus shifts to an elaboration of how she developed herself as a career project (Cochran, 1992). The outcomes of a "virtual" self- and career construction counseling-based interview conducted with her (based on information gathered from numerous publications and interviews) are used to uncover her key life themes. This interview is subsequently analyzed, and mission and vision statements are proposed for her. Next, the chapter discusses how Dolly Parton enacted her mission and vision and influenced the lives of countless other people positively (and continues to do so). More particularly, she provided and continues to provide a holding environment for millions of people. I explain how self- and career construction principles are realized in Dolly Parton's career-life story before the chapter is concluded.

12.1 Orientation

Many years ago as an ardent fan of Dolly Parton's music, I began incorporating some of her songs and comments and life story into my lectures and presentations,

J. G. (Kobus) Maree, *Innovating Counseling for Self- and Career Construction*,
https://doi.org/10.1007/978-3-030-48648-8_12

in South Africa and abroad. The "message" that I hope to convey through this book is that career counseling, too, can be excitement-filled, creative, inspirational, and life-changing. Dolly Parton's two honorary doctorates for her creative and humanitarian contributions, as well as the UT's introduction of an honors course on her work, shows that her work is valued and respected as much by the scholarly community as it is by the public in general. The chapter draws on her inspiring career-life story to demonstrate how counseling for self- and career construction counseling theory is practically and "naturally" enacted in numerous real-life contexts. Watching her remarkable career unfold over the past four decades, I have been particularly interested in observing the overlap between the theory and practice of self- and career construction counseling and the evolution of Dolly Parton's life story (Hinckley, 2017). The way in which she has succeeded in actively mastering what she had passively suffered (Savickas, 2001), for instance, has been well documented by numerous authors. Her inspiring "story" has also been captured in musical form especially but also in many books, movies, and articles of various kinds. Below, I elaborate further on this topic.

12.2 Dolly Parton's Timeless Conversation with Music

Dolly Parton entered into a remarkable conversation with music at a very early age, and key facets of her career-life story have been captured in her timeless songs. In her own words: "Songs ... They're just stories put to music (Netflix, 2019)." The deeply moving autobiographical song *Coat of many colors* (Globazik Media, 2018), her own favorite, signature song from among the roughly 3000 songs she has written, is of particular interest from the perspective of this book, and the following two lines from the song in particular have become embedded in the hearts and minds of many millions of people across the world:

a. "One is only poor if [one] choose[s] to be", and
b. "Although we had no money, I was rich as I could be in my coat of many colors that my mama made for me." (Photograph 12.1)

The embedded messages conveyed by these lines lie at the heart of this book, and the approach developed by Savickas and advocated here provides a powerful strategy to realize it. The messages also provide a good place to talk about resilience and thriving in the face of discrimination. Two issues should resonate with all career counselors: First, Dolly Parton had an excellent "audience" in her mother who reminded her constantly about how special she was (career counselors often represent the supportive audience their clients need). Second, she chose not to accept the negative stories of others about her that she was "poor". Instead, she defined "poorness" not in terms of money but rather in terms of lack of character (H. Sensoy-Briddick, personal communication, October 20, 2019).

To set the scene for the rest of the chapter, I begin by reporting briefly on Dolly Parton's biography.

Photograph 12.1 *Dolly Parton's Coat of Many Colors* coat displayed in the Country Music Hall of Fame and Museum in Nashville, Tennessee. *Source* Wikimedia Commons, https://commons.wikimedia.org/wiki/File:Coat_of_Many_Colors_coat.jpg

12.3 Background to Dolly Parton's Life: Brief Biography

Dolly Rebecca Parton was born on 19 January 1946 in a one-room cottage on the banks of the Little Pigeon River in the small town of Pittman Center, Sevier County (in the Great Smoky Mountains, East Tennessee) (Parton, 2010; Schmidt, 2017). The family lived a simple life, slept on straw beds, and had no electricity, gas, or running water. Her father (Robert Lee) was a sharecropper while her mother (Avie Lee) was a housewife. The family consisted of 12 children (six boys and six girls), six of whom became professional musicians. A 13th member of the family died shortly after birth. His passing was traumatic for Dolly, the more so because, according to the tradition in that part of the world at the time, she had the job of looking after him. As a result, many of her current social outreach projects are aimed at helping children in need. Her own family barely made a living, with the children growing up in extreme poverty.

Dolly's entire life has been closely interwoven with music activities. She wrote her first song (*Little tiny Tasseltop,* a song about a little doll her father had made for her, while her mother had made the doll a dress) at the age of five and went on to write more than 3000 songs. She began to play the guitar at the age of seven, and her first record (*Puppy love*) was released when she was 13 years old. She always wanted to be a singer and took a bus to Nashville ("Music city") immediately after she had graduated from high school. The rest is indeed "history".

12.4 Overview of Some of Dolly Parton's Milestone Achievements

A global icon and role model, Dolly Parton is the most celebrated singer-songwriter in the history of country music. A gifted singer, songwriter, multi-instrumentalist, record producer, philanthropist, actress, and businesswoman, she has received global recognition for her innovative contributions to the world of music over many decades, coupled with her humanitarian projects. Her philanthropic work includes the promotion of children's reading and education. In 1988, she founded the Dollywood Foundation to inspire children in her home county to achieve educational success. The foundation finances Dolly Parton's Imagination Library, a book-gifting and -distribution program that distributes books across the world. To date, the program has distributed 130 million books to pre-school aged children for free. Children receive a free book for five years (every month from the day they are born until they reach kindergarten). The first book they receive is *The little engine that could* (Piper, 2001), and *Look out Kindergarten, here I come*! (Carlson, 2004) is the last. Sandwiched between these two books, children receive books that are chosen by a panel of literary experts. All books relate to the themes of inspiration and imagination (CNN Library, 2019; Dembling, 2011; Schmidt, 2017).

Dolly Parton has received 47 Grammy Award nominations and has also been nominated for three Academy Awards as well as two Emmys and a Tony Award. She has sold over 160 million albums globally (*News Sentinel Staff*, 2009) and has been awarded two honorary doctorates. The first was awarded by Carson-Newman College for her commitment to education in Appalachia. The second was awarded by the University of Tennessee (UT), which bestowed only the second honorary doctorate in "Humane and musical letters" ever to Dolly Parton in 2009. The Chancellor of UT (Jimmy Cheek) explained that she received the degree "because of her career not just as a musician and entertainer, but for her role as a cultural ambassador, philanthropist and lifelong advocate for education" (*News Sentinel Staff*, 2009, p. 1). Dolly's active mastery over the things she encountered as a child resulted in her achieving success as well as in her giving back to others. During her acceptance speech, she commented that education and the arts were hugely important to her and that the degree was something that "makes me and would have made my parents very proud" (*News Sentinel Staff*,2009, p. 1).

This section of the chapter on Dolly Parton would be incomplete without reference to Dollywood, the theme park conceptualized and seen through to completion by Dolly (see my earlier comments in this regard). When, in 1986, her lawyers recommended that she drop the idea of Dollywood, she again refused and, instead, fired them. Today, Dollywood is the largest single entertainment park in the USA, employing many thousands of people (approximately 3000 people are on its payroll, making Dollywood the single largest employer in the area).

Below, I report on the outcomes of a "virtual" or simulated self- and career construction counseling interview (based on information obtained from numerous publications and actual interviews given by her) with Dolly Parton to shed more light on just how she had succeeded in developing herself as a life and career project (Cochran, 1992). This enabled her to appreciate the dynamic forces that shaped and continue to shape her central self—a process that ends in and embodies self-construction that has enabled her to negotiate numerous transitions throughout her life. In other words, a process that illustrates the advancement of her sense of self and her career and life identity or sense of who she really is (Guichard, 2008a, 2008b). This interview will also enable us to uncover Dolly's key life themes.

12.5 Outcomes of a "Virtual" Self- and Career Construction Counseling-Based Interview with Dolly Parton: Uncovering her Key Life Themes

Dolly Parton's responses to a number of career-story questions/statements appear below. (**It should be emphasized, though, that these responses are based purely on information gathered from numerous publications and actual interviews given by her.**)

1. Her greatest strengths:

   Much has been written about Dolly Parton's greatest strengths, and it is not possible to list all of them here. However, the following strengths (Crowder, 2014; Parton, 2016) are probably representative of her specific uniqueness.

   a. She is extremely loyal—to her family, her home state, her followers, and her country. After having expressed her support for the LGBT(QIA) community, for instance, she received threats from various people but refused to be bullied into withdrawing her support.
   b. She is splendidly unique. A person who never allows stale, worn-out rules to limit her self- and career construction. Instead, she is renowned for her own signature look, style of singing, acting, dressing, working, re-inventing herself, and reaching out to others.
   c. She is resilient, readily acknowledges her own limitations and mistakes, which confirms the strength and intactness of her sense of self (her identity; who she really is). It shows that, beneath the wigs, the make-up, and the self-deprecating comments, she is an emotionally stable human being who has nothing to prove by pretending to be someone she is not, nor someone who never makes mistakes.

d. Once she is motivated to do something, she will do everything she can to actualize that dream. In her own words, "24/7, 365, I was going to make a success of my life" (Parton, 2011, n.p.). She is a living example of a person who is not afraid to pursue her dreams tirelessly.
e. She does not allow herself to be defined by, for instance, other people, the extreme poverty she grew up in, and the hurt and rejection she suffered early in life. Instead, she displays a remarkable and inspiring capacity to turn hurt into hope evidenced by, for instance, the manner in which she dealt with the rejection and humiliation she suffered when she was mocked by her classmates when she wore her coat of many colors to school.
f. She stands up for what she believes in.
g. She is sincere, compassionate, and really cares about people. Her mother describes her as a genuinely caring person who is sensitive to the needs of other people and finds it hard to see others suffer.
h. She is action-orientated and a living example of a person who does things instead of merely talking about what must or can be done. Examples of her industry are the large number of songs she had composed (generally regarded as 3000^{+}) (Sawyers, 2019), the books she has written, her participation in several movies, her book distribution project, and the theme park she conceptualized and brought to fruition (Barnes, 2019).
i. She is not swayed by the opinions of others but, rather, draws on her own life story for advice, a theme that pervades her life story. A few examples can illustrate this: When she decided to follow a career as a solo artist, she was sued by her singing partner, Porter Wagoner. However, she did not give in. Her decision was vindicated in the years after the split when she became globally renowned and contributed hugely to the popularity of country music (Parton, 2016).

2. Her areas for development:

   She could probably sleep and rest more.

3. What she values most.

   Helping others in need, using her talents to entertain and bring happiness to others, using her wealth to make a difference in the lives of others, promoting education and the arts, and writing and singing songs that people can go to in their greatest need. In addition, she says: "I've always felt like my music was more my ministry than a job" (Mitas, 2020, p. 2).

4. She admired the following person when she was young:

   "The local town 'tramp': I thought she was the most beautiful person I'd ever seen when we were little kids." She added that that woman was "the lady that I actually patterned myself after because she left an impression" (Sprankles & Brolley, 2019, n.p.). It wasn't until much later, Dolly admitted, that she learned that the woman was actually a local prostitute. She admired the woman for the fact that her style was unique, and to this day she continues to admire her because of her unique style. Dolly is very clear on the matter: She never judged the woman, nor does she judge anyone else. All that mattered to her then and matters to her today is that the woman was unique, different, and "stylish". Dolly Parton herself is arguably one of the most unique women in show business; a woman with her very own style. (This example also illustrates the principle that the important thing about people's role models is what it is about the role models that people take from them.)

5. What others say about her:

> "She is extremely sensitive. She has a gift to see and identify with the hurt and pain of others. She cares deeply about others and is distressed to see any one being sad or hurt. A gifted songwriter, she started composing songs before she could write them down. Her music has always been her way to express herself (Parton, 2016, n.p). She is as kind and nice as she is in person (if not more) as she is on stage."

6. Six of her favorite mottos or quotations (BrainyQuote, n.d, n.p.):

> "One is only poor, only if one chooses to be."
>
> "Find out who you are and do it on purpose."
>
> "Dream more, learn more, care more, and be more."
>
> "If you see someone without a smile, give them yours."
>
> "If you don't like the road you're walking on, start paving another one."
>
> "We cannot direct the wind but we can adjust the sails."

7. Her favorite book or movie or book turned into a movie:

   Here, Dolly repeatedly cites two books. The first is *Coat of Many Colors* (Dolly Parton, in Bonaguro, 2018, p. 3), the main theme of which is that one is poor only if one chooses to be poor. And how vividly does she not actualize this theoretical principle in her own life!

   Her other favorite book is *The Little Engine That Could* because "[i]t shows children that you can do it if you think you can ... that's my philosophy in life" (Dolly Parton, in Bonaguro, 2018, p. 3). What she is saying is that realizing the aims of achieving success, helping to lighten the load of others, and experiencing a sense of meaning and purpose in life is not dependent on how strong or talented or whatever one is. Rather, perseverance, enthusiasm, kindness, and dedication are what enables one to achieve these aims.

8. She wants to be remembered as ...

   Dolly repeatedly says that she would much rather be called the "book lady" (Parton, 2020, n. p.) than the "queen of country music" (Miller, 2008) because her father never had the chance to go to school. In other words, her biggest wish is to be remembered as a person who contributed to the development of children. Moreover, she states: "I suppose the only other desire I ever had [other than becoming a singer-entertainer] was to become a missionary" (Miller, 2008, p. 43).

9. So far, three of her biggest successes have been:

a. Her numerous personal achievements and awards.
b. Establishing the Imagination Library, which has already distributed more than a 130 million books among young children under the age of six across the world. The book *Coat of Many Colors* (adapted from her classic song—her favorite among the more than 3000 songs she has written so far) was the 100 millionth book to be distributed (*Business wire*, 2018).
c. Dollywood.

10. She experienced the following three challenges/"problems" when she was young and doesn't want others to suffer or go through them as well (Bonaguro, 2018):

    a. Losing her baby brother shortly after he was born. (She subsequently wrote a song *Angel hill* in his memory to help ease her pain.)
    b. Her family was desperately ('dirt') poor when she was young. It broke her heart to see her mother in particular suffer.
    c. "She was mocked and bullied because they were poor, and she had to wear ragged clothes."
    d. "I've struggled enough in my life to be appreciated and understood. I've had to go against all kinds of people through the years just to be myself. I think everybody should be allowed to be who they are" (Parton, in Abraham, 2019, p. 63).

11. The first things she remembers about her life (or her earliest recollections)

Dolly often recounts one particular earliest recollection that gave rise to her signature song *Coat of many colors.* This is more or less how the story goes: When Dolly was six, her mother, in the middle of the Tennessee winter, was given a box containing pieces of cloth from a wealthy neighbor. Since Dolly needed a coat, her mother stitched the pieces together and made her a multicolored coat. While she was sewing the coat together, Dolly's mother told her the Old Testament Bible story of Joseph and his amazing coat and said her coat was more or less the same as Joseph's coat. Feeling very proud of her new coat, Dolly couldn't wait to wear it to school, expecting the other children also to like the coat and be proud of her mother's handiwork. So, the next day, she put it on and rushed off to school … only to be mocked and laughed at over her precious "coat of rags". The other children even tried to tear it from her body and shove her into a closet. A tearful Dolly tried her best to tell them that her beautiful coat was as pretty to her and meant more to her than their expensive coats meant to them. She also told them that no matter what they thought, a person is only as poor as she or he wishes to be and that money alone cannot make people happy. They would not listen, and Dolly eventually ran home, feeling hurt, sad, and unhappy and crying bitterly (Hinckley, 2017). (Also see the next section for the sequel to this recollection about how Dolly managed to actively master the pain she suffered at the time.) Her second signature song *I will always love you*, written when she was splitting from her former "employer" and singing partner, Porter Wagoner, is one of many instances during her life when she drew on her almost uncanny ability to articulate (narrate) her micro-life stories to deal with her pain. (Moreover, that song has come to mean a great deal to countless others.)

The first recollection revolves around three central life themes: First, a poor little girl being mocked, rejected, and hurt by her peers because of her coat of many colors made from cloth remnants. After leaving school, Dolly embarked on a career as a singer, actress, and entertainer, wearing wigs and colorful, extravagant dresses. Numerous magazine writers have made fun of her, and she is constantly "mocked" for her extraordinary attire and appearance—quite similar to what happened in her earliest recollection. However, in behaving in this fashion, she has actively mastered her passive suffering. She is not at all fazed by others' snipes and comments. Her self-deprecatory comments such as "it costs a lot of money to look this cheap" (BrainyQuote, n.d.; Harper, 2019) are admired and considered indicative of her high emotional-social intelligence.

The second key theme is that one does not need to allow oneself to be hurt by what others think or say about you. Instead, what really matters is what one prefers to believe about oneself. Dolly Parton believes that people should not be defined by their socioeconomic status (in her case, poverty). While not denying that people suffer many kinds of pain, she maintains that one's mindset or view on a particular matter is key to dealing with all "pain". Her life story demonstrates how pain or suffering can be converted into social contributions as exemplified by her humanitarian contributions such as providing free books to poor children and writing songs such as her famous *Coat of many colors* with its inspiring message. Hers is a remarkable story: She is who she is, and she makes no attempt to hide behind her celebrity status.

This theme also resonates with a therapeutic truism in clinical hypnotherapy, namely that all hypnosis is self-hypnosis and that people who do not wish to get healthy emotionally cannot be compelled to seek such health.

The third theme, too, is reflected in words from the *Coat of many colors*: "Although we had no money, I was rich as I could be in my coat of many colors that my momma made for me" (Parton, 2000, n.p.). Here, she states that it is love and the belief that one can feel happy, irrespective of one's circumstances that make one happy. Money, fame, or possessions by themselves cannot bring real happiness.

No wonder that in real life Dolly Parton is a well-loved and revered artist, a rare human being who tirelessly reaches out to people in need.

12.6 Dolly Parton's Integrated Career-Life Story Narrative

Dolly Parton's responses to a number of career-story questions/statements appear below. **(It should be emphasized, though, that these responses are based purely on information gathered from numerous publications and actual interviews given by her.)**

12.6.1 Dolly Parton's Identity, Value, or Power Statement

Dolly is a musically gifted, creative, dynamic, kind, and loyal person who unfailingly stands by those that she loves and cares about. She will never allow stale, non-sensical, rules limit her self- and career construction or influence her unique style of singing, acting, dressing, and working. Her capacity to reinvent herself constantly is a rare gift in these turbulent times. Many people deride her because of her signature style (always dressed extravagantly, wearing wigs and heavy make-up). She even does so herself, tongue in cheek. As she often says: "You have no idea how much it costs to look this cheap!" Yet, she is perfectly sure of who she is, and no amount of derision or attempted humiliation ever bothers her because, according to her, "no book should ever be judged by its cover alone". Beneath the wigs and the make-up and the self-deprecating comments, inside, she is "a real good book;" a real good "story"! (Parton, 2008, n.p.).

If Dolly believes in something, nothing will stop her achieving her goal. She works "24/7, 365" (Parton, 2011, n.p.) to realize her dreams and to continue to make a success of her life. Yes, she, too, does wonder occasionally whether what she is achieving is really worth the sacrifice—which simply proves that she is only human after all! (Parton, 2011).

Dolly has never allowed herself to be defined by what others say about her. Yes, she grew up in extreme poverty, and, yes, she experienced humiliation, rejection, and hurt in her early as well as her later life. Yet, as can be seen, God gave her the wonderful gift of being able to turn hurt into hope.

Dolly is an active, dynamic, living example of someone who does things instead of merely talking about what must or can be done. Above all, she never shies away from finding a way to help people who are poor or who have lost what was precious to them. To this end, she draws on her God-given capacity to write songs, to sing, to create work opportunities for others, to promote young children's education, and to make people laugh or cry (depending on their need at the time). She is a visionary who inspires others to follow and never let go of their dreams. As happy as she is to help people, she never asks them for advice or gives them advice on what they should do because she believes that only they know deep inside what they really want and need and how best to draw on their own life stories for advice. She maintains that they are the experts on themselves—not she (*Skynews*, 2019, n.p.).

If I (the author) were to sum up her story, it would be in the following words: We can all be stars, can be happy, and can be successful. However, nobody can help us to be happy, successful, helpful, or kind if we do not want to be.

Careers and associated fields of study associated with Dolly Parton's key life themes and identity, value, or power statement include entertainer (singer, actress, and songwriter) businesswoman, educator, psychologist, therapist, philanthropist, social worker, hairdresser, innovator, and author.

12.7 Dolly Parton's Chosen Career and Her Mission and Vision Statements (as Inferred from the Above Discussion)

To enable her to experience a sense of meaning and purpose in her life, she became a singer, songwriter, movie star, producer, entrepreneur, businesswoman, and philanthropist (**occupational choice**).

12.7.1 Mission Statement (Personal Meaning)

She is happy and successful in her career-life because of her ability to express herself in numerous ways and on numerous forums—by writing and singing hit songs, by acting in acclaimed movies, by writing books, by actualizing her potential as a businesswoman, and by inspiring countless others. She has worked tirelessly, has made the most of her talents, and has become a global star; a rare icon and living legend (Girley, 2019). By making the most of her God-given talents, and in her own inimitable way, she has achieved great success in the fields of music, philanthropy, education, and psychology. A rare celebrity, a genuine star; she has realized her dreams and allows herself to keep on dreaming (Parton, 2012).

12.7.2 Vision Statement (Social Meaning)

Dolly experiences a sense of purpose in her career-life because of the substantial social contributions she has made and is still making, such as helping millions of people deal with their sadness, sorrow, poverty, hurt, and, even more importantly, making their hurt a gift to other people. This includes helping those less fortunate (financially and emotionally) survive even the most serious challenges, promoting the education and dreams of many others, soothing their pain, creating job opportunities, developing the reading ability (education) of countless young people, and sparking the creative powers and hopes of millions of others. Doing so helps her honor the legacy of her beloved parents, whom she will miss sorely until the day she lays her head down (*News Sentinel Staff*, 2009).

This scenario illustrates Dolly Parton's reasons for working as hard as she always has to actualize her potential in the service of not only herself but in the interests of others as well.

Below, I show how Dolly Parton actualizes her career-life story narrative and advances key aspects of life design counseling in the lives of countless other people.

12.8 How Dolly Parton Developed Herself as a Career Project

From a life design perspective that focuses on reflexive consciousness and self-making (Hartung & Santili, 2018; Savickas et al., 2009), Dolly Parton has developed her "self" and career as a project (Cochran, 1992). Put differently: She has used herself (Hartung & Santili, 2018) "as a project for making meaning [that] most values narratability" (p. 11) or, in other words, she has developed the capacity to narrate her own life story, along with adaptability and intentionality as the main outcomes that helped her answer the question: "What purpose does work serve in my life?" (p. 11). Her narrations take the form of verbal discourses, books, and, especially, a large number of songs, numerous radio and TV interviews, transmedia storytelling (Edwards, 2018), as well as interviews with representatives of a broad spectrum of the print media.

Dolly Parton's actions show how self- and career construction counseling principles are actualized in an authentic, natural way in numerous everyday real-world contexts. A remarkable overlap can be seen between her endeavors and the theory and practice of career construction. She consistently recounts two kinds of stories alluded to by Savickas (1995), namely "those that reveal the client's preoccupation or central life concern and those that reveal the plot or what they plan to do about the preoccupation". I connect these stories with "the thread of continuity that is [her] life theme" (p. 4).

Below, I explain in more detail how Dolly Parton's career-life confirms Savickas' (2009a) assertion that theory follows practice. The practical enactment of a number of theoretical aspects of career construction counseling (see **bold** below) in Dolly Parton's career-life are discussed briefly. Stated differently: I show how counseling for self- and career construction theory building is premised on practice, as exemplified by the career-life story of Dolly Parton.

12.8.1 How Dolly Parton's Career-Life Confirms Savickas' (2009) Assertion That Theory Follows Practice

Dolly Parton **enacts various career-life roles** (e.g. entertainer, actress, singer, song-writer, innovator, employer, entrepreneur, and philanthropist) that enable her to construct her career and herself by participating in a broad array of activities. She is highly adept at **narratability** (recounting or narrating her life story). Her recollection of wearing her coat of many colors to school and being mocked by children, for instance, is an example of the kind of story that reveals a person's **preoccupation or central life concern**. The kind of story that reveals **the plot** or what the person plans to do about the preoccupation is illustrated by what is arguably Dolly Parton's **most central recollection** (about the coat of many colors). She recounts how she carried the pain, rejection, and hurt inside her for several years. Then, roughly 10 years after the incident, one day, she woke up and wrote the song *Coat of many colors*. She recounts that many people with disabilities or had had suffered rejection had told her how much the song meant to them and its healing influence. The message that they took from the song was that people should not allow adversity and challenge to define them. Instead, **they should turn disability, rejection, or rejection into a gift to others**.

We should rather strive to make meaning of our hurt, find a way to overcome hindrances, and thus master actively what we have suffered or are suffering passively. In time, we should **transform the "pain" or situation into triumph and make a social contribution**, much as Dolly Parton and many others have done. The pain she suffered passively became "formative wounds in the Dolly Parton creation story" (Zoladz, 2019, p. 21). In doing so, we **enhance our own experience of a sense of purpose in our lives**. This is possible if we believe we can do so and **actively work towards mastering challenge**s thus adding a sense of meaning, hope, and purpose to our lives. Moreover, Dolly Parton repeatedly states that she **never "advises"** people on issues. This is what she said during her commencement (acceptance) speech in 2009: "[I am] nervous because I know that I am supposed to say something meaningful to you. Maybe some good advice for you to always remember. Now I usually try not to give advice. Information, yes; advice, no" (Parton, 2009, September 14, n.p.). Elsewhere, she says: "I don't try to tell other people what do. People are always asking, 'What kind of advice would you give?' and I answer, 'I don't give advice. I have some information if you want to know some facts and sometimes how I dealt with something' " (*Skynews*, 2019, n.p.).

Perusal of Dolly Parton's storyline also uncovers what Savickas (1995) refers to as "the thread of continuity that is [her] life theme" (p. 4). Her stories encourage authenticity narratives (Edwards, 2018) to clarify her **career identity**, which she constantly draws on to elicit inner advice (**autobiographicity**). Sharing these stories also advances her **career adaptability and employability**, and makes her more **career resilient** (enhances her ability to perform competently in rapidly changing, challenging, multidimensional, and often disabling contexts or circumstances) (Rochat, Masdonati, & Dauwalder, 2017). Woven together into a grand narrative, her micro-life stories lucidly and spontaneously reveal who she is from a work and career perspective: **a great artist and entertainer, an educator, an entrepreneur, a therapist, a philanthropist; the kind of work that enables her to convert her preoccupations** or key life themes (Krieshok, Black, & McKay, 2009) **into occupations**. Consistent with counseling for career construction theory, she believes that **each person is unique** and has to establish her or his career identity (*SkyNews*, 2019, n.p.): "Everybody has a right to be themselves. Everybody has their own path and their own road to walk. And everybody's talent is different."

Put differently: Dolly Parton's **career-life identity** as an artist, a healer, and a philanthropist is revealed by the telling, sharing, and performing of her life stories (LaPointe, 2010) in a way that helps and **inspires** millions of others and enhances their **sense of imagination and creativity** (Maree, 2019a, 2019b; Marr, 2018). Those who listen to her telling (reading, singing, performing) her stories are inspired by watching her "perform" these stories. Her **self-awareness, (critical) self-reflection,**

and reflexivity shape and fine-tune her **career identity**, which she promotes by carefully examining and using her reflections (**reflexivity**) to help her map out her future with a clear plan of positive action to promote forward movement and experience the "ultimate" purposeful life in which she constructs herself and her career (Guichard & Dumora, 2010; Guichard, Pouyaud, De Calan, & Dumora, 2012).

What inspires and impresses me personally, more than any other aspect of Dolly Parton's career-life, is how she has devoted her entire life to providing holding environments for others.

12.9 Providing a Holding Environment for Millions of People

A brief glance at Dolly Parton's life-time achievements reveals positive action, forward movement, innovation, and many other career construction-related endeavors. However, above all, they reveal how she has succeeded in providing a sacred space or holding environment for millions of people. Zoladz (2019, p. 21) argues that "much of her music is grounded by an authentic sense of insecurity that she's worked hard to overcome". Moreover, Glenville (in Harper, 2019) points out that she clearly has durability—a key 'holding' trait that restores a sense of stability in a constantly and rapidly changing and uncertain world. By living out the principle of actively mastering what she has passively suffered, she inspires countless others to draw on their own sense of creativity and imagination to do likewise. The following story illustrates this claim. Dolly's father was unable to read or write and consequently felt inferior and incompetent his whole life. Dolly's Imagination Library Book project (referred to earlier) is an example of how she has helped so many people to convert hurt into hope and social contributions. It shows also how she has succeeded in healing herself (dealing with her own pain, namely sadness at the plight of her father who was "crippled" by his inability to read or write) by helping others. Doing so serves as example of making social contributions, making meaning of her situation, instilling hope, and promoting the living of purposeful lives (Bonaguro, 2018).

Knoepp (2019) states that no matter what measure one applies, Dolly Parton's philanthropical contributions to humanity are staggering and legendary. To back this up, he recalls that two days after the devastating runaway veld fires in western North Carolina and Gatlinburg (Tennessee) in 2016, Dolly Parton established the My People's Fund to help survivors of the disaster. Around $12.5 million were raised for Sevier County residents (where Dolly grew up) to help reconstruct their community. In addition, Dolly recently donated $1 million towards research in search of a cure for the coronavirus (Reuter, 2020).

12.10 Summary

Dolly Parton's inspiring career-life story illustrates the overlap between the theory and practice of self- and career construction counseling and, to a significant extent, also life design counseling. Dolly Parton has been implementing self- and career construction counseling theory in practice in her own career-life to improve the lives of countless others. She has done this without any knowledge of the theory that has underpinned her achievements. I have long maintained that we, as career psychologists, can learn a great deal about our field by observing artists, as is indeed confirmed by this chapter.

After having presented numerous keynote addresses and workshops on self- and career construction and life design intervention, I can state unequivocally that Dolly Parton's life story provides exceptionally helpful material for understanding the theory and mastery of the skills associated with self- and career construction and life design intervention. Unfailingly, after presentations, participants express admiration for and appreciation of Dolly Parton's insight into aspects of our profession (without realizing it). Moreover, careful analysis of her career-life story confirms what many researchers have been saying for years, namely that theory follows practice, and not the other way around.

Chapter 13 is the final chapter of the book.

References

Barnes, H. (2019). *9 things to know about Dolly Parton*. Retrieved from https://popculture.com/country-music/2019/01/18/9-things-to-know-about-dolly-parton/.

Bonaguro, A. (2018). *How Dolly Parton's father inspires her every day*. Retrieved from http://www.cmt.com/news/1797943/how-dolly-partons-father-inspires-her-every-day/.

BrainyQuote. (n.d.) *Dolly Parton quotes*. Retrieved from https://www.brainyquote.com/authors/dolly-parton-quotes.

Business wire. (2018). Retrieved from https://www.businesswire.com/news/home/20180228005041/en/Dolly-Parton%E2%80%99s-Imagination-Library-Reaches-100-Million.

Carlson, N. (2004). *Look out Kindergarten, here I come!*. London, England: Penguin.

CNN Library. (2019). *Dolly Parton fast facts*. Retrieved from https://edition.cnn.com/2015/07/01/us/dolly-parton-fast-facts/index.html.

Cochran, L. R. (1992). The career project. *Journal of Career Development, 18*(3), 187–197.

Crowder, C. (2014). 7 surprising reasons to admire Dolly Parton. Retrieved from https://celebs.allwomenstalk.com/surprising-reasons-to-admire-dolly-parton/7/.

Dembling, S. (2011). *Dolly Parton's been writing songs for 60 years*. Retrieved from https://www.dallasobserver.com/music/dolly-partons-been-writing-songs-for-60-years-6426138.

Edwards, L. H. (2018). *Dolly Parton: Gender and country music*. Bloomington, IN: Indiana University Press.

Girley, B. (2019). *Dolly Parton: My music is more my ministry than a job*. Retrieved from https://ambotv.com/blog/entertainment/dolly-parton-my-music-is-more-my-ministry-than-a-job/

Globazik Media (2018, February 28). *Coat of many colors*. Retrieved from https://www.youtube.com/watch?v=Mikj3KQhTMA.

Guichard, J. (Ed.). (2008a). *La nouvelle découverte des activités professionnelles et projets personnels* [The discovery of occupational activities and personal plans: An updated workshop method]. Paris, France: Editions qui plus est.

Guichard, J. (2008b). Proposition d'un schema d'entretien constructiviste de conseil en orientation pour des adolescents ou de jeunes adultes [Outline of a life designing counseling interview for adolescents and young adults]. *L'orientation Scolaire et Professionnelle, 37,* 413–440.

Guichard, J., & Dumora, B. (2010). A constructivist approach to ethically grounded vocational development intervention for young people In J. A. Athanasou & R. van Esbroeck (Eds), *International handbook of career guidance* (pp. 187–208). Dordrecht, The Netherlands: Springer Science.

Guichard, J., Pouyaud, J., De Calan, C., & Dumora, B. (2012). Identity construction and career development interventions with emerging adults. *Journal of Vocational Behavior, 81,* 52–58.

Harper, L. (2019). *How Dolly Parton's 'cheap' signature look conquered fashion*. Retrieved from https://www.theguardian.com/music/2019/nov/29/dolly-parton-cheap-look-conquered-fashion.

Hartung, P. J., & Santili, S. (2018). *My Career Story*: Description and initial validity evidence. *Journal of Career Assessment, 26*(2), 308–321.

Hinckley, D. (2017). *Dolly Parton's Coat of many colors & several hankies*. Retrieved from https://www.huffingtonpost.com/david-hinckley/dolly-partons-coat-of-man_b_8755510.html.

Knoepp, L. (2019). How Dolly Parton gave $12.5 million and unprecedented research to Sevier County. Retrieved from http://www.bpr.org/post/how-dolly-parton-gave-125-million-and-unprecedented-research-sevier-county#stream/0.

Krieshok, T. S., Black, M. D., & McKay, R. A. (2009). Career decision making: The limits of rationality and the abundance of non-conscious processes. *Journal of Vocational Behavior, 75,* 75–290.

LaPointe, K. (2010). Narrating career, positioning identity: Career identity as a narrative practice. *Journal of Vocational Behavior, 77,* 1–9.

Maree, J. G. (2019a, June). *Career Development in Africa: Decent work for all: Brief photomontage*. Keynote Address at the Annual Career Development Practitioner Congress, Emperors Palace Conference Centre, Kempton Park, South Africa.

Maree, J. G. (2019b). Postmodernising career counseling in a deep rural context. In J. G. Maree (Ed.), *Handbook of innovative career counseling* (pp. 577–596). New York, NY: Springer.

Marr, B. (2018). *7 Job skills of the future (that AIs and robots can't do better than humans)*. Retrieved from https://www.forbes.com/sites/bernardmarr/2018/08/06/7-job-skills-of-the-future-that-ais-and-robots-cant-do-better-than-humans/#10a27e676c2e.

Miller, S. (2008). *Smart blonde: Dolly Parton*. New York, NY: OmnibusPress.

Mitas, M. (2020, March 25). Dolly Parton's post on instagram is the reminder we all need right now. Retrieved from https://www.cheatsheet.com/entertainment/dolly-partons-post-on-instagram-is-the-reminder-we-all-need-right-now.html/.

Netflix. (2019, November 5). *Dolly Parton's Heartstrings: Official Trailer, Netflix* [Video file]. Retrieved from https://www.youtube.com/watch?v=eNo-Qxsp-mk.

News Sentinel Staff. (2009). *UT to grant Dolly Parton an honorary doctorate degree*. Retrieved from http://archive.knoxnews.com/entertainment/pop-culture/ut-to-grant-dolly-parton-an-honorary-doctorate-degree-ep-410361058-359583561.html.

Parton, D. (2000, November 23). *Dolly Parton—Coat of many colors*. Retrieved from https://www.youtube.com/watch?v=QTmjlsDWi3o.

Parton, D. (2008, May 10). *Backwoods Barbie by Dolly Parton* – Retrieved from https://www.youtube.com/watch?v+VJBz1U6Y-pg.

Parton, D. P. (2009, September 14). *Dolly Parton delivers commencement address at the University of Tennessee 2009*. Retrieved from https://www.youtube.com/watch?v=EuOm2lLIOoU.

Parton, D. (2010, August 05). *Dolly Parton on Oprah*. Retrieved from https://www.youtube.com/watch?v=xnerhSulS8c.

Parton, D. (2011, November 15). *Dolly Parton: The sacrifice (official music video)*. Retrieved from https://www.youtube.com/watch?v=6Ywoy9IBRM8.

Parton, D. (2012). *Dream more*. London, Great Britain: Bantam Press.
Parton, A. L. (2016). *Mama's memories – from Avie Lee Parton*. Retrieved from https://dollyparton.com/front-porch-stories/mamas-memories-from-avie-lee-parton/11278.
Parton, D. (2020, March 31). *Dolly Parton is helping with bed time by reading stories for fans*. Retrieved from https://www.youtube.com/watch?v=QKR2-7-6z00.
Piper, W. (2001). *The little engine that could*. New York, NY: Penguin.
Reuter, A. (2020, April 01). *Dolly Parton donates $1 million to Vanderbilt Hospital, aiding ongoing research for coronavirus cure*. Retrieved from https://www.billboard.com/articles/columns/country/9348404/dolly-parton-vanderbilt-hospital-donation.
Rochat, S., Masdonati, J., & Dauwalder, J. (2017). Determining career resilience. In J. G. Maree (Ed.), *The psychology of career adaptability, career resilience, and employability* (pp. 125–141). New York, NY: Springer.
Savickas, M. L. (1995). Examining the personal meaning of inventoried interests during career counseling. *Journal of Career Assessment, 3*(2), 188–201.
Savickas, M. L. (2001). Toward a comprehensive theory of career development: Disposition concerns and narratives. In F. T. L. Leong & A. Barak (Eds.), *Contemporary models in vocational psychology: A honor of Samuel H. Osipow* (pp. 295–320). Mahwah, NJ: Lawrence Erlbaum.
Savickas, M. L. (2009a, April). *The essentials of life design counseling*. Invited public lecture. Pretoria, South Africa: The University of Pretoria.
Savickas, M. L. (2009b, April). *Utilizing early anecdotes in counseling in the 21st century*. Keynote presentation, SA Society for Clinical Hypnosis. Pretoria, South Africa.
Savickas, M. L. (2009c, June). *The role of values in careers: Meaning and mattering in life design*. Keynote at the Biennial Society for Vocational Psychology Conference, University of St Louis, Missouri.
Savickas, M. L. (2009d). Career-style counseling. In T. J. Sweeney (Ed.), *Adlerian counseling and psychotherapy: A practitioner's approach* (5th ed., pp. 183–207). New York, NY: Routledge.
Savickas, M. L., Nota, L., Rossier, J., & Dauwalder, J. P., Duarte, M. E., Guichard, J., …Van Vianen, A. E. M. (2009). Life designing: A paradigm for career construction in the 21st century. *Journal of Vocational Behavior, 75*, 239-250.
Sawyers, B. J. (2019). The 15 Best Dolly Parton songs. Retrieved from https://www.wideopencountry.com/dolly-parton-songs-ranked/.
Schmidt, R. L. (Ed.). (2017). *Dolly on Dolly: Interviews and encounters with Dolly Parton*. Chicago, IL: Chicago Review Press.
Sky News. (2019, February 18). Dolly Parton: '9 to 5' in #MeToo era is as relevant as ever. Retrieved from https://www.youtube.com/watch?v=3Hx_ybX7wvs.
Sprankles, J., & Brolley, B. (2019). *The untold truth of Dolly Parton*. Retrieved from https://www.thelist.com/94995/untold-truth-dolly-parton/.
Zoladz, L. (2019). *Is there anything we can all agree on? Yes: Dolly Parton*. Retrieved from https://www.nytimes.com/2019/11/21/arts/music/dolly-parton.html.

Part VI
Closure

Chapter 13
Closing Chapter

It's easy to come up with new ideas; the hard part is letting go of what worked for you two years ago, but will soon be out of date.
(Roger von Oech)

Abstract In this chapter, I first discuss the lens that should be used to understand and interpret the contents of the book. Next, I consider the key issue as to whether it is advisable to continue using tests (in conjunction with qualitative assessment instruments) in career counseling. The main caveats for the success of the approach espoused in the book are discussed, key aspects of counselors' role in career counseling are examined, and a brief synthesis of the integrative model proposed in Chap. 10 is provided before the chapter is concluded.

13.1 Orientation

The approach advocated in this book is based on self- and career construction counseling principles. Given its successful implementation in Global North contexts and the need for new, innovative, feasible career counseling interventions in Global South contexts, I have presented many workshops and made many presentations to promote the approach. My "mission" started with workshops on the theory and practice of the *CCI,* and my research on the effectiveness and value of the integrative approach (see, for instance, Maree, 2017, 2018b, 2019b) has yielded promising results, with positive feedback from counselors and clients alike on its usefulness in multiple contexts.

The aim of this chapter is to capture the essence of what the book is about and highlight a few of the most salient points that have led to the success of the integrative approach.

J. G. (Kobus) Maree, *Innovating Counseling for Self- and Career Construction*,
https://doi.org/10.1007/978-3-030-48648-8_13

13.2 Suggested Lens to Promote Understanding and Interpretation of the Book

Members of Division 16 of the International Association for Applied Psychology (IAAP) were recently invited by the Chair: Division 16 (Paul Hartung) to list up to three ideas or challenges that are central in the field of career psychology today. My three ideas are given below.

First, we should **join hands internationally** to promote multi-disciplinary, inter-disciplinary, and cross-disciplinary collaboration beyond artificial boundaries to help people retain or regain control over an occupational situation that is portrayed by many as spiraling out of control. To this end, **it is key to think innovatively; differently than before**. Moreover, collectively, we should understand, accept, and act as if we believe ourselves that change itself is a given; an implicit generator and creator of opportunities instead of a "problem". What is a "problem" is our inability to exploit change by using what we have and drawing on technological advances to convert ever-evolving challenges into opportunities for all.

Second, it is important to prioritize professionally and **help vulnerable people actively** such as those living in poverty and with disabilities, migrants, and those who are "different", rejected, or disrespected for whatever reason become employable and access sustainable, "decent" employment. Rekindle their sense of self, of self-respect, of dignity, and of career identity. Above all, we should understand that the "problem" is not that there are insufficient resources and opportunities for all. Rather, the focus should be on sharing available resources equitably to meet the ideal of providing contemporary career counseling for all (Rossier, 2015)—those who are disadvantaged especially. Doing so should start early in their school lives. Regrettably, though, at school level, learners in affluent contexts such as private schools are mostly taught by well-trained educators and have access to innovative, cutting- edge career counseling intervention; however, this not the case with learners from resource-scarce environments. Providing the kind of educating, training, and career counseling these learners need to help them do well in the future remains a huge challenge. Sadly, in Global South contexts especially, well-intended measures to "improve" the situation of such learners are often not well planned and executed and serve only to widen the gap between the "haves" and the "have nots".

Third, the individual and collective response of career psychology to global occupational changes should **be innovative and continue to center on challenging accepted "truths"**. More specifically, it is imperative to innovate and update the theory of, research on, and practice of career psychology in a way that advances people's career adaptability, employability, career resilience, career agility, and career creativity. Doing so is essential if we want to help them understand and accept that change is a constant and a generator (creator) of major opportunities and that work-related threats should be seen as ways of devising and accessing exciting new job opportunities. Accordingly, the onus rests on us to update the language of our discourse to reflect a sense of hope and purpose.

To achieve these three outcomes, career counselors should, in my view, be able to identify proactively what is referred to as "fifth wave-related changes" (Work 5.0) in occupational contexts if they are sincere in their efforts to provide contemporary, relevant career counseling.

13.3 Clarifying the Issue Regarding the Continued Use of Tests (in Conjunction with Qualitative Assessment Instruments) in Career Counseling

As mentioned earlier, there appears to be a widespread misconception that using an approach and intervention based on career construction theory precludes the use of traditional tests. Workshop attendees and audience members during presentations at scholarly conferences alike have mentioned that they find it hard to reconcile the use of qualitative, narrative, or storied interventions with the use of tests. More specifically, people often want to know how I explain the relationship between the *MCM* (a traditional test) and the theoretical model that I advocate, namely counseling for self- and career construction.

Given the frequency of these questions and reservations, I need to repeat that the differential approach (which alludes to quantitative assessment and the use of tests) constitutes one of the three cornerstones of career construction theory. Therefore, questioning the use of tests during career construction (as well as life design) counseling is based on a misunderstanding of the key theoretical traditions that form the basis of career construction (and life design) counseling and intervention. Also, to promote triangulation of assessment outcomes and the rigor of interventions, I personally prefer to use tests as well when administering career construction counseling, especially in group contexts.

Where experienced career counselors work with individual, psychologically healthy clients in particular, they may choose to use qualitative assessment (eliciting "stories") alone. However, career counselors with inadequate training in the qualitative assessment modality are urged to obtain sufficient practical experience in the use of qualitative interventions (under the supervision of skilled mentors) first. This is because the success of qualitative intervention depends largely on the level of training and experience of individual career counselors. The style of assessment and the combination of tests and qualitative assessment strategies depends also on clients' life phase (in relation to the transitions they are facing at any given point in time) as well on the unique crossroads confronting them. Even in individual contexts, clients could be requested to respond to any number of additional qualitative questions (and perhaps even complete a traditional test or tests such as the *MCM* and/or the *MBTI*), especially if the career counselor is inexperienced. Conversely, the *My Career Story* (*MCS*) (Savickas & Hartung, 2012) (a questionnaire and intervention strategy designed for use in either individual or group contexts to help people author and re-author their career-life stories) may be used either on its own or in conjunction with the *CIP* and/or the *MCM*. According to Hartung and Santili (2018), the *MCS* was designed to simulate the *Career Construction Interview* (*CCI*) and broaden its application possibilities.

13.4 Enhancing the Implementation of the Integrative Approach

Below, I elaborate on steps that can be taken to enhance the implementation of the integrative approach. First, attending workshops to master the basic principles of the approach is essential. Second, appreciating the importance of helping people listen carefully to and hear themselves instead of believing that it is the task of counselors to become experts on them and "tell" them what to do is equally important. In the end, people should be provided with sufficient information to enable them to advise themselves on what decisions might be in their best interests regarding the handling of unique career-life transitions. Third, steps should be taken to promote triangulation and crystallization of the intervention in order to enhance its validity, credibility, and trustworthiness[1]. This also includes (where possible) securing the services of an external coder (interrater) to increase the trustworthiness of qualitative (for instance, thematic) analysis (uncovering of life themes) as well as a "blind" scorer of psychometric tests. This is because our deep involvement with the intervention and our subjective interpretation of information may inadvertently impact and limit our ability to analyze the information ("data") correctly. Fourth, more research involving larger and diverse groups of people is needed to establish the effectiveness of the approach espoused here in different contexts, especially in Global South contexts. Fifth, counselors and clients should endeavor jointly to elicit clients' key life themes. Career counselors' prompting of clients should be minimal; instead, they should together reflect on clients' answers to questions (meta-reflection) to facilitate reflexivity. Sixth, the aim of authorizing clients' life themes is to promote their choice-making status and readiness. Unless this aim is achieved, clients may well refuse to accept responsibility for their decisions and choices. Seventh, counselors need to observe clients carefully and ask them to validate or invalidate their observations and interpretations of observations. Likewise, eighth, it is important to clarify, rephrase, and reframe clients' questions and comments. Ninth, clients need to be reminded that their (perceived) limitations should be regarded as the springboard to converting pain, weaknesses, and challenges ("weaknesses") into strengths, triumphs, social contributions, and enhancement of their sense of purpose in their career-lives. Lastly, creating a safe space of trust between counselors and clients is essential for establishing and promoting the therapeutic relationship between the two parties.

---

[1] See, for instance, Maree (2018a, 2019c) for examples of how rigor of the intervention can be enhanced.

13.5 Examination of Key Aspects of the Counselor's Role in Career Counseling

From my vantage point, clients can best be understood and helped when counselors consciously attempt to get to know them from an integrative perspective that focuses on objective and subjective dimensions of their career-life stories. To promote their understanding of clients, career counselors should view them through the three-fold theoretical lens of social actorship, motivated agency, and autobiographical authorship and integrate these three constructs in a way that augments extension, furtherance, and integration of their smaller and larger life stories (McAdams, 2010, 2013; Savickas, 2011, 2016). Examining the extent to which clients have mastered (or have not mastered) key developmental tasks during their crucial formative years can provide vital information regarding not only their signature strengths but also their signature non-successes or developmental milestones that they did not master during their developmental years. Once these strengths and non-successes or unsuccessfully mastered key developmental milestones have been uncovered, a strategy can be devised and operationalized jointly to enable clients to master incomplete developmental tasks successfully in order to advance their self- and career construction. Key to the success of such strategies is developing clients' self-sufficiency, self-reliance, resourcefulness, and adaptive capacities and focusing on their unique emotions, cognitions, volitions, and passions (Cochran, 1997; Littleton, Arthur, & Rousseau, 2000; Savickas, 2019a, 2019b). Above all, career counselors should strive to devise and implement an active, forward movement-orientated approach. Viewing clients as passive "patients" is not conducive to beneficial counseling for them.

I agree with Phares (1992) that career counselors' primary allegiance in psychology should be to "best" ways to help them understand clients and their idiosyncratic career counseling needs instead of "clinging" to specific theoretical approaches, assessment techniques, strategies, and interventions that may no longer suffice in changing times.

Assessing the effectiveness of career counseling interventions is essential. Doing so involves establishing if and to what extent interventions have contributed to or produced significant changes in the career-life stories of clients (Savickas et al., 2009; Soresi, Nota, Ferrari, & Solberg, 2008). Changes in this context may manifest in differing ways and to differing extents and should be assessed in various ways and at various levels. This includes monitoring clients' evolving career-life stories, obtaining feedback on how they are coping and in what respects, and to what extent they have moved forward on account of the intervention. Lastly, and pivotally, career counselors need to keep abreast of the latest developments in career psychology, renew and innovate their practice, and upskill themselves continuously. Refining, updating, and improving their theory base and innovating their practice are key constituents of a strategy aimed at re-invigorating and innovating their own careers and life stories and promoting a sense of purpose in their career-lives too.

For the sake of convenience, a brief synthesis of the integrative model proposed in Chap. 10 is provided below.

Brief explanation of Table 13.1. First, the *MCM* is completed and then the *CIP*. (The questionnaires can be completed either online or in hard copy format.) Second, clients' responses are analyzed and synthesized (see Tables 10.1 and 10.2). Depending on whether the questionnaires were completed online or in hard copy format, the online reports or the template are/is used to (a) craft clients' identity, value, or power statements; (b) identify clients' integrated main interest categories/patterns; (c) help clients decide where they want to study after completing school; and (d) craft clients' mission and vision statements. Next, (e) action plans are devised to facilitate thorough job analysis; and (f) short-, medium-, and longer-term feedback is obtained to help researchers and practitioners assess the effectiveness of their intervention and guide them in their efforts to continue to render a useful service.

Table 13.1 Brief synthesis of the integrative model proposed in Chap. 10

Phase	Step	Detailed explanation	Analyzing and synthesizing clients' responses
1: Eliciting the life story		Clients complete the *MCM* (followed by the *CIP*) in hard copy format OR: Clients complete the *MCM* (followed by the *CIP*) online	
2: Authorizing (validating) the life story	1	Completed hard copy versions of the *CIP* and *MCM* are reflected on OR: Online assessment: Presenting and reflecting on clients' responses	Online: See Table 10.1 Hard copy: See Table 10.2
	2	Making sense of the reflections by "connecting the dots"	See Tables 10.1 and 10.2
	3	Formulating clients' personal meaning (mission) and social meaning (vision) statements	See Tables 10.1 and 10.2
3: Facilitating forward movement	1	Devising action plans to facilitate action and forward movement	See Tables 10.1 and 10.2
	2	Obtaining regular feedback	See Tables 10.1 and 10.2

13.6 Discussion

Designing and developing career counseling assessment instruments that can work for people across the diversity spectrum is often regarded as an overly optimistic aim. However, as the case studies presented in this book have shown individually and collectively, this aim can be achieved. While career counselors endeavor to respond appropriately to major changes in the occupational world, the integrative approach delineated and demonstrated here opens up exciting possibilities to help clients uncover and enact their key life themes and rekindle a sense of meaning and purpose in their career-lives. The approach holds great promise as a strategy that can enhance clients' self-worth, sense of self, self-efficacy, and sense of purpose, and enable them to perceive the future as full of promise and excitement instead of daunting, negative, discouraging, and threatening.

Counselors are obliged to continue to provide a career counseling service that will enable clients to retain, promote, and, in some instances, regain their employability in the gig economy. Using storytelling in conjunction with or without clients' scores on tests seems to be the best foundation for intervention in today's world. Hallmark features of the current and projected economy include uncertainty about the future, mounting fear that "robots" will eventually take over almost all kinds of work, and frustration and anger about workers' and work-seekers' inability to find meaningful employment. In many ways, the counseling for self- and career construction approach helps career counselors rise above many of the challenges associated with traditional approaches to career counseling intervention (Cardoso, Janeiro, & Duarte, 2017; Maree, 2019a, 2019b). Qualitative assessment techniques supplement quantitative assessment techniques and vice versa. The net result is contemporary career counseling that meets the career counseling needs of present-day workers. Contemporary career counseling theories and goals, premised on and merging the historical and philosophical underpinnings of both qualitative and quantitative approaches, are integrated to produce a framework for the examination, interpretation, explanation, and guidance of career choice-related behavior (Duarte, 2010; Maree, 2010d; Savickas et al., 2009).

The integrative approach is consistent with the view that career counseling and career decision-making should be recognized as a multifaceted process and not simply "three interviews and a cloud of dust" (Crites, 1981, p. 49). This approach complies with the key criteria for advancing rigor in research and practice, namely trustworthiness, validity, and reliability. Integrative intervention is versatile (one of its key features) in that it can be applied in various ways (depending on the idiosyncratic needs of clients) in individual and in group contexts. Moreover, the approach facilitates the administration of telehealth (telepsychology, teletherapy, and tele-career counseling). Both the *MCM* and the *CIP* can, for instance, be administered either online or in hard copy format. Clients can be guided in a respectful, inspiring, and uncomplicated manner to advise themselves regarding their career decision questions by identifying and constructing their often painful and traumatic key life themes and subsequently transcending the hard times they may have experienced and finding a way to convert hurt into hope. Once this aim has been achieved, "[the logical] next step is for counselors to help clients connect what they view as their life purpose or role in the larger society with their activity within the work role" (Duffy & Dik, 2009, p. 441).

Some aspects of the new approach to career counseling remain open to further debate. However, what cannot be contested is that we as career counselors are obliged to help clients advise themselves on career-related decisions instead of being "advised" by others. In addition, as evidenced by feedback from research participants and clients across the world, the integrative approach can transform the "process" of administering and receiving career counseling into an experience that is akin to "the stroke of midnight on New Year's Eve [offering] the possibility of a new beginning" (Epston, in O'Hanlon, 1994, p. 3). Every client that I ever see, or every group of clients, brings up this picture in my mind. Suddenly, it is a few seconds before midnight on New Year's Eve. We are bidding farewell to the "old" and welcoming and embracing the "new". I hear cheerful music, exuberant singing, corks popping, balloons bursting, people singing excitedly, and happy songs playing. We all are looking forward to experiencing the newness of the new dawn. We are about to convert hurt and anguish (where it exists) into renewed hope, defeat into victory, and challenges into opportunities. We are also about to make meaning in our work-lives, choose and construct careers that will enhance a sense of hope in our lives, ignite our potential to unleash "magic" in our personal career-life stories, design ourselves, lead successful lives, and make meaningful social contributions—in short to live purposeful lives.

So then, is Dolly Parton right when she sings the following words?

But they didn't understand it
And I tried to make them see
That one is only poor
Only if they choose to be
Now I know we had no money
But I was rich as I could be
In my coat of many colors
My mama made for me
How very true.

13.7 Conclusion

We all experience pain, rejection, lack of fulfillment, disappointment, heartache, and sadness from time to time. However, people's circumstances and challenges do not define who they are or can become. Just the opposite. If we want to, and with the necessary support structures and mechanisms to rise to challenges, we have the power and innovativeness to convert our greatest challenges into opportunities and successes, inaction into action, "problems" into growth areas and strengths, questions into answers (and answers into further questions), and subconscious life themes into conscious motivations to make a success of our lives. Humankind has consistently done so throughout the ages. No matter how overwhelming the challenges facing us, we can master actively what we have suffered or are suffering (often passively). Or, in the words of Norah Lofts (1958): "Heaven isn't something that lies about us in our infancy and then is lost; nor is it something that be attained by the exercise of impossible virtues. Heaven is something that you can hold in your hand" (p. 15). In other words, we can decide and advise ourselves whether we should choose to be happy, successful, contented … (please add whichever words you wish here). Just as one cannot be hypnotized by another person, one cannot blame one's personal circumstances for being negative; for acting imprudently; for being unable to convert hurt into hope, challenge and defeat into victory, stuckness into forward movement; or for not succeeding in finding a way to experience a sense of purpose in one's daily work.

Likewise, each of us can choose to look through a lens of despair at the future of work, at our individual and collective (perceived or real) threatened career-life prospects, and at whether the notion of purposeful work is about to disappear forever. Conversely, we can choose to regard constant change as a source of hope and inspiration. I propose that we adopt individually and collectively an innovative, proactive, positive, hopeful career counseling approach, make the most of change to advance this approach, and join hands to help people live hope-filled and purposeful lives, which I regard as a the ultimate aim of research, theory, praxis, and policy development in the career counseling field.

Lastly: The reality and the good news is that we do have a choice. This principle lies at the heart of the innovation that I am trying to advance through this book, and the integrative approach provides a formidable strategy to achieve this aim.

If this book has succeeded in gently nudging the notion of counseling for self- and career construction forward to wider use and helped even one person understand that heaven is indeed in our hands, then I would consider all the effort that has gone into the writing of the book worth the time and trouble.

References

Cardoso, P., Janeiro, I. N., & Duarte, M. E. (2017). Life design counseling group intervention with Portuguese adolescents. *Journal of Career Development, 1,* 1–14. https://doi.org/10.1177/0894845316687668.

Cochran, L. R. (1997). *Career counseling: A narrative approach.* Pacific Grove, CA: Thousand Oaks.

Crites, J. O. (1981). *Career counseling. Models, methods, and materials.* New York, NY: McGraw-Hill Book Company.

Duarte, M. E. (2010, July). *Restructuring career counseling: Objectives and instruments.* 27th International Congress of Applied Psychology, Melbourne, Australia.

Duffy, R. D., & Dik, B. J. (2009). Beyond the self: External influences in the career development process. *The Career Development Quarterly, 58,* 29–43.

Hartung, P. J., & Santili, S. (2018). *My Career Story*: Description and initial validity evidence. *Journal of Career Assessment, 26*(2), 308–321.

Littleton, S. M., Arthur, M. B., & Rousseau, D. M. (2000). The future of boundaryless careers. In A. Collin & R. A. Young (Eds.), *The future of career* (pp. 101–114). New York, NY: Cambridge University.

Lofts, N. (1958). *Heaven in your hand*. Greenwich, CT: Fawcett Publications.

Maree, J. G. (2010d). Critical appraisal of the system of education and prospects of meeting the manpower and developmental needs of South Africa. *Africa Insight, 40*, 85–108.

Maree, J. G. (2018a). Advancing career counselling research and practice using a new quantitative + qualitative approach to elicit clients' advice from within. *South African Journal of Higher Education, 32*(4), 149–170.

Maree, J. G. (2018b). Using life design counseling for career construction to facilitate sustainable employability and decent work in a developing country context. In V. Cohen-Scali, J. Pouyaud, M. Podgórny, V. Drabik-Podgórny, G. Aisenson, J.-L. Bernaud, I. Moumoula., J. Guichard (Eds.). *Interventions in career design and education* (pp. 195–214). New York, NY: Springer.

Maree, J. G. (2019a, June). *Career development in Africa: Decent work for all: Brief photomontage*. Keynote Address at the Annual Career Development Practitioner Congress, Emperors Palace Conference Centre, Kempton Park, South Africa.

Maree, J. G. (2019b). Postmodernising career counseling in a deep rural context. In J. G. Maree (Ed.), *Handbook of innovative career counseling* (pp. 577–596). New York, NY: Springer.

Maree, J. G. (2019c). Innovative career construction counselling for a creative adolescent. *British Journal of Guidance and Counselling*. https://doi.org/10.1080/03069885.2018.1504202.

Maree, J. G. (Ed.). (2017). *Handbook of career adaptability, employability, and resilience*. New York, NY: Springer.

McAdams, D. P. (2010). The problem of meaning in personality psychology from the standpoints of dispositional traits, characteristic adaptations, and life stories. *Japanese Journal of Personality, 18*, 173–186.

McAdams, D. P. (2013). The psychological self as actor, agent, and author. *Perspectives on Psychological Science, 8*(3), 272–295.

O'Hanlon, B. (1994). The third wave. *Family Therapy Networker, 18*(6), 19–29.

Phares, E. J. (1992). *Clinical psychology: Concepts, methods and profession*. Pacific Grove, CA: Brooks/Cole Publishing Company.

Rossier, J. (2015). Personality assessment and career interventions. In P. J. Hartung, M. L. Savickas, & W. B. Walsh (Eds.), *APA handbook of career intervention: Foundations* (Vol. 1, pp. 327–350). Washington, DC: American Psychological Association. https://doi.org/10.1037/1438-018.

Savickas, M. L. (2011). Reshaping the story of career counseling. In K. Maree (Ed.), Shaping the story—A guide to facilitate narrative counseling (pp. 1–3). Boston/Rotterdam, The Netherlands: Sense.

Savickas, M. L. (2016, July). *Meaning at work: Work at meaning*. Closing keynote presentation, National Career Development Association Conference, Chicago, United States of America.

Savickas, M. L. (2019a). *Theories of psychotherapy series. Career counseling* (2nd ed.). Washington, DC: American Psychological Association.

Savickas, M. L. (2019b, September). *Designing a self and constructing a career in post-traditional societies*. Keynote address at the 43rd international association for educational and vocational guidance Conference, Bratislava, Slovakia.

Savickas, M. L., & Hartung, P. J. (2012, June). *My career story: An autobiographical workbook for life-career success*. Retrieved from www.vocopher.com.

Savickas, M. L., Nota, L., Rossier, J., & Dauwalder, J. P., Duarte, M. E., Guichard, J., …Van Vianen, A. E. M. (2009). Life designing: A paradigm for career construction in the 21st century. *Journal of Vocational Behavior, 75*, 239–250.

Soresi, S., Nota, L., Ferrari, L., & Solberg, S. (2008). Career guidance for persons with disabilities. In J. A. Athanasou & R. Van Esbroeck (Eds.), *International handbook of career guidance* (pp. 405–417). Dordrecht: Springer Science.

Epilogue: Innovating Counseling for Self- and Career Construction

Within the literature and lore of career counseling there are occasional reminders that qualitative and quantitative data are not incompatible, and that they are complementary ways of knowing a person. Jepsen (1994) reminds that Donald Super, author of the treatise *The Psychology of Careers* (1957), pioneered narrative and actuarial approaches to career assessment. Again, in this post-postmodern era in which the paradigm scuffles have settled, Kobus Maree reminds that career assessment is integral to career counseling, and that career assessment is both qualitative and quantitative, not one or the other.

In this latest statement on the art and science of career assessment and counseling, Kobus Maree builds on decades of research and development, exemplified by his opus *Counselling for Career Construction: Connecting life themes to construct life portraits. Turning pain into hope* (Maree, 2013), with its signature subtitle, *Connecting Life Themes to Construct Life Portraits: Turning Pain Into Hope.* Turning pain into hope is the totem of Kobus Maree's endeavor to produce practical means by which practitioners can inspire individuals to find ways out from their confusion in a complex world-of-work, to ways forward into new meanings in work and career. How? In this present work, *Innovating Counseling for Self- and Career Construction*, Kobus Maree again reminds career practitioners and scholars that individuals are deserving of sophisticated means of career assessment and counseling that integrate all the data—not just some of it—that can meaningfully represent their exquisite uniqueness as individuals. The counseling and assessment methods described within this book practically operationalize the three dimensions to the question, "What do we know when we know a person?" (McAdams, 1995). Those three dimensions of knowing a person—dispositional traits, characteristic adaptations, and life stories—are practically brought into focus by the methods herein. Furthermore, the methods enable an operationalization of the career construction theory (Savickas, 2005) and its rendering of an answer to McAdams' question by way of a vocational traits, career adaptability, and life themes.

On many occasions I have heard Kobus Maree mention a source of his inspiration, Dolly Parton and her famous *Coat of Many Colors*. That symbolic coat, patches stitched into a garment, epitomizes the axiom: the whole is greater than the sum of

J. G. (Kobus) Maree, *Innovating Counseling for Self- and Career Construction*,
https://doi.org/10.1007/978-3-030-48648-8

its parts. Likewise, in his approach to career assessment and counseling, Kobus Maree artfully stitches patches of qualitative and quantitative data together meaningfully into a whole more than its patches. We scholars and practitioners of career assessment and counseling can learn much more from Kobus Maree and his colorful coat.

Professor Peter McIlveen
Australian Collaboratory for Career Employability & Learning for Living
Institute for Resilient Regions
University of Southern Queensland
Toowoomba, Australia

References

Goldschmidt, A. J. W., & Hilbert, J. (2009). *Health economy in Germany – economical field of the future (Gesundheitswirtschaft in Deutschland - Die Zukunftsbranche).* Germany: Wikom Publishing House.

Seymour, V. (2016). The human– nature relationship and its impact on health: A critical review. *Frontiers in Public Health, 4*, 260. https://doi.org/10.3389/fpubh.2016.00260.

Jepsen, D. A. (1994). The thematic-extrapolation method: Incorporating career patterns into career counseling. *Career Development Quarterly, 43*(1), 43. https://doi.org/10.1002/j.2161-0045.1994.tb00845.x

Maree, K. (2013). *Counselling for career construction: Connecting life themes to construct life portraits: Turning hope into pain.* Rotterdam, The Netherlands: Sense Publishers.

McAdams, D. P. (1995). What do we know when we know a person? *Journal of Personality, 63*(3), 366–396. https://doi.org/10.1111/j.1467-6494.1995.tb00500.x

Savickas, M. L. (2005). The theory and practice of career construction. In S. D. Brown & R. W. Lent (Eds.), *Career development and counseling: Putting theory and research to work* (pp. 42–70). Hoboken, NJ: Wiley.

Super, D. E. (1957). *The psychology of careers.* New York, NY: Harper and Row.

Notes

1. I thank Mr. Tim Steward for his editing of the text.
2. Likewise, I thank the participants for participating in the research and for permitting me to report on their stories.
3. The two people who participated in making the DVD (see Chapter 8, p. 128) went on to excel at various levels. The female participant focused on a career in entertainment and has become a well-known, award-winning actress and motivational speaker (she has also written several self-help books). The male participant enrolled on a course in law (including modules in psychology) and has completed a master's degree in law (human rights advocacy and litigation). He is currently completing a second master's degree in international economic law and policy. He is employed by a law firm and specializes in human rights advocacy and litigation. Both participants report that they are experiencing a profound sense of meaning, purpose, and hope in their career-lives.

J. G. (Kobus) Maree, *Innovating Counseling for Self- and Career Construction*,
https://doi.org/10.1007/978-3-030-48648-8

Addendum A: Crafting a Career-Life Story Narrative

"Integrative career choice and construction conversation" template

The following seven-step document will assist you in integrating all your career information into a concrete and feasible career plan. This document will require you to have your *Career Interest Profile* (*CIP*) answer sheets and your *Maree Career Matrix* (*MCM*) report available. You may also include other information you have available.

Name and Surname:

....

Step 1: Summarize Some Main Patterns from Your Career-Story Narratives (*Career Interest Profile*)

Strengths	
Areas for Growth	
Values	
Central Life Themes	
Now combine all of the above (your strengths, areas for growth, values and central life themes) into two or three sentences that communicate your uniqueness. Begin with the words "I am …	
I am	

Step 2: Please Complete the Following Table by Referring to Your *CIP* Answer Sheet, *MCM* Report, and School Marks (You May Also Include Other Relevant Information)

J. G. (Kobus) Maree, *Innovating Counseling for Self- and Career Construction*,
https://doi.org/10.1007/978-3-030-48648-8

Career Interest Profile (CIP)			*Maree Career Matrix (MCM)*		School marks per subject at the end of last year	
Sevenpreferredinterest categories	Fivepreferred careers	Seven careers Underlined ingreen	preferred (Interest and confidence) career categories	Specific careersyouscored both high interest (2) and confidence (2)	Subject	Mark
1.	1.	1.	1.	1.	1.	
2.	2.	2.	2.	2.	2.	
3.	3.	3.	3.	3.	3.	
4.	4.	4.	4.	4.	4.	
5.	5.	5.	5.	5.	5.	
6.	6.	6.	6.	6.	6.	
7.	7.	7.	7.	7.	7.	
8.	8.	8.	8.	8.	8.	

career interest profile MAREE CAREER MATRIX

Step 3: Identify YourIntegratedMain Interest Categories/ Patterns (Based on the Information Provided in the Table Above)

Interest category or field	
1	
2	
3	
4	
5	
6	

Step 4: Where do you Want to Study After Having Completed Grade 12?

Summarised possible career choices		University	University of technology	TVET College/Private training
1				
2				
3				
4				
5				

Some Useful Websites and Phone Numbers

www.onetonline.org/find/

www.careers24.com

www.gostudy.net

www.jobspace.co.za

www.careersunlimimited.co.za

www.labour.gov.za/DOL/legislation/acts/how-tos/skill-development/how-to-join-a-learnership-if-you-are-unemployed;

www.interns24.co.za/list-available-learnerships-south-africa/?gclid=EAIaIQobChMI__XiraT-2gIVg7DtCh0LgwBzEAAYASAAEgIgB_D_BwE

www.careerexpo.co.za; www.careers.co.za; http://www.careerjunction.co.za/;

www.careersportal.co.za; www.careerplanet.co.za; www.saqa.org.za(**for critical skills career list**);www.pacecareers.com/; www.skillsportal.co.za;

pace. www.gostudy.mobi; http://www.nqf.org.za/; http://ncap.careerhelp.org.za/occupations;

DHET Helpline 0800 8722 222; DHET Career Development Services: 0860 35 66 35 or careerhelp@dhet.gov.za; www.careerhelp.org.za

Step 5: My Personal Career Plan

Integrate all the Information from all the Above Steps and Complete the Following:

I want to study (field(s) of study)

……………………………………………………………………………………………

………………………………………………………………………

……………………………………………………………………………………………

………………………………………………………………………

so that I can (personal meaning)

……………………………………………………………………………………………

………………………………………………………………………

……………………………………………………………………………………………

………………………………………………………………………

and in the process (social meaning)

……………………………………………………………………………………………

………………………………………………………………………

……………………………………………………………………………………………

………………………………………………………………………

STEP 6: THOROUGH JOB ANALYSIS

STEP 7: FEEDBACK.

My very best wishes for a bright future accompany you.

Addendum B: Example of a 'Postmodern' career Counseling Report

Narrative career counseling report[1]

Name	: ...
School	: ...
Date of birth	: ...
Date of assessment	: ...
Age	: ...

My Story So Far: The Tale of Fairy

What you need to know before my Fairy tale begins.[2]

Hi there! My name is "Fairy". Those closest to me call me Fairy. I am X years old and I am currently in Grade 10 at YYY. I am at a stage in my career development where I need to reflect on the subject choices that I made at the end of last year. Both my parents and I wonder if I made the best choices that I could have made. As such, I want to explore whether the subjects I currently take are the most suitable selections for my aptitudes, personality and interests.

I also want to make sure that these subjects will allow me to follow a career trajectory that makes it possible to undertake tertiary studies, to use my unique personal talents and, hopefully, to lead to personal success in whatever I do. I realise that the choice of subjects that may lead to certain career options in future, is an important step during which my personal attributes and values must be considered. Feel free to spend some time with me as I embark on this personal journey of self-exploration.

[1] This report is the exclusive property of the client and may not be used for forensic purposes.

[2] Some of the tests/questionnaires that were used in this test situation were either standardized some time ago, or were not designed/have not been standardized in South Africa. The information has throughout been interpreted from a narrative perspective, and the results have to be treated with great care.

J. G. (Kobus) Maree, *Innovating Counseling for Self- and Career Construction*,
https://doi.org/10.1007/978-3-030-48648-8

Learning to Fly: My School Life.

I like going to school but I sometimes find it difficult dealing with the pressure of schoolwork. I find Mathematics and Science especially challenging, even though I try my best. Also, I do not particularly like working with numbers. English and Afrikaans are okay. I really enjoy Biology and I find Home Economics fun as it allows me to be creative with both cooking and designing.

I expect a lot from myself. I put much effort into my schoolwork and, when I obtain poor results despite my hard work, it can cause me to feel quite despondent. Exams are particularly stressful for me, as I get very nervous and anxious about them. I sometimes find keeping on top of all my schoolwork rather challenging too. I want to know what I can do to improve my marks.

I was a prefect in Grade 7 and I have been a member of the Representative Council of Learners (RCL) every year since I started high school. It is a lot of work but I enjoy it nonetheless. I like to be a leader and to be influential in the organisation of events as well as with intervention around issues at school.

What this Fairy Likes To Do To Rest Her Wings: My Free Time Activities.

At school, I play softball and rugby. I aided in setting up the girls' rugby team. Sport is one of my favourite pastimes and I am a very active person. In my personal leisure moments I love to spend time with my friends and they come to me when they want us to arrange to do something together. I enjoy dancing and I listen to a variety of music. Sometimes a like to be creative and I will then make things. I also find personal joy in learning about astrology and all things spiritual in nature. Believe it or not, I can cook too!

A Fairy's Nearest and Dearest: My Family.

I have a wonderful, loving and supportive family. It seems as if they know me fairly well. I am the eldest of three daughters. My sisters are quite a bit younger than me so they are closer to each other. My Mom is one of my confidants in life and my Dad is a role model who inspires me in my future aspirations and to become more confident in myself. My Dad thinks that I would enjoy working with people, possibly in the corporate world or in the helping professions. He views me as both a leader and a negotiator. He thinks that I have a strong, confident personality.

Both my parents want me to study after school and follow my dreams. Education is very important to them and they feel that this is one of the most significant values they can impart to me in my life. I understand this and want to study when I finish school too.

What enchants this Fairy and Causes Her Wings to Flutter: My Interests.

If we look at my present interests, I like to be involved in leadership, negotiation and organisational activities. I also like variety in whatever I do. I enjoy being around people and spending time with others and I love to talk to them. I especially like the idea of working in the travel and tourism industry, artistic, creative environments and the health field or anything to do with sports.

According to my results on the *Rothwell-Miller Interest Blank*, I am most interested in artistic/ aesthetic activities. This means that careers in art, clothing or interior design, the beauty industry or craft production appeal to me. I am also interested in practical, service-oriented careers that allow for hands-on involvement in my work. Furthermore, careers that allow me to be persuasive such as training, management, communications, sales or marketing are other interests that attract my attention. I do not think that working with figures or with anything in the medical field will be an interesting future prospect. Neither do I want to be involved in the operation of machinery and equipment.

I also completed the *South African Vocational Interest Inventory*. My results on this questionnaire, once again, reflect that I am interested in management, sales, promotion and persuasion. Also, I do not mind the idea of working with administrative tasks in an office environment. My interest in creative design came to the fore again here.

A Fairy's Personal Gifts: My Aptitudes.

My talents are a key factor to bear in mind, especially if we want to know about what aptitudes I have. I am creative and very good at organising. I am also a natural negotiator.

According to the *Senior Aptitude Tests*, my memory and motor skill aptitudes are my most prominent talents. I have an average ability to adequately memorise and remember material. I am also sufficiently skilled in hands-on tasks that require speed and hand-eye coordination. My ability to see patterns and relationships between visual objects in my environment is also average.

I need to work on my verbal comprehension and reasoning as well as my ability to work with mathematical calculations quickly and accurately.

A Fairy's Wishes: My Values and Needs in Life.

First and foremost, I want to be happy in my career and in my life. Self- development and personal growth are essential goals attached to this need for personal contentment. Education and my personal, spiritual well-being are vital for this too. This is in essence what I view personal success to be. I rate highly the need for a personal sense of freedom and independence in whatever I do.

I do want stability or balance in life as well as certainty and security in anything I do. Money is important to me for these reasons. As I already mentioned, my family is a cherished part of my life. I place high regard on their support, love and care. My friends are also central in my life for this. It is important to me that I make my family proud.

Fairylike charm: My Personality.

My personality involves those aspects of myself that best describe me as a person. I am inquisitive, friendly, open and talkative. I readily share my life experiences with others. As such, I am extroverted in nature under most circumstances. However, sometimes I need a little bit of personal space when I want to figure things out for myself. I am very contemplative and reflective about my life.

I have a firm sense of what is fair in life. I do tend to stand up for others and myself when I experience unfair treatment. I am very supportive and caring towards those around me. I am intuitive about the feelings and wishes of others. I do not always need the support of others but it is something that I like to have in my life. Trust in relationships is important to me. I can be rather hard on myself as I expect a lot from myself, especially scholastically. Sometimes I worry and can get quite down when things do not go as I had planned and prepared for. I do not cope very well in situations that create pressure and I can then feel quite stressed, tense and anxious.

I have a strong, independent character. I am more of a leader than a follower in life. Others accept me as such. I am action-orientated too as I like to organise, plan and do things rather than just talk about them. I am dynamic, energetic and I like variety in my life. I am committed to whatever I decide to undertake. I am not too fond of routine but I can deal with these sorts of activities if I need to.

Possible obstacles in My Flight Trajectory.

Some challenging things have happened in my life over the past few years. These events are still very much on my mind. I find it hard to be a teenager sometimes as there are so many new and demanding aspects of life to deal with.

I can be quite tough on myself and this may cause me to feel sad, stressed and anxious at times. I need to find a way to work through my concerns and, sharing these worries with others is something that I am contemplating doing so that they can support me as I try to find ways of coping and thriving in my life. My personal strengths and positive outlook will help in this process, as I firmly believe that people grow from the challenges they negotiate in life.

Well, here I am, this is me ... and although I already know myself very well, I am looking forward to learning more about myself as I discover new things and situations in my life. I want to grow as a person and be successful in whatever I do.

How can I Spread My Wings and Fly? Suggestions for Further Exploration.

I have the following characteristics that I would like to use in my future career:

- Creativity
- An aesthetic orientation
- Clerical, organisational and management abilities
- Persuasive, negotiating abilities
- A sociable, outgoing nature
- Person-orientation and sensitivity to the needs of others
- Contemplativeness
- A need for freedom, variety and action

Occupational fields that I might like begin starting to explore include the following:

- Artistic, Practical and Persuasive Careers
  - Dressmaking/Clothing Design
  - Graphic/Interior Design
  - Somatology
  - Catering
  - Photography
  - Graphic Design
  - Advertising

- Management & Persuasive Careers
  - Retail Buyer
  - Business Management
  - Sales
  - Marketing
  - Human Resources
  - Personnel Management
  - Public Relations
  - Hotel Management
  - Travel and Tourism
  - Sports Instructor
  - Estate Agent
  - Training Consultant

I will also consider replacing Physical Sciences with Business Studies if my school can accommodate this change. Before doing this, I will have to explore what the different study fields that fit my unique attributes require as well as my interest in these fields. I may also try taking Biology on higher grade next year as I would like to try to do so. Also, extra English classes might help me to improve my English marks. It will be a great idea for me to undertake further career facilitation when I am busy completing my Grade 12 school year.

… and the provisional conclusion of this Fairy tale[3]?

I realise that it is now up to me to explore the afore-mentioned career fields for future career planning and for consideration of my subject choices. I plan to search for job-shadowing opportunities for hands-on career exploration purposes. This entails that I will seek out people and organisations in my proposed career fields so as to discuss these occupations and to gain first-hand experiences of careers from them.

I propose that I will attend open days at Universities, Universities of Technology and further education and training colleges to find out more about career fields that appeal to me. I will undertake personal Internet searches for job information purposes

[3]Despite the fact that X has exceptional potential, sustained/continued success will to a large extent be co-determined by her consistent display of personality traits such as her will to achieve, perseverance, responsibility, diligence, self-discipline, her ability to adequately manage time and stress, and emotional stability.

too. I can consult with my career facilitator at any time during this process in order to discuss my feelings and to address any difficulties I may be experiencing both with my career development and in coping with being a teenager.

Future … here I come!

Addendum C: *Career-Life Story Narrative Exemplar*

Career-Life Story Narrative

1. **Identifying details**

Name	: Sharné (pseudonym)
Birth date	: …
Assessment date	: …
Age	: 17 years
Grade	: 12
School	: …

2. **Reason for assessment**

Sharné's parents referred her for counseling on the choice of a career. In her own words: 'To make sure that my career choice "fits" my personality profile.'

3. **Career-life history**

Sharné is the first of two children in an intact family. Her developmental milestones were reached within the accepted time limits and there appears to be a high degree of closeness and good communication between Sharné and her parents. Sharné's parents who have always been extremely supportive of her. Both parents are entrepreneurs and small business owners. They recently started their own paint store.

4. **Personal profile**

4.1 Observed profile

Sharné comes across as a pleasant, vivacious, cooperative young woman capable of establishing excellent interpersonal relationships.

4.2 Interest profile

4.2.1 Qualitative outcomes

J. G. (Kobus) Maree, *Innovating Counseling for Self- and Career Construction*,
https://doi.org/10.1007/978-3-030-48648-8

According to the *Career Interest Profile* (this questionnaire yields qualitative career-related information), Sharné's preferred interest categories are currently **Social, care-giving, and community services and teaching**; **Persuasive (Marketing)**; **Adventure, plants, animals, and the environment**; **Entrepreneurship, running, and maintaining a personal business; Executive and management practice**; and **Sport**.

4.2.2 Quantitative outcomes

According to the *Maree Career Matrix*, (a quantitative career inventory), her preferred interest and confidence categories are currently **Sport; Persuasive (Marketing)**; **Social, care-giving, and community services and teaching**; **Executive and management practice**; **Adventure, plants, animals and the environment;** and **Tourism**.

Sharné's career matrix is shown below.

4.3 Personality profile

Taking her age into account, Sharné's sense of self appears adequate. According to information gained from diverse sources, Sharné is an honourable young woman who is also dedicated, committed to her studies, and trustworthy. She exhibits natural leadership skills and is confident in her own decisions. Creatively inclined, well-mannered, and cooperative, she has a phlegmatic temperament and strong moral values. She is interested in sport (especially horse riding), enjoys the company of others, and is described as a good 'listener'. She integrates easily with groups while at the same time being self-reliant and confident in her own decisions. Sharné enjoys challenges. Areas for growth include an overly strong inclination to do things in her way. She could also be more considerate of the opinions of others. She sometimes finds it hard to deal with disparaging or negative comments and can occasionally be swayed by the views of others. She sometimes gets emotionally attached to others too easily and at times finds it hard to stay focused.

4.4 Key career-life themes

Careful analysis of Sharné's responses and reflections revealed a number of central career-life themes, including the following:

- Being there for and helping others deal with hurt and making a change in their lives;
- being an inspirational leader;
- using sport (horse riding especially) as a vehicle to help others express themselves and enhance their sense of self and self-worth; and
- Standing up for the rights of others.

4.5 Summarized reflections

Sharné currently exhibits a satisfactory degree of academic 'maturity' (development) (although she could still work much harder!) and many of the personality traits associated with academic success. Her main career interest and confidence categories are apparent and vest in the following fields currently: **Sport; Persuasive (Marketing); Social, care-giving, and community services and teaching; Executive and management practice; Adventure, plants, animals and the environment; and Tourism**.

5.1 **Recommendations**

5.1.1 The following fields of study at university level should be explored:

- **B.Ed** (e.g. Early Childhood Development and Foundation, Senior, or Further Education and Training Phase OR Human Movement Sciences and Sports Management). Sharné could then perhaps apply for acceptance into a **B.Ed** (Hons: Educational Psychology) programme and eventually into a **M.Ed** (Educational Psychology) programme
- **B.A/ B.Com** Human Resource Management
- **B.A** Communication/ **B.Com** Marketing Communication
- **B.Com** Marketing Management
- **B.Admin** (Business Management) **OR B.Com** Business Management.

Could also be considered:

- **B.A** Health Sciences (specialising in Biokinetics)
- **B.A** Sport, Health, and Leisure Science: Human Movement Science and Recreation Science (followed by a Postgraduate Certificate in Education (**PGCE**) (specialising in Biokinetics or Children Kinetics)
- **B.A** Sport and Leisure Studies
- **B.A** Tourism Development/ **B.Com** Tourism Management.

5.1.2 At university of technology level

- Equine Science.

5.1.3 At private higher education and training level

- Airline Cabin Crew Member.

5.1.4 Hobby-orientated activities: Sharné could participate in the following types of activities:

- Sport (including horse riding)
- Reading and writing
- Listening to music/Watching TV and movies
- Spending time with friends.

5.2 Work analysis[4] is essential. This includes attendance of open days, visits to educational institutions/employers, discussions with occupational practitioners, part-time work, work shadow, surfing of the Internet; visit e.g. skillsportal.co.za; careersportal.co.za; www.careers.co.za; http://www.careerjunction.co.za; https://www.onetonline.org/find/; https://www.saqa.org.za (for critical skills career list); SAQA Helpline: Send an SMS to 072 204 5056 with your question or send a "Please Call Me" and one of the Career Advisors will call you back; phone 086 999 0123 (Mon-Fri: 08:00-16:30); e-mail: careerhelp@dhet.gov.za.
5.3 Sharné should aim for an average of 65-70% in her Grade 12 examinations.
5.4 Small group work (with motivated students) is strongly recommended.
5.5 **Sharné should read more**.
5.6 Sharné should contact any relevant authority for training in regard to writing the *National Benchmark Tests* (*NBT*).
5.7 Sharné is urged to heed her own 'words of wisdom' (quotes) to inspire herself, namely:

- "*For we walk by faith and not by sight*" (build your life around things that have eternal significance).
- "*Every day is a new beginning – treat it that* way" (take action to make your dreams come true and give your life new meaning).
- "*You will never influence the world by trying to be like it*" (be unique; stand out).

5.8 Continuous report-back as well as monitoring her progress is essential.

My best wishes accompany Sharné. I expect a great deal from her.

[4]**Visit the following websites: ...**

Bibliography

Abraham, J. (2018). *Fascinating: Dolly parton's life story and secrets*. Retrieved from https://www.parentsdome.com/fascinating-dolly-partons-life-story-and-secrets/

BrainyQuote. (n.d.) *Dolly parton quotes*. Retrieved from https://www.brainyquote.com/authors/dolly-parton-quotes

Cardoso, P., Savickas, M. L., & Gonçalves, M. M. (2020). Facilitating narrative change in career construction counselling. *Journal of Career Development, 29*(1), 1–14. https://doi.org/10.1177/0894845319898872.

Career indecision. (n.d.) Available at https://psychology.iresearchnet.com/counseling-psychology/career-counseling/career-indecision/

Flum, H. (2015). Relationships and career development: An integrative approach. In P. J. Hartung, M. L. Savickas, & W. B. Walsh (Eds.), *APA handbook of career intervention* (Vol. 1, pp. 145–158). Washington, DC: American Psychological Association.

Girley, B. (2019). *Dolly parton: My music is more my ministry than a job*. Retrieved from https://ambotv.com/blog/entertainment/dolly-parton-my-music-is-more-my-ministry-than-a-job/

Goldschmidt, A. J. W., & Hilbert, J. (2009). *Health economy in Germany – economical field of the future (Gesundheitswirtschaft in Deutschland – Die Zukunftsbranche)*. Berlin, Germany: Wikom Publishing House.

Holland, J. L., & Gottfredson, G. D. (1975). Predictive value and psychological meaning of vocational aspirations. *Journal of Vocational Behavior, 6*, 349–363.

How does group counseling differ from individual counseling? (n.d.) Retrieved from https://onlinedegrees.bradley.edu/blog/how-does-group-counseling-differ-from-individual-counseling/

Jacaranda FM. (2015). *Die windpomp trailer*. Retrieved from https://www.youtube.com/watch?v=GC68LxWK9J4

Maree, K. (1996). *Trial match*. Cape Town, South Africa: Nb Publishers.

Maree, K. (2005). *Zweepi: the spinning game*. Pretoria, South Africa: Aktua Press.

Morgan, T., & Ness, D. (2003). Career decision-making difficulties of first-year students. *The Canadian Journal of Career Development, 2*(1), 33–39.

Mpofu, E., Ntinda, K., Maree, K., & Oakland, T. (2017). *Meeting learner support needs in a developing country context: Developing the Botswana Learner Appraisal System (BLAS)*. Gaborone, Botswana: ASDE.

Richardson, L. (2000). Writing: A method of inquiry. In N. K. Denzin & Y. S. Lincoln (Eds.), *The Sage handbook of qualitative research* (2nd ed., pp. 923–948). Thousand Oaks, CA: Sage.

Rūmī, J. M., & Barks, C. (1996). *The essential Rumi. 1st HarperCollins* (paperback ed.). San Francisco, CA: Harper.

Soresi, S., Nota, L., Ferrari, L., & Solberg, S. (2008). Career guidance for persons with disabilities. In J. A. Athanasou & R. Van Esbroeck (Eds.), *International handbook of career guidance* (pp. 405–417). Dordrecht: Springer Science.

J. G. (Kobus) Maree, *Innovating Counseling for Self- and Career Construction*,
https://doi.org/10.1007/978-3-030-48648-8

Stevens, G., Duncan, N., & Sonn, C. C. (2013). Memory, narrative and voice as liberatory praxis in the apartheid archive. In G. Stevens, N. Duncan, & D. Hook (Eds.), *Race, memory and the apartheid archive: Towards a transformative psychosocial praxis* (pp. 25–44). London/Johannesburg: Palgrave Macmillan/Wits University Press.

Villiers, A. (2020). *Why we should stop using 'soft' skills.* Retrieved from https://www.ncda.org/aws/NCDA/pt/sd/news_article/278124/_PARENT/CC_layout_details/false

Whiteman, D. L. (1997). *Contextualization: The theory, the gap, the challenge.* Retrieved from http://spu.edu/temp/denuol/context.htm

Index

J. G. (Kobus) Maree, *Innovating Counseling for Self- and Career Construction*,
https://doi.org/10.1007/978-3-030-48648-8

The manufacturer's authorised representative in the EU is Springer Nature Customer Service Centre GmbH, Europaplatz 3, 69115 Heidelberg, Germany. If you have any concerns regarding our products, please contact ProductSafety@springernature.com

Printed and bound by CPI Group (UK) Ltd, Croydon, CR0 4YY
05/10/2026
02228126-0010